Great American Classics Cookbook

Great American Classics Cookbook

Edited by Susan Westmoreland

FOOD DIRECTOR
GOOD HOUSEKEEPING

Hearst Books
A Division of Sterling Publishing Co., Inc.
NEW YORK

Good Housekeeping

EDITOR IN CHIEF: Ellen Levine
FOOD DIRECTOR: Susan Westmoreland
ASSOCIATE FOOD DIRECTOR: Susan Deborah Goldsmith
SPECIAL PROJECTS DIRECTOR: Richard Eisenberg

Good Housekeeping Great American Classics Cookbook Credits

WRITER: Beth Allen
CULINARY CONSULTANT AND EDITOR: Deborah Mintcheff
CULINARY HISTORIAN: Jan Longone
COPY EDITOR: Brenda Goldberg
PROOFREADERS: Synde Matus, Diane Boccadoro, and Barbara Machtiger

Photo Credits

Angelo Caggiano: pg. 12, 187; **Brian Hagiwara:** 62, 92, 99, 102, 142, 147, 157, 174, 247, 251, 257; **Rita Maas:** 13, 16, 63, 77, 160, 161, 175, 188, 221; **Simon Metz:** 199; **Steven Mark Needham:** 78, 126, 192, 204, 217, 230, 232, 258, 273, 276, 296, 306, 313; **David Murray & Jules Selmes:** 31; **Ann Stratton:** 21, 30, 37, 46, 79, 90, 110, 214, 222, 231, 248, 259, 281, 290, 295; **Mark Thomas:** 52, 56, 87, 93, 115, 116, 117, 133, 139, 163, 193, 213, 218, 225, 227, 265, 300, 301, 303, 305, 309, 310, 314, 317, 323.

Illustration Credits

Illustration on pg. 9 from the booklet, *Knox Gelatine Dainty Desserts Candies.* Copyright, 1931. Charles B. Knox Gelatine Co., Inc., Johnstown, New York.

Illustrations on pgs. 10 & 11 from the booklet, *The Recipe Book For Club Aluminum Ware With Personal Service.* The Club Alumninum Company, Chicago, Illinois.

Hearst Books

PUBLISHER: Jacqueline Deval
MANAGING EDITOR: Maryanne Bannon
ASSISTANT PROJECT EDITOR: Cindy Lutzke
DESIGN: Celia Fuller
TYPOGRAPHY: Laura Smyth
COVER DESIGN: Celia Fuller

Library of Congress Cataloging-in-Publication Data

Good Housekeeping great American classics cookbook / edited by Susan Westmoreland.
    p. cm.
    Includes index.
    ISBN 1-58816-280-X
    1. Cookery, American. I. Title: Great American classics cookbook. II. Westmoreland, Susan. III. Good Housekeeping (New York, N.Y.)
TX715.G6542 2004
641.5973--dc22

2004000933

10 9 8 7 6 5 4 3 2 1

Published by Hearst Books
A Division of Sterling Publishing Co., Inc.
387 Park Avenue South, New York, NY 10016

Good Housekeeping is a trademark owned by Hearst Magazines Property, Inc., in USA, and Hearst Communications, Inc., in Canada. Hearst Books is a trademark owned by Hearst Communications, Inc.

The Good Housekeeping Cookbook Seal guarantees that the recipes in this cookbook meet the strict standards of the Good Housekeeping Institute, a source of reliable information and a consumer advocate since 1900. Every recipe has been triple-tested for ease, reliability, and great taste.

www.goodhousekeeping.com

Distributed in Canada by Sterling Publishing
c/o Canadian Manda Group, One Atlantic Avenue, Suite 105
Toronto, Ontario, Canada M6K 3E7

Distributed in Australia by Capricorn Link (Australia) Pty. Ltd.
P.O. Box 704, Windsor, NSW 2756 Australia

Printed in China

ISBN 1-58816-280-X

Contents

FOREWORD 7 ★ INTRODUCTION 9

★ CHAPTER 1 ★
Dips, Dunks & Nibbles
12

★ CHAPTER 2 ★
Soups & Sandwiches
30

★ CHAPTER 3 ★
Best-Dressed Salads
62

★ CHAPTER 4 ★
Eggs & Cheese–Plain & Fancy
78

★ CHAPTER 5 ★
Chicken Every Sunday
92

★ CHAPTER 6 ★
From the Butcher's Block
116

★ CHAPTER 7 ★
A Mess of Fish
142

★ CHAPTER 8 ★
Pasta, Grains & Beans
160

★ CHAPTER 9 ★
Eat Your Vegetables!
174

★ CHAPTER 10 ★
From the Bread Basket
192

★ CHAPTER 11 ★
What's for Dessert Tonight?
230

★ CHAPTER 12 ★
A Piece of Cake, A Slice of Pie
258

★ CHAPTER 13 ★
Our Best Cookies & Candies
300

BIBLIOGRAPHY 329 ★ INDEX 330

Foreword

We all love a great home-cooked meal—especially when it features familiar favorites like Mom's meat loaf and apple pie. And those all-American foods we've grown up with are exactly what this book is all about.

Many of us prepare dishes that have been handed down from one generation to the next. My favorite is my grandmother's 3-Layer Devil's Food Cake, something I still enjoy making when my brood gets together. Of course, I've changed it a little, by icing it with Creamy Fudge Frosting instead of her Fluffy White Icing, but basically it's still the same cake.

Here at *Good Housekeeping*, we take seriously our role in preserving our country's food heritage and shaping new ways to cook traditional foods. Inside *Good Housekeeping Great American Classics* you'll find a book that does all this and more.

First and foremost, it's a recipe book—a compilation of over 300 selections that have become a living part of our nation's history. You'll find dishes dating back to the early days in America, when the Pilgrims refined Native American techniques for cooking plentiful foods such as corn, fish, and fowl. As our forefathers discovered local ingredients in various regions, down-home specialties became everyday favorites, and we've got them, too—from New England chowder to Southern batter-fried chicken and San Francisco sourdough. Later, as immigrants began arriving, they taught us how to layer lasagna and stir-fry, so you'll find recipes with an international flavor here as well.

But *Good Housekeeping Great American Classics* is much more than a delicious compilation of heirloom recipes with beautiful color photos. Each recipe comes with a story of how it became part of our heritage. For example, did you know that Caesar salad was created from ingredients that Caesar Cardini of Caesar's Palace managed to scrape together when he ran low on food in his kitchen? All of these food gems make this book a cultural history to enjoy reading at your leisure.

Like many of our earlier cookbooks, *Great American Classics* was compiled by our talented *Good Housekeeping* Food Director, Susan Westmoreland, and her staff, who spend their days developing and triple-testing recipes to ensure that you have success with each one.

So from our kitchens to yours, enjoy sharing the greatest foods from around this great nation.

ELLEN LEVINE, Editor in Chief

A Short History
Of
American Cooking

Long before Columbus voyaged to America, Native Americans had embraced a variety of indigenous foods and incorporated them into their diet. Deer, bison, moose, and small game roamed the woodlands. Flocks of migrating birds were plentiful, and the oceans, rivers, and lakes were treasure troves of fish and shellfish. Wild and cultivated foods abounded, including beans, corn, squash, and wild rice. The array of available wild fruits was also very impressive: blueberries, cranberries, currants, elderberries, strawberries, grapes, and plums dotted the countryside.

TURNING OLD WAYS INTO NEW

The settlers who ventured forth into the New World in the 1600 and 1700s brought their cherished recipes and styles of cooking with them. The English settled in Jamestown and Plymouth, the Dutch gravitated to the mouth of the Hudson River, the Swedes traveled to the banks of the Delaware River, and the Germans settled in the Pennsylvania farmland.

Much of the fish, fowl, and plants the settlers found were unfamiliar, but they adapted their family recipes to the local ingredients: bread was made with corn instead of wheat, and dried berries stood in for raisins in their beloved scones. They used corn flour in their English puddings and added molasses and spices, creating a new favorite called Indian pudding. The settlers also discovered different ways to use both old and new ingredients. Pumpkin and barley became bases for beer, apples were turned into cider, and soups, hashes, and stews were made with turkey and venison instead of beef or chicken. Fresh herbs, and homemade chutneys and ketchups were popular, perhaps because they could mask the flavor of foods that were past their prime.

From the natives, the Pilgrims who lived in and around Plymouth learned how to grow corn, beans, and squash and how to make *msickquatash* (succotash). The Virginians added squirrel and corn to another native recipe, creating Brunswick Stew. New Englanders learned how to steam corn and shellfish in a pit lined with hot stones and seaweed, possibly creating some of the first clambakes. By the time the Revolutionary War rolled around, the colonists were eating well.

EXPANDING THEIR HORIZONS

After the Revolutionary War, adventurous Americans headed west across the Appalachians. Small trading posts marked new settlements, which in time grew into villages, towns, and cities.

As settlers made their homes in various regions, they developed recipes that reflected the local ingredients. New England cooks enjoyed baked beans, Boston brown bread, and boiled dinners of meats and fresh vegetables, while the Germans in Pennsylvania added wursts and sauerkraut to their daily fare. The wealthiest New Yorkers and Philadelphians took advantage of all of the best available foods and ate lavishly on fresh pineapples, excellent beef, and over sixty kinds of fresh fish. Southern plantation owners feasted regularly on dishes influenced by their African-American cooks: fried chicken, beaten biscuits, candied sweet potatoes, benne seed wafers, elaborate coconut cakes, and pecan pies .

From New Orleans and the southern Louisiana bayou country came Creole and Cajun cooking, with jambalayas, gumbos, pilaus, beignets (doughnut puffs),

pralines, and chicory coffee. America's heartland became known for "hog and hominy" as well as for fresh produce. Cattle, too, became a major industry, with the first beef stockyard opening in Chicago in 1827. As prospectors joined the rush west for gold, San Francisco was turned into a boom town, complete with fancy hotels, French chefs serving elegant meals, and saloons where imported liquor was poured with abandon. Many Southern Chinese immigrants joined the rush for gold, staying on in California to work on the railroads, cook in homes and mining camps, and contribute their stir-frying techniques to dishes.

By this time, Thomas Jefferson had traveled widely in Europe and returned home with "new inventions." He introduced us to homemade noodles "served like macaroni," waffles from Holland, and even a dessert resembling baked Alaska.

INFLUENCING HOW WE EAT

In 1796, *American Cookery* by Amelia Simmons was published. It was the first cookbook written by an American and printed in America. Many of its recipes reflected the English style of cooking, but others were truly American in spirit, such as Johny [sic] Cake or Hoe Cake and A Nice Indian Pudding. In the nineteenth century, other notable culinary writers helped to create an American cuisine. The century ended with the 1896 publication of *The Boston Cooking-School Cook Book* by Fannie Farmer, whose readers were instructed on the importance of measuring ingredients precisely for guaranteed success. Magazines such as *Woman's Home Companion* in 1873 and *Good Housekeeping* in 1885 taught novice cooks the basics and offered accomplished home cooks exciting recipes. Others had their impact, too, including Sarah Josepha Hale, who, as editor of *Godey's Lady's Book* for forty years, successfully lobbied President Lincoln to make Thanksgiving a national holiday.

DEVELOPING FOOD TECHNOLOGY

By the second half of the nineteenth century, owning an icebox was all the rage. The commercial canning of meats, oysters, vegetables, and fruits began as early as 1819, and by the 1900s the sales of canned foods topped well over a billion dollars. Free-standing wood cookstoves replaced hearth cooking in many New England homes by the 1850s. These stoves made it easier to control the cooking temperature and were also much safer than stirring a pot near open flames.

After the Civil War, more inventions impacted the food Americans ate. The Continental railroad and the telegraph system drew Americans closer. Housewives across the country were able to purchase beef from Chicago stockyards at their local butcher, fresh ocean fish at their neighborhood fishmonger, and wheels of Wisconsin cheese at the local general store. And by the 1890s, safe pasteurized milk was being hand-delivered right to one's back door.

DISCOVERING NEW FOODS

Newly created ingredients turned housewives into successful bakers: sweetened condensed milk led to the creation of Key Lime Pie, the invention of baking powder and self-rising flour in the 1850s inspired spectacular layer cakes, and cake yeast, and the improved milling of white flour made it easy to bake an excellent loaf of light leavened bread. In the 1890s, breakfast was forever changed thanks to Quaker oatmeal and to Dr. John H. Kellogg and his brother Will, who created cornflakes. Charles B. Knox packaged Sparkling Granulated Gelatine in 1893, propelling us into the age of the molded salad. Soon after, Pearl B. Wait and Orator Woodward introduced Jell-O brand gelatin, making shimmering fruit-gelatin desserts an easy everyday happening.

Right before the turn of the twentieth century and until World War I, the Age of Optimism, life for many Americans was good. The Waldorf-Astoria Hotel, which opened its elaborate doors in 1893, regaled its diners with elegant chafing dishes filled with crab Louis. Gas stoves with thermostatically controlled ovens became available in 1915, with the electric refrigerator following the next year. And by the 1940s, almost half of American homes had both of these appliances.

Not to be overlooked were the approximately 20 million immigrants who came here between 1880 and 1920. These Italians, Germans, Chinese, and Jews lived in ethnic enclaves in the large cities and introduced their American neighbors to old-world favorites, including pizza, sauerbraten, egg foo yong, and overstuffed pastrami sandwiches.

SURVIVING THE WAR YEARS

When America entered World War I in 1917, President Woodrow Wilson appointed Herbert Hoover to head the newly established U.S. Food Administration. His campaign encouraged meatless Tuesdays and Fridays and supported the use of food stamps to ration such foods as butter and sugar. He encouraged all citizens to plant vegetable gardens, giving birth to the famous liberty gardens, later followed by the successful victory gardens in World War II. During the Roaring Twenties, processed foods became menu staples. Betty Crocker, with the continuing help of Fannie Farmer, taught housewives to cook using precise step-by-step recipes. These were the days of pineapple upside-down cake (using canned pineapple), Swiss steak, and home versions of elegant hotel dishes such as eggs Benedict.

Following the stock market crash of 1929, housewives learned to stretch leftovers into hash or potpie and how to extend meat to create tasty one-pot dishes such as lasagna, shepherd's pie, and vegetable-meat stews. At this time, another favorite, the po'boy sandwich became even more popular, and meatless meals of macaroni and cheese were frequently on the menu. In 1930, Clarence Birdseye started the frozen-food industry, enabling Americans to enjoy a variety of healthful and tasty vegetables year-round.

Through both world wars, food manufacturers made great advancements in preserving food for the troops: from instant mashed potatoes to precooked frozen meals. These would soon take their rightful place in supermarkets to be heartily embraced by consumers.

EATING FINER AND FASTER THAN EVER BEFORE

After World War II, the soldiers retuned home with newly acquired tastes for foreign foods. Almost overnight, yogurt, Dutch cocoa, Chinese teas, Scottish shortbread, and even South African rock lobster tails became affordable and available. Mixes became the fastest and most foolproof way to bake cakes, Kraft packaged presliced processed cheese that was ready for sandwiches, and Swanson's offered three-course dinners

in the freezer case. The first Pillsbury Bake-Off was held in 1949, and delicate chiffon cakes debuted the following year. New kitchen appliances, such as electric skillets, tabletop rotisseries, and electric knives and can openers sped up basic kitchen tasks. And James Beard brought his culinary expertise to homemakers via their television sets.

COOKING GOURMET

Beginning in the 1960s, Julia Child's TV program, "The French Chef," came into living rooms across the country, taking the mystique out of French dishes, such as beef Wellington and crepes Suzette, and turning dinner parties into memorable gourmet feasts. Menus went continental, with Flemish beef carbonnade, Japanese sukiyaki, and Greek moussaka. Iceberg lettuce took a backseat to to Bibb lettuce, arugula and the popular Caesar salads. Nouvelle cuisine, which called for the best ingredients cooked as little as possible, arrived from France. Alice Waters started the revolutionary California cuisine by using only the freshest and finest-quality ingredients at her restaurant, Chez Panisse. Food larders grew, too, with such gourmet additions as leeks, shallots, purple potatoes, and miniature vegetables. The Cuisinart made slicing and dicing faster than ever thought possible, and bread machines, pasta machines, espresso makers, and cooking schools helped turn more and more Americans into expert cooks.

Here, in the twenty-first century, farmers' markets, organic superstores, specialty cheese shops, fishmongers, and butchers focus on bringing high-quality ingredients to consumers on a daily basis. Much like our forefathers centuries ago, we continue to embrace the finest and freshest foods that America has to offer.

Keeping in mind that culinary history is not an exact science and that much research is still being done, we bring you this book, which chronicles the evolution of American culinary traditions through the centuries, for your enjoyment.

Chapter 1

Dips, Dunks & Nibbles

The Age of Elegance was at its height in America during the last half of the nineteenth century. Formal seven-course dinners were common in some upper-class homes. The food was served in the latest style: *a la russe*. Instead of bringing it to the table all at once (in true English style), the butlers plated each course in the kitchen and presented them to each guest from gold and silver servers.

After the 1920s, despite Prohibition, this elaborate style of entertaining gave way to the cocktail party: those warm and friendly gatherings at home, where guests sipped, dipped, dunked, and nibbled, often well past the cocktail hour and long into suppertime. With this social phenomenon came finger foods that could be eaten without muss or fuss. Hostesses began stuffing celery, potting meats and seafood, broiling clams and oysters, baking cheese puffs, and creating dips for everything from raw oysters to crunchy vegetable crudités. By the 1930s, women's magazines and cookbooks were featuring recipes for fancy ribbon sandwiches, quick dips, spicy nuts, and cream cheese balls rolled in everything imaginable.

Popular, too, was the cocktail buffet table, which was often adorned with a chafing dish (which had been very popular at the turn of the century) to keep such favorites as cheese fondue, meatballs, or crab cakes warm for an hour or two. Punch bowls frequently made an appearance at these parties. In the '30s, punch bowls were filled with fruit juice, sometimes alcohol, slices of fresh fruit, and a simple ice ring, which floated on top and kept it all cold. During the holidays, fruit punch was replaced by festive eggnog sprinkled with ground nutmeg or by hot wassail. By the late '40s and through the '50s, fruit punches became dressier. Ice rings were tinted a pretty pink and fresh fruit was decoratively arranged within the ice, turning a simple fruit punch into a real showstopper. Today bite-size foods are classics, so nibble away to your heart's content!

◀ *Chafing-Dish Meatballs, Hot Cheddar Puffs, and Half-Moon Empanadas*

South-of-the-Border Guacamole

From south of the border down Mexico way comes an avocado dip that is heated up with chile peppers. Its name comes from the Spanish word *ahuacamolli* (avocado sauce). One recipe appeared in a 1942 *Good Housekeeping Cook Book*. As ethnic and regional specialties took over dinner parties in the 1950s, guacamole caught on quickly and remains a cocktail-party standby.

PREP: 5 minutes ★ **MAKES** about 1½ cups

2 medium or 1 large ripe Hass avocado*

2 tablespoons minced onion

2 tablespoons chopped fresh cilantro

1 tablespoon fresh lime juice

2 serrano or jalapeño chiles, seeded and minced

½ teaspoon salt

¼ teaspoon coarsely ground black pepper

1 ripe plum tomato, chopped

tortilla chips

Cut each avocado lengthwise in half; remove each pit. With spoon, scoop flesh from peel into medium bowl. Add onion, cilantro, lime juice, chiles, salt, and pepper. With potato masher, coarsely mash mixture; stir in tomato. Transfer to small serving bowl and serve or cover and refrigerate up to 2 hours. Serve with tortilla chips.

*Choose perfectly ripened avocados that yield to gentle pressure when lightly squeezed in the palm of the hand.

EACH TABLESPOON: About 35 calories, 1g protein, 2g carbohydrate, 3g total fat (1g saturated), 0mg cholesterol, 45mg sodium.

Maryland Crab Dip

In the 1950s, hostesses coast to coast entertained friends at fancy cocktail parties and informal backyard barbecues. This hot dip, made with chunks of crab, a hint of curry, and slivers of almonds, was often served regardless of what else was on the menu. Our recipe uses Old Bay seasoning in place of curry powder.

PREP: 5 minutes ★ **BAKE:** 23 minutes ★ **MAKES** 1½ cups

⅓ cup slivered almonds

½ pound lump crabmeat, picked over

½ cup mayonnaise

⅓ cup sour cream

2 tablespoons minced onion

2 tablespoons chopped fresh parsley

1 teaspoon Old Bay seasoning

crackers

1. Preheat oven to 350°F. Grease 9-inch pie plate.

2. Spread almonds on cookie sheet. Bake, stirring occasionally, until lightly browned and fragrant, about 8 minutes; cool.

3. In medium bowl, combine crabmeat, mayonnaise, sour cream, onion, parsley, and seasoning. Turn into prepared pie plate and spread evenly.

4. Bake until heated through, about 15 minutes. Sprinkle with almonds. Serve with crackers.

EACH TABLESPOON: About 62 calories, 2g protein, 1g carbohydrate, 6g total fat (1g saturated), 14mg cholesterol, 82mg sodium.

Seven-Layer Tex-Mex Dip

This dip appeared at almost every party in Texas in the early 1980s. Count the layers (there were usually seven): bean dip, mashed avocados, sour cream, green onions, chopped tomatoes, black olives, and a generous topping of shredded cheese. For our recipe, you can assemble all the layers and chill them until ready to serve. Then warm the bean and cheese layers through and top with guacamole and sour cream.

PREP: 35 minutes ★ **BAKE:** 15 minutes
MAKES 24 servings

1 can (15 to 19 ounces) pinto beans, rinsed and drained

1 cup mild to medium salsa

2 green onions, finely chopped

1 small garlic clove, minced

4 ounces Monterey Jack cheese, shredded (1 cup)

1 can (2.25 ounces) sliced ripe black olives, rinsed and drained

2 ripe medium Hass avocados

⅓ cup chopped fresh cilantro

3 tablespoons finely chopped red onion

2 tablespoons fresh lime juice

½ teaspoon salt

1 cup sour cream

tortilla chips

1. Preheat oven to 350°F. In medium bowl, combine beans, 3 tablespoons salsa, half of green onions, and garlic. Mash until well combined but still slightly chunky. Spread in bottom of 9-inch glass pie plate.

2. Sprinkle Jack cheese over bean mixture, then spread with remaining salsa and sprinkle with olives. Bake until hot, about 15 minutes.

3. Meanwhile, cut each avocado in half; remove each pit. With spoon, scoop flesh from peel into same medium bowl. Mash avocados until slightly chunky. Stir in ¼ cup cilantro, red onion, lime juice, and salt. Spoon avocado mixture over hot dip; spread sour cream on top. Sprinkle with remaining green onions and remaining cilantro. Serve with tortilla chips.

EACH SERVING: About 83 calories, 3g protein, 4g carbohydrate, 6g total fat (2g saturated), 9mg cholesterol, 206mg sodium.

Chicken Liver Pâté

The more Americans traveled overseas in the 1960s and 1970s, the more they developed a taste for sophisticated foods, such as French pâté. Our silky smooth version is seasoned the traditional way: with a splash of brandy, some black pepper, and dried thyme.

PREP: 25 minutes plus chilling ★ **COOK:** 23 minutes
MAKES about 1½ cups

2 tablespoons butter or margarine

1 small onion, finely chopped

1 garlic clove, finely chopped

1 pound chicken livers, trimmed

2 tablespoons brandy

½ cup heavy or whipping cream

½ teaspoon salt

¼ teaspoon dried thyme

¼ teaspoon ground black pepper

assorted crackers, toast, or thinly sliced apples

1. In 10-inch skillet, melt butter over medium-high heat. Add onion; cook, stirring frequently, until tender and golden, about 10 minutes. Stir in garlic and livers; cook until livers are lightly browned but still pink inside, about 5 minutes. Stir in brandy; cook 5 minutes longer.

2. In blender or in food processor with knife blade attached, puree chicken-liver mixture, cream, salt, thyme, and pepper until smooth, stopping blender occasionally and scraping down sides with rubber spatula.

3. Spoon mixture into small bowl; cover and refrigerate at least 3 hours or up to overnight. Let stand 30 minutes at room temperature before serving. Serve with crackers, toast, or apples.

EACH TABLESPOON: About 54 calories, 4g protein, 1g carbohydrate, 4g total fat (2g saturated), 92mg cholesterol, 75mg sodium.

Entertaining Through the Centuries

After the Revolutionary War, the new nation welcomed a wave of immigrants. Many became household servants for the upper classes. The availability of such help changed the way Americans entertained, giving rise to dinner soirées in the mid- and late 1800s. Dinner invitations were usually engraved, menus were hand-calligraphed on porcelain slates, and waiters formally served seven-course dinners featuring French-inspired cuisine.

By the turn of the twentieth century and through the Roaring Twenties, servants were harder to find. Yet gracious entertaining remained in vogue. Women planned parties at home to show off their cooking skills. They gave formal teas, joined dinner clubs, and threw themed supper parties, often featuring four-course menus straight from a recent issue of one of the women's magazines.

When the century began sinking into the Great Depression, the protocol, pomp, and servants of yesteryear gradually gave way to informal at-home suppers, which were frequently prepared with the help of packaged goods and Betty Crocker. These were also the days of Prohibition. Even though liquor was illegal, bootleggers flourished. Wealthier Americans stashed liquor and wine at home, and cocktail parties, where drinks were served with finger foods, became stylish.

After World War II, young couples moved to newly developed suburban communities and discovered the ease of entertaining at informal backyard parties and casual dinners. Menus often featured classic favorites, such as hamburgers and steaks. In the 1960s, Julia Child brought *The French Chef* to television. More Americans were traveling too. Dinner parties offered a chance to cook ethnic specialties and to show off recently acquired cooking skills. By the beginning of the twenty-first century, continental cuisine became commonplace, restaurant entertaining grew even more popular, and culinary gurus whisked their way to stardom through increasingly popular television cooking shows that were enjoyed at home.

Potted Shrimp

Lacking refrigeration, the early settlers preserved seafood and meats by "potting" them. They first cooked the food, then potted and sealed it with plenty of fat, often butter. Potting food is still quite popular throughout the Deep South, especially in the Carolinas.

PREP: 15 minutes plus chilling ★ **COOK:** 3 minutes
MAKES about 2 cups

8 tablespoons (1 stick) unsalted butter, softened (do not use margarine)

1 pound medium shrimp, shelled and deveined

¾ teaspoon salt

¼ teaspoon ground red pepper (cayenne)

2 tablespoons dry sherry

sesame crackers or toast

1. In 10-inch skillet, melt 1 tablespoon butter over medium-high heat. Add shrimp, salt, and ground red pepper. Cook, stirring frequently, until shrimp are opaque throughout, about 2 minutes. Add sherry and cook 30 seconds.

2. Transfer shrimp and pan juices to food processor with knife blade attached and pulse until shrimp is finely chopped. Add remaining butter; process until blended.

3. Transfer shrimp mixture to serving bowl. Cover and refrigerate up to 24 hours. Let stand 30 minutes at room temperature before serving. Serve with sesame crackers or toast.

EACH TABLESPOON: About 39 calories, 2g protein, 0g carbohydrate, 3g total fat (2g saturated), 25mg cholesterol, 72mg sodium.

Classic Onion Dip

The tasty mixtures we now call dips started out as sauces that were ladled over foods. In the mid-nineteenth century, *dip* referred to a sauce of pork fat ladled over fish. At 1950s dinner parties, cream cheese–based onion and clam dips were two of the most popular offerings. In 1952, the Lipton Soup Company made preparing onion dip even easier by developing a dehydrated onion-soup mix. A consumer, however, is credited with creating the first dip using the soup mix, which Lipton has featured ever since. "Just open a couple of packages and fold into a cup of sour cream." Instantly, this never-fail onion party dip was ready for guests. Soon it became known as California Dip. Our onion dip is even better, for it's made the old-fashioned way: from slow-simmered onions folded into—of course—sour cream.

PREP: 10 minutes plus cooling ★ **COOK:** 30 minutes
MAKES 1 2/3 cups

2 large onions (12 ounces each), finely chopped (2 cups)
2 cups canned chicken broth or Old-Fashioned Chicken Broth (page 45)
1 tablespoon minced garlic
1/2 bay leaf
1/4 teaspoon dried thyme
1 teaspoon red wine vinegar
1 cup sour cream
1/8 teaspoon salt
1/8 teaspoon ground black pepper
crackers or potato chips

1. In 2-quart saucepan, combine onions, broth, garlic, bay leaf, and thyme; heat to boiling over high heat. Reduce heat and cook until liquid has almost completely evaporated, about 25 minutes.

2. Transfer mixture to medium bowl; stir in vinegar. Cool to room temperature.

3. Stir in sour cream, salt, and pepper. Cover and refrigerate up to overnight. Serve with crackers or potato chips.

EACH TABLESPOON: About 27 calories, 1g protein, 2g carbohydrate, 2g total fat (1g saturated), 4mg cholesterol, 93mg sodium.

Hot Cheddar Puffs

(pictured on page 12)

As cocktail parties became the rage in the '50s, every good hostess began collecting recipes for favorite finger foods to serve at parties. Often some form of cheesy puffs appeared. Ours are special: hot, spicy, crispy, and melt-in-your-mouth delicious!

PREP: 20 minutes ★ **BAKE:** 25 minutes
MAKES about 8 dozen puffs

2 teaspoons curry powder
1/2 teaspoon ground coriander
1/2 teaspoon ground cumin
1/4 teaspoon ground red pepper (cayenne)
6 tablespoons butter or margarine, cut into pieces
1/2 teaspoon salt
1 cup water
1 cup all-purpose flour
4 large eggs
4 ounces Cheddar cheese, shredded (1 cup)

1. Preheat oven to 400°F. Grease two large cookie sheets.

2. In 3-quart saucepan, combine curry powder, coriander, cumin, and ground red pepper. Cook over medium heat, stirring constantly, until very fragrant, about 1 minute. Stir in butter, salt, and water; heat to boiling over high heat. Remove from heat. With wooden spoon, stir in flour all at once. Return pan to medium-low heat, stirring constantly, until mixture forms a ball and leaves side of pan. Remove from heat.

3. Stir in eggs, one at a time, beating well after each addition, until batter is smooth and satiny. Stir in Cheddar. Spoon batter into large pastry bag fitted with 1/2-inch plain tip. Pipe batter, about 1 inch apart, on cookie sheets, forming 1-inch-wide and 3/4-inch-high mounds. Alternatively, drop teaspoons of dough on cookie sheets. With fingertip dipped in cool water, smooth peaks.

4. Bake puffs until deep golden, 25 to 30 minutes, rotating cookie sheets between oven racks halfway through baking. Transfer to wire racks to cool. Repeat with remaining batter.

5. Serve puffs at room temperature or reheat in 400°F oven 5 minutes to serve hot.

EACH PUFF: About 20 calories, 1g protein, 1g carbohydrate, 1g total fat (0g saturated), 10mg cholesterol, 30mg sodium.

Half-Moon Empanadas

(pictured on page 12)

In Spanish *empanar* means "to wrap in dough." These half-moon pastry turnovers are filled with *picadillo,* the Mexican-spiced beef filling. Recipes for empanadas first appeared here in print in the 1920s, and these savories are now a staple in Mexican-American fare.

PREP: 1 hour 15 minutes ★ **BAKE:** 15 minutes per batch
MAKES about 54 turnovers

Flaky Turnover Pastry (opposite)
2 teaspoons vegetable oil
1 small onion, finely chopped
1 large garlic clove, minced
¼ teaspoon ground cinnamon
¼ teaspoon ground red pepper (cayenne)
4 ounces ground beef chuck
¼ teaspoon salt
1 cup canned tomatoes with juice
3 tablespoons chopped golden raisins
3 tablespoons chopped pimiento-stuffed olives
    (salad olives)
1 large egg beaten with 2 tablespoons water

1. Prepare Flaky Turnover Pastry. Wrap in plastic wrap; set aside.

2. In 10-inch skillet, heat oil over medium heat. Add onion; cook, stirring frequently, until tender, about 5 minutes. Stir in garlic, cinnamon, and ground red pepper; cook 30 seconds. Increase heat to medium-high. Add ground beef and salt; cook, breaking up meat with side of spoon, until beef begins to brown, about 5 minutes. Stir in tomatoes with their juice, raisins, and olives, breaking up tomatoes with side of spoon. Cook over high heat until liquid has almost evaporated, 7 to 10 minutes. Remove from heat.

3. Preheat oven to 425°F. Divide dough into four equal pieces. On floured surface, with floured rolling pin, roll one piece of dough until ¹⁄₁₆ inch thick. Keep remaining dough covered. With 3-inch round biscuit cutter, cut out as many rounds as possible, reserving trimmings. On one half of each dough round, place 1 level measuring teaspoon of filling. Brush edges of rounds with some egg mixture. Fold dough over to enclose filling. With fork, press edges together to seal dough; prick tops. Brush tops of empanadas lightly with egg mixture. With spatula, lift turnovers and place, 1 inch apart, on ungreased large cookie sheet.

4. Bake turnovers just until golden, 15 to 17 minutes. Repeat with remaining dough, filling, and egg mixture. Press together dough trimmings and reroll.

Flaky Turnover Pastry

In large bowl, combine *3 cups all-purpose flour, 1½ teaspoons baking powder,* and *¾ teaspoon salt.* With pastry blender or two knives used scissor-fashion, cut in *1 cup vegetable shortening* until mixture resembles coarse crumbs. Sprinkle with about *6 tablespoons cold water,* 1 tablespoon at a time, mixing with fork after each addition, until dough is just moist enough to hold together. Shape into ball. Refrigerate pastry if not assembling turnovers right away.

EACH TURNOVER: About 70 calories, 1g protein, 6g carbohydrate, 5g total fat (2g saturated), 5mg cholesterol, 80mg sodium.

Bite-Size Quiche Lorraine

In the 1960s, Julia Child started a gourmet revolution by giving women the skills and recipes with which to cook classic French cuisine. Bacon-and-cheese pie from the south of France, called quiche Lorraine, quickly became an American standard. Julia called it "just a custard in a fancy dress."

PREP: 1 hour plus chilling ★ **BAKE:** 20 minutes
MAKES 36 mini quiches

Pastry Dough for 2-Crust Pie (page 298)
1 tablespoon butter or margarine, melted
1 package (8 ounces) bacon, finely chopped
1 cup half-and-half or light cream
2 large eggs
1/4 teaspoon salt
3 ounces Swiss cheese, shredded (3/4 cup)

1. Prepare Pastry Dough for 2-Crust Pie. Grease and flour thirty-six 1¾-inch mini-muffin-pan cups.

2. On lightly floured surface, with floured rolling pin, roll dough until ⅛ inch thick. Using 3-inch fluted round cookie cutter, cut pastry dough into 36 rounds, rerolling trimmings.

3. Line muffin-pan cups with dough rounds; brush lightly with melted butter. Cover and refrigerate.

4. Preheat oven to 400°F. In 12-inch skillet, cook bacon over medium heat until browned. Transfer bacon to paper towels to drain.

5. In small bowl, beat half-and-half, eggs, and salt. Divide bacon and cheese evenly among pastry cups. Spoon about 1 tablespoon egg mixture into each cup. Bake until knife inserted in center of quiche comes out clean, 20 to 25 minutes. Remove quiches from pan and serve hot, warm, or at room temperature.

EACH QUICHE: About 111 calories, 3g protein, 7g carbohydrate, 8g total fat (4g saturated), 26mg cholesterol, 118mg sodium.

Nachos

As the story goes, in the 1940s, a group of Texas women were lunching at the Victory Club in Piedras Negras, Mexico (just across the border from Eagle Pass, Texas). Chef Ignacio "Nacho" Anaya was running low on his usual specials, so he quickly threw some ingredients together for a snack. He spread a little cheese on toasted tortillas, topped each with a jalapeño slice, and called them *Nacho's Especiales.*

PREP: 30 minutes ★ **BAKE:** 5 minutes per batch
MAKES 36 nachos

36 unbroken large tortilla chips
3 large ripe plum tomatoes, cut into 1/4-inch pieces
1/3 cup chopped fresh cilantro
1/4 teaspoon salt
1 tablespoon vegetable oil
1 fully cooked chorizo sausage (3 ounces), finely chopped, or 3/4 cup finely chopped pepperoni (3 ounces)
1 medium onion, finely chopped
1 garlic clove, finely chopped
1/2 teaspoon ground cumin
1 can (15 to 19 ounces) black beans, rinsed and drained
4 ounces Monterey Jack cheese, shredded (1 cup)
2 pickled jalapeño chiles, very thinly sliced

1. Preheat oven to 400°F. Arrange as many tortilla chips as will fit in single layer on two ungreased large cookie sheets. In small bowl, combine tomatoes, cilantro, and salt.

2. In 10-inch skillet, heat oil over medium heat. Add chorizo, onion, garlic, and cumin; cook, stirring, until onion is tender, about 5 minutes. Stir in beans, mashing with back of spoon; cover and cook until heated through.

3. Place 1 tablespoon mashed bean mixture on each tortilla chip. Sprinkle Jack cheese over beans and top each nacho with 1 slice jalapeño. Bake until cheese begins to melt, about 5 minutes.

4. Spoon about 1 teaspoon tomato mixture on each nacho. Transfer nachos to platter; keep warm. Repeat with remaining chips, bean mixture, cheese, and tomato mixture. Serve warm.

EACH NACHO: About 51 calories, 2g protein, 4g carbohydrate, 3g total fat (1g saturated), 5mg cholesterol, 112mg sodium.

Texas Cheese Straws

In the mid-1950s, fancy tea parties, complete with turn-of-the-century elegance, were popular in bustling Texas cities. The tea tables were usually covered with linen and lace and set with the finest china. Sterling trays were laden with petite open-faced tea sandwiches, rich buttery cookies, carved vegetables, and creamy dips. These flaky, twisted, crispy cheese straws were often present, displayed in a circular pattern on a cut-crystal plate.

PREP: 30 minutes ★ **BAKE:** 20 minutes per batch
MAKES about 48 cheese straws

1 tablespoon paprika

½ teaspoon dried thyme

¼ to ½ teaspoon ground red pepper (cayenne)

¼ teaspoon salt

1 package (17¼ ounces) frozen puff-pastry sheets, thawed

1 large egg white, lightly beaten

8 ounces sharp Cheddar cheese, shredded (2 cups)

1. Grease two large cookie sheets. In small bowl, combine paprika, thyme, ground red pepper, and salt.

2. Unfold 1 puff-pastry sheet. On lightly floured surface, with floured rolling pin, roll pastry into 14-inch square. Lightly brush with egg white. Sprinkle pastry with half of paprika mixture. Sprinkle half of Cheddar over half of pastry. Fold pastry over to enclose cheese, forming rectangle. With rolling pin, lightly roll over pastry to seal layers together. With pizza wheel or knife, cut pastry crosswise into ½-inch-wide strips.

3. Preheat oven to 375°F. Place strips, ½ inch apart, on prepared cookie sheets, twisting each strip twice to form spiral and pressing ends against cookie sheet to prevent strips from uncurling during baking. Bake cheese straws until golden, 20 to 22 minutes. With spatula, carefully transfer straws to wire racks to cool.

4. Repeat with remaining puff-pastry sheet, egg white, paprika mixture, and cheese. Store in airtight container up to 1 week.

EACH STRAW: About 75 calories, 2g protein, 5g carbohydrate, 6g total fat (2g saturated), 9mg cholesterol, 65mg sodium.

Peppery Nuts

During the 1950s, many of the more affluent families moved from the cities to the suburbs, where they often threw cocktail parties "to get to know the neighbors." These soirées inspired the creation of drinks and fancy tidbits to accompany them. Bowls of spiced nuts, flavored with Worcestershire sauce and a dash of hot pepper, were among the most popular offerings. The type of nuts used depended on where you lived. Walnuts and almonds were popular in California, while pecans were the nut of choice in the Deep South.

PREP: 5 minutes plus cooling ★ **BAKE:** 20 minutes
MAKES about 2 cups

8 ounces walnuts (2 cups)

2 tablespoons sugar

1 tablespoon vegetable oil

1½ teaspoons Worcestershire sauce

½ teaspoon ground red pepper (cayenne)

¼ teaspoon salt

1. Preheat oven to 350°F. Place walnuts in jelly-roll pan. Bake, stirring occasionally, until toasted, about 20 minutes.

2. Meanwhile, in small bowl, combine sugar, oil, Worcestershire, ground red pepper, and salt.

3. Drizzle spice mixture over hot nuts and toss until thoroughly coated. Spread nuts in single layer; cool completely in pan on wire rack. Store at room temperature in tightly covered container up to 1 month.

EACH ¼ CUP: About 210 calories, 4g protein, 9g carbohydrate, 19g total fat (2 g saturated), 0mg cholesterol, 80mg sodium.

Texas Cheese Straws ▶

Pineapple Punch

To make a fascinating violet-tinted punch of delicate flavor, put one cup of grated pineapple with one pint of water, cook for fifteen minutes. Strain through cheesecloth, pressing out all the juice. Add one pint of water and two cups of sugar, which have been boiled ten minutes, half a cup of freshly made tea, the juice of three oranges and three lemons, one cup of grape juice and two and one-half quarts of water. Put in a punch bowl with a large lump of ice. Serve perfectly chilled in sherbet glasses.

—Good Housekeeping Everyday Cook Book, 1903

Firecracker Party Mix

In 1955, the home economists at Ralston Purina's Checkerboard Square in St. Louis created a party snack using Chex cereal squares to bolster sales. They tossed the cereal with pretzel sticks, nuts, and a spicy butter spiked with Worcestershire sauce. Over the years, numerous variations have evolved. This one mirrors the original recipe with one exception: the nuts have been replaced with popped corn.

PREP: 10 minutes plus cooling ★ **BAKE:** 30 minutes per batch
MAKES about 25 cups

¼ cup Worcestershire sauce

4 tablespoons butter or margarine

2 tablespoons brown sugar

1½ teaspoons salt

½ to 1 teaspoon ground red pepper (cayenne)

12 cups popped corn (about ⅓ cup unpopped)

1 package (12 ounces) oven-toasted corn cereal squares

1 package (8 to 10 ounces) thin pretzel sticks

1. Preheat oven to 300°F. In 1-quart saucepan, combine Worcestershire, butter, brown sugar, salt, and ground red pepper; heat over low heat, stirring often, until butter has melted.

2. Place half each of popped corn, cereal, and pretzels in large roasting pan; toss with half of Worcestershire-butter mixture.

3. Bake popcorn mixture 30 minutes, stirring once halfway through baking. Cool mixture in very large bowl or on surface covered with waxed paper. Repeat with remaining ingredients.

EACH ½ **CUP:** About 65 calories, 1g protein, 13g carbohydrate, 1g total fat (0 g saturated), 0mg cholesterol, 245mg sodium.

Oysters Rockefeller

Chef Jules Alciatore of the famous Antoine's restaurant in New Orleans created this dish, which is truly "as rich as Rockefeller himself" in 1899. The original recipe has never been revealed, though legend has it that a New York chef recorded notes from Chef Alciatore himself. One was instructed to "Take the tail and tips of small green onions. Take celery, take chervil, take tarragon leaves and the crumbs of stale bread. Take Tobasco sauce and the best butter obtainable. Pound all these into a mixture in a mortar, so that all the fragrant flavorings are blended. Add a dash of absinthe. Force the mixture through a fine-meshed sieve. Place one spoonful on each oyster as it rests in its own shell and in its own juice on the crushed rock salt, the purpose of which is to keep the oyster piping hot . . ." Numerous versions have been created over the years, using ingredients such as spinach, shallots, herbs, anchovies, lettuce, lime juice, and even anise. Here fresh oysters on the half shell are cooked until sizzling hot under a bed of seasoned chopped spinach and buttered bread crumbs.

PREP: 30 minutes ★ **BAKE:** 10 minutes
MAKES 4 first-course servings

1 dozen oysters, shucked, bottom shells reserved

kosher or rock salt (optional)

1 bunch spinach (10 to 12 ounces), tough stems trimmed, washed, and dried very well

1 tablespoon plus 2 teaspoons butter or margarine

2 tablespoons finely chopped onion

pinch ground red pepper (cayenne)

¼ cup heavy or whipping cream

1 tablespoon Pernod or other anise-flavored liqueur

pinch salt

2 tablespoons plain dried bread crumbs

1. Preheat oven to 425°F. Place oysters in shells in jelly-roll pan lined with ½-inch layer of kosher salt to keep them flat, if desired; refrigerate.

2. In 2-quart saucepan, cook spinach over high heat until wilted; drain. Rinse spinach with cold running water; drain well. Finely chop spinach. Wipe saucepan dry with paper towels.

3. In same clean saucepan, melt 1 tablespoon butter over medium heat. Add onion; cook until tender, about 3 minutes. Stir in ground red pepper. Stir in spinach, cream, Pernod, and salt. Cook over high heat, stirring, until liquid has reduced and thickened. Remove from heat.

4. In small saucepan, melt remaining 2 teaspoons butter over low heat. Remove from heat; stir in bread crumbs until evenly moistened.

5. Spoon spinach mixture evenly on top of oysters. Sprinkle with buttered bread crumbs. Bake until edges of oysters curl, about 10 minutes.

EACH SERVING: About 166 calories, 6g protein, 9g carbohydrate, 12g total fat (7g saturated), 57mg cholesterol, 228mg sodium.

Clams Casino

The year was 1917, and Mrs. Paran Stevens was hosting a luncheon for her society friends at the Casino at Narragansett Pier in New York City. Maitre d'Hotel Julius Keller created a dish for the occasion featuring clams on the half shell baked with bacon and seasonings. He didn't know what to call it but decided on Clams Casino in honor of the restaurant. Many books include a recipe for Oysters Casino, which is also quite tasty.

PREP: 30 minutes ★ **BAKE:** 10 minutes
MAKES 6 first-course servings

2 dozen littleneck clams, scrubbed and shucked, bottom shells reserved

kosher or rock salt (optional)

3 slices bacon

1 tablespoon olive oil

½ red pepper, very finely chopped

½ green pepper, very finely chopped

¼ teaspoon coarsely ground black pepper

1 garlic clove, finely chopped

1 cup fresh bread crumbs (about 2 slices bread)

1. Preheat oven to 425°F. Place clams in shells in jelly-roll pan lined with ½-inch layer of kosher salt to keep them flat, if desired; refrigerate.

2. In 10-inch skillet, cook bacon over medium heat until browned; transfer to paper towels to drain. Discard drippings from skillet. Add oil, red and green peppers, and black pepper to skillet. Cook, stirring occasionally, until peppers are tender, about 5 minutes. Stir in garlic and cook 30 seconds; remove from heat.

3. Finely chop bacon; stir bacon and bread crumbs into pepper mixture in skillet. Spoon crumb mixture evenly over clams. Bake until crumb topping is light golden, about 10 minutes.

EACH SERVING: About 107 calories, 9g protein, 6g carbohydrate, 5g total fat (1g saturated), 23mg cholesterol, 122mg sodium.

Shrimp Cocktail

The outfitting of shrimp boats with refrigeration in the early twentieth century made it possible to transport fresh shrimp to more American cities. Shrimp cocktail served with spicy red shrimper's (cocktail) sauce remains an all-American favorite to this day. The original Rémoulade Sauce, based on mayonnaise and subtly spiced with mustard and horseradish, comes from France. When parsley is added it becomes Rémoulade Verte. For a Cajun rendition, forget the tarragon and Dijon and heat it up with some Creole mustard and cayenne.

PREP: 25 minutes plus chilling ★ **COOK:** 25 minutes
MAKES 8 appetizer servings

1 lemon, thinly sliced

4 bay leaves

20 whole black peppercorns

10 whole allspice berries

2 teaspoons salt

24 extra-large shrimp (1 pound), shelled and deveined

Red Cocktail Sauce (opposite)

Rémoulade Verte (opposite)

12 small romaine lettuce leaves

24 (7-inch) bamboo skewers

1. In 5-quart Dutch oven, combine *2 quarts water*, lemon, bay leaves, peppercorns, allspice berries, and salt; heat to boiling. Cover and boil 15 minutes.

2. Add shrimp; cook just until opaque throughout, 1 to 2 minutes. Drain and rinse with cold running water to stop cooking. Cover and refrigerate shrimp up to 24 hours.

3. Prepare Red Cocktail Sauce and/or Rémoulade Verte.

4. Just before serving, place bowls of sauces in center of platter; arrange romaine leaves around bowls, leaf tips facing out. Thread each shrimp on a bamboo skewer and arrange skewers on romaine.

EACH SERVING WITHOUT SAUCE: About 51 calories, 10g protein, 1g carbohydrate, 1g total fat (0g saturated), 70mg cholesterol, 141mg sodium.

Red Cocktail Sauce

PREP: 15 minutes ★ MAKES about 1 cup

1 cup bottled cocktail sauce
2 tablespoons chopped fresh cilantro
2 tablespoons minced jalapeño chile
2 teaspoons fresh lime juice

In small bowl, combine cocktail sauce, cilantro, jalapeño, and lime juice until well blended. Cover and refrigerate up to 24 hours.

EACH TABLESPOON: About 18 calories, 0g protein, 4g carbohydrate, 0g total fat (0g saturated), 0mg cholesterol, 191mg sodium.

Rémoulade Verte

PREP: 20 minutes ★ MAKES about 2/3 cup

1/3 cup mayonnaise
2 tablespoons sour cream
3 tablespoons finely chopped dill pickle
1 tablespoon chopped fresh parsley
3/4 teaspoon chopped fresh tarragon or 1/4 teaspoon dried tarragon
1/2 teaspoon chopped fresh chives
1 anchovy fillet, finely chopped
1 teaspoon capers, drained and chopped
1 teaspoon Dijon mustard

In small bowl, combine mayonnaise, sour cream, pickle, parsley, tarragon, chives, anchovy, capers, and mustard; stir until well blended. Cover and refrigerate up to 24 hours.

EACH TABLESPOON: About 61 calories, 0g protein, 0g carbohydrate, 6g total fat (1g saturated), 6mg cholesterol, 143mg sodium.

Dilly Shrimp

Pickling foods not only preserves them but also adds extra flavor. The food is first boiled, then pickled with vinegar, spices, and fresh dill. Pickled shrimp is best made a day ahead and refrigerated overnight, making it great for parties.

PREP: 20 minutes plus overnight to marinate
COOK: 5 minutes ★ MAKES 24 appetizer servings

1/4 cup dry sherry
3 teaspoons salt
1/4 teaspoon whole black peppercorns
1 bay leaf
3 pounds large shrimp, shelled and deveined, leaving tail part of shell on, if desired
2/3 cup fresh lemon juice (about 4 large lemons)
1/2 cup distilled white vinegar
1/2 cup vegetable oil
3 tablespoons pickling spices, tied in cheesecloth bag
2 teaspoons sugar
2 dill sprigs

1. In 4-quart saucepan, combine *6 cups water,* sherry, 2 teaspoons salt, peppercorns, and bay leaf; heat to boiling over high heat. Add shrimp; heat to boiling. Shrimp should be opaque throughout when water returns to boil; if needed, cook about 1 minute longer. Drain.

2. In large bowl, combine lemon juice, vinegar, oil, pickling spices, sugar, dill, and remaining 1 teaspoon salt. Add shrimp and toss well to coat. Spoon into ziptight plastic bags, press out air, and seal. Refrigerate shrimp overnight to marinate, turning bags occasionally.

3. Remove shrimp from marinade and arrange in chilled bowl. Serve with cocktail picks.

EACH SERVING: About 69 calories, 9g protein, 1g carbohydrate, 2g total fat (0g saturated), 70mg cholesterol, 166mg sodium.

The Chafing Dish

Culinary historian Evan Jones cites the chafing dish as "an important part of American dining room paraphernalia as early as the mid-1800s." Delmonico's in New York City was one of the first restaurants to serve food in a sterling-silver covered dish set over a low flame. Other restaurants quickly followed suit. Chafing dishes often featured foods such as turkey tetrazzini: diced cooked turkey dressed up with a rich cream sauce. By the mid-1900s, chafing dishes started appearing on buffet tables everywhere to keep such popular foods as chicken à la king hot until guests helped themselves.

Buffalo Chicken Wings

On an otherwise rather typical day in 1964, Teressa Bellissimo, owner of the Anchor Bar in Buffalo, New York, accidentally received too many chicken wings from one of her suppliers. She fried them, swished them in butter, spiced them up with hot sauce, and served the wings with her cooling blue-cheese dressing on the side. This recipe saves on some calories by broiling the wings instead of frying them.

PREP: 15 minutes ★ **BROIL:** 20 minutes
MAKES 18 appetizers

4 ounces blue cheese, crumbled (1 cup)

½ cup sour cream

¼ cup mayonnaise

¼ cup milk

¼ cup chopped fresh parsley

1 tablespoon fresh lemon juice

½ teaspoon salt

3 pounds chicken wings (18 wings), tips discarded, if desired

3 tablespoons butter or margarine

¼ cup hot pepper sauce

1 medium bunch celery, cut into sticks

1. Preheat broiler. In medium bowl, combine blue cheese, sour cream, mayonnaise, milk, parsley, lemon juice, and ¼ teaspoon salt. Cover and refrigerate.

2. Arrange chicken wings on rack in broiling pan; sprinkle with remaining ¼ teaspoon salt. Broil 5 inches from heat source 10 minutes. Turn wings; broil until golden, 10 to 15 minutes longer.

3. Meanwhile, in 1-quart saucepan, melt butter with hot pepper sauce over low heat, stirring occasionally; keep sauce warm.

4. In large bowl, toss wings with seasoned butter to coat well. Arrange chicken wings and celery on platter along with blue-cheese sauce and serve.

EACH APPETIZER (WITHOUT WINGTIP): About 169 calories, 10g protein, 3g carbohydrate, 13g total fat (5g saturated), 39mg cholesterol, 349mg sodium.

Chafing-Dish Meatballs

(pictured on page 12)

These mini meatballs, flavored with typical Mexican spices, make great party fare, especially when served from an elegant chafing dish.

PREP: 30 minutes ★ **COOK:** 40 minutes
MAKES 20 appetizer servings

1½ pounds ground beef chuck

¾ cup plain dried bread crumbs

I large egg

3 garlic cloves, minced

1¼ teaspoons salt

½ teaspoon ground black pepper

¼ cup water

I can (28 ounces) plum tomatoes

I chipotle chile in adobo*

2 teaspoons vegetable oil

I small onion, finely chopped

I teaspoon ground cumin

I cup canned chicken broth or **Old-Fashioned Chicken Broth** (page 45)

¼ cup coarsely chopped fresh cilantro

I. In large bowl, combine ground beef, bread crumbs, egg, one-third of garlic, 1 teaspoon salt, pepper, and water just until well blended but not overmixed. Shape mixture into ¾-inch meatballs, handling meat as little as possible.

2. In blender, at low speed, puree tomatoes with their juice and chipotle chile until smooth.

3. In nonreactive 5-quart Dutch oven, heat oil over medium heat. Add onion; cook, stirring often, until tender, about 5 minutes. Stir in cumin and remaining garlic; cook 30 seconds. Stir in tomato mixture, broth, and remaining ¼ teaspoon salt; heat to boiling over high heat.

4. Add meatballs; heat to boiling. Reduce heat and simmer, uncovered, 30 minutes. Transfer mixture to chafing dish and sprinkle with cilantro. Serve with cocktail picks.

*Canned chipotle chiles in adobo (smoked jalapeño chiles in a vinegary marinade) are available in Hispanic markets and in the ethnic section of some supermarkets.

EACH SERVING: About 125 calories, 8g protein, 5g carbohydrate, 8g total fat (3 g saturated), 31mg cholesterol, 310mg sodium.

Sausage-Stuffed Mushrooms

American settlers frequently found mushrooms growing wild but avoided eating them, fearing they might be poisonous. It wasn't until the nineteenth century that cultivated mushrooms from France were imported. By the 1920s, white mushrooms were being cultivated here. They rapidly grew in popularity, and by the 1960s, stuffed mushrooms had become a popular hors d'oeuvre.

PREP: 50 minutes ★ **BAKE:** 15 minutes
MAKES 30 appetizers

1½ pounds medium white mushrooms (about 30)

8 ounces sweet or hot Italian-sausage links, casings removed

½ cup shredded mozzarella cheese

¼ cup seasoned dried bread crumbs

I. Remove stems from mushrooms; chop stems. Set mushroom caps and chopped stems aside.

2. Heat 10-inch skillet over medium heat. Add sausage; cook, breaking up meat with side of spoon, until well browned, about 8 minutes. With slotted spoon, transfer sausage to paper towels to drain. Spoon off all but 2 tablespoons drippings from skillet.

3. Add mushroom stems to hot drippings in skillet. Cook, stirring, until tender, about 10 minutes. Remove from heat; stir in sausage, mozzarella, and bread crumbs.

4. Preheat oven to 450°F. Fill mushroom caps with sausage mixture. Place stuffed mushrooms in jelly-roll pan. Bake until heated through, about 15 minutes. Serve hot.

EACH APPETIZER: About 39 calories, 2g protein, 2g carbohydrate, 3g total fat (1g saturated), 6mg cholesterol, 90mg sodium.

Deviled Eggs

Church suppers and picnics were extremely popular in the mid-twentieth century. At least one platter of deviled eggs was usually served.

PREP: 40 minutes ★ MAKES 24 deviled eggs

12 large eggs
¼ cup sliced pimientos, chopped
¼ cup low-fat mayonnaise dressing
1 tablespoon plus 1 teaspoon Dijon mustard
½ teaspoon ground red pepper (cayenne)
¼ teaspoon salt

1. In 3-quart saucepan, place eggs and enough *cold water* to cover by at least 1 inch; heat to boiling over high heat. Immediately remove saucepan from heat and cover tightly; let stand 15 minutes. Pour off hot water and run cold water over eggs to cool. Peel eggs.

2. Cut eggs lengthwise in half. Gently remove yolks and place in small bowl; with fork, finely mash yolks. Stir in pimientos, mayonnaise dressing, mustard, ground red pepper, and salt until well mixed.

3. Place egg-white halves in jelly-roll pan lined with paper towels (to prevent eggs from rolling). Spoon egg-yolk mixture into egg halves. Cover and refrigerate up to 4 hours.

EACH DEVILED EGG: About 45 calories, 3g protein, 1g carbohydrate, 3g total fat (1g saturated), 0g fiber, 106mg cholesterol, 100mg sodium.

Swiss Fondue

This ever-popular hot cheese specialty from Switzerland was reintroduced and popularized in the 1950s, just when Americans were discovering new "foreign" dishes. The name comes from the French word *fondre* (to melt). This classic version uses Swiss cheese, Gruyère cheese, and white wine to create the perfect balance of flavors.

PREP 15 minutes ★ COOK 15 minutes
MAKES 6 first-course servings

1 garlic clove, cut in half
1½ cups dry white wine
1 tablespoon kirsch or brandy
8 ounces Swiss or Emmental cheese, shredded (2 cups)
8 ounces Gruyère cheese, shredded (2 cups)
3 tablespoons all-purpose flour
⅛ teaspoon ground black pepper
pinch ground nutmeg
1 loaf (16 ounces) French bread, cut into 1-inch cubes

1. Rub inside of fondue pot or heavy nonreactive 2-quart saucepan with garlic; discard garlic. Pour wine into fondue pot. Heat over medium-low heat until very hot but not boiling; stir in kirsch.

2. Meanwhile, in medium bowl, toss Swiss cheese, Gruyère, and flour until mixed. Add cheese mixture, one handful at a time, to wine, stirring constantly and vigorously until cheese has melted and mixture is thick and smooth. If mixture separates, increase heat to medium, stirring just until smooth. Stir in pepper and nutmeg.

3. Transfer fondue to table; place over tabletop heater to keep hot, if you like. To eat, spear cubes of French bread onto long-handled fondue forks and dip into cheese mixture.

EACH SERVING: About 567 calories, 29g protein, 45g carbohydrate, 25g total fat (14g saturated), 76mg cholesterol, 689mg sodium.

Ribbon Sandwiches

Tea parties became a favorite way for American women to entertain their friends in the 1960s—and the fancier the food, the better! Thin ribbons of elegant "stacked" sandwiches were frequently found on tea trays. To make the most attractive sandwiches, choose breads of contrasting colors and fill the sandwiches with a variety of creamy fillings, such as cream cheese with minced nuts and pimiento-stuffed olives, chicken salad, finely chopped ham salad, and egg salad with minced sweet pickles.

PREP: 40 minutes ★ **MAKES** 24 ribbon sandwiches

1 package (8 ounces) cream cheese, softened
2 small green onions, finely chopped
3 tablespoons chopped fresh parsley
4 radishes, minced
$\frac{1}{8}$ teaspoon salt
$\frac{1}{8}$ teaspoon ground black pepper
18 very thin slices whole-wheat bread
12 very thin slices white bread

1. Line jelly-roll pan with damp paper towels.

2. In small bowl, combine cream cheese, green onions, parsley, radishes, salt, and pepper until well blended. For each stack, gently spread cream cheese mixture on 2 slices whole-wheat bread and 2 slices white bread. Alternately stack slices, beginning with whole-wheat and ending with white. Place another slice whole-wheat bread on top of stack. Repeat with remaining bread to make 6 stacks.

3. Gently press down on each stack. With serrated knife, trim crusts. Place stacks in prepared pan; cover with additional damp paper towels to keep bread from drying out. Cover pan tightly with plastic wrap and refrigerate up to 4 hours.

4. Cut each stack crosswise into quarters. Arrange on a platter and serve.

EACH SANDWICH: About 79 calories, 2g protein, 9g carbohydrate, 4g total fat (2g saturated), 10mg cholesterol, 128mg sodium.

Chapter 2

Soups & Sandwiches

The earliest soups served in America resembled stews, as they were made from a pot of water, raw meat, and green vegetables. Martha Washington's was a classic: "pretty piece of beef…a marrow bone or two…end of a neck of muton or veale…a little bacon…some sorrel & spinnage, & cabbedg leaves, green pease, what salt you like." These substantial home-made main-dish soups were practical as well as delicious, for they used fresh local ingredients that were readily available: there were shrimp and crawfish gumbos in the Louisiana bayou country, she-crab soup in Charleston, hearty fish and potato chowders in New England, fresh vegetable soups from the Midwestern farmlands, and lentil preaching soups in Amish villages. Americans so loved these regional soups that they soon became part of our country's culinary heritage.

Nineteenth-century cookbook authors advised readers that the best way to pull the flavor out of meat and vegetables for a soup was to always use cold water and to simmer (never boil) soup. In her 1886 cookbook, Fannie Farmer instructs readers that some of the most flavorful soups take advantage of tasty leftovers, such as a piece of bacon or ham.

She advises that a small piece of ham or bacon adds great flavor to a soup pot. In her Split Pea Soup, she suggests thinning the soup with the water left from boiling a ham. With the twentieth century came soups from the can, the freezer, and in pouches that were heated in a microwave oven.

Eating a sandwich with a cup of soup is traditionally American. As early as the late 1800s, sandwiches began appearing. In the first part of the twentieth century, old-fashioned sandwich and soda shops became popular meeting-and-eating spots. Generations of school children have grown up on a cup of tomato soup and a toasted cheese sandwich for lunch. Today sandwiches have also gone regional and ethnic. Pulled pork from the South, fajitas from Mexico, lobster rolls from Maine, steak sandwiches from the Midwestern plains, and Cuban sandwiches from Miami have all become commonplace.

Creamy Asparagus Cup

As early as the 1740s, Swedish naturalist Peter Kalm recorded that asparagus grew wild and in cultivated fields in New Jersey. William Byrd, founder of Richmond and fellow of the Royal Society, reported in *The National History of Virginia, or the Newly Discovered Eden* in 1737 that Virginians had long been growing all manner of Euoprean fruits and vegetables including "very large and long asparagus of splendid flavor." By the end of the century, asparagus recipes began appearing in cookbooks. This delicate first-course soup is always elegant, whether it's served hot or cold.

PREP: 10 minutes ★ **COOK:** 25 minutes
MAKES about 5 cups or 4 first-course servings

- 2 tablespoons butter or margarine
- 1 medium onion, chopped
- 12 ounces asparagus, trimmed and cut into 1-inch pieces (3 cups)
- 3 tablespoons all-purpose flour
- 1/4 teaspoon salt
- 1/8 teaspoon ground black pepper
- 1 can (14 1/2 ounces) chicken or vegetable broth or 1 3/4 cups Old-Fashioned Chicken Broth (page 45)
- 1 cup half-and-half or light cream

1. In 3-quart saucepan, melt butter over medium heat. Add onion and cook, stirring frequently, until tender and golden, about 10 minutes. Add asparagus; cook 1 minute.

2. With wire whisk, stir in flour, salt, and pepper until blended. Gradually whisk in broth until smooth; heat to boiling, stirring constantly. Reduce heat; cover and simmer until asparagus is tender, 5 to 10 minutes.

3. Spoon half of mixture into blender. Cover, with center part of cover removed to let steam escape; puree until smooth. Pour into bowl. Repeat with remaining asparagus mixture.

4. Return puree to same clean saucepan; stir in half-and-half. Heat through (do not boil). Serve soup hot, or cover and refrigerate to serve chilled later. If chilled soup is too thick, stir in some milk.

EACH SERVING: About 194 calories, 6g protein, 14g carbohydrate, 14g total fat (8g saturated), 38mg cholesterol, 657mg sodium.

Cream of Cauliflower Soup

Prepare as directed but substitute *3 cups small cauliflower flowerets* for asparagus, use *1 1/4 cups half-and-half or light cream*, and add *dash of ground red pepper (cayenne)*. If desired, stir in *4 ounces sharp Cheddar cheese, shredded* (1 cup), and *1/2 teaspoon Dijon mustard* when heating through. Makes about 5 cups or 4 first-course servings.

Cream of Broccoli Soup

Prepare as directed but substitute *3 cups small broccoli flowerets* for asparagus. Makes about 4 1/2 cups or 4 first-course servings.

Cream of Spinach Soup

Prepare as directed but substitute *2 packages (10 ounces each) frozen chopped spinach*, thawed, for asparagus and omit the 5 to 10 minutes of cooking time in Step 2. Makes about 4 1/2 cups or 4 first-course servings.

Black Bean Soup

For thousands of years, black beans have been popular throughout Mexico and Venezuela. But it wasn't until 1970 that this soup began appearing on American menus. The Coach House restaurant in New York began serving a pureed black bean soup that contained a splash of sherry and was topped with a slice of lemon and some chopped hard-cooked egg.

PREP: 20 minutes plus overnight to soak beans
COOK: 2 hours 30 minutes
MAKES about 13 cups or 12 first-course servings

1 pound dry black beans
3 tablespoons olive oil
3 large carrots, peeled and chopped
3 medium onions, chopped
3 stalks celery with leaves, chopped
4 garlic cloves, peeled
2 bay leaves
1/2 teaspoon dried thyme
2 smoked ham hocks (1 1/2 pounds)
10 cups water
1 teaspoon coarsely ground black pepper
1/2 cup chopped fresh parsley
3 tablespoons dry sherry
2 teaspoons salt
12 paper-thin lemon slices

1. In large bowl, place beans with enough *water* to cover by 2 inches. Soak overnight.

2. Drain and rinse beans. In 5-quart Dutch oven, heat oil over medium heat. Add carrots, onions, and celery; cook, stirring, until tender, about 10 minutes. Add garlic, bay leaves, and thyme; cook 1 minute.

3. Add beans, ham hocks, water, and pepper to Dutch oven; heat to boiling over high heat. Reduce heat; cover and simmer until beans are very tender, about 2 hours. Discard ham hocks and bay leaves.

4. Spoon one-fourth of bean mixture into blender. Cover, with center part of cover removed to let steam escape; puree until very smooth. Pour into bowl. Repeat with remaining mixture. Return puree to same clean Dutch oven; stir in all but 2 tablespoons parsley, sherry, and salt. Cook 5 minutes.

5. To serve, ladle soup into bowls, garnish with lemon slices, and sprinkle with remaining 2 tablespoons parsley.

EACH SERVING: About 207 calories, 10g protein, 32g carbohydrate, 5g total fat (1g saturated), 2mg cholesterol, 788mg sodium.

The Senate's Famous Bean Soup

Several stories exist about the origin of the mandate for serving this famous white-bean soup in the Senate dining rooms. One attributes the tradition, as well as the creation of the recipe, to Senator F. Dubois of Idaho in the early 1900s. Some documents indicate that Senator Knute Nelson of Minnesota, chairman of the Senate committee on Rules in 1907, enjoyed the soup so much that he decreed that the soup should be served on a daily basis in the Senate dining rooms. Senator Dubois' version of the soup included mashed potatoes, but the soup served in the Senate today does not include them. It is interesting to note that in the House of Representatives, the Honorable Joseph Cannon, Speaker of the House from 1903 to 1911, passed a resolution requiring that a hearty bean soup be served in the House dining rooms every day. Representative Bob Traxler of Michigan (1974–1993) later decreed that the soup be made only with Michigan white navy beans.

Serves 8

2 pounds dried Michigan white navy beans
Four quarts hot water
1 1/2 pounds smoked ham hocks
1 onion, chopped
2 tablespoons butter
Salt and pepper to taste

Wash the navy beans and run hot water through them until they are slightly whitened. Place the beans in a pot with the hot water. Add the ham hocks; simmer approximately three hours in a covered pot, stirring occasionally. Remove ham hocks and set aside to cool. Dice the meat and return to soup. Lightly brown the onion in butter. Add to soup. Before serving, bring to a boil and season with salt and pepper.

Source: original recipe from the United States Senate

Calico Cheese Soup

The American colonists brought their love of cheese with them from their homeland. Indeed, most of the cheeses they ate were imported from England, but by the early 1800s, they had developed their own. These early cheeses were based on the methods used for making English Cheshires, the cheese-making methods of the German immigrants in Pennsylvania, and the sophisticated cheese-making techniques of the Swiss in the mid-Atlantic colonies.

PREP: 15 minutes ★ COOK: 15 minutes
MAKES about 6 cups or 6 first-course servings

4 tablespoons butter or margarine

1 small garlic clove, crushed with garlic press

2 cups (½-inch) fresh bread pieces (about 6 slices crustless firm white bread)

1 large onion (12 ounces), chopped

2 carrots, peeled and chopped

½ cup chopped celery

¼ cup all-purpose flour

¼ teaspoon ground red pepper (cayenne)

3 cups canned chicken broth or Old-Fashioned Chicken Broth (page 45)

1 cup half-and-half cream or light cream

8 ounces sharp Cheddar cheese, shredded (2 cups)

1. Preheat oven to 350°F. Melt 1 tablespoon butter. In medium bowl, combine melted butter and garlic. Add bread cubes, tossing to coat. Spread cubes in single layer in small baking pan. Bake, stirring once, until golden, about 15 minutes; set aside to cool.

2. In large saucepan, melt remaining 3 tablespoons butter over medium heat. Add onion, carrots, and celery. Cover and cook, stirring occasionally, until tender but not browned, about 10 minutes.

3. With wire whisk, stir in flour and ground red pepper until blended; cook, stirring, 2 minutes. Gradually whisk in broth and half-and-half until smooth; heat to boiling. Reduce heat to low. Stir in Cheddar; heat until melted (do not boil). Serve with croutons.

EACH SERVING WITH CROUTONS: About 384 calories, 15g protein, 22g carbohydrate, 26g total fat (16g saturated), 77mg cholesterol, 511mg sodium.

Bacon-Corn Chowder

(pictured on page 30)

Our ancestors quickly recognized the attributes of *maize* (Indian corn) from the Native Americans and developed tasty ways to serve it. One of the most beloved preparations is thick, creamy corn chowder. In our version, we use bacon, which imparts a delicate smoky quality.

PREP: 25 minutes ★ COOK: 30 minutes
MAKES about 9½ cups or 8 first-course servings

6 medium ears corn, husks and silk removed

4 slices bacon, cut into ½-inch pieces

1 medium red onion, chopped

1 jalapeño chile, seeded and finely chopped

1 garlic clove, finely chopped

2 tablespoons all-purpose flour

½ teaspoon salt

⅛ teaspoon ground black pepper

1 pound red potatoes (6 medium), cut into ½-inch pieces

2 cans (14½ ounces each) chicken broth or 3½ cups Old-Fashioned Chicken Broth (page 45)

2 cups half-and-half or light cream

1 ripe medium tomato (8 ounces), peeled, seeded, and chopped

thinly sliced fresh basil leaves

1. Cut kernels from corncobs (about 3 cups), reserving 3 corncobs; discard remaining corncobs.

2. In 5-quart Dutch oven, cook bacon over medium heat until browned. With slotted spoon, transfer bacon to paper towels to drain; crumble.

3. To bacon drippings in Dutch oven, add onion and jalapeño; cook, stirring, until onion is tender, about 5 minutes. Add garlic; cook 1 minute longer. With wire whisk, whisk in flour, salt, and pepper; cook, stirring, 1 minute longer.

4. Stir in potatoes, corncobs, broth, and half-and-half; heat to boiling over high heat. Reduce heat; cover and simmer until potatoes are tender, 10 to 15 minutes.

5. Discard corncobs; stir in corn kernels and heat through. Ladle chowder into tureen. Stir in tomatoes and sprinkle with bacon and basil.

EACH SERVING: About 272 calories, 7g protein, 29g carbohydrate, 15g total fat (7g saturated), 30mg cholesterol, 693mg sodium.

Chunky Gazpacho

In the 1824 cookbook *The Virginia House-wife,* Mary Randolph offers a recipe called Gaspacho-Spanish, which is a layered tomato salad. "Put some biscuit or toasted bread in the bottom of a sallad bowl, put in a layer of tomatos with their skins taken off, and one of sliced cucumbers...and chopped onion...stew some tomatos quite soft, strain the juice, mix in some mustard, oil, and water, and pour over it. . . . " Recipes for gazpacho as we know it today began appearing in cookbooks by 1845.

PREP: 30 minutes plus chilling
MAKES about 5 cups or 4 first-course servings

2 medium cucumbers (about 8 ounces each), peeled

1 medium yellow pepper

¼ small red onion

2 pounds ripe tomatoes (about 6 medium), peeled, seeded, and chopped

½ to 1 small jalapeño chile, seeded

3 tablespoons fresh lime juice

2 tablespoons extravirgin olive oil

¾ plus ⅛ teaspoon salt

¼ cup light sour cream or plain lowfat yogurt

1 tablespoon milk

5 teaspoons finely chopped fresh cilantro

1. Chop half of 1 cucumber, half of yellow pepper, and all of onion into ¼-inch pieces; set aside. Cut remaining cucumbers and yellow pepper into large pieces.

2. In blender or food processor with knife blade attached, puree large pieces of cucumber and yellow pepper, tomatoes, jalapeño, lime juice, oil, and ¾ teaspoon salt until smooth. Pour into medium bowl; add cut-up cucumber, yellow pepper, and onion. Cover and refrigerate until well chilled, at least 6 hours or up to overnight.

3. Prepare cilantro cream: In small bowl, stir sour cream, milk, cilantro, and remaining ⅛ teaspoon salt until smooth. Cover and refrigerate.

4. To serve, ladle soup into chilled bowls and top with dollops of cilantro cream.

EACH SERVING WITH CILANTRO CREAM: About 165 calories, 4g protein, 21g carbohydrate, 9g total fat (1g saturated), 6mg cholesterol, 505mg sodium.

German Lentil Soup

German immigrants settled in the lush farmlands of Pennsylvania in the mid-eighteenth century. As this was well before the days of central heating, they needed foods that would sustain them during the long, cold winters. The Old Order of House Amish held their Sabbath services in various homes in the villages. A hearty stew-like soup of beans, smoked pork butt, and ham was served during the breaks between preachings and was therefore nicknamed "preaching soup." According to author and food historian Evan Jones, "The soup is said to fortify both preacher and the gathered faithful." Our stick-to-your-ribs soup is a faithful rendition.

PREP: 25 minutes ★ **COOK:** 1 hour 30 minutes
MAKES about 11 cups or 6 main-dish servings

4 slices bacon, cut into ½ inch pieces

2 medium onions, chopped

2 carrots, peeled and chopped

1 large stalk celery, chopped

1 package (16 ounces) lentils, rinsed and picked through

1 smoked ham hock (about 1 pound)

2 quarts water

1 bay leaf

1 teaspoon salt

½ teaspoon dried thyme

½ teaspoon ground black pepper

2 tablespoons fresh lemon juice

1. In 5-quart Dutch oven, cook bacon over medium-low heat until lightly browned. Add onions, carrots, and celery; cook over medium heat until vegetables are tender, 15 to 20 minutes. Add lentils, ham hock, water, bay leaf, salt, thyme, and pepper; heat to boiling over high heat. Reduce heat; cover and simmer until lentils are tender, 50 to 60 minutes. Remove and discard bay leaf.

2. Transfer ham hock to cutting board; cut off meat and discard skin and bones. Cut meat into bite-size pieces and return to soup. Heat through; stir in lemon juice.

EACH SERVING: About 390 calories, 25g protein, 52g carbohydrate, 10g total fat (3g saturated), 13mg cholesterol, 1,1027mg sodium.

Cream of Mushroom Soup

Recipes for creamy mushroom soup appeared around 1926, shortly after white mushrooms were first cultivated in Pennsylvania. As the story goes, Lewis Downing of Downingtown, Pennsylvania, noticed pure white mushroom spores popping up among his other mushrooms. He propagated the new white types, which soon evolved into a new industry. Pennsylvania now leads the nation in mushroom production. Our recipe calls for white mushrooms, but almost any favorite mushroom (or mix of mushrooms) will work well.

PREP: 20 minutes ★ **COOK:** 35 minutes
MAKES about 6 cups or 6 first-course servings

3 tablespoons butter or margarine

I pound white mushrooms, trimmed and thinly sliced

I medium onion, thinly sliced

2 tablespoons all-purpose flour

2 cups water

I can (14½ ounces) chicken broth or 1¾ cups Old-Fashioned Chicken Broth (page 45)

½ teaspoon fresh thyme or ¼ teaspoon dried thyme

½ teaspoon salt

⅛ teaspoon ground black pepper

½ cup heavy or whipping cream

1. In 5-quart Dutch oven, melt 2 tablespoons butter over medium-high heat. Add mushrooms; cook, stirring occasionally, until mushrooms are tender and begin to brown, about 15 minutes. Transfer to bowl.

2. In same Dutch oven, melt remaining 1 tablespoon butter over medium heat. Add onion; cook until tender and golden, about 10 minutes. With wire whisk, stir in flour until blended; cook 1 minute. Gradually stir in water, broth, thyme, salt, pepper, and half of mushrooms; heat to boiling, stirring constantly.

3. Spoon half of mushroom mixture into blender. Cover, with center part of cover removed to let steam escape; puree until smooth. Pour puree into bowl. Repeat with remaining mushroom mixture.

4. Return puree to same clean Dutch oven; stir in cream and remaining mushrooms with their juice. Heat through (do not boil).

EACH SERVING: About 167 calories, 3g protein, 9g carbohydrate, 14g total fat (8g saturated), 43mg cholesterol, 548mg sodium.

French Country Onion Soup

The soldiers who served in France during World War II came home with a newfound love for onion soup. Its deep, rich flavor comes from the slow caramelization of the onions—a step that mustn't be omitted.

PREP: 15 minutes
COOK/BAKE: 1 hour 55 minutes
MAKES 6½ cups or 4 main-dish servings

3 tablespoons butter or margarine

7 medium onions (about 2½ pounds), each cut lengthwise in half and thinly sliced

¼ teaspoon salt

4 cups water

I can (14½ ounces) beef broth

¼ teaspoon dried thyme

4 slices (½ inch thick) French bread

4 ounces Gruyère or Swiss cheese, shredded (1 cup)

1. In nonstick 12-inch skillet, melt butter over medium heat. Add onions and salt; cook, stirring occasionally, until onions are very tender and begin to caramelize, about 45 minutes. Reduce heat to low; cook, stirring frequently, until onions are deep golden brown, about 15 minutes longer.

2. Transfer onions to 3-quart saucepan. Add ½ cup water to skillet; heat to boiling over high heat, stirring to scrape up browned bits from bottom of pan. Pour water from skillet into saucepan with onions. Add broth, thyme, and remaining 3½ cups water; heat to boiling over high heat. Reduce heat to low; cover and simmer until onions are very tender, about 30 minutes.

3. Meanwhile, preheat oven to 450°F. Arrange bread slices in single layer on cookie sheet; bake until lightly toasted, about 5 minutes.

4. Place four 2½-cup ovenproof bowls in jelly-roll pan for easier handling. Ladle soup into bowls and top with toasted bread, gently pressing toast into soup. Sprinkle evenly with Gruyère. Bake until cheese has melted and begins to brown, 12 to 15 minutes.

EACH SERVING: About 368 calories, 15g protein, 36g carbohydrate, 19g total fat (11g saturated), 56mg cholesterol, 837mg sodium.

French Country Onion Soup ▶

Bear Mountain Butternut Squash Soup

The Native Americans introduced squash to the early American settlers, and it has been a staple ever since. This creamy soup uses the large pear-shaped butternut variety, which gives this bright orange soup just a hint of sweetness. Be sure to serve the soup with the cinnamon-spiced croutons, just the way they like it in the Bear Mountain foothills of New York State.

PREP: 35 minutes ★ **COOK:** 35 minutes
MAKES about 8¾ cups or 8 first-course servings

Cinnamon Croutons (opposite)

1 medium leek

3 tablespoons butter or margarine

2 carrots, peeled and coarsely chopped

1 medium onion, coarsely chopped

1 medium butternut squash (about 2½ pounds), peeled and cut into 1-inch pieces

2¼ cups water

1 can (14½ ounces) chicken broth or 1¾ cups Old-Fashioned Chicken Broth (page 45)

½ teaspoon salt

½ cup half-and-half or light cream

1. Prepare Cinnamon Croutons.

2. Cut off root and trim dark green top from leek; cut leek lengthwise in half. Cut white and pale green part crosswise into ¼-inch-thick slices; discard dark green part. Rinse leek in bowl of cold water, swishing to remove sand. Transfer to colander to drain, leaving sand in bottom of bowl.

3. In 5-quart Dutch oven or saucepot, melt butter over medium-high heat. Add carrots, onion, and leek; cook, stirring occasionally, until lightly browned, about 10 minutes. Add squash, water, broth, and salt; heat to boiling. Reduce heat to low; cover and simmer until squash is very tender, 15 to 20 minutes.

4. Spoon half of squash mixture into blender. Cover, with center part of cover removed to let steam escape; puree until smooth. Pour into bowl. Repeat with remaining vegetable mixture.

5. Return puree to same clean Dutch oven; stir in half-and-half. Heat through (do not boil). Serve soup hot with Cinnamon Croutons.

Cinnamon Croutons

Preheat oven to 400°F. Cut *4 ounces French bread (½ loaf)* into ¾-inch pieces (4 cups); place in bowl. Add *3 tablespoons melted butter, ¼ teaspoon ground cinnamon,* and *⅛ teaspoon salt;* toss to coat. Spread bread pieces in jelly-roll pan. Bake until golden, 10 to 12 minutes.

EACH SERVING WITH CROUTONS: About 219 calories, 4g protein, 28g carbohydrate, 11g total fat (7g saturated), 29mg cholesterol, 590mg sodium.

How to Peel Butternut Squash

To peel butternut squash, we've found that it's best to cut it crosswise in half using a chef's knife. Then cut the larger bottom section lengthwise in half so you can scoop out the seeds. Next, cut all of the squash into 1- to 1½-inch-thick slices. Place each slice, skin side up, on a board and use a paring knife to remove the tough skin. Other winter squashes, such as acorn and Hubbard, can be even tougher to peel and are best cut into pieces and baked with the skin on.

—The Good Housekeeping Test Kitchen

Split Pea with Ham Soup

In the 1841 book *The Good Housekeeper, or, the Way to Live Well, and to be Well While We Live*," Sarah Josepha Hale sites a recipe for Old Pease Soup: "Put a pound and a half of split peas on in four quarts of water, with roast-beef or mutton bones, and a ham bone, two heads of celery, and four onions . . ." Ever since, this soup has been a favorite way to use a leftover ham bone.

PREP: 10 minutes ★ **COOK:** 1 hour 10 minutes
MAKES 11 cups or 6 main-dish servings

2 tablespoons vegetable oil

2 white turnips (6 ounces each), peeled and chopped (optional)

2 carrots, peeled and finely chopped

2 stalks celery, finely chopped

1 medium onion, finely chopped

1 package (16 ounces) dry split peas, rinsed and picked through

2 smoked ham hocks (1 1/2 pounds)

2 quarts water

1 bay leaf

1 teaspoon salt

1/4 teaspoon ground allspice

1. In 5-quart Dutch oven, heat oil over medium-high heat. Add turnips, if using, carrots, celery, and onion. Cook, stirring frequently, until carrots are tender-crisp, about 10 minutes. Add split peas, ham hocks, water, bay leaf, salt, and allspice; heat to boiling over high heat. Reduce heat; cover and simmer 45 minutes.

2. Discard bay leaf. Transfer ham hocks to cutting board; discard skin and bones. Finely chop meat. Return meat to soup. Heat through.

EACH SERVING: About 343 calories, 21g protein, 52g carbohydrate, 7g total fat (1g saturated), 3mg cholesterol, 1,174mg sodium.

Fresh Tomato Soup

Bring back those fond childhood memories with a hearty pot of cream of tomato soup. This one's a fresh take on the old-fashioned favorite. It starts with four pounds of garden-ripe tomatoes. To turn it into the creamy version we've all come to love, stir in some heavy cream just before serving.

PREP: 20 minutes ★ **COOK:** 1 hour 10 minutes
MAKES about 8 cups or 8 first-course servings

1 tablespoon butter or margarine

1 medium onion, chopped

1 stalk celery, chopped

1 carrot, peeled and chopped

1 garlic clove, crushed with garlic press

2 teaspoons fresh thyme or 1/2 teaspoon dried thyme

4 pounds ripe tomatoes, coarsely chopped

1 can (14 1/2 ounces) chicken broth or 1 3/4 cups Old-Fashioned Chicken Broth (page 45)

1/2 cup water

1 bay leaf

3/4 teaspoon salt

1/4 teaspoon coarsely ground black pepper

snipped chives

1. In nonreactive 5-quart Dutch oven, melt butter over low heat. Add onion, celery, and carrot; cook, stirring occasionally, until tender, about 10 minutes. Stir in garlic and thyme; cook 1 minute.

2. Add tomatoes, broth, water, bay leaf, salt, and pepper; heat to boiling over high heat. Reduce heat; simmer, uncovered, until tomatoes are broken up and mixture has thickened slightly, about 45 minutes. Discard bay leaf.

3. Spoon one-third of mixture into blender. Cover, with center part of cover removed to let steam escape; puree until smooth. Pour puree into large bowl. Repeat with remaining mixture.

4. To serve hot, return soup to same clean Dutch oven and heat through. Ladle soup into bowls and sprinkle with chives. To serve cold, refrigerate at least 6 hours.

EACH SERVING: About 81 calories, 3g protein, 14g carbohydrate, 3g total fat (1g saturated), 4mg cholesterol, 475mg sodium.

Vichyssoise

Everyone agrees that it was Chef Louis Diat, of New York's Ritz-Carlton, who served the first bowl of vichyssoise. Some historians say the year was 1910; others claim it was around 1917. In any case, Chef Diat based his *potage* (soup) on his mother's hot potato and leek porridge, a dish he remembered from his childhood in France. He particularly recalled the plump, tender leeks he pulled up from their garden for the porridge. For his creation, he pureed the vegetables, added heavy cream, and topped it off with chives. He then named the soup for the town of Vichy near his birthplace in France.

PREP: 20 minutes plus chilling ★ COOK: 50 minutes
MAKES about 8 cups or 8 first-course servings

4 medium leeks (1 1/4 pounds)

2 tablespoons butter or margarine

1 pound all-purpose potatoes (3 medium), peeled and thinly sliced

2 cans (14 1/2 ounces each) chicken broth or 3 1/2 cups Old-Fashioned Chicken Broth (page 45)

1/2 cup water

1 teaspoon salt

1/4 teaspoon ground black pepper

1 cup milk

1/2 cup heavy or whipping cream

1. Cut off roots and trim dark green tops from leeks; cut each leek lengthwise in half. Slice enough of white and pale green parts to equal 4 1/2 cups. (Reserve any leftover leeks for another use.) Rinse leeks in large bowl of cold water, swishing to remove sand. Transfer to colander to drain, leaving sand in bottom of bowl.

2. In 4-quart saucepan, melt butter over medium heat. Add leeks and cook, stirring, 8 to 10 minutes. Add potatoes, broth, water, salt, and pepper; heat to boiling over high heat. Reduce heat; cover and simmer 30 minutes.

3. Spoon half of mixture into blender. Cover, with center part of cover removed to let steam escape; puree until smooth. Pour puree into bowl. Repeat with remaining vegetable mixture.

4. Stir milk and cream into puree. To serve hot, return soup to same clean saucepan. Heat through over low heat (do not boil). To serve cold, cover and refrigerate at least 4 hours or until very cold.

EACH SERVING: About 161 calories, 4g protein, 14g carbohydrate, 10g total fat (6g saturated), 32mg cholesterol, 778mg sodium.

New England Clam Chowder

The name of this signature New England dish is derived from the French word *chaudière* (large cauldron). As the story goes, Bretons always threw their daily catch into cauldrons to make communal stew. This custom traveled from Newfoundland to Nova Scotia and down into New England, where white clam chowder remains a staple today.

PREP: 20 minutes plus cooling ★ COOK: 45 minutes
MAKES about 9 cups or 8 first-course servings

1 cup water

1 1/2 dozen chowder or cherrystone clams, scrubbed

2 ounces salt pork or bacon, chopped

1 medium onion, finely chopped

1 tablespoon all-purpose flour

1/8 teaspoon ground black pepper

1 pound all-purpose potatoes (3 medium), peeled and chopped

4 cups half-and-half or light cream

1/2 teaspoon salt

1. In 4-quart saucepan, heat water to boiling over high heat. Add clams; heat to boiling. Reduce heat; cover and simmer until clams open, 5 to 10 minutes, transferring clams to bowl as they open. Discard any clams that have not opened.

2. When cool enough to handle, remove clams from their shells and coarsely chop. Discard shells. Strain clam broth through sieve lined with paper towels into measuring cup; if necessary add enough *water* to equal 2 cups.

3. In same clean saucepan, cook salt pork over medium heat until lightly browned. With slotted spoon, remove salt pork and discard. Add onion to drippings in pan; cook, stirring occasionally, until tender, about 5 minutes.

4. With wire whisk, stir in flour and pepper until well blended; cook 1 minute. Gradually whisk in clam broth until smooth. Add potatoes; heat to boiling. Reduce heat; cover and simmer until potatoes are tender, about 15 minutes. Stir in half-and-half and clams; heat through (do not boil). Taste for seasoning; add salt if necessary.

EACH SERVING: About 227 calories, 7g protein, 16g carbohydrate, 15g total fat (9g saturated), 52mg cholesterol, 232mg sodium.

Manhattan Clam Chowder

By the mid-1800s, chowders had become so popular that cooks throughout New England had their own versions: in Rhode Island, cooks frequently tossed tomatoes into the pot, along with the potatoes, vegetables, and clams. Sometime in the 1930s, this hearty red soup became known as Manhattan clam chowder. One of the most famous versions is served at the Oyster Bar in Grand Central Terminal.

PREP: 30 minutes plus cooling ★ **COOK:** 50 minutes
MAKES about 12 cups or 12 first-course servings

5 cups water

3 dozen chowder or cherrystone clams, scrubbed

5 slices bacon, finely chopped

1 large onion (12 ounces), finely chopped

2 large carrots, peeled and finely chopped

2 stalks celery, finely chopped

1 pound all-purpose potatoes (3 medium), peeled and finely chopped

½ bay leaf

1¼ teaspoons dried thyme

¼ teaspoon ground black pepper

1 can (28 ounces) plum tomatoes

2 tablespoons chopped fresh parsley

¾ teaspoon salt

1. In nonreactive 8-quart saucepot, heat 1 cup water to boiling over high heat. Add clams; heat to boiling. Reduce heat; cover and simmer until clams open, 5 to 10 minutes, transferring clams to bowl as they open. Discard any clams that have not opened.

2. When cool enough to handle, remove clams from shells and coarsely chop. Discard shells. Strain clam broth through sieve lined with paper towels into bowl.

3. In same clean saucepot, cook bacon over medium heat until browned; add onion and cook until tender, about 5 minutes. Add carrots and celery; cook 5 minutes.

4. Add clam broth to bacon mixture in saucepot. Add potatoes, remaining 4 cups water, bay leaf, thyme, and pepper; heat to boiling. Reduce heat; cover and simmer 10 minutes. Add tomatoes with their liquid, breaking them up with side of spoon. Simmer 10 minutes longer.

5. Stir in chopped clams and heat through. Discard bay leaf and sprinkle with parsley. Taste for seasoning; add salt if necessary.

EACH SERVING: About 117 calories, 5g protein, 12g carbohydrate, 6g total fat (2g saturated), 12mg cholesterol, 342mg sodium.

Shrimp Bisque

Typically, a bisque is a thick, rich, creamy soup made by pureeing stock that contains cooked seafood and sometimes vegetables. Ours gets an extra flavor boost from the shrimp shells that are simmered in the stock before it is strained. Lacing the soup with cream and brandy just before serving makes it even more delicious.

PREP: 20 minutes ★ COOK: 1 hour 20 minutes
MAKES about 10 cups or 10 first-course servings

3 tablespoons butter or margarine

1 pound medium shrimp, shelled and deveined, shells reserved

2 cans (14½ ounces each) low-sodium chicken broth or 3½ cups Old-Fashioned Chicken Broth (page 45)

1 cup dry white wine

½ cup water

1 large onion (12 ounces), chopped

2 carrots, peeled and chopped

2 stalks celery, chopped

2 tablespoons regular long-grain rice

1 bay leaf

1¼ teaspoons salt

⅛ to ¼ teaspoon ground red pepper (cayenne)

1 can (14½ ounces) diced tomatoes

1 cup half-and-half or light cream

2 tablespoons brandy or dry sherry

1. In nonreactive 5-quart Dutch oven, melt 1 tablespoon butter over medium heat. Add shrimp shells and cook, stirring frequently, 5 minutes. Add broth, wine, and water; heat to boiling. Reduce heat; cover and simmer 15 minutes. Strain broth mixture through sieve into bowl; with spoon, press on shrimp shells to extract any remaining liquid. Discard shells.

2. In same clean Dutch oven, melt remaining 2 tablespoons butter over medium-high heat. Add shrimp and cook until opaque throughout, about 3 minutes. With slotted spoon, transfer shrimp to separate bowl. Add onion, carrots, and celery to Dutch oven; cook, stirring, until celery is tender, about 10 minutes. Add shrimp broth, rice, bay leaf, salt, and ground red pepper; heat to boiling over high heat. Reduce heat; cover and simmer until rice is tender, about 20 minutes. Add tomatoes with their juice and cook 10 minutes longer. Remove from heat and discard bay leaf. Stir in shrimp.

3. Spoon one-fourth of shrimp mixture into blender. Cover, with center part of cover removed to let steam escape; puree until very smooth. Pour puree into bowl. Repeat with remaining mixture.

4. Return puree to clean Dutch oven; stir in half-and-half and brandy. Heat through over medium heat (do not boil).

EACH SERVING: About 149 calories, 10g protein, 9g carbohydrate, 7g total fat (4g saturated), 74mg cholesterol, 667mg sodium.

Yankee Fish Chowder

Down East in Maine and throughout New England, local cooks have made good use of rich cod catches by stuffing it, baking it, frying it, and turning it into the all-time favorite thick, creamy codfish chowder. This hearty soup is an easy supper-in-a-bowl. Serve hot popovers or pan biscuits alongside, if you like.

PREP: 20 minutes ★ **COOK:** 45 minutes
MAKES about 10 cups or 5 main-dish servings

4 slices bacon

3 carrots, peeled and each cut lengthwise in half, then crosswise into $\frac{1}{4}$-inch-thick slices

3 stalks celery, chopped

1 medium onion, finely chopped

1 pound all-purpose potatoes (3 medium), peeled and cut into $\frac{1}{2}$-inch pieces

3 bottles (8 ounces each) clam juice

1 can (14$\frac{1}{2}$ ounces) chicken broth or 1$\frac{3}{4}$ cups Old-Fashioned Chicken Broth (page 45)

1 bay leaf

1 pound cod fillet, cut into 1$\frac{1}{2}$-inch pieces

1 cup half-and-half or light cream

$\frac{1}{4}$ teaspoon ground black pepper

1. In 5-quart Dutch oven, cook bacon over medium heat until browned. Using slotted spoon, transfer to paper towels to drain; crumble.

2. Discard all but 2 tablespoons bacon drippings from Dutch oven. Add carrots, celery, and onion; cook, stirring occasionally, until lightly browned, 12 to 15 minutes. Add potatoes, clam juice, broth, and bay leaf; heat to boiling. Reduce heat; cover and simmer until vegetables are tender, about 15 minutes.

3. Add cod; cover and cook until fish is just opaque throughout, 2 to 5 minutes. Gently stir in half-and-half and pepper; heat through (do not boil). Discard bay leaf. Ladle soup into tureen or soup bowls. Sprinkle with crumbled bacon.

EACH SERVING: About 316 calories, 24g protein, 25g carbohydrate, 14g total fat (6g saturated), 65mg cholesterol, 930mg sodium.

Billi Bi

This superb fish soup was named after William Brand, an American who lived in Paris in 1925 and was a regular at Maxim's restaurant. Brand happened to love mussels, so Chef Louis Barthe created this soup for him, calling it "Billi" for his first name and "Bi" for the first initial of his last name. In an authentic Billi Bi, the mussels are removed before the soup is strained. However, many cooks in France and in America stir the mussels back in right before serving, as we've done here.

PREP: 20 minutes plus cooling ★ **COOK:** 20 minutes
MAKES about 3$\frac{1}{3}$ cups or 4 first-course servings

2 pounds mussels, scrubbed and debearded

1 large onion (12 ounces), thinly sliced

1 cup dry white wine

1 cup water

5 sprigs plus 1 tablespoon chopped fresh parsley

pinch dried thyme

2 tablespoons all-purpose flour

$\frac{1}{2}$ cup heavy or whipping cream

pinch ground red pepper (cayenne)

salt (optional)

1. In nonreactive 5-quart Dutch oven, combine mussels, onion, wine, water, parsley sprigs, and thyme. Cover and heat to boiling over high heat. Reduce heat to medium; cook until mussels open, about 5 minutes, transferring mussels with slotted spoon to bowl as they open. Discard any mussels that have not opened.

2. When cool enough to handle, remove mussels from shells and discard mussel shells. Strain mussel broth through sieve lined with paper towels into nonreactive 3-quart saucepan.

3. Heat mussel broth to boiling over high heat. In cup, with wire whisk, stir flour into cream until smooth; gradually whisk into broth and heat to boiling, whisking constantly. Add ground red pepper; reduce heat and simmer, whisking occasionally, 2 minutes. Stir in mussels and heat through; do not overcook or mussels will become tough. Taste for seasoning; add salt if necessary. Stir in chopped parsley.

EACH SERVING WITHOUT SALT: About 236 calories, 10g protein, 12g carbohydrate, 13g total fat (7g saturated), 59mg cholesterol, 205mg sodium.

Noodles for Soup

Noodles are an excellent accompaniment to soup and very easily made. Beat one egg slightly, add half a teaspoon of salt, then work in as much flour as the wetting will take up. Knead it well, toss on a floured board and roll out as thin as a sheet of paper. Cover with a towel and set aside for twenty minutes. Cut into fancy shapes with French vegetable cutters. There may be diamonds, hearts, clover leaves or circles. The sheet may be shredded finely with a sharp vegetable knife or rolled like a jelly roll and cut into the finest shavings. Set aside to dry and use when required, cooking the noodles for twenty minutes before they are needed in boiling salted water. Drain and add to the soup just before sending to the table. Noodles may also be cooked in stock, seasoned and served as a side dish.

—Good Housekeeping Everyday Cook Book, 1903

Chicken-Noodle Soup

After the Revolutionary War, the pioneers moved westward. By the early 1800s they had reached the American heartland, where they settled on the gloriously rich farmlands. Every farm had its chickens; an invaluable source of meat and eggs for the settlers. One could often count on a pot of soup quietly simmering away on the back of the kitchen stove. Homemade chicken soup was a favorite then and still is today. Over the years egg noodles have been added, making this one of the most loved soups.

PREP: 25 minutes plus making broth ★ **COOK:** 25 minutes
MAKES 11 cups or 4 main-dish servings

2 quarts Old-Fashioned Chicken Broth (page 45)

2 cups shredded chicken (from Old-Fashioned Chicken Broth)

2 cups medium egg noodles (about 3 ounces)

1 cup frozen peas

2 tablespoons chopped fresh parsley

1$\frac{1}{2}$ teaspoons salt

$\frac{1}{8}$ teaspoon ground black pepper

1. In 4-quart saucepan, heat broth to boiling; reduce heat and add chicken.

2. Meanwhile, cook noodles as label directs. Drain. Add cooked noodles, peas, parsley, salt, and pepper to soup; heat through.

EACH SERVING: About 312 calories, 31g protein, 25g carbohydrate, 9g total fat (3g saturated), 90mg cholesterol, 1,194mg sodium.

Chicken and Rice Soup

outh Carolina is the birthplace of the American rice industry, and the South Carolineans developed an exclusive rice cookery. By the late seventeenth century, the rice crop was thriving, and cooks were finding different uses for the newfound grain. It's no accident that plantation and farm kitchens had kettles of chicken soup simmering away, frequently with rice added to the pot. As it cooked, the rice thickened the soup to just the right consistency.

PREP: 10 minutes plus making broth ★ **COOK:** 30 minutes
MAKES about 10 cups or 6 main-dish servings

3 carrots, peeled and chopped

1 stalk celery, chopped

5 cups Old-Fashioned Chicken Broth (opposite)

1 teaspoon salt

2 cups cooked chicken (from Old-Fashioned Chicken Broth), cut into bite-size pieces

1 cup regular long-grain rice, cooked as label directs

In 3-quart saucepan, combine carrots, celery, broth, and salt; heat to boiling over high heat. Reduce heat; simmer until vegetables are very tender, about 15 minutes. Stir in chicken and rice; heat through.

EACH CUP: About 247 calories, 19g protein, 31g carbohydrate, 5g total fat (2g saturated), 45mg cholesterol, 538mg sodium.

Old-Fashioned Chicken Broth

s James Beard stated unequivocally, "Chicken broth... is virtually indispensable in the well-run kitchen." This recipe is easy to double or triple. Freeze any extra in sturdy containers for up to three months.

PREP: 20 minutes plus cooling ★ **COOK:** 3 hours 30 minutes
MAKES about 12 cups

1 chicken (3½ to 4 pounds), including neck (reserve giblets for another use)

2 pounds chicken wings

2 carrots, peeled and cut into 2-inch pieces

1 stalk celery, cut into 2-inch pieces

1 medium onion, cut into quarters

5 parsley sprigs

1 garlic clove

½ teaspoon dried thyme

½ bay leaf

salt (optional)

1. In 6-quart saucepot, combine chicken, chicken neck, chicken wings, carrots, celery, onion, parsley, garlic, thyme, bay leaf, and enough *water* to cover; heat to boiling over high heat. Skim foam from surface. Reduce heat and simmer 1 hour, skimming occasionally.

2. Remove from heat; transfer whole chicken to large bowl (leave chicken wings in pot). When cool enough to handle, remove skin and bones from chicken. (Reserve chicken meat for another use, such as Chicken-Noodle Soup, opposite.) Return skin and bones to saucepot; heat to boiling. Skim foam; reduce heat and simmer 2 hours.

3. Strain broth through colander into large bowl; discard solids. Strain again through sieve into containers; cool. Cover and refrigerate to use within 3 days, or freeze up to 4 months.

4. To use, skim and discard fat from surface of broth. If using in place of canned chicken broth in a recipe, season broth to taste with salt.

EACH CUP: About 35 calories, 3g protein, 3g carbohydrate, 2g total fat (1g saturated), 4mg cholesterol, 108mg sodium.

Beefy Vegetable Soup

I n the 1824 cookbook *The Virginia House-Wife*, women were instructed to make beef soup this way: "Take the hind shin of beef, cut off all the flesh off the leg-bone, which must be taken away entirely, or the soup will be greasy." Fortunately, today all you have to do is pick up ready-to-use beef shanks from your supermarket.

PREP: 25 minutes plus overnight to soak beans
COOK: 1 hour 50 minutes
MAKES about 14 cups or 8 main-dish servings

---

8 ounces dry large lima beans (1¼ cups)

1 tablespoon vegetable oil

2 pounds bone-in beef shank cross cuts, each
   1½ inches thick

2 medium onions, chopped

3 garlic cloves, finely chopped

⅛ teaspoon ground cloves

4 large carrots, peeled and cut into ½-inch pieces

2 stalks celery, chopped

½ small head green cabbage (8 ounces),
   cored and cut into ½-inch pieces (about 5 cups)

4½ cups water

1 can (14½ ounces) beef broth

2 teaspoons salt

½ teaspoon dried thyme

½ teaspoon coarsely ground black pepper

1 pound (3 medium) all-purpose potatoes, peeled
   and cut into ¾-inch pieces

1 can (14½ ounces) diced tomatoes

1 cup frozen whole-kernel corn

1 cup frozen peas

¼ cup chopped fresh parsley

1. In large bowl, place beans and enough *water* to cover by 2 inches. Soak overnight. Drain and rinse beans.

2. In nonreactive 8-quart saucepot, heat oil over medium-high heat until hot. Add beef, in batches, and cook until well browned, transferring meat to bowl as it is browned. Reduce heat to medium; add onions and cook, stirring, until tender, about 5 minutes. Stir in garlic and cloves; cook 30 seconds. Return beef to saucepot; add carrots, celery, cabbage, water, broth, salt, thyme, and pepper; heat to boiling. Reduce heat; cover and simmer until beef is tender, about 1 hour.

3. Meanwhile, in 4-quart saucepan, combine beans and enough *water* to cover by 2 inches; heat to boiling over high heat. Reduce heat; cover and simmer until beans are just tender, about 30 minutes; drain beans. Add potatoes and beans to saucepot; heat to boiling. Reduce heat; cover and simmer 5 minutes. Stir in tomatoes with their juice; cover and simmer until potatoes are tender, about 10 minutes longer.

4. With slotted spoon, transfer beef to cutting board. Cut beef into ½-inch pieces; discard bones and gristle. Return beef to saucepot; add frozen corn and peas. Heat through. Ladle into bowls and sprinkle with parsley.

EACH SERVING: About 375 calories, 27g protein, 44g carbohydrate, 11g total fat (4g saturated), 38mg cholesterol, 990mg sodium.

◄ *Beefy Vegetable Soup*

Rest-of-the-Turkey Soup

Thanksgiving has always meant enjoying a bountiful feast that features a roasted turkey and all the trimmings. In many homes, a large pot of soup made from the leftover turkey is a day-after-Thanksgiving ritual. This recipe starts with homemade stock, which is made by slowly simmering the turkey carcass in water with vegetables and seasonings.

PREP: 15 minutes plus overnight to chill ★ **COOK:** 5 hours
MAKES about 13 cups or 12 first-course servings

6 carrots, peeled

3 stalks celery

roasted turkey carcass plus 2 cups cooked turkey meat, finely chopped

2 medium onions, each cut into quarters

5 parsley sprigs

1 garlic clove, peeled

¼ teaspoon dried thyme

½ bay leaf

1¼ teaspoons salt

1 cup regular long-grain rice, cooked as label directs

2 tablespoons fresh lemon juice or 1 tablespoon dry sherry

1. Cut 2 carrots and 1 stalk celery into 2-inch pieces. In 12-quart stockpot, combine turkey carcass, carrot and celery pieces, onions, parsley sprigs, garlic, thyme, bay leaf, and enough *water* to cover; heat to boiling over high heat. Skim foam from surface. Reduce heat and simmer, skimming occasionally, 4 hours.

2. Strain broth through colander set over large bowl; discard solids. Strain again through sieve into several containers; cool. Cover and refrigerate overnight.

3. Skim and discard fat from surface of broth; measure broth and pour into 5-quart saucepot. If necessary, boil broth over high heat until reduced to 10 cups to concentrate flavor.

4. Cut remaining 4 carrots and remaining 2 stalks celery into ½-inch pieces; add to broth. Add salt and heat soup to boiling. Reduce heat; simmer until vegetables are tender, about 15 minutes. Stir in cooked rice and turkey; heat through. Remove from heat; stir in lemon juice.

EACH SERVING: About 113 calories, 10g protein, 12g carbohydrate, 2g total fat (1g saturated), 21mg cholesterol, 355mg sodium.

All-American Club

The origin of the club sandwich is somewhat unclear. Some say it first appeared in the double-decker club cars during the late 1800s. Others contend it was first served in casino gambling rooms or in private men's clubs. According to James Beard, the original clubs were made with only two slices of bread (always toasted and buttered). "On this goes a leaf of lettuce, a bit of mayonnaise, slices of chicken breast, slices of peeled ripe tomatoes, a sprinkle of salt, crisp bacon rashers, more mayonnaise, and a second piece of toast." Over the years, a third slice of bread was added, and turkey was used instead of chicken.

PREP: 20 minutes ★ **MAKES** 2 main-dish servings

6 slices bacon

6 slices white bread, toasted

mayonnaise

lettuce leaves

2 large slices cooked turkey

salt

ground black pepper

1 large tomato, sliced

1. In 10-inch skillet, cook bacon over medium heat until crisp; transfer to paper towels to drain.

2. Spread one side of each bread slice with mayonnaise. Arrange lettuce leaves on 2 slices; top each with turkey. Sprinkle with salt and pepper, then cover each with another bread slice, mayonnaise side up. Top each sandwich with more lettuce, half of tomato slices, 3 bacon slices, and bread slice, mayonnaise side down.

3. Cut each sandwich on diagonal into quarters. Use frilled toothpicks to secure, if you like. Arrange, cut sides up, on individual plates.

EACH SERVING: About 540 calories, 14g protein, 44g carbohydrate, 35g total fat (7g saturated), 35mg cholesterol, 878mg sodium.

Variations

Prepare as directed but substitute *2 large slices cooked ham, corned beef, pastrami,* or *roast beef* for turkey. Substitute *2 slices Swiss cheese* or *4 slices cooked Canadian bacon* for bacon.

Tales of The Coney Island Dog

Thanks to America's German immigrants, hot German sausages (wienerwursts) were being sold from pushcarts on the streets of New York City by the 1860s. At the St. Louis World Fair in the 1904, Antoine Feuchtwanger introduced fairgoers to a frankfurter in a roll, named for his birthplace, Frankfurt, Germany. While in 1901 at New York City's Polo Grounds, a concessionaire noticed that his cold foods weren't selling. So his vendors supplied hot dachshund sausages and sold them by calling out "Red Hots! Get your red hots here!" Sports cartoonist T. A. "Tad" Dorgan, created a talking sausage in his newspaper cartoons, giving birth to the name "hot dog."

Sometime in the next few years, it is believed that Charles Feltman, owner of Feltman's Restaurant, a Coney Island beer garden and dinner house, was the first to put "boiled nibs of meat" on a warm roll and sell them for a dime. He employed Nathan Handwerker as a roll-cutter and delivery boy, as well as piano player Eddie Cantor and singer Jimmy Durante. The sandwich was a hit, but not everyone could afford this dime specialty. As the story goes, Cantor and Durante persuaded Handwerker to open up his own stand and loaned him $300 for the venture.

In 1916, Handwerker opened Nathan's Famous Frankfurter Stand in Coney Island and featured his five-cent hot dog, which was made from a recipe handed down from his wife Ida's grandmother. Most of his customers liked them so much that a smear of ketchup and Nathan's special golden brown mustard was all they added. Occasionally, though, regular customers asked for fried onions on top, which Nathan gladly served, even though they were meant for his five-cent hamburgers. He offered other specialties too: roast beef sandwiches for a nickel, crinkle-cut fries (called potato chips in those days) for ten cents, sodas for five cents, malted milk and milk shakes for six cents, and ice-cream sodas for a dime. In fact, Handwerker's stand was likely the very first fast-food restaurant in America: a place where one could walk up to a counter and order a complete meal.

The rest is history—red-hot history! When the BMT elevated subway line was extended to Coney Island in 1923, thousands of New Yorkers were able to travel to Coney Island (often called the poor man's Riviera) for a nickel to enjoy a day at the beach. Nathan's business boomed as did the publicity. Politicians, show-business stars, and sports heroes were often photographed munching on a "Coney Island" (a Nathan's frankfurter). The names read like a who's who: Buddy Hackett, Carol Channing, Red Buttons, and even Jacqueline Kennedy.

Before long, Coney Island hot dogs were being enjoyed across America. By the 1970s, when Nathan's Famous rolled into cities far from New York, vendors realized that customers wanted a Coney Island "their way." To satisfy their demands, they set up a condiment bar that offered toppings such as sauerkraut and relish in addition to ketchup and Nathan's famous mustard. In 1984, they added chili, and three years later an aged Cheddar cheese sauce.

From that first hot dog sold at Nathan Handwerker's stand in the early 1900s for just five cents grew the famous Coney Island red hot, still known by that same name today.

The Earl of Sandwich—Jimmy Twitcher

As with other American classics, the sandwich is believed to have had its beginning in England. In the eighteenth century, in the court of George III, the fourth Earl of Sandwich was a gentleman named John Montagu. Around the gambling tables, John was better known as Jimmy Twitcher. In 1762, during a twenty-four-hour gambling marathon, he ordered some meat dishes to be placed between pieces of bread and brought to the gaming tables so he could continue playing. In his honor, these combinations were called sandwiches, and a whole new way of eating was born.

During the Victorian era and into the early 1900s, sandwiches were usually made with very thin slices of bread and cut into squares or fancier hearts or diamonds. The bread was covered with a delicate layer of sweet creamy butter or heartier fillings, such as egg or chopped chicken salad, or even chunks of lobster or fried oysters. Dainty open-faced canapés were popular fare for parties.

Gradually sandwiches became heartier and often contained several layers, giving birth to such all-American classics as the club, the hero, and diner favorites, such as hamburgers, Sloppy Joes, and BLTs. Regional roots also play a big part in the sandwich menu. Philadelphia cheese steaks, muffulettas in New Orleans, and the popular western sandwich are some good examples. Through the years sandwiches have indeed become an American way of eating, and it doesn't appear that their popularity will ever wane.

Turkey Divan

Tearooms were popular lunch places for women in the mid-1900s, especially in the South and Midwest. This open-faced sandwich was almost always on the menu. Originally it was made with chicken, buttery puff pastry, and often with delicate spears of asparagus.

PREP: 25 minutes ★ **BAKE:** 10 minutes
MAKES 4 main-dish servings

3 tablespoons butter or margarine

3 tablespoons all-purpose flour

I cup chicken broth

½ cup half-and-half

½ cup freshly grated Parmesan cheese

pinch ground black pepper

3 cups broccoli flowerets

4 slices firm white bread, toasted

8 ounces sliced cooked turkey or chicken

1. In 2-quart saucepan, melt butter over medium-low heat. With wire whisk, stir in flour; cook, whisking, 1 minute. Gradually whisk in broth and half-and-half until smooth; heat to boiling over high heat, whisking frequently. Reduce heat; simmer, stirring occasionally, 5 minutes. Reserve 2 tablespoons Parmesan cheese. Whisk in remaining cheese and pepper. Remove from heat and set aside.

2. Preheat oven to 450°F. Grease 13" by 9" baking dish.

3. Place broccoli in medium skillet. Add enough *water* to cover by ½ inch; heat to boiling over high heat. Reduce heat and simmer until broccoli is tender-crisp, about 2 minutes. Drain well.

4. Arrange bread slices in bottom of prepared dish. Spoon ½ cup sauce over bread. Layer turkey and broccoli on top. Spoon remaining sauce over and sprinkle with reserved cheese. Bake until lightly browned and bubbly, 10 to 12 minutes.

EACH SERVING: About 401 calories, 29g protein, 25g carbohydrate, 20g total fat (11g saturated), 88mg cholesterol, 813mg sodium.

Monte Cristo

How this sandwich got its name remains a mystery. Its ingredients, however—buttered bread, Gruyère or Swiss cheese, and ham—do resemble those of the grilled sandwich, the croque monsieur. But, unlike its French "cousin," the Monte Cristo is dipped in batter. As it grills, the cheese melts and the butter coating turns golden and crispy. To make a Monte Carlo, use roasted turkey instead of ham.

PREP: 10 minutes ★ **COOK:** 10 minutes
MAKES 4 main-dish servings

2 large eggs

1/3 cup milk

1/4 teaspoon salt

1 1/2 teaspoons Dijon mustard

8 slices "toasting" white bread

4 ounces thinly sliced baked ham

4 ounces thinly sliced Swiss or Gruyère cheese

4 tablespoons butter or margarine

1. In pie plate, with fork, beat eggs, milk, and salt until well blended.

2. Spread mustard on one side of 4 bread slices. Layer with ham and cheese. Top with remaining bread slices. Dip sandwiches in egg mixture, including edges, letting soak briefly.

3. In nonstick large skillet, melt 2 tablespoons butter over medium-low heat. Add sandwiches, in batches if necessary, and cook until browned, about 4 minutes per side, adding remaining butter as needed.

4. To serve, cut each sandwich on diagonal in half.

EACH SERVING: About 434 calories, 22g protein, 27g carbohydrate, 26g total fat (14g saturated), 182mg cholesterol, 1,030mg sodium.

Muffuletta

An enterprising Italian immigrant named Salvatore Lupo created this New Orleans specialty at the Central Grocery in 1906. It resembled a Sicilian sandwich he recalled from his childhood: a round loaf of hollowed-out bread that was stuffed with ham, salami, cheese, and pickled vegetables known as olive salad. He called his sandwich a muffuletta, Sicilian for "hollow bread."

PREP: 25 minutes plus chilling ★ **MAKES** 6 main-dish servings

1 1/4 cups finely chopped celery with leaves

1 cup drained giardiniera (Italian mixed pickled vegetables), chopped

3/4 cup green and black Mediterranean olives, such as Gaeta or Kalamata, pitted and chopped

1/3 cup chopped fresh parsley

1 garlic clove, minced

1/4 cup olive oil

1/4 teaspoon ground black pepper

1 round soft loaf (8 to 10 inches) French bread

4 ounces thinly sliced smoked ham

4 ounces thinly sliced Provolone cheese

4 ounces thinly sliced Genoa salami

1. In medium bowl, combine celery, giardiniera, olives, parsley, garlic, oil, and pepper until well mixed. Cover and refrigerate at least 4 hours or up to overnight to blend flavors.

2. Cut bread horizontally in half. Remove enough soft center from each half to make room for filling. (Reserve soft bread for another use.) Onto bottom half of bread, spoon half of celery-olive mixture; layer ham, provolone, and salami on top. Spoon remaining celery-olive mixture over all. Replace top half of bread.

3. Wrap sandwich in foil and refrigerate at least 4 hours or up to 24 hours to blend flavors and allow juices to soften bread. To serve, let stand at room temperature about 30 minutes, then cut into 6 wedges.

EACH SERVING: About 399 calories, 17g protein, 28g carbohydrate, 24g total fat (8g saturated), 41mg cholesterol, 1,615mg sodium.

Hero

"**Y**ou'd have to be a hero to eat it!" stated noted food writer Clementine Paddleford in the 1930s when asked her opinion of this sandwich. It is called by many names: grinder in New England, submarine in Connecticut, bomber in Upstate New York, wedge or hoagie in Philadelphia, po' boy in New Orleans, Italian meat sandwich in Chicago, and Cuban sandwich in Miami. Where you eat it not only determines what it's called but also what it's stuffed with. This popular version contains meats, cheeses, shredded lettuce, and tomatoes and is drizzled with a spicy oil-and-vinegar dressing.

PREP: 15 minutes ★ **MAKES** 4 main-dish servings

¼ cup vinaigrette of choice

1 large loaf (12 ounces) Italian bread

4 ounces thinly sliced hot and/or sweet capocollo, prosciutto, soppressata, and/or salami

4 ounces mozzarella cheese, preferably fresh, thinly sliced

additional ingredients, such as shredded romaine lettuce or arugula, peperoncini, fresh basil leaves, roasted red peppers, very thinly sliced red onions, pesto, olivada, and/or sliced ripe tomatoes

1. Prepare vinaigrette. Cut bread horizontally in half. Remove enough soft center from each half to make room for filling. (Reserve soft bread for another use.)

2. Brush vinaigrette evenly over cut sides of bread. Layer meats and mozzarella on bottom half of bread. Top with additional ingredients of your choice. Replace top half of bread. If not serving right away, wrap sandwich in foil and refrigerate up to 4 hours. Cut crosswise into 4 pieces.

EACH SERVING: About 430 calories, 20g protein, 36g carbohydrate, 23g total fat (7g saturated), 48mg cholesterol, 1,226mg sodium.

Reuben Sandwiches

Many say that the Reuben was the inspiration of Reuben Kulakofsky, owner of the Central Market in Omaha, Nebraska, who happened to be a regular at a weekly poker group at the Blackstone Hotel in the 1920s. One night he served up grilled sandwiches of corned beef, sauerkraut, and Swiss cheese between two slices of dark rye; it soon became known as a Reuben.

PREP: 45 minutes ★ **COOK:** 8 minutes
MAKES 4 main-dish servings

½ cup mayonnaise

1 tablespoon finely chopped green pepper

1 tablespoon chili sauce

8 slices rye bread

4 slices Swiss cheese, halved crosswise

8 ounces sliced corned beef

8 ounces refrigerated bagged sauerkraut, drained (1 cup)

2 tablespoons butter or margarine

1. In small bowl, combine mayonnaise, green pepper, and chili sauce. Spread about 1 tablespoon mayonnaise mixture on each bread slice. Top each of 4 bread slices with 1 slice Swiss cheese, one-fourth of corned beef, one-fourth of sauerkraut, and another cheese slice. Cover with remaining bread slices, mayonnaise side down.

2. In 12-inch skillet, melt butter over medium heat. Add sandwiches and cook until browned, about 4 minutes. Turn and cook, adding more butter as necessary, until bread has browned and cheese melts, about 4 minutes. Cut each sandwich crosswise in half.

EACH SERVING: About 677 calories, 24g protein, 36g carbohydrate, 48g total fat (16g saturated), 113mg cholesterol, 1,751mg sodium.

◄ *Hero*

"The Original" Pat's King of Steaks®
Philadelphia Cheese Steak

Back in the 1930s, Philadelphia restaurateur Pat Olivieri wooed a lot of customers with fried steak and onions served up on a crispy Italian-style roll. Some time after, he topped if off with a slice of American cheese and later added sautéed peppers. Today, his family is still frying up the "real original" at Pat King's Steaks in the City of Brotherly Love.

Serves 4

24 oz thin sliced rib eye or eye roll steak

6 tablespoons of soy bean oil

Cheese (we recommend Cheez Whiz® but American or Provolone works fine)

4 crusty Italian rolls

I large Spanish onion

Optional
Sweet green and red peppers sautéed in oil
Mushrooms sautéed in oil

ASSEMBLY

Heat an iron skillet or a nonstick pan over medium heat

Add 3 tablespoons of oil to the pan and sauté the onions to desired doneness

Remove the onions

Add the remaining oil and sauté the slices of meat quickly on both sides

Melt the Cheez Whiz® in a double boiler or in the microwave

Place 6 oz. of the meat into the rolls

Add onions and pour the Cheez Whiz® over top

Garnish with hot or fried sweet peppers, mushrooms, ketchup

Put on the theme song to the first Rocky movie and enjoy!

Source: original recipe from Pat's King of Steaks®

Western Sandwiches

The chuck wagon was a vital part of every wagon train. Due to a lack of refrigeration, however, eggs would frequently get "high" (past their prime) during the journey over the hot trail. Some believe that the women often mixed onions and any seasonings they had on hand to mask the off taste. Other food historians link the tradition of combining eggs, onion, and spices with chuck-wagon cooks of later days. Over the years, green peppers and ham were added to the mix. Out West this sandwich is known as a Denver.

PREP: 10 minutes ★ **COOK:** 3 minutes
MAKES I main-dish serving

I large egg, lightly beaten

2 tablespoons milk

2 tablespoons chopped baked ham

I tablespoon minced onion

I tablespoon minced green pepper

pinch salt

pinch ground black pepper

I teaspoon butter or margarine

I Kaiser roll, split and warmed

I. In medium bowl, combine egg, milk, ham, onion, green pepper, salt, and black pepper.

2. In 8-inch nonstick skillet, melt butter over medium heat. Pour egg mixture into skillet and cook until almost set, about 2 minutes. With wide metal spatula, turn and cook 1 minute longer. Place egg mixture on bottom of roll; replace top of roll.

EACH SERVING: About 331 calories, 17g protein, 33g carbohydrate, 14g total fat (5g saturated), 237mg cholesterol, 830mg sodium.

Tuna Melt

This favorite sandwich became popular in the late 1960s and early 1970s. Typically, tuna salad was piled high on white toast, covered with a slice of American cheese or Velveeta®cheese, then broiled until hot and melted. Sometimes the sandwich was made with two slices of toast, and sometimes tomato was added. No one knows who created the first tuna melt, but its great taste is obvious to all.

PREP: 10 minutes ★ **COOK:** 5 minutes
MAKES 4 main-dish servings.

- **1 can (12 ounces) solid white tuna packed in water, drained and flaked**
- **1 stalk celery, thinly sliced**
- **¼ cup mayonnaise**
- **8 slices rye bread**
- **4 ounces sliced Cheddar or Swiss cheese**
- **1 tablespoon butter or margarine**

1. In small bowl, with fork, combine tuna, celery, and mayonnaise. Spread one side of 4 bread slices with tuna mixture. Top each with one-fourth of cheese and 1 bread slice.

2. In nonstick 12-inch skillet, melt butter over medium-high heat. Arrange sandwiches in skillet. Cover and cook, turning sandwiches once, until cheese has melted and bread is toasted, about 5 minutes.

EACH SERVING: About 513 calories, 34g protein, 32g carbohydrate, 27g total fat (10g saturated), 79mg cholesterol, 1,024mg sodium.

Dilly Egg Tea Sandwiches

No tea tray is ever complete unless it includes egg sandwiches. Fanny Farmer advised her readers: "Chop finely the whites of hard boiled eggs; force the yolks through a strainer or potato ricer." Her words hold true to this day. To keep the bread from becoming soggy, spread one side of each slice with a little soft butter before piling on the egg filling.

PREP: 20 minutes ★ **MAKES** 18 tea sandwiches

- **3 large hard-cooked eggs, peeled and finely shredded**
- **¼ cup mayonnaise**
- **2 tablespoons chopped fresh dill**
- **¼ teaspoon freshly grated lemon peel**
- **¼ teaspoon ground black pepper**
- **12 very thin slices white or whole-wheat bread**

1. In medium bowl, combine eggs, mayonnaise, dill, lemon peel, and pepper. Spread evenly on 6 bread slices; top with remaining bread slices. Trim crusts and cut each sandwich into 3 equal rectangles.

2. If not serving right away, line jelly-roll pan with damp paper towels. Place sandwiches in pan; cover with additional damp paper towels to keep bread from drying out. Cover pan tightly with plastic wrap and refrigerate up to 4 hours.

EACH SANDWICH: About 68 calories, 2g protein, 6g carbohydrate, 4g total fat (1g saturated), 37mg cholesterol, 95mg sodium.

A Spot of Tea...

English colonists brought their love of taking tea to America. It was usually enjoyed at four in the afternoon: a pleasant way to break up a busy day and to spend time with family and friends. And happily this elegant tradition continues today. A proper tea begins with a teapot, preferably earthenware or glazed china, filled with freshly brewed tea (steeped about three to five minutes). Sugar cubes, warmed milk or light cream (the true English way), and slices of lemon or orange studded with whole cloves are popular offerings.

True to the tradition established in the 1800s, various savories and sweets are also offered. Elegant teahouses serve them on a three-tiered pedestal made of sterling or hand-painted porcelain. Guests are instructed to "start at the bottom tier and eat your way to the top." The bottom tier usually holds fancy open-faced or ribbon sandwiches filled with a few favorites, such as smoked salmon, cream cheese with chopped chives, egg salad with watercress, or paper-thin slices of smoked ham. The second shelf is stacked with warm scones or thin tea biscuits with pots of cream and jam on the side. The top tier is piled high with all that is fancy, rich, and creamy: miniature éclairs, tiny fruit-filled tarts, delicate cake fingers, one-bite macaroons, and buttery shortbread cookies.

Classic Hamburgers—with the works!

By the mid-1800s, a pounded beefsteak hot off the grill was popular fare in the city of Hamburg, Germany. According to James Trager in *The Food Chronology*, the popular sandwich made its American debut in New Haven, Connecticut, in 1900: "Louis Lassen grinds 7¢/LB. lean beef, broils, it and serves it between two slices of toast (no catsup or relish) to customers at his 5-year-old three-seat Louis Lunch." Other historians cite different beginnings. Jeffrey Tennyson claims that when teenager Charles Nagreen was frying up ground beef patties at the Wisconsin Ouagamic County Fair in 1885, he noticed that his customers loved them but wanted to eat them "on the run." So he sandwiched the patties between two slices of bread and sent them on their way. Other stories abound, but most everyone agrees that hamburgers got their first national exposure at the 1904 St. Louis World's Fair. And an American tradition was born.

PREP: 5 minutes ★ **COOK:** 8 minutes
MAKES 4 main-dish servings

1¼ **pounds ground beef chuck**

½ **teaspoon salt**

¼ **teaspoon ground black pepper**

1. Shape ground beef into 4 patties, each ¾ inch thick, handling meat as little as possible. Sprinkle patties with salt and pepper.

2. Heat 12-inch skillet over high heat until hot. Add patties and cook about 4 minutes per side for medium or until desired doneness.

EACH BURGER: About 243 calories, 29g protein, 0g carbohydrate, 14g total fat (6g saturated), 88mg cholesterol, 391mg sodium.

Grilled Hamburgers

Prepare outdoor grill. Shape patties as directed. Place patties on grill over medium heat; cook about 4 minutes per side for medium or until desired doneness.

Tex-Mex Burgers

Before shaping into patties, combine *2 tablespoons finely chopped onion, 2 tablespoons bottled salsa, 1 teaspoon salt,* and *1 teaspoon chili powder* with *ground beef* just until well blended but not overmixed. Panfry or grill as directed.

EACH BURGER: About 249 calories, 29g protein, 1g carbohydrate, 14g total fat (6g saturated), 88mg cholesterol, 771mg sodium.

Seven Backyard Burger Secrets

1. Buy only ground chuck, which is 81 to 85 percent lean, and be sure to buy 1¼ pounds for 4 burgers; 5 ounces of raw beef cooks down to 4 ounces. Lean ground beef (sirloin or round, 90 to 95 percent lean) won't give you a plump, juicy burger. If you must use lean meat, make it moister by mixing in 1 or 2 tablespoons of water, red or white wine, broth, or milk per pound of beef.
2. If not using the meat right away, refrigerate in its supermarket wrapping up to 2 days. (And don't let the meat or its juice touch other foods; the spread of *E. coli* and other bacteria is a real risk.) For longer storage, rewrap in freezer wrap or foil and freeze; use within 3 months.
3. Handle the beef gently when shaping it so you don't end up with a "hockey puck." Start with a mound, flatten it slightly, and smooth the edges all around the patty.
4. Make sure the grill is hot before putting on the burgers. A heated grill will sear the meat so it won't stick. And a quick searing retains juices.
5. Don't flatten the patties with a spatula. Pressing squeezes out the flavorful juices and won't speed up the cooking.
6. Cook burgers to at least medium: 160°F on an instant-read thermometer inserted horizontally (the center should no longer be pink).
7. Cheese lovers: Don't get more cheese on the grill slats than on the burgers! Once the patties are cooked to medium, blanket the top with Cheddar, Swiss, or another favorite cheese, and cook with the grill lid down for about 1 minute.

◄ *Tex-Mex Burgers*

Kentucky Hot Brown

The year was 1923, the place The Brown Hotel in Louisville, Kentucky, and the occasion one of their famous dinner dances. Each evening when the band took a break around midnight, the guests headed for the restaurant for something to eat. The orders were always the same: ham and eggs and more ham and eggs, night after night.

Chef Fred K. Schmidt had an idea. He would make an open-faced turkey sandwich and smother it with mornay sauce. In 1923 this was quite innovative, as turkey was primarily eaten at Thanksgiving and Christmas, but at the hotel they had just begun serving turkey year-round. Hotel Manager Rudy Suck thought that the sandwich would taste a bit flat, but the Chef had planned on browning the sandwich under the broiler. The maitre d' felt that the sandwich needed a bit of color, so Schmidt suggested putting two strips of bacon on top. The hotel manager made the final suggestion of adding some pimiento, and a southern tradition was born.

Today the Hot Brown is served to folks before the steeple chases, the races, Kentucky Derby Parties, and every day at The Brown Hotel. The recipe has changed a little over the years, but it is still just as delicious.

Makes four traditional Hot Browns

4 ounces butter ($^1/_2$ cup)

Flour to make a roux (about 6 tablespoons)

3 to 3$^1/_2$ cups milk

6 tablespoons grated Parmesan cheese

I beaten egg

I ounce heavy cream ($^1/_4$ cup), whipped

Salt and pepper to taste

8 slices of toast, such as brioche or other white bread (crusts trimmed)

8 wedges of fresh tomato

Slices of roast turkey

Extra Parmesan for topping

Pinch of paprika

8 strips fried bacon

Chopped fresh parsley

Melt the butter and add enough flour to make a reasonably thick roux (enough to absorb all of the butter). Add the milk and Parmesan cheese. Bring the mixture to a simmer stirring frequently. Cook the milk at medium heat an additional 5 minutes, stirring frequently and being careful not to scorch the sauce. Reduce the heat to low and fold in the egg to thicken the sauce, but do not allow the sauce to boil. Remove from the heat. Fold in the whipped cream. Add salt and pepper to taste.

Toast the 8 slices of bread. Cut 4 slices of the toast diagonally into 2 triangles each (you will have 8 triangles and 4 whole slices).

For each Hot Brown, place one whole slice of toast on the bottom of a metal or flameproof dish. Place 2 triangles of toast on opposite sides and tuck in a wedge of tomato on top of each triangle. Cover the toast with a liberal amount of turkey. Sprinkle with extra Parmesan cheese. Then pour on a generous amount of sauce, sprinkle with additional Parmesan, and a pinch of paprika. Place the entire dish under a broiler until the sauce is speckled brown and bubbly. Remove from the broiler, cross two pieces of bacon on top, sprinkle with some parsley, and serve immediately.

Source: original recipe from The Brown Hotel

Sloppy Joes

The credit for creating the first loose-meat sandwich most often goes to a café cook named Joe. It happened in Sioux City, Iowa, in the 1930s. Fun to make and to eat, Sloppy Joes have been a hit ever since.

PREP: 20 minutes ★ **COOK:** 35 minutes
MAKES 6 main-dish servings

4 teaspoons olive oil
I medium onion, chopped
2 garlic cloves, finely chopped
I medium red pepper, chopped
I small green pepper, chopped
I stalk celery, chopped
2 pounds ground beef chuck
I can (28 ounces) whole tomatoes in puree, chopped
2 tablespoons light (mild) molasses
I tablespoon cider vinegar
I teaspoon salt
$\frac{1}{4}$ teaspoon ground black pepper
6 hamburger buns, split

1. In nonstick 12-inch skillet, heat oil over medium heat. Add onion and garlic and cook until onion is tender, about 5 minutes.

2. Add red and green peppers and celery; cook until tender, about 5 minutes. Stir in ground beef and cook, breaking up meat with side of spoon, until meat is no longer pink, about 5 minutes. Stir in tomatoes with their puree, molasses, vinegar, salt, and black pepper; heat to boiling. Reduce heat and simmer until sauce has slightly thickened, about 10 minutes.

3. Place split buns on dinner plates and top with Sloppy Joe mixture.

EACH SERVING: About 481 calories, 36g protein, 39g carbohydrate, 20g total fat (7g saturated), 94mg cholesterol, 936mg sodium.

Hot Open-Faced Steak Sandwiches

Diners began appearing in cities and towns by the early 1900s, and good home cooking was always on the menu. Hot open-faced sandwiches, traditionally topped with homemade gravy, became a standby. In this version, sautéed mushrooms replace the gravy.

PREP: 15 minutes ★ **COOK:** 35 minutes
MAKES 4 main-dish servings

2 tablespoons butter or margarine, softened
I tablespoon plus I teaspoon chopped fresh tarragon
$\frac{3}{8}$ teaspoon ground black pepper
I loaf (8 ounces) French bread, cut horizontally in half
3 teaspoons vegetable oil
I beef flank steak (1$\frac{1}{4}$ pounds)
$\frac{3}{4}$ teaspoon salt
I medium onion, thinly sliced
12 ounces white mushrooms, trimmed and sliced
pinch dried thyme
$\frac{1}{3}$ cup dry red wine

1. In small bowl, combine butter, 1 tablespoon tarragon, and $\frac{1}{8}$ teaspoon pepper until well blended. Spread tarragon butter evenly on cut sides of bread. Cut each bread half crosswise into 4 pieces.

2. In heavy 12-inch skillet (preferably cast iron), heat 2 teaspoons oil over medium-high heat until very hot. Pat steak dry with paper towels and sprinkle with $\frac{1}{4}$ teaspoon salt and $\frac{1}{8}$ teaspoon pepper. Add steak to skillet and cook 6 to 8 minutes per side for medium-rare or until desired doneness. Transfer steak to cutting board. Set aside.

3. Add remaining 1 teaspoon oil and onion to skillet; cook over medium heat, stirring frequently, until tender, about 5 minutes. Stir in mushrooms, thyme, remaining $\frac{1}{2}$ teaspoon salt, and remaining $\frac{1}{8}$ teaspoon pepper. Cook over medium-high heat until mushrooms are tender and liquid has evaporated, about 8 minutes. Stir in wine and boil 2 minutes. Remove from heat. Keep warm.

4. Holding knife almost parallel to cutting board, cut steak into thin slices across the grain; arrange on bread. Spoon mushroom mixture on top; sprinkle with remaining 1 teaspoon tarragon.

EACH SERVING: About 544 calories, 35g protein, 38g carbohydrate, 26g total fat (11g saturated), 89mg cholesterol, 946mg sodium.

Steak Fajitas

This is typical Tex-Mex fare: marinated skirt steak grilled over mesquite coals and rolled up in tortillas. Its name comes from the Spanish word *faja* (girdle or "strip"). Its true origin is hazy, but fajitas were probably first served at the Roundup restaurant in McAllen, Texas, in the 1930s. Here's our take on this favorite: thin slices of broiled skirt steak rolled up with grilled peppers and onions in a soft flour tortilla.

PREP: 15 minutes plus marinating ★ COOK/BROIL: 20 minutes
MAKES 6 main-dish servings

3 tablespoons fresh lime juice

3 tablespoons fresh orange juice

3/4 teaspoon salt

1/2 teaspoon dried oregano, crumbled

1 beef skirt steak (1 3/4 pounds)

1 tablespoon olive oil

2 medium onions, thinly sliced

2 garlic cloves, thinly sliced

3 large red peppers, cut into 1/2-inch-thick strips

1 large green pepper, cut into 1/2-inch-thick strips

2 teaspoons finely chopped pickled jalapeño chile

12 (6-inch) flour tortillas

1. In cup, combine lime and orange juices, 1/2 teaspoon salt, and oregano. Transfer to ziptight plastic bag; add meat, turning to coat. Seal bag, pressing out as much air as possible. Refrigerate beef 1 hour to marinate, turning bag once.

2. Preheat broiler. Meanwhile, in 12-inch skillet, heat oil over medium heat. Add onions and garlic; cook, stirring frequently, until onions are tender, about 5 minutes. Add red and green peppers, jalapeño, and remaining 1/4 teaspoon salt. Cook, stirring frequently, until red and green peppers are tender, about 7 minutes.

3. Remove meat from marinade and place on rack in broiling pan. Broil steak 6 inches from heat source, 3 to 4 minutes per side for medium-rare or until desired doneness. Cut meat into thin slices across the grain and serve with tortillas and pepper mixture.

EACH SERVING: About 418 calories, 30g protein, 34g carbohydrate, 17g total fat (6g saturated), 66mg cholesterol, 531mg sodium.

Barbecued Pulled Pork Sandwiches

Southerners slowly smoke pork for hours, then hand-pull it off the bone and stir it into spicy barbecue sauce. This easy indoor version simmers on the stove top.

PREP: 10 minutes plus cooling ★ COOK: 3 hours
MAKES 10 main-dish servings

3 pounds boneless pork shoulder-blade roast, trimmed and tied

1/2 teaspoon salt

1/4 teaspoon ground black pepper

1 tablespoon vegetable oil

2 cups water

1 cup ketchup

1/4 cup distilled white vinegar

1/4 cup Worcestershire sauce

1/3 cup packed brown sugar

1 tablespoon dry mustard

1/4 to 1/2 teaspoon crushed red pepper

10 hamburger buns, split

1. Pat pork dry with paper towels. Sprinkle roast with salt and pepper. In nonreactive 5-quart Dutch oven, heat oil over high heat until very hot. Add roast and cook until browned on all sides, about 15 minutes. Transfer pork to plate; discard drippings from pot.

2. Combine water, ketchup, vinegar, Worcestershire, brown sugar, dry mustard, and crushed red pepper in Dutch oven. Add pork and heat to boiling over high heat. Reduce heat; cover and simmer 2 hours 30 minutes, turning roast every 30 minutes.

3. Transfer roast to plate; cool. Boil pot liquid until it has reduced and thickened, about 5 minutes.

4. When roast is cool enough to handle, discard string. Separate meat into chunks, removing as much fat as possible. With hands or fork, shred meat into bite-size pieces. Return pork to Dutch oven, stirring well; heat through. Serve pulled pork on hamburger buns.

EACH SERVING: About 408 calories, 31g protein, 37g carbohydrate, 15g total fat (4g saturated), 93mg cholesterol, 806mg sodium.

New Orleans Oyster Po' Boy

One story traces the very first po' boy to the Martin Brothers Grocery in New Orleans in the 1920s. The sandwiches were either given away for free or were sold for fifteen cents to streetcar workers who were on strike. Po' boys can be filled with a variety of meats or seafood. When made with fried oysters, as in this recipe, it's also known as an oyster loaf.

PREP: 20 minutes ★ **COOK:** 30 seconds per batch
MAKES 4 main-dish servings

vegetable oil for frying

¼ cup mayonnaise

1 tablespoon minced shallot

1 tablespoon chopped fresh parsley

1 tablespoon capers, drained and chopped

¼ teaspoon hot pepper sauce plus additional for serving

1 cup fine cracker crumbs

¼ teaspoon ground red pepper (cayenne)

1 pint shucked oysters, drained

4 soft French bread rolls, each cut horizontally in half and lightly toasted

1 cup very thinly sliced iceberg lettuce

1. In heavy 3-quart saucepan, heat 2 inches oil over medium-high heat until temperature reaches 375°F on deep-fat thermometer.

2. Meanwhile, in small bowl, combine mayonnaise, shallot, parsley, capers, and ¼ teaspoon hot pepper sauce until well blended.

3. On waxed paper, combine cracker crumbs and ground red pepper. Coat 6 oysters with crumb mixture. With slotted spoon, carefully add oysters, all at once, to hot oil; cook until golden, about 30 seconds. With slotted spoon, transfer oysters to paper towels to drain. Repeat coating and frying with remaining oysters.

4. Spread mayonnaise mixture evenly on bottoms of toasted rolls. Top with lettuce and oysters. Replace tops of rolls. Serve with hot pepper sauce.

EACH SERVING: About 504 calories, 16g protein, 49g carbohydrate, 27g total fat (4g saturated), 78mg cholesterol, 898mg sodium.

Chapter 3

Best-Dressed Salads

Americans have always had their own style when it comes to salads. In Eliza Leslie's 1848 *Directions for Cookery in Its Various Branches,* there are two coleslaw recipes: Excellent Cold Slaw, which is made with shredded white cabbage, tossed with a boiled dressing, and set aside until cold, and

Warm Slaw, which starts with warmed-up red cabbage that is doused with hot vinegar dressing and then covered (to keep it warm) and brought to the table. Salads of cucumbers, beets, and onions in spicy vinegar were also popular at that time and are still an important part of our salad repertoire. Burpee developed iceberg lettuce in 1894. It was often tossed with extras, such as grapefruit segments, avocado slices, and red onion rings. Salads were "dressed up" for parties with fresh fruit, nuts, cream cheese, and sweet whipped-cream dressings. Often they were then frozen and decorated with maraschino cherries. In 1905, Charles Knox ran a recipe contest, which started the Age of the Molded Salad. Perfection Salad, which contained bits of celery, cabbage, and red pepper, appeared in a Knox recipe booklet. It was so popular that it continued to be printed through the twentieth century with only some minor changes.

Perhaps Americans' all-time favorite salad is potato salad, especially when made with a creamy dressing. Of course, macaroni salad and three-bean salad are popular at church suppers, while egg salad and chicken salad are enjoyed for lunch and light suppers year-round. Waldorf salad comes from the famous hotel in New York City, the cobb salad from a Hollywood restaurant, and Caesar salad from a restaurateur in Tijuana, Mexico.

Americans also have unique ways of dressing salads. Whether a salad is drizzled with Russian dressing containing chili sauce and caviar, tossed with a creamy ranch buttermilk dressing, or crowned with green goddess or other dressing, they take on their own delicious taste. It's no wonder that salads are so popular and so much a part of our dining ritual.

During the last half of the twentieth century, the greens in our salad bowls became more sophisticated. We went from iceberg lettuce to mesclun, Belgian endive, radicchio, watercress, and dandelions.

◄ *Cobb Salad*

Classic Chicken Salad

All manner of salads became very popular by the late nineteenth century; hardly a meal went by that didn't include a salad course. Fannie Farmer offers three chicken salads in her 1896 cookbook. In one salad, she uses the classic French technique of marinating cut up warm food (in this case chicken) in a simple French dressing so it can more easily absorb all the flavor. In our recipe, letting the just-cooked chicken rest in its cooking broth achieves the same result: a moist chicken that is also very flavorful.

PREP: 20 minutes plus cooling ★ **COOK:** I hour
MAKES 4 main-dish servings

I chicken (3 pounds)
1½ teaspoons salt
3 stalks celery, finely chopped
¼ cup mayonnaise
2 teaspoons fresh lemon juice
¼ teaspoon ground black pepper

I. In 4-quart saucepan, place chicken, 1 teaspoon salt, and enough *water* to cover; heat to boiling over high heat. Reduce heat; cover and gently simmer until chicken loses its pink color throughout, about 45 minutes. Remove from heat and let stand 30 minutes; drain (reserve broth for another use). When chicken is cool enough to handle, discard skin and bones; cut meat into bite-size pieces.

2. In large bowl, combine celery, mayonnaise, lemon juice, remaining ½ teaspoon salt, and pepper; stir until blended. Add chicken and toss to coat. Transfer to serving bowl. Cover and refrigerate until ready to serve.

EACH SERVING: About 337 calories, 36g protein, 2g carbohydrate, 20g total fat (4g saturated), 117mg cholesterol, 779mg sodium.

Basil-and-Dried-Tomato Chicken Salad

Prepare as directed but add *¼ cup chopped fresh basil* and *2 tablespoons finely chopped oil-packed dried tomatoes*, drained, to mayonnaise mixture.

Curry-Grape Chicken Salad

Prepare as directed but add *2 cups red or green seedless grapes*, cut in half, *1 teaspoon curry powder*, and *1 teaspoon honey* to mayonnaise mixture.

Lemon-Pepper Chicken Salad

Prepare as directed but use *1 tablespoon fresh lemon juice* and *½ teaspoon coarsely ground black pepper*, and add *½ teaspoon freshly grated lemon peel* to mayonnaise mixture.

Chef's Salad

It's generally believed by many food historians that Louis Diat created the first chef's salad in the kitchen of the Ritz-Carlton hotel in New York City. His recipe called for smoked ox tongue as one of the meats and watercress as the green. Chicken and ham have happily replaced the ox tongue, and romaine or iceberg lettuce often serves as the green.

PREP: 25 minutes ★ **MAKES** 4 main-dish servings

10 cups bite-size pieces assorted salad greens, such as romaine, endive, escarole, or red leaf

Classic French Vinaigrette (page 77), Blue Cheese Dressing (page 75), or Thousand Island Dressing (page 76)

1/4 teaspoon salt

4 ounces smoked or baked ham, cut into long, thin strips

4 ounces Swiss cheese, cut into long, thin strips

2 hard-cooked large eggs, peeled and quartered

2 carrots, peeled and coarsely shredded or 1/2 cup sliced radishes

1 small red onion, thinly sliced

1/2 cup sliced peeled cucumber

In large serving bowl, toss greens with 1/3 cup salad dressing and salt. Decoratively arrange ham, cheese, egg, carrots, red onion, and cucumber on top. Serve with remaining dressing alongside.

EACH SERVING WITH CLASSIC FRENCH VINAIGRETTE:
About 343 calories, 19g protein, 13g carbohydrate, 24g total fat (8g saturated), 146mg cholesterol, 923mg sodium.

EACH SERVING WITH BLUE CHEESE DRESSING:
About 339 calories, 22g protein, 13g carbohydrate, 23g total fat (10g saturated), 160mg cholesterol, 909mg sodium.

EACH SERVING WITH THOUSAND ISLAND DRESSING:
About 315 calories, 20g protein, 14g carbohydrate, 20g total fat (8g saturated), 169mg cholesterol, 862mg sodium.

Crab Louis

Three chefs (all named Louis) are given credit for inventing Crab Louis. One was the chef at Solari's restaurant in San Francisco in 1914, another, the chef at the Olympic Club in Seattle, and the third, the chef at the St. Francis Hotel in San Francisco.

PREP: 1 hour ★ **MAKES** 4 main-course servings

1 cup mayonnaise

3 tablespoons ketchup

2 tablespoons chopped green onion

1 tablespoon Worcestershire sauce

1 tablespoon red wine vinegar

2 teaspoons fresh lemon juice

1/2 teaspoon salt

1/8 teaspoon ground white pepper

1 container (16 ounces) lump crabmeat, picked over

lettuce leaves

3 hard-cooked large eggs, peeled and sliced

1 cucumber, sliced

1 ripe tomato, sliced

1. In medium bowl, combine mayonnaise, ketchup, onion, Worcestershire, vinegar, lemon juice, salt, and pepper. Cover and refrigerate 30 minutes.

2. In center of platter, mound crab. Arrange lettuce, eggs, cucumber, and tomato around crab. Serve with dressing.

EACH SERVING: About 605 calories, 30g protein, 10g carbohydrate, 50g total fat (8g saturated), 305mg cholesterol, 1,147mg sodium.

Taco Salad

Glen Bell, owner of the very first Taco Bell in Downey, California, helped popularize the Mexican-American sandwich in a taco shell in 1962. Soon those same ingredients took the form of a generously proportioned salad that has become a favorite from coast to coast.

PREP: 30 minutes ★ **COOK:** 20 minutes
MAKES 6 main-dish servings

2 teaspoons vegetable oil

I medium onion, chopped

I garlic clove, finely chopped

2 tablespoons chili powder

I teaspoon ground cumin

I pound ground beef chuck

I can (8 ounces) tomato sauce

I head iceberg lettuce, cut into quarters and very thinly sliced

I large ripe tomato (10 ounces), chopped

I ripe avocado, peeled, pitted, and chopped

4 ounces sharp Cheddar cheese, shredded (I cup)

3 tablespoons sour cream

I cup loosely packed small fresh cilantro leaves

5 ounces tortilla chips

I. In 10-inch skillet, heat oil over medium heat. Add onion and cook, stirring occasionally, until tender, about 5 minutes. Stir in garlic, chili powder, and cumin; cook 30 seconds. Add ground beef, breaking up meat with side of spoon; cook until no longer pink, about 5 minutes. Stir in tomato sauce; cook 5 minutes longer.

2. Divide lettuce among dinner plates. Spoon warm beef mixture on top of lettuce. Top with tomato, avocado, and Cheddar. Top each serving with some sour cream and sprinkle with cilantro. Tuck tortilla chips around edge of each plate.

EACH SERVING: About 506 calories, 22g protein, 21g carbohydrate, 38g total fat (15g saturated), 87mg cholesterol, 504mg sodium.

Cobb Salad

(pictured on page 62)

One late night in 1937, Robert Cobb of Hollywood's Brown Derby restaurant tossed up this chopped salad for a guest from "a little of this and a little of that." He not only ended up pleasing his guest but also created a California tradition.

PREP: 25 minutes ★ **BROIL/COOK:** 8 minutes
MAKES 6 main-dish servings

12 ounces skinless, boneless chicken breast halves

$1/4$ teaspoon salt

$1/8$ teaspoon ground black pepper

6 slices bacon, coarsely chopped

I head iceberg lettuce, thinly sliced

3 hard-cooked large eggs, peeled and coarsely chopped

I large ripe tomato (10 ounces), cut into $1/2$-inch pieces

I ripe avocado, peeled, pitted, and cut into $1/2$-inch pieces

3 ounces Roquefort cheese, crumbled ($3/4$ cup)

Classic French Vinaigrette (page 77)

I. Preheat broiler. Place chicken on rack in broiling pan and sprinkle with salt and pepper. Place pan in broiler 6 inches from heat source. Broil until chicken loses its pink color throughout, about 4 minutes per side. When cool enough to handle, cut into $1/2$-inch pieces.

2. Meanwhile, in 10-inch skillet, cook bacon over medium heat until browned. Transfer bacon to paper towels to drain.

3. Line large platter with lettuce. Arrange eggs, tomato, avocado, Roquefort, chicken, and bacon in striped pattern over lettuce. Pass dressing separately.

EACH SERVING (WITHOUT DRESSING): About 272 calories, 24g protein, 9g carbohydrate, 16g total fat (6g saturated), 157mg cholesterol, 537mg sodium.

Classic Egg Salad

In the 1926 edition of the *The Boston Cooking-School Cook Book,* Fannie Farmer describes egg salad as resembling old-fashioned stuffed eggs. The mashed yolks were flavored with a little oil dressing, shaped into balls, then stuffed back into the whites. Today egg salads are made from whole eggs, which are chopped, flavored, and often served up as a sandwich filling. Many favor an egg-salad sandwich on white toast accompanied by pickles and potato chips, which makes for a very satisfying lunch.

PREP: 10 minutes ★ **COOK:** 10 minutes plus standing
MAKES 2 cups or 4 main-dish servings

6 large eggs
¼ cup mayonnaise
1½ teaspoons Dijon or spicy brown mustard
¼ teaspoon salt

1. In 3-quart saucepan, place eggs and enough *cold water* to cover by at least 1 inch; heat to boiling over high heat. Immediately remove from heat and cover tightly; let stand 15 minutes. Pour off hot water and run cold water over eggs to cool. Peel eggs.

2. Coarsely chop eggs and transfer to medium bowl. Add mayonnaise, mustard, and salt and stir to combine. If not serving right away, cover and refrigerate up to 4 hours.

EACH SERVING: About 217 calories, 10g protein, 1g carbohydrate, 19g total fat (4g saturated), 327mg cholesterol, 359mg sodium.

Curried Egg Salad

Prepare as directed but add *4 teaspoons chopped mango chutney* and *½ teaspoon curry powder* to egg mixture.

Caesar-Style Egg Salad

Prepare as directed but use only *⅛ teaspoon salt.* Add *2 tablespoons freshly grated Parmesan cheese* and *1 teaspoon anchovy paste* to egg mixture.

Mexican-Style Egg Salad

Prepare as directed but add *⅓ cup chopped fresh cilantro* and *½ teaspoon hot pepper sauce* to egg mixture.

Deli-Style Egg Salad

Prepare as directed but add *¼ cup chopped celery* and *¼ cup chopped red onion* to egg mixture.

Caesar Salad

During the days of Prohibition, Hollywood movie stars often crossed the Mexican border to Tijuana for a fun night out. One popular spot was Caesar's Palace. On the night of July 24, 1924, Caesar Cardini had just about run out of food in the kitchen. He improvised and whipped up a salad with the few things he could scrape together: romaine lettuce, some good olive oil, a little cheese, and a few eggs. He entertained his guests by dramatically preparing the salad tableside, which created an immediate sensation. The original Caesar salad contained raw eggs. Due to salmonella concerns, our dressing is made with mayonnaise.

PREP: 15 minutes   Bake: 7 minutes
MAKES 4 first-course servings

6 slices (½ inch thick) Italian bread
2 garlic cloves, each cut in half
3 tablespoons olive oil
¼ cup mayonnaise
¼ cup freshly grated Parmesan cheese
3 tablespoons fresh lemon juice
2 tablespoons water
2 teaspoons anchovy paste
1 head romaine lettuce, torn into bite-size pieces

1. Preheat oven to 400°F. Rub bread slices with cut sides of garlic. Brush both sides of bread with 2 tablespoons oil. Cut bread into ½-inch pieces; place in jelly-roll pan. Bake until golden brown and crisp, about 7 minutes.

2. Meanwhile, prepare dressing: In large salad bowl, with wire whisk, mix mayonnaise, Parmesan, lemon juice, water, remaining 1 tablespoon oil, and anchovy paste until blended. Add lettuce and croutons; toss to coat.

EACH SERVING: About 367 calories, 9g protein, 27g carbohydrate, 25g total fat (5g saturated), 14mg cholesterol, 604mg sodium.

Spinach with Hot Bacon Dressing

German immigrants are often given credit for the combination of crisp spinach leaves and hot bacon dressing. They were already known for tossing hot cooked potatoes with that particular dressing and also for making wilted lettuce salads.

PREP: 15 minutes ★ **COOK:** 12 minutes
MAKES 6 first-course servings

2 bunches (10 to 12 ounces each) spinach, washed and dried very well, tough stems trimmed

6 slices bacon, coarsely chopped

1 small onion, finely chopped

2 tablespoons sugar

1/3 cup cider vinegar

2 tablespoons olive oil

1/2 teaspoon salt

1. Tear spinach into bite-size pieces and place in large serving bowl.

2. In 10-inch skillet, cook bacon over medium heat until browned. With slotted spoon, transfer bacon to paper towels to drain. Discard all but 2 tablespoons drippings from skillet.

3. Add onion to skillet and cook over low heat until tender, about 5 minutes. Add sugar, stirring to coat. Stir in vinegar, oil, and salt; heat to boiling. Pour hot dressing over spinach. Add bacon and toss until well mixed and coated with dressing. Serve immediately.

EACH SERVING: About 152 calories, 4g protein, 10g carbohydrate, 11g total fat (3g saturated), 8mg cholesterol, 376mg sodium.

Carrot-Raisin Salad

This cheery, bright orange salad dotted with dark raisins is a regular at church suppers and in school cafeterias. The traditional recipe uses only carrots and raisins; we've added small chunks of apple.

PREP: 15 minutes ★ **MAKES** 6 accompaniment servings

1 orange

1/4 cup mayonnaise

1/4 cup sour cream

1/2 teaspoon sugar

1/2 teaspoon salt

1 pound carrots, peeled and shredded

1 Granny Smith apple, cut in half, cored, and chopped

1/4 cup dark seedless raisins

1. From orange, grate 1/4 teaspoon peel and squeeze 2 tablespoons juice.

2. In large serving bowl, with wire whisk, mix orange peel and juice, mayonnaise, sour cream, sugar, and salt until blended. Fold in carrots, apple, and raisins until well blended.

EACH SERVING: About 224 calories, 2g protein, 24g carbohydrate, 14g total fat (4g saturated), 14mg cholesterol, 412mg sodium.

Wilted Dilly Cucumbers

In *American Food,* Evan Jones cites historian Robert Beverley, who wrote that Virginians cultivated "all the Culinary Plants that grow in England." And cucumbers were among them. In Dutch and in German communities, smothering cucumber slices until they wilted was a highly regarded tradition.

PREP: 15 minutes plus standing and chilling
MAKES 6 accompaniment servings

2 English (seedless) cucumbers, not peeled, thinly sliced

2 teaspoons salt

½ cup sour cream

2 tablespoons chopped fresh dill

1 tablespoon distilled white vinegar

⅛ teaspoon ground black pepper

1. In colander set over large bowl, toss cucumbers and salt; let stand 30 minutes at room temperature. Discard liquid in bowl. Pat cucumbers dry with paper towels.

2. In same clean bowl, combine sour cream, dill, white vinegar, and pepper. Add cucumbers, stirring to coat. Cover and refrigerate at least 1 hour to blend flavors or up to 4 hours.

EACH SERVING: About 60 calories, 2g protein, 5g carbohydrate, 4g total fat (3g saturated), 8mg cholesterol, 203mg sodium.

Creamy Coleslaw

Whether the Dutch or the Germans are the originators of the first coleslaw remains a mystery. In their native countries, they both ate cabbage salads: the Dutch called it *koolsla,* and the Germans called it *kole.* Americans were introduced to these appealing salads by the late 1700s. The first slaws were usually tossed with boiled dressing, which was later replaced by mayonnaise or sour cream.

PREP: 25 minutes ★ **MAKES** 12 accompaniment servings

2 lemons

½ cup mayonnaise

¼ cup sour cream

1 tablespoon sugar

1 teaspoon salt

½ teaspoon coarsely ground black pepper

¼ teaspoon celery seeds, crushed

1 large head green cabbage (3 pounds), thinly sliced, tough ribs discarded (12 cups)

4 carrots, peeled and shredded

1. From lemons, grate 1 teaspoon peel and squeeze ¼ cup juice. In large bowl, with wire whisk, mix lemon peel and juice, mayonnaise, sour cream, sugar, salt, pepper, and celery seeds until blended.

2. Add cabbage and carrots to dressing in bowl; toss to coat. Serve at room temperature, or cover and refrigerate up to 4 hours.

EACH SERVING: About 114 calories, 2g protein, 9g carbohydrate, 8g total fat (2g saturated), 8mg cholesterol, 274mg sodium.

Three-Bean Salad

In the late 1950s, attendees at family reunions, picnics, or church suppers were likely to see a salad made from three different beans. It became an immediate party favorite for one reason: the longer the salad stood on the buffet table the better its flavor.

PREP: 25 minutes plus chilling ★ **COOK:** 13 minutes
MAKES 8 accompaniment servings

8 ounces green beans, trimmed and cut into
    1-inch pieces (2 cups)
8 ounces wax beans, trimmed and cut into
    1-inch pieces (2 cups)
1½ teaspoons salt
3 tablespoons olive or vegetable oil
3 tablespoons cider vinegar
2 tablespoons sugar
1 can (15 to 19 ounces) red kidney beans, rinsed and
    drained
¼ cup chopped onion

1. In 4-quart saucepan, heat *3 inches water* to boiling over high heat. Add green and wax beans and ½ teaspoon salt; heat to boiling. Cook until tender-crisp, 6 to 8 minutes; drain. Rinse beans with cold running water to cool slightly; drain.

2. Meanwhile, prepare dressing: In large bowl, with wire whisk, mix oil, vinegar, sugar, and remaining 1 teaspoon salt until well blended. Add green and wax beans, kidney beans, and onion; toss until mixed and coated with dressing. Cover and refrigerate salad at least 2 hours to blend flavors or up to 24 hours.

EACH SERVING: About 118 calories, 4g protein,
14g carbohydrate, 5g total fat (1g saturated),
0mg cholesterol, 441mg sodium.

Iowa Corn Salad

To Native Americans, corn was known as the staff of life and was closely linked to their religious beliefs and rituals. It is no wonder then that even today corn is a basic part of our diet, especially in the Midwest. In this recipe, we have combined corn with other favorite farm-stand vegetables for a great-tasting summer salad that can be prepared several hours ahead.

PREP: 30 minutes ★ **COOK:** 10 minutes
MAKES 12 accompaniment servings

12 ears corn, husks and silk removed
12 ounces green beans, trimmed and cut into
    ¼-inch pieces
½ cup cider vinegar
¼ cup olive oil
¼ cup chopped fresh parsley
1 teaspoon salt
½ teaspoon coarsely ground black pepper
1 red pepper, finely chopped
1 small sweet onion, such as Vidalia or Walla Walla,
    finely chopped

1. In 8-quart saucepot, heat *2 inches water* to boiling over high heat; add corn. Heat to boiling. Reduce heat; cover and simmer 5 minutes. Drain. When cool enough to handle, cut kernels from corncobs.

2. Meanwhile, in 2-quart saucepan, heat *1 inch water* to boiling over high heat; add green beans and heat to boiling. Reduce heat and simmer until tender-crisp, 3 to 5 minutes. Drain. Rinse with cold running water; drain.

3. Prepare dressing: In large bowl, with wire whisk, mix vinegar, oil, parsley, salt, and black pepper until blended.

4. Add corn, green beans, red pepper, and onion to dressing in bowl; toss to coat. Serve, or cover and refrigerate up to 2 hours.

EACH SERVING: About 179 calories, 5g protein,
31g carbohydrate, 6g total fat (1g saturated),
0mg cholesterol, 219mg sodium.

Old-Fashioned Potato Salad

The credit goes to the German immigrants for introducing Americans to potato salad. Theirs was served hot, was spiked with a vinegar dressing, and contained bits of smoked bacon. In New England, the colonists tossed potatoes with a homemade mayonnaise dressing. Mayonnaise was probably named after the city of Mahon on the island of Minorca. One story is that the chef to the duc de Richelieu created mayonnaise in honor of a French victory at Port Mahon in 1756. Most historians agree that the word *mayonnaise* is of French origin. Here is the classic mayonnaise-dressed potato salad, which has been toted to community fund-raisers, church suppers, and potluck dinners over the years, especially since the 1950s.

PREP: 20 minutes ★ **COOK:** 35 minutes
MAKES 10 accompaniment servings

3 pounds all-purpose potatoes (9 medium), not peeled
½ cup mayonnaise
½ cup milk
2 tablespoons distilled white vinegar
2 tablespoons chopped green onion
1 teaspoon sugar
1 teaspoon salt
¼ teaspoon coarsely ground black pepper
2 large stalks celery, thinly sliced

1. In 4-quart saucepan, combine potatoes and enough *water* to cover; heat to boiling over high heat. Reduce heat; cover and simmer until tender, 25 to 30 minutes. Drain. When cool enough to handle, peel potatoes and cut into ¾-inch pieces.

2. Meanwhile, prepare dressing: In large bowl, with wire whisk, mix mayonnaise, milk, vinegar, green onion, sugar, salt, and pepper until blended. Add potatoes and celery to dressing; toss to coat. If not serving right away, cover and refrigerate up to 4 hours.

EACH SERVING: About 198 calories, 3g protein, 27g carbohydrate, 9g total fat (2g saturated), 8mg cholesterol, 315mg sodium.

Lemony Potato Salad

Prepare as directed but substitute *3 tablespoons fresh lemon juice* and *1 teaspoon freshly grated lemon peel* for distilled white vinegar.

Church-Supper Macaroni Salad

Through the centuries, American life has often centered around the church. An old-fashioned church supper just wouldn't be complete without a big bowl of this classic and satisfying macaroni salad.

PREP: 25 minutes ★ **COOK:** 7 minutes
MAKES 6 accompaniment servings

8 ounces elbow macaroni
2¾ teaspoons salt
4 carrots, peeled and chopped
about 2 lemons
⅔ cup mayonnaise
⅓ cup milk
2 stalks celery, chopped
2 green onions, thinly sliced

1. In large saucepot, cook pasta as label directs, using 2 teaspoons salt. Add carrots to pasta water 2 minutes before pasta has completed cooking. Cook until carrots are tender-crisp and pasta is done, 1 to 2 minutes longer.

2. Meanwhile, from lemon, grate 1 teaspoon peel and squeeze 3 tablespoons juice. Prepare dressing: In large bowl, with wire whisk, mix mayonnaise, milk, lemon peel and juice, and remaining ¾ teaspoon salt until blended.

3. Drain pasta and carrots; add to dressing in bowl along with celery and green onions; toss until mixed and well coated with dressing. Serve at room temperature, or cover and refrigerate up to 4 hours.

EACH SERVING: 351 calories, 6g protein, 36g carbohydrate, 21g total fat (3g saturated), 16mg cholesterol, 598mg sodium.

Waldorf Salad

Maître d'Hotel Oscar Tschirky of the Waldorf-Astoria hotel in New York City created this food classic in 1896. The original version was made with apples, celery, and mayonnaise, but by 1928, when *The Rector Cook Book* was printed, chopped walnuts had been added. And that version is still on the hotel menu today.

PREP: 30 minutes ★ MAKES 8 accompaniment servings

⅓ cup mayonnaise

¼ cup sour cream

1 tablespoon fresh lemon juice

1 teaspoon honey

¼ teaspoon salt

3 red apples, such as Braeburn, Cortland, or Red Delicious, cored and cut into ½-inch pieces

2 stalks celery, each cut lengthwise in half, then thinly sliced

½ cup walnuts, toasted and coarsely chopped

⅓ cup dark seedless raisins (optional)

Prepare dressing: In medium bowl, with wire whisk, mix mayonnaise, sour cream, lemon juice, honey, and salt until blended. Add apples, celery, walnuts, and raisins, if using, to dressing in bowl; toss until mixed and coated with dressing.

EACH SERVING: About 181 calories, 2g protein, 16g carbohydrate, 14g total fat (2g saturated), 9mg cholesterol, 135mg sodium.

Tomato Aspic Mold

In the early 1900s, Americans discovered the wonders of making molded salads with gelatin. One of the first was tomato aspic. Originally it was molded with homemade calf's-foot jelly. At the turn of the century, following the suggestion of a Philadelphia cooking-school teacher, Charles Knox granulated his sheet gelatin, and a new era in salad making began.

PREP: 15 minutes plus chilling ★ COOK: 20 minutes
MAKES 8 accompaniment servings

4 cups tomato juice

¼ cup celery leaves

6 whole allspice berries

2 whole cloves

2 envelopes unflavored gelatin

2 tablespoons fresh lemon juice

1 tablespoon sugar

½ teaspoon hot pepper sauce

1 container (8 ounces) sour cream

2 tablespoons mayonnaise

2 tablespoons chopped fresh dill

1. In 3-quart saucepan, heat 3½ cups tomato juice to boiling. Add celery leaves, allspice berries, and cloves. Reduce heat and simmer 15 minutes.

2. Meanwhile, pour remaining ½ cup tomato juice into large bowl and evenly sprinkle with gelatin. Let stand 2 minutes to soften gelatin slightly.

3. Strain hot tomato-juice mixture through sieve over softened gelatin. Stir until gelatin has completely dissolved. Stir in lemon juice, sugar, and hot pepper sauce. Pour into 8½" by 4½" glass loaf pan or 5-cup nonreactive decorative mold. Cover and refrigerate until set, at least 6 hours or up to overnight.

4. To unmold, dip pan in large bowl of hot water 10 seconds. Invert onto platter; remove bowl. In small bowl, combine sour cream, mayonnaise, and dill; stir until blended. Serve tomato aspic with dilled sour cream.

EACH SERVING: About 120 calories, 3g protein, 9g carbohydrate, 9g total fat (4g saturated), 14mg cholesterol, 487mg sodium.

Molded Salads, Plain and Fancy!

By 1896, manufacturers had already discovered the positive effect that professional endorsements and helpful booklets had on the sales of new or improved products. One of these companies, Knox Gelatine, published *Dainty Desserts for Dainty People*, a booklet of recipes that used Knox's Sparkling Calves Head Gelatine. The booklet was offered free, compliments of grocers, to introduce customers to the newly granulated gelatin.

Until 1893, Knox Gelatine had been available only in shredded form. After receiving a number of requests from prominent cooking teachers, Mr. Knox responded by manufacturing the gelatin in granulated form, making it easier to accurately measure out. One of these requests came from teacher and cookbook author Miss Sarah T. Rorer, who wrote: "May I suggest to you to granulate your Gelatine, and keep same up to its present high standard of quality? So many new recipes call for a small amount of Gelatine, and the ordinary household scales do not weigh less than an ounce…"

The four-by-six-inch booklet was typical of advertising booklets of that time; it touted the advantages of the product in the opening pages: "This is Worth Reading: KNOX GELATINE IS NOT LIKE PIE, IT'S HEALTHY… [it's] the purest made … It has no odor or taste to disguise, so requires less flavoring …"

The recipes in the thirty-two page booklet, which included specialties of the day such as tomato jelly, caramel ice cream, cantaloupe frappé, almond Bavarian cream, and Italian tutti fruitti, used the new granulated gelatin. In 1931, Knox published another booklet, *Plain and Fancy Salads*, that offered a collection of salads, including an early version of Perfection Salad that closely resembled the original 1905 recipe. The booklet described it as "A delicious accompaniment to cold sliced chicken or veal."

Perfection Salad

In 1905, Mrs. John Cooke entered a recipe contest sponsored by Knox Gelatin. Her Perfection Salad took third prize and helped launch a whole generation of proud hostesses who served molded-salad creations.

PREP: 20 minutes plus chilling
MAKES 8 accompaniment servings

5 cups cold water

4 envelopes unflavored gelatin

1 cup sugar

1½ teaspoons salt

1 cup cider vinegar

¼ cup fresh lemon juice (about 2 large lemons)

3 cups finely shredded cabbage

1⅓ cups diced celery (about 3 stalks)

1 jar (4 ounces) diced pimientos

lettuce leaves (optional)

1. In 1-quart saucepan, heat 2 cups water to boiling. In medium bowl, mix gelatin, sugar, and salt. Add boiling water, stirring until gelatin has completely dissolved. Stir in vinegar, lemon juice, and remaining 3 cups cold water. Refrigerate until mixture mounds slightly when dropped from a spoon, about 30 minutes.

2. Gently fold in cabbage, celery, and pimientos with their liquid. Pour mixture into 2½-quart decorative mold; cover and refrigerate until set, about 3½ hours.

3. To unmold salad, dip mold in large bowl of hot water 10 seconds. Invert onto large flat plate lined with lettuce leaves, if desired. Remove mold.

EACH SERVING: About 128 calories, 4g protein, 30g carbohydrate, 0g total fat (0g saturated), 0mg cholesterol, 468mg sodium.

Fruit Salad

Blanch the meat of two dozen English walnuts and break in pieces. Skin and seed two dozen white grapes, cut one pineapple in slices and slices in cubes. Slice three bananas. Separate the sections of two large oranges and remove all skin. Arrange each in separate piles. Pour over a dressing made of one-half cup of Madeira wine, one cup of sugar, two tablespoons of lemon juice and one-half cup of orange juice. Garnish with Maraschino cherries.

—**Good Housekeeping Everyday Cook Book,** 1903

Heavenly Fruit Salad

During the 1950s and 1960s, this molded salad, which often contained canned fruit cocktail or pineapple, graced many dinner tables, especially around the holidays. It can also be made with fresh fruits, as we have suggested here.

PREP: 20 minutes plus chilling ★ **COOK:** 2 minutes
MAKES 8 servings

2 tablespoons fresh lemon juice

1 teaspoon unflavored gelatin

1 package (3 ounces) cream cheese, softened

1/4 cup mayonnaise

2 tablespoons sugar

1/2 cup heavy or whipping cream, whipped

1 3/4 cups assorted fresh fruit, such as sliced strawberries, sliced peaches, and blueberries

1/4 cup chopped walnuts or pecans

1/4 cup maraschino cherries, quartered

lettuce leaves (optional)

1. Spoon lemon juice into 1-quart saucepan. Evenly sprinkle gelatin over lemon juice. Let stand 1 minute to soften gelatin slightly. Heat mixture over medium-low heat, stirring, until gelatin has completely dissolved, about 1 minute.

2. Meanwhile, in medium bowl, with mixer at medium speed, beat cream cheese, mayonnaise, and sugar until smooth. Beat in gelatin mixture. With rubber spatula, fold in whipped cream, then fold in fruit, nuts, and cherries. Pour mixture into 8½" by 4½" glass loaf pan. Cover and refrigerate until set, at least 4 hours.

3. To unmold, dip loaf pan in large bowl of hot water 10 seconds. Invert onto platter lined with lettuce leaves, if desired. Remove loaf pan.

EACH SERVING: About 198 calories, 2g protein, 11g carbohydrate, 17g total fat (7g saturated), 36mg cholesterol, 78mg sodium.

Blue Cheese Dressing

This creamy dressing is a favorite for green salads as well as assorted raw vegetables. Try Stilton or Roquefort, or go American and use Maytag blue, a fabulous handmade Iowa cheese that is as good as blue cheese gets.

PREP: 10 minutes ★ **MAKES** about 1 cup

---

4 ounces blue cheese, crumbled (1 cup)

3 tablespoons half-and-half or light cream

1/2 cup mayonnaise

2 tablespoons white wine vinegar

1 teaspoon Dijon mustard

1/8 teaspoon salt

1/8 teaspoon ground black pepper

In small bowl, with fork, mash blue cheese with half-and-half until creamy. With wire whisk, mix in mayonnaise, vinegar, mustard, salt, and pepper until well blended. Cover and refrigerate up to 3 days.

EACH TABLESPOON: About 79 calories, 2g protein, 1g carbohydrate, 8g total fat (2g saturated), 10mg cholesterol, 165mg sodium.

Russian Dressing

The earliest versions of this dressing were made with Russian caviar, which is how the dressing got its name. By the twentieth century, however, the caviar was eliminated because of its cost.

PREP: 10 minutes ★ **MAKES** about 1 cup

3/4 cup mayonnaise

1/4 cup chili sauce

2 tablespoons finely chopped green pepper

1 tablespoon snipped fresh chives (optional)

1/4 teaspoon dry mustard

1/4 teaspoon Worcestershire sauce

3 drops hot pepper sauce

In small bowl, stir mayonnaise, chili sauce, green pepper, chives, if using, mustard, Worcestershire, and hot pepper sauce until well mixed. Cover and refrigerate up to 3 days.

EACH TABLESPOON: About 78 calories, 0g protein, 1g carbohydrate, 8g total fat (1g saturated), 6mg cholesterol, 117mg sodium.

Poppy-Seed Dressing

Just who whisked up the first poppy-seed dressing is not known. Helen Corbitt, food guru at the Houston Country Club and at Neiman Marcus in Dallas in the 1950s, however, certainly helped make it famous. Whatever the season, Helen's guests could always count on delicious fresh fruit salads with this excellent dressing ladled over.

PREP: 10 minutes ★ **MAKES** 1½ cups

---

1 cup vegetable oil

1/3 cup cider vinegar

1/2 cup sugar

1 tablespoon grated onion

1 tablespoon poppy seeds

1 teaspoon dry mustard

1 teaspoon salt

In blender, combine oil, vinegar, sugar, onion, poppy seeds, dry mustard, and salt; process until mixture has thickened and is smooth. Transfer to bowl or jar; cover and refrigerate up to 2 days. Stir well before using.

EACH TABLESPOON: About 99 calories, 0g protein, 4g carbohydrate, 9g total fat (1g saturated), 0mg cholesterol, 97mg sodium.

Ranch Buttermilk Dressing

Several stories exist regarding the origin of ranch dressing. The most quoted one traces it to Alaska in the mid-twentieth century, where Steve Henson created a dry mix of herbs and spices that he blended with mayonnaise and buttermilk to create a creamy dressing. In the 1950s, in Santa Barbara, California, he ran a 120-acre dude ranch called the Hidden Valley® Guest Ranch. The menu often included salad, so Steve perfected his dressing and served it in the dining room. It was so popular that it became the only dressing served at the ranch. Not surprising, guests often requested jars of the dressing to take home. Steve quickly realized that it would be much easier to package the dry mix and let people add in the mayonnaise and buttermilk at home. The simple mix of dry herbs and spices grew into a multi-million dollar mail-order business. And that's how one of America's favorite salad dressings came to be.

PREP: 10 minutes ★ **MAKES** about ¾ cup

½ **cup buttermilk**

⅓ **cup mayonnaise**

1 tablespoon chopped fresh parsley

½ **teaspoon grated onion**

¼ **teaspoon salt**

¼ **teaspoon ground black pepper**

1 garlic clove, cut in half

In small bowl, with wire whisk, mix buttermilk, mayonnaise, parsley, onion, salt, and pepper until blended; stir in garlic. Cover and refrigerate up to 3 days. Remove garlic before serving.

EACH TABLESPOON: About 48 calories, 0g protein, 1g carbohydrate, 5g total fat (1g saturated), 4mg cholesterol, 93mg sodium.

Thousand Island Dressing

Legends abound about the creation of thousand island dressing. One story suggests that the first recipe came from the Thousand Islands in the St. Lawrence River. Another popular tale is that the bits and pieces in the dressing resemble thousands of islands in a sea of dressing.

PREP: 15 minutes ★ **MAKES** 1 cup

½ **cup mayonnaise**

¼ **cup chopped pimiento-stuffed olives (salad olives)**

1 hard-cooked large egg, peeled and coarsely chopped

2 tablespoons chili sauce

1 tablespoon sweet pickle relish

1 tablespoon finely chopped fresh parsley

1 tablespoon finely chopped green onion

⅛ **teaspoon ground black pepper**

In small bowl, stir mayonnaise, olives, egg, chili sauce, relish, parsley, green onion, and pepper until well mixed. Cover and refrigerate up to 3 days. Stir well before using.

EACH TABLESPOON: About 60 calories, 1g protein, 1g carbohydrate, 6g total fat (1g saturated), 17mg cholesterol, 129mg sodium.

Green Goddess Dressing

In the mid-1920s, George Arliss appeared in William Archer's play *The Green Goddess*. Since he was staying at San Francisco's Palace Hotel, he frequently dined at the hotel's Palm Court restaurant. In Arliss's honor, the chef created The Green Goddess: a salad of romaine, escarole, and chicory tossed in a salad bowl that was first rubbed with garlic. It was then topped with a creamy dressing that was subtly flavored with anchovy paste. The original recipe used only mayonnaise; sour cream makes it even more "goddesslike."

PREP: 10 minutes ★ **MAKES** about ¾ cup

½ cup mayonnaise

¼ cup sour cream

½ cup loosely packed fresh parsley leaves

2 tablespoons fresh tarragon leaves

2 tablespoons chopped green onion

1 tablespoon snipped fresh chives

1 tablespoon red wine vinegar

1 teaspoon anchovy paste

¼ teaspoon ground black pepper

In blender, combine mayonnaise, sour cream, parsley, tarragon, green onion, chives, vinegar, anchovy paste, and pepper; puree until smooth, scraping down sides of blender occasionally. Transfer to bowl or jar; cover and refrigerate up to 3 days.

EACH TABLESPOON: About 78 calories, 0g protein, 1g carbohydrate, 8g total fat (2g saturated), 8mg cholesterol, 79mg sodium.

Classic French Vinaigrette

Early salad dressings were simple mixtures stirred up from homemade tarragon or wine vinegar, vegetable oil, and dry mustard. By the mid-twentieth century, imported olive oils and vinegars were readily available, and Julia Child was teaching Americans the proper French way to dress a salad. Using the best red or white wine vinegar and virgin olive oil along with some salt, pepper, and a hint of dry mustard was the secret. In time, mustard from Dijon, France, which is made from mustard seeds, white wine, and unfermented grape juice became all the rage and is still included in many recipes.

PREP: 5 minutes ★ **MAKES** about ¾ cup

¼ cup red wine vinegar

1 tablespoon Dijon mustard

¾ teaspoon salt

½ teaspoon coarsely ground black pepper

½ cup olive oil

In medium bowl, with wire whisk, mix vinegar, mustard, salt, and pepper until blended. In thin, steady stream, whisk in oil until blended. Cover and refrigerate dressing up to 1 week.

EACH TABLESPOON: About 82 calories, 0g protein, 0g carbohydrate, 9g total fat (1g saturated), 0mg cholesterol, 175mg sodium.

On Lettuce, circa 1699

In *A Discourse of Sallets* in 1699, John Evelyn writes about the importance of reaching that delicate, harmonious balance between the lettuce in a *sallet* (salad) and the other ingredients: "By reason of its soporifous [dull and boring] quality, lettuce ever was, and still continues, the principal foundation of the universal tribe of sallets, which is to cool and refres . . . . We have said how necessary it is that in the composure of a sallet, every plant should come in to bear its part, without being overpowe'd by some herb of a stronger taste, so as to endanger the native sapor and virtue of the rest; but fall in to their places, like the notes in music, in which there should be nothing harsh or grating."

Chapter 4

Eggs & Cheese– Plain & Fancy

"Two eggs over easy with toast" is a familiar breakfast cry in diners and cafés across America—and it has been for centuries. But eggs were not always plentiful or inexpensive enough to eat every day. The Native Americans ate wild fowl eggs, including turkey, pigeon, and goose. When the English settlers arrived in Jamestown they had chickens with them. From then until the late nineteenth century, chickens and eggs were popular but costly in urban areas. They were reserved for special occasions, except for the well-to-do, who could afford to serve eggs more often.

Nineteenth-century cookbooks include various ways to cook eggs: gently poached and served on buttered toast (known as dropped eggs in New England); soft boiled for breakfast; cooked up into griddle cakes; turned into omelets with oysters, ham, or asparagus tips; and souffléd into light and airy egg puffs. Since 1864, eggs have been scrambled, fricasseed with bread crumbs, fried in lard, turned into deviled eggs, scalloped, and baked au gratin.

The commercial breeding of chickens in 1934 revolutionized the egg industry. Eating eggs as often as one liked finally became a reality. During the twentieth century, eggs went Mexican as *huevos rancheros* and cheesy stratas showed up on brunch tables and open-faced Italian omelets, called *frittatas,* turned pantry staples into gourmet meals.

High-quality cheese was a treasured commodity that was sometimes given as a presentation gift. In 1802, a 1,235-pound Cheshire cheese from Massachusetts was given to President Thomas Jefferson on New Year's Day.

Up until the time of industrialization, cheese making had been women's work. The cheese-making industry developed when the English brought over their techniques, the Germans applied their production methods, and the Scandinavians set up operations in the Midwest. Today cheeses made in America and those imported from European countries are readily available and enjoyed on a daily basis.

Creamy Scrambled Eggs for a Crowd

Short-order cooks seem to have a way of turning out delicious, creamy eggs cooked to everyone's liking. It's not difficult, but it does require good technique. Here's how: Cook the eggs slowly, gently pushing them into the center of the skillet as they cook, which makes soft, creamy curds.

PREP: 10 minutes ★ **COOK:** 10 minutes
MAKES 8 main-dish servings

14 large eggs

¼ teaspoon ground black pepper

3 tablespoons butter or margarine

2 packages (3 ounces each) cream cheese, cut into 1-inch cubes

1. In large bowl, with wire whisk, beat eggs and pepper until well blended. In nonstick 12-inch skillet, melt butter over medium heat; add eggs. With heat-safe rubber spatula, gently push egg mixture into center as it begins to set to form soft curds, about 3 minutes.

2. When eggs are partially cooked, top with cream cheese. Continue cooking, stirring occasionally, until eggs have thickened and no visible liquid egg remains. Transfer to warm platter.

EACH SERVING: About 243 calories, 13g protein, 2g carbohydrate, 20g total fat (10g saturated), 407mg cholesterol, 217mg sodium.

Scrambled Eggs with Cream Cheese and Salmon

Prepare as directed but sprinkle *4 ounces smoked salmon, chopped (¾ cup),* over eggs with cream cheese. To serve, top with *¼ cup chopped green onions.*

EACH SERVING: About 260 calories, 15g protein, 2g carbohydrate, 21g total fat (10g saturated), 410mg cholesterol, 501mg sodium.

Denver Omelet

Ranch hands in the Rocky Mountains rise early to complete their morning chores. Mid-morning they feast on hearty dishes like this omelet stuffed with ham, onion, and green pepper. In most states, it's known as a western omelet.

PREP: 20 minutes ★ **COOK:** 2 minutes per omelet
MAKES 4 main-dish servings

FILLING

1 tablespoon olive oil

1 small onion, chopped

1 green pepper, chopped

1 red pepper, chopped

1 piece cooked ham (4 ounces), finely chopped (1 cup)

OMELETE

8 large eggs

½ cup water

½ teaspoon salt

4 teaspoons butter or margarine

1. Prepare filling: In nonstick 10-inch skillet, heat oil over medium heat. Stir in onion and green and red peppers. Cook, stirring occasionally, until vegetables are tender, about 10 minutes. Add ham and heat through.

2. Prepare omelet: In medium bowl, with wire whisk, beat eggs, water, and salt.

3. In another 10-inch nonstick skillet, melt 1 teaspoon butter over medium-high heat. Pour ½ cup egg mixture into skillet. Cook, gently lifting edge of eggs with heat-safe rubber spatula and tilting pan to allow uncooked eggs to run underneath, until eggs are set, about 1 minute. Spoon one-fourth of filling over half of omelet. Fold unfilled half of omelet over filling and slide onto warm plate. Repeat with remaining butter, egg mixture, and filling. If desired, keep omelets warm in 200°F oven until all omelets are cooked.

EACH SERVING: About 284 calories, 20g protein, 6g carbohydrate, 20g total fat (7g saturated), 452mg cholesterol, 881mg sodium.

Italian Ham and Potato Frittata

Italian omelets (frittatas) began popping up in American homes, especially for weekend brunches, around the mid-1900s. Unlike a French omelet, where the filling ingredients are folded inside the eggs, in a frittata all of the ingredients are cooked together. It is often finished off in the oven or lightly browned under the broiler and served in wedges right from the skillet.

PREP: 10 minutes ★ **COOK/BAKE:** 45 minutes
MAKES 6 main-dish servings

10 ounces all-purpose potatoes (2 medium), peeled, cut lengthwise in half, then thinly sliced

1¼ teaspoons salt

3 tablespoons vegetable oil

1 piece cooked ham (4 ounces), cut into ½-inch pieces (1 cup)

1 medium onion, thinly sliced

8 large eggs

¼ cup water

¼ teaspoon coarsely ground black pepper

pinch dried thyme

1. Preheat oven to 425°F. In 2-quart saucepan, combine potatoes, enough *cold water* to cover, and 1 teaspoon salt; heat to boiling over high heat. Cook until tender, about 10 minutes; drain.

2. In oven-safe nonstick 10-inch skillet (if skillet is not oven-safe, wrap handle with double layer of foil), heat 1 tablespoon oil over medium-high heat. Add ham and cook, stirring occasionally, until lightly browned, about 3 minutes. With slotted spoon, transfer ham to plate.

3. Add 1 tablespoon oil to skillet. Add onion and cook, stirring occasionally, until tender and golden, about 10 minutes. Transfer onion to ham on plate.

4. In large bowl, with wire whisk, beat eggs, water, remaining ¼ teaspoon salt, pepper, and thyme until well blended. Stir in potatoes, ham, and onion. Heat remaining 1 tablespoon oil in skillet over medium heat. Pour in egg mixture; cover and cook until egg mixture begins to set around edge, about 3 minutes. Remove cover and place skillet in oven. Bake until frittata is set, 8 to 10 minutes.

5. To serve, loosen frittata from skillet and slide onto warm platter; cut into 6 wedges.

EACH SERVING: About 232 calories, 14g protein, 10g carbohydrate, 15g total fat (4g saturated), 294mg cholesterol, 663mg sodium.

Egg Foo Yong

In the nineteenth and early twentieth centuries, Chinese chefs cooked for railroad gangs, in logging camps, and in elegant homes in California. Chinese-style dishes, such as these egg pancakes filled with bits of vegetables and shrimp, became popular fare.

PREP: 20 minutes ★ **COOK:** 20 minutes
MAKES 4 main-dish servings

6 large eggs

2 teaspoons Asian sesame oil

1 teaspoon sugar

¾ teaspoon salt

6 teaspoons vegetable oil

1 stalk celery, cut lengthwise in half and thinly sliced

1 package (8 ounces) mushrooms, trimmed and chopped

3 green onions, thinly sliced

2 tablespoons grated, peeled fresh ginger

8 ounces medium shrimp, shelled, deveined, and cut crosswise in half

soy sauce (optional)

1. In large bowl, with wire whisk, mix eggs, sesame oil, sugar, and salt until blended; set aside.

2. In nonstick 12-inch skillet, heat 2 teaspoons vegetable oil over medium-high heat. Add celery and cook, stirring occasionally, 2 minutes. Add mushrooms, green onions, and ginger; cook until mushrooms are light brown, about 5 minutes. Stir in shrimp and cook 1 minute. Set aside until cool, about 10 minutes.

3. Stir cooled shrimp mixture into beaten egg mixture. In nonstick 8-inch skillet, heat 1 teaspoon vegetable oil over medium heat. Pour in one-fourth (about 3/4 cup) of egg mixture. Cook until eggs have almost set, about 3 minutes. With wide spatula, turn egg pancake over; cook 1 minute longer. Transfer to platter; cover and keep warm. Repeat with remaining oil and egg mixture.

EACH SERVING: About 270 calories, 20g protein, 7g carbohydrate, 17g total fat (3g saturated), 390mg cholesterol, 575mg sodium.

Eggs in a Hole

As its name implies, in this dish an egg is placed in a hole that is cut in a slice of bread and then cooked. Hot off a griddle, it's a delicious and a fun way to serve "one egg over easy with toast."

PREP: 5 minutes ★ **COOK:** 5 minutes ★ **MAKES** 4 servings

---

2 tablespoons butter or margarine

4 slices white bread

4 large eggs

1/8 teaspoon salt

pinch ground black pepper

1. In 12-inch nonstick skillet, melt 1 tablespoon butter over medium heat. While butter melts, with biscuit cutter or glass, cut a 2-inch circle from center of each slice of bread; reserve bread rounds for another use.

2. Arrange bread slices in single layer in skillet. Break 1 egg into each hole. Sprinkle eggs with salt and pepper. Cook until eggs are set on bottom, 2 to 3 minutes. Add remaining 1 tablespoon butter to skillet; carefully turn bread slices with spatula, letting butter run under. Cook eggs to desired degree of doneness, 1 to 2 minutes.

EACH SERVING: About 182 calories, 8g protein, 11g carbohydrate, 12g total fat (5g saturated), 228mg cholesterol, 309mg sodium.

Huevos Rancheros

This ever-popular brunch dish is best known outside of Mexico. In Spanish, *huevos rancheros* means "ranch-style eggs." The authentic dish consists of fried eggs placed on crisp corn tortillas that are covered with chili-infused red sauce and topped with crumbled *queso fresco* (fresh cheese). Other recipes, like ours, call for toppings such as sour cream, avocado, and cilantro.

PREP: 10 minutes ★ **COOK/BAKE:** 20 minutes
MAKES 4 main-dish servings

---

2 tablespoons vegetable oil

1 medium onion, coarsely chopped

1 garlic clove, finely chopped

1 jalapeño chile, seeded and finely chopped

1 can (14 to 16 ounces) tomatoes

1/4 teaspoon salt

4 (6-inch) corn or flour tortillas

3 tablespoons butter or margarine

4 large eggs

1 ripe medium avocado, pitted, peeled, and cut crosswise into thin slices (optional)

2 tablespoons sour cream

1 tablespoon chopped fresh cilantro

1. Preheat oven to 350°F. In nonreactive 2-quart saucepan, heat 1 tablespoon oil over medium-high heat. Add onion, garlic, and jalapeño; cook, stirring, until onion is tender, about 5 minutes. Stir in tomatoes with their juice and salt; heat to boiling over high heat, breaking up tomatoes with side of spoon. Reduce heat; cover and simmer, stirring, 5 minutes.

2. Wrap tortillas in foil; place in oven until heated through, about 10 minutes.

3. Meanwhile, in 10-inch skillet, melt butter over medium heat. Break 1 egg into small cup. Holding cup close to skillet, slip egg into skillet; repeat with remaining eggs. Reduce heat to low; cook slowly, spooning butter over eggs to baste them and turning eggs to cook on both sides, until egg whites are completely set and egg yolks begin to thicken but are not hard, 3 to 5 minutes.

4. Place tortillas on warm plates. Place 1 fried egg on each tortilla and spoon 2 tablespoons tomato sauce over each. Top with avocado and some sour cream; sprinkle with cilantro. Serve with remaining tomato sauce on the side.

EACH SERVING: About 403 calories, 11g protein, 25g carbohydrate, 31g total fat (10g saturated), 239mg cholesterol, 521mg sodium.

Eggs Benedict

Culinary historians cite two possible origins of this classic, both in New York City. One attributes the first eggs Benedict to the chef at Delmonico's restaurant in Manhattan. As the story goes, Mrs. Le Grand Benedict, a regular customer, became upset when no new items were added to the menu. To appease her, eggs Benedict was created. The other tale concerns the Waldorf-Astoria hotel and Wall Street broker Lemuel Benedict, who came up with eggs Benedict from offerings on the hotel's famous buffet table in 1894.

PREP: 25 minutes ★ **COOK:** 10 minutes
MAKES 8 main-dish servings

Hollandaise Sauce (page 176)
8 slices Canadian bacon
4 English muffins, split and toasted
8 large eggs

1. Prepare Hollandaise Sauce; keep warm.

2. In jelly-roll pan, arrange toasted English muffins and top each with slice of Canadian bacon; keep warm.

3. Poach eggs: In 12-inch skillet, heat 1½ inches *water* to boiling. Reduce heat to medium-low. Break 1 egg into small cup; holding cup close to surface of water, slip into simmering water. Repeat with remaining eggs. Cook until egg whites have set and egg yolks begin to thicken but are not hard, 3 to 5 minutes.

4. Place jelly-roll pan with bacon-topped muffins next to poaching eggs. With slotted spoon, carefully remove eggs, one at a time, from water and very briefly drain (still held in spoon) on paper towels; set 1 egg on top of each slice of Canadian bacon. Spoon Hollandaise Sauce over. Serve hot.

EACH SERVING: About 311 calories, 15g protein, 15g carbohydrate, 21g total fat (10g saturated), 337mg cholesterol, 786mg sodium.

Baked Eggs Au Gratin

The American version of English Cheddar (store cheese) could be found in most New England grocery stores in the nineteenth century. By the 1900s, recipes for eggs au gratin were appearing in cookbooks.

PREP: 10 minutes ★ **BAKE:** 10 minutes
MAKES 8 servings

4 ounces sliced Swiss cheese
1 cup heavy or whipping cream
8 large eggs
¼ teaspoon salt
⅛ teaspoon ground black pepper
pinch paprika
8 slices white or whole-wheat bread, toasted

1. Preheat oven to 425°F. Butter 9-inch deep-dish pie plate.

2. Line pie plate with overlapping slices of Swiss cheese; pour in cream. Break 1 egg into small cup; holding cup close to surface of cream, slip egg into cream. Repeat with remaining eggs, placing them side by side. Sprinkle eggs with salt, pepper, and paprika.

3. Bake until eggs are done as desired, 10 to 15 minutes. Serve with toast.

EACH SERVING: About 302 calories, 13g protein, 14g carbohydrate, 21g total fat (11g saturated), 268mg cholesterol, 322mg sodium.

Pickled Beets with Eggs

The Amish and Moravians from the German Alps and the Rhineland immigrated to rural Pennsylvania in the eighteenth century. They loved pickled dishes, such as ours, which consists of hard-cooked eggs and sliced beets. As the eggs marinate, they turn a colorful, appetizing pink.

PREP: 15 minutes plus cooling and chilling overnight
COOK: 30 minutes ★ **MAKES** 12 first-course servings

6 large eggs
5 medium beets (about 1½ pounds, including tops)
1 cup cider vinegar
⅓ cup sugar

1. In 2-quart saucepan, place eggs and enough *cold water* to cover eggs by at least 1 inch; heat to boiling over high heat. Immediately remove from heat and cover tightly; let stand 15 minutes. Pour off hot water; run cold water over eggs to cool. Peel eggs; set eggs aside to cool.

2. Meanwhile, trim tops from beets, leaving about 1 inch of stems attached. Scrub beets well with cold running water. In 3-quart saucepan, place beets and enough *water* to cover; heat to boiling over high heat. Reduce heat to medium-low; cover and simmer until beets are tender, 20 to 25 minutes. Drain; reserve 1 cup beet cooking liquid. Immediately, peel beets under cold running water and cut into ¼-inch-thick slices.

3. Place whole eggs in medium bowl or 1½-quart wide-mouth jar; layer sliced beets on top. In nonreactive 1-quart saucepan, combine vinegar, sugar, and reserved beet cooking liquid; heat to boiling over high heat. Pour vinegar mixture over eggs and beets. Set aside until egg-beet mixture is cool; with spoon, gently turn eggs occasionally for even color. Cover and refrigerate at least 24 hours before serving. Refrigerate up to 1 week.

4. To serve, cut the eggs lengthwise in half and serve with sliced beets.

EACH SERVING: About 55 calories, 4g protein, 5g carbohydrate, 3g total fat (1g saturated), 107mg cholesterol, 50mg sodium.

Skillet French Toast

Who would have ever guessed that a dish as humble as French toast would become a classic breakfast and brunch dish. It's best prepared with slightly stale or day-old bread, so it can soak up as much of the egg-milk batter and flavorings as possible. Some recipes (including ours) suggest dipping the bread in the batter right before cooking. But real French toast aficionados know that this dish is at its best when the bread is allowed to soak for at least an hour, or better yet overnight, in the batter. When cooked the next day, the French toast comes out lighter, higher, even slightly souffléd (or perhaps it just seems so).

PREP: 5 minutes ★ **COOK:** 15 minutes
MAKES 4 main-dish servings

3 large eggs
¾ cup milk
⅛ teaspoon salt
4 tablespoons butter or margarine
8 slices (½ inch thick) sourdough or other firm white bread
softened butter or margarine, maple syrup, or honey

1. In pie plate, with wire whisk, beat eggs, milk, and salt until well blended. In nonstick 12-inch skillet, melt 2 tablespoons butter over medium-high heat.

2. Dip 4 bread slices, one at a time, in beaten egg mixture to coat both sides well. Place in skillet and cook until browned, about 4 minutes per side. Transfer to cookie sheet; keep warm to 200°F oven. Repeat with remaining 2 tablespoons butter and remaining 4 bread slices. Serve hot with butter, maple syrup, or honey.

EACH SERVING WITHOUT BUTTER, SYRUP, OR HONEY: About 341 calories, 11g protein, 32g carbohydrate, 18g total fat (10g saturated), 197mg cholesterol, 605mg sodium.

Pain Perdu

As its name suggests, French toast originated in France, where it was called *ameritte* or *pain perdu* (lost bread). In America, the French Acadians embraced *pain perdu,* and it soon became a classic dish. This popular brunch dish has also been known as German toast and nun's toast. *The Picayune's Creole Cook Book* features two recipes: one for Lost Bread that is flavored with orange flower water and the other for Spanish Toast that is spiked with brandy or rum. Whatever it's called, this dish is made from white bread (preferably a little stale) dipped into an egg-milk batter and cooked to golden perfection. In restaurants it almost always arrives at the table with a pat of melting butter, a sprinkling of confectioners' sugar, and a pitcher of warm maple syrup.

Cream Waffles

Before the Pilgrims sailed for the New World, they spent time in Holland, where they discovered *wafels:* light Dutch batter cakes cooked on a wafflelike griddle. It is also believed that the early Dutch settlers contributed their knowledge of waffles. By the end of the eighteenth century, waffle parties were all the rage in America.

PREP: 15 minutes ★ **BAKE:** 5 minutes per batch
MAKES eleven 4" by 4" waffles or 4 servings

2 cups all-purpose flour

1 tablespoon baking powder

½ teaspoon salt

2 cups light cream

2 tablespoons butter or margarine, melted

2 large eggs, lightly beaten

softened butter or margarine, and maple syrup

1. Preheat waffle baker as manufacturer directs. In large bowl, combine flour, baking powder, and salt. Add light cream, melted butter, and eggs; whisk until smooth.

2. When waffle baker is ready, pour in batter until it spreads to within 1 inch of edges. Cover and bake as manufacturer directs (do not lift cover during baking).

3. When waffle is done, lift cover and loosen waffle with fork. Serve immediately with butter and maple syrup, or keep warm in oven (place waffles directly on oven rack in 250°F oven to keep crisp). Reheat waffle baker before pouring in more batter. If batter becomes too thick upon standing, thin with a little milk.

EACH SERVING: About 551 calories, 13g protein, 53g carbohydrate, 32g total fat (19g saturated), 201mg cholesterol, 1,110mg sodium.

Griddle Cakes

Flat cakes cooked on a griddle are as old as America itself. Indian cakes, which are made from cornmeal, were prepared in the early 1600s. Dutch immigrants stirred up *pannekoeken* (buckwheat cakes) in the mid-1700s, and hoe cakes were baked on the blade of a hoe in the ashes of a fire. During the 1800s, griddle cakes made from white flour were called flapjacks at first, then pancakes later on. Out West there were slapjacks, while in the South there were delicate batter cakes. In the northwest logging camps, hotcakes were known as flannel cakes, perhaps because their texture resembled that of the loggers' flannel shirts. They were also called flat cars because they looked like the open railroad cars that were used for shipping lumber.

PREP: 15 minutes ★ **COOK:** 4 minutes per batch
MAKES 3 main-dish servings

1 cup all-purpose flour

2 tablespoons sugar

2 teaspoons baking powder

½ teaspoon baking soda

½ teaspoon salt

1¼ cups buttermilk, or 1 cup plain yogurt plus ¼ cup milk

3 tablespoons butter or margarine, melted

1 large egg, lightly beaten

vegetable oil for brushing pan

1. In large bowl, combine flour, sugar, baking powder, baking soda, and salt. Add buttermilk, melted butter, and egg; stir just until flour is moistened.

2. Heat griddle or 12-inch skillet over medium heat until drop of water sizzles; brush lightly with oil. Pour batter by scant ¼ cups onto hot griddle, making a few pancakes at a time. Cook until tops are bubbly, some bubbles burst, and edges look dry, about 2 minutes. With wide spatula, turn pancakes and cook until underside is golden. Transfer to platter; keep warm in 200°F oven.

3. Repeat with remaining batter, brushing griddle with more oil if necessary.

EACH SERVING: About 366 calories, 10g protein, 46g carbohydrate, 16g total fat (8g saturated), 106mg cholesterol, 1,167mg sodium.

Sour Cream Pancakes

Prepare as directed but substitute *1 container (8 ounces) sour cream* and *¼ cup milk* for buttermilk.

Griddle Cakes ▶

German Puffed Pancake

The German immigrants loved pancakes. They were, however, different from the pancakes Americans were used to. A batter was whipped up, poured into a skillet, and partially cooked on the stove top. It was then placed in the oven until golden and puffed. The pancake was rushed to the table and topped with melted butter, sugar, and fresh lemon juice. Southern plantation cooks made their own versions of these puffed cakes. They were cooked in the "family" cast-iron skillet until moist and puffy, closely resembling Yorkshire pudding. To keep the pancake puffed for as long as possible, it was served right from the skillet. Our version begins with sautéed apples that are caramelized before the batter is added to the skillet, making this one of the most delicious versions ever.

PREP: 15 minutes ★ **COOK/BAKE:** 30 minutes
MAKES 6 main-dish servings

2 tablespoons butter or margarine

½ cup plus 2 tablespoons sugar

¼ cup water

6 medium Granny Smith or Newtown Pippin apples (2 pounds), each peeled, cored, and cut into 8 wedges

3 large eggs

¾ cup milk

¾ cup all-purpose flour

¼ teaspoon salt

1. Preheat oven to 425°F. In oven-safe 12-inch skillet (if skillet is not oven-safe, wrap handle with double layer of foil), combine butter, ½ cup sugar, and water; heat to boiling over medium-high heat. Add apples; cook, stirring occasionally, until apples are golden and sugar mixture begins to caramelize, about 15 minutes.

2. Meanwhile, in blender or in food processor with knife blade attached, blend eggs, milk, flour, remaining 2 tablespoons sugar, and salt until smooth.

3. Pour batter over apples. Place skillet in oven and bake until pancake has puffed and is golden, about 15 minutes. Cut into wedges and serve hot.

EACH SERVING: About 301 calories, 6g protein, 54g carbohydrate, 8g total fat (4g saturated), 121mg cholesterol, 181mg sodium.

Classic Cheese Soufflé

(pictured on page 78)

Thanks to cooking teachers Julia Child and James Beard, twentieth-century housewives could open a cookbook, take a cooking class, or watch a television program and learn something about gourmet cooking. Child's and Beard's recipes were so precisely written and detailed that many a novice in the kitchen felt confident enough to tackle *coq au vin*, an apple Charlotte, or a cheese soufflé such as ours.

PREP: 25 minutes ★ **BAKE:** 55 minutes
MAKES 6 main-dish servings

2 tablespoons plain dried bread crumbs or freshly grated Parmesan cheese

4 tablespoons butter or margarine

¼ cup all-purpose flour

¼ teaspoon salt

⅛ teaspoon ground red pepper (cayenne)

1½ cups milk

8 ounces sharp Cheddar cheese, shredded (2 cups)

5 large eggs, separated

1 large egg white

1. Preheat oven to 325°F. Grease 2-quart soufflé dish; sprinkle evenly with bread crumbs.

2. In heavy 3-quart saucepan, melt butter over low heat. Stir in flour, salt, and ground red pepper until blended; cook, stirring, 1 minute. With wire whisk, gradually whisk in milk. Cook, stirring constantly with wooden spoon, until mixture has thickened and boils. Stir in Cheddar; cook, stirring, just until cheese has melted and sauce is smooth. Remove from heat.

3. In small bowl, with wire whisk or fork, lightly beat egg yolks; gradually whisk in ½ cup hot cheese sauce. Gradually whisk egg-yolk mixture into cheese sauce in saucepan, stirring rapidly to prevent curdling. Set aside to cool.

4. In large bowl, with mixer at high speed, beat egg whites until stiff peaks form when beaters are lifted. With rubber spatula, gently fold one-third of beaten egg whites into cool cheese mixture. Fold in remaining whites, just until blended.

5. Pour mixture into prepared soufflé dish. If desired, to create top-hat effect (center will rise higher than edge), with back of spoon, make 1-inch-deep indentation all around top of soufflé mixture about 1 inch from edge of dish. Bake until soufflé has puffed, is golden brown, and knife inserted 1 inch from edge comes out clean, 55 to 60 minutes. Serve hot.

EACH SERVING: About 355 calories, 18g protein, 9g carbohydrate, 27g total fat (15g saturated), 246mg cholesterol, 520mg sodium.

Corn and Pepper Jack Soufflé

Grease 2½- to 3-quart soufflé dish. Prepare as directed, but in Step 1, after mixture has thickened and boils, cook, stirring frequently, 2 minutes. Substitute *8 ounces Monterey Jack cheese with jalapeño chiles*, shredded (2 cups), for Cheddar and stir *1 cup fresh corn kernels* into cheese mixture before folding in beaten egg whites.

EACH SERVING: About 375 calories, 19g protein, 15g carbohydrate, 27g total fat (14g saturated), 246mg cholesterol, 540mg sodium.

Gruyère-Spinach Soufflé

Prepare as directed but substitute *8 ounces Gruyère cheese*, shredded (2 cups), for Cheddar. Stir *1 package (10 ounces) frozen chopped spinach*, thawed and squeezed dry, into Gruyère cheese mixture before folding in beaten egg whites. Substitute *pinch ground nutmeg* for ground red pepper (cayenne).

EACH SERVING: About 370 calories, 21g protein, 11g carbohydrate, 27g total fat (15g saturated), 248mg cholesterol, 445mg sodium.

Southwestern Soufflé

Prepare as directed but substitute *8 ounces Monterey Jack cheese*, shredded (2 cups), for Cheddar and stir *½ cup chopped cooked ham* into cheese mixture before folding in beaten egg whites.

EACH SERVING: About 365 calories, 21g protein, 9g carbohydrate, 27g total fat (15g saturated), 253mg cholesterol, 660mg sodium.

Cheese, American Style

America's love for cheese goes back to the birth of the nation. Most of the cheeses enjoyed by the colonists were the expensive Cheshires imported from England. After the revolution, however, high taxes were placed on such treasured commodities. Cheeses were often the "honored guest" at presidential celebrations. In 1837, 10,000 citizens attended Andrew Jackson's last reception at the White House and feasted on a 1,400-pound wheel of cheese.

As the pleasure of eating cheese caught on in America, the cheese-making industry developed. In the nineteenth century, Cheddar was the most popular cheese, thanks in part to Joseph Harding's improved manufacturing techniques. Varieties from Vermont and New York became well known. After the Gold Rush, Monterey Jack, a cheese similar to one made by the Spanish friars, was created by farmer David Jacks. In Wisconsin, around 1850, a Swiss farmer named Adam Blumer developed an imitation Swiss cheese, complete with their signature holes. Limburger, which was first made in Belgium, was produced by the German immigrants in Upstate New York. This strong-flavored, strong-smelling cheese was served in slabs, in beer halls alongside dark beer and pumpernickel bread.

In 1903, Chicago grocery clerk J. H. Kraft began wrapping cheese for his customers and selling it door-to-door by horse and wagon. The rest is history—big-business history. The United States is now the largest producer of cheese in the world.

Overnight Cheese Strata

Leave it to the Americans to devise a way to turn day-old bread into a never-fail type of cheese soufflé. The strata became popular in the mid-1900s. In its simplest form, it consisted of buttered slices of bread that were alternately layered with shredded cheese in a casserole and covered with a mixture of milk and eggs. Back then it was known as cheese pudding and scalloped cheese.

PREP: 15 minutes plus chilling ★ **BAKE:** 1 hour
MAKES 6 main-dish servings

8 slices firm white bread

8 ounces extrasharp Cheddar cheese, shredded (2 cups)

1 tablespoon butter or margarine, softened

6 large eggs

2 cups milk

1 teaspoon Dijon mustard

¼ teaspoon salt

pinch ground red pepper (cayenne)

1. Lightly grease 8-inch square baking dish. Arrange 4 bread slices in bottom of dish. Sprinkle with Cheddar. Spread butter on one side of remaining 4 bread slices and arrange, butter side up, on top of cheese.

2. In large bowl, with wire whisk, beat eggs, milk, mustard, salt, and ground red pepper until well blended. Slowly pour egg mixture over bread slices. Press bread down to absorb egg mixture and spoon egg mixture over any uncoated bread. Cover and refrigerate at least 4 hours or up to overnight.

3. Preheat oven to 350°F. Remove cover and bake strata until golden and knife inserted in center comes out clean, about 1 hour. Let stand 10 minutes before serving.

EACH SERVING: About 401 calories, 21g protein, 24g carbohydrate, 24g total fat (13g saturated), 269mg cholesterol, 675mg sodium.

Party Cheese Mold

By the end of the nineteenth century, molded creations became easy to make and no-fail, thanks to the folks at the Knox Gelatine Company. Ours, which is surrounded by fresh fruits, is an impressive addition to a buffet table.

PREP: 20 minutes plus chilling
MAKES 6 accompaniment servings

1 envelope unflavored gelatin

¾ cup cold water

1 container (16 ounces) cottage cheese

1 package (8 ounces) cream cheese, softened

2 tablespoons confectioners' sugar

¾ teaspoon freshly grated lemon peel

⅛ teaspoon salt

honeydew melon wedges, strawberries, blueberries, and seedless green grapes

honey (optional)

1. In small saucepan, evenly sprinkle gelatin over cold water; let stand 2 minutes to soften gelatin slightly. Cook over medium-low heat, stirring constantly, until gelatin has completely dissolved. Remove from heat.

2. Press cottage cheese through sieve into large bowl. Add cream cheese, confectioners' sugar, lemon peel, salt, and gelatin mixture. With mixer at medium speed, beat mixture until smooth; pour into 4-cup mold or bowl. Cover and refrigerate until set, about 4 hours.

3. To unmold, run tip of paring knife around edge and tap side sharply to break seal. Invert onto chilled large plate; remove mold. Arrange fresh fruits around mold. Drizzle with honey, if you like.

EACH SERVING: About 224 calories, 13g protein, 6g carbohydrate, 17g total fat (10g saturated), 53mg cholesterol, 469mg sodium.

Dyeing Easter Eggs

The egg, which represents fertility, new beginnings, and new life is synonymous with Easter. So it is no wonder that the custom of dyeing eggs at Easter has been a treasured tradition the world over.

Each group of immigrants who came here had its own way of decorating eggs. The Greeks dyed eggs crimson to honor the blood of Christ, while German and Austrian immigrants colored them green and exchanged them with friends on Maunday Thursday (Thursday before Easter). The Ukrainians liked to use complex designs and various colors to create their *pysanki* eggs. Nowadays eggs are dyed and decorated as simply or as elaborately as one likes.

In Washington, D.C., on the day after Easter, there's lots of egg rolling going on at the White House. This fun tradition dates back to 1816, when Dolley Madison organized the first national Easter Egg Roll on the beautiful sloping lawn of the Capitol. In the 1880s, it was moved to the White House lawn. Rolling eggs is so popular now that thousands of eggs are dyed each year for this special event.

Chapter 5

Chicken Every Sunday

Americans have always craved chicken. The settlers quickly learned from the Native Americans how to slowly spit-roast chicken on green-wood sticks until "smoked to a turn." They also knew that a great stew pot was something to be cherished (the luckiest brides were given one) and that

even the toughest fowl would become succulent after a few hours of simmering. They soon discovered that the broth was delicious and the pot even better when they added dumplings and cooked them until plump and tender.

Pit-barbecued chickens "arrived" in New York society when they made their debut at political rallies in the 1700s. As the economy cycled over the years, the poor became poorer and chickens became harder to come by. But that didn't stop folks from carving up this versatile, juicy bird whenever possible.

Nineteenth-century cookbooks offered few poultry recipes because of the greater availability of game and wild fowl. Eliza Leslie in her 1848 book *Directions for Cookery in Its Various Branches*, provides only ten poultry recipes. Her Baked Chicken Pie recipe advises: "It will be much improved by the addition of a quarter

of a hundred oysters; or by interspersing the pieces of chicken with slices of cold boiled ham. You may add also some yolks of eggs boiled hard."

In the 1930s, Louisiana Senator Huey P. Long rallied the vote of the poor by promising them "a chicken in every pot." He used the example of Henri IV, who attempted to attract the support of the hungry by promising them a "chicken in [their] pot every Sunday."

Today almost everyone has a favorite way of preparing chicken. Southerners batter and fry it, smoke it, barbecue it, and turn it into fricassée, while Midwesterners love to roast it. Californians stir-fry their chicken, and Cajuns toss it into the gumbo pot. However you choose to serve the bird, you can count on chicken being on the menu—not just on Sunday but any day of the week.

Sunday Roast Chicken

(pictured on page 92)

The Pilgrims brought domesticated chickens to our shores. Ever since then, roast chicken has been America's favorite Sunday dinner. This one is stuffed the simplest way, with just a couple of sprigs of fresh thyme tucked beneath the skin.

PREP: 20 minutes ★ **ROAST:** 1 hour
MAKES 4 main-dish servings

---

1 chicken (3½ pounds)

2 sprigs plus 1 tablespoon chopped fresh thyme

¾ teaspoon salt

¼ teaspoon coarsely ground black pepper

⅛ teaspoon ground allspice

1 jumbo onion (1 pound), cut into 12 wedges

¼ cup water

2 teaspoons olive oil

2 large Granny Smith apples, each cored and cut into quarters

2 tablespoons applejack brandy or Calvados

½ cup canned chicken broth or Old-Fashioned Chicken Broth (page 45)

1. Preheat oven to 450°F. Remove giblets and neck from chicken; reserve for another use. Rinse chicken inside and out with cold running water; drain. Pat chicken dry with paper towels.

2. With fingertips, gently separate skin from meat on chicken breast. Place 1 thyme sprig under skin of each breast half. In cup, combine chopped thyme, salt, pepper, and allspice.

3. With chicken breast side up, lift wings up toward neck, then fold wing tips under back of chicken so wings stay in place. Tie legs together with string.

4. In medium roasting pan (14" by 10"), toss onion, chopped thyme mixture, water, and oil. Push onion mixture to sides of pan. Place chicken, breast side up, on small rack in center of roasting pan.

5. Roast chicken and onion mixture 40 minutes. Add apples to pan; roast about 20 minutes longer. Chicken is done when temperature on meat thermometer inserted in thickest part of thigh, next to body, reaches 175° to 180°F and juices run clear when thigh is pierced with tip of knife.

6. Transfer chicken to warm platter; let stand 10 minutes to set juices for easier carving.

7. Meanwhile, remove rack from roasting pan. With slotted spoon, place onion mixture around chicken on platter. Skim and discard fat from drippings in pan. Add applejack to pan drippings; cook 1 minute over medium heat, stirring constantly. Add broth; heat to boiling. Serve pan-juice mixture with chicken. Remove skin from chicken before eating, if desired.

EACH SERVING WITH SKIN: About 589 calories, 49g protein, 22g carbohydrate, 33g total fat (9g saturated), 159mg cholesterol, 708mg sodium.

EACH SERVING WITHOUT SKIN: About 441 calories, 43g protein, 22g carbohydrate, 20g total fat (5g saturated), 132mg cholesterol, 686mg sodium.

Herb-Roasted Chicken with Moist Bread Stuffing

One of the simplest (and best) ways to stuff a chicken is to mix up a bowl of old-fashioned bread stuffing. Many of the stuffings in the earliest cookbooks were bread stuffings, including two in the 1796 cookbook, *American Cookery*. All are listed under the heading "To Stuff and Roast a Turkey, or Fowl." Our stuffing recipe is rather straightforward: simple to mix up and very delicious. If you bake the stuffing outside the bird, tightly covering the dish with foil will keep it moist. This allows the stuffing to steam, somewhat imitating the way it cooks when inside a bird.

PREP: 10 minutes ★ **ROAST:** 1 hour
MAKES 4 main-dish servings

1 chicken (3½ pounds)
3 tablespoons butter or margarine, softened
2 tablespoons chopped fresh chives
1 tablespoon chopped fresh parsley
¼ teaspoon salt
¼ teaspoon coarsely ground black pepper
Moist Bread Stuffing (opposite)

1. Preheat oven to 450°F. Remove giblets and neck from chicken; reserve for another use. Rinse chicken inside and out with cold running water; drain. Pat chicken dry with paper towels.

2. In cup, combine butter, chives, and parsley until very well blended. With fingertips, gently separate skin from meat on chicken breast and thighs. Rub herb mixture on meat under skin. Sprinkle salt and pepper on outside of chicken. With chicken breast side up, lift wings up toward neck, then fold wing tips under back of chicken so wings stay in place. Tie legs together with string.

3. Place chicken, breast side up, on rack in small roasting pan (13" by 9"). Roast chicken about 1 hour. Chicken is done when temperature on meat thermometer inserted in thickest part of chicken thigh, next to body, reaches 175° to 180°F and juices run clear when thigh is pierced with tip of knife.

4. Transfer chicken to warm platter; let stand 10 minutes to set juices for easier carving. Remove skin from chicken before eating, if desired. Serve with Moist Bread Stuffing.

EACH SERVING WITH SKIN AND WITHOUT STUFFING: About 469 calories, 48g protein, 0g carbohydrate, 30g total fat (10g saturated), 169mg cholesterol, 275mg sodium.

EACH SERVING WITHOUT SKIN OR STUFFING: About 321 calories, 41g protein, 0g carbohydrate, 16g total fat (6g saturated), 142 mg cholesterol, 254 mg sodium.

Moist Bread Stuffing

In 4-quart saucepan, melt *4 tablespoons butter or margarine* over medium heat. Add *3 stalks celery*, coarsely chopped, and *1 small onion*, finely chopped; cook, stirring occasionally, until tender, about 12 minutes.

Remove saucepan from heat. Add *1 loaf (16 ounces) sliced firm white bread*, cut into ¾-inch cubes, *1 can (14½ ounces) chicken broth or 1¾ cups Old-Fashioned Chicken Broth* (page 45), *¼ cup chopped fresh parsley*, *½ teaspoon dried thyme*, *½ teaspoon salt*, *¼ teaspoon dried sage*, and *¼ teaspoon coarsely ground black pepper*; toss to combine well.

Use to stuff chicken or serve in baking dish alongside chicken. Spoon stuffing into greased 9" by 9" baking dish; cover with foil. Bake in preheated 325°F oven until heated through, about 30 minutes. Makes about 5 cups stuffing.

EACH ½ CUP STUFFING: About 170 calories, 4g protein, 24g carbohydrate, 6g total fat (3 g saturated), 13mg cholesterol, 473 mg sodium.

Chicken, Baltimore Style

Split a young chicken down the back as for broiling; take out the breast-bone and cut off the tips of the wings. Cut into four pieces, dredge with salt and pepper, dip them in egg and crumbs and put in a pan with enough melted butter poured over each piece to moisten it. Roast in a hot oven about twenty minutes. Make a rich cream sauce or Bechamel sauce, pour on a dish and place the chicken on it. Garnish with slices of fried bacon.

—Good Housekeeping Everyday Cook Book, 1903

Barbecued Chicken, North Carolina Style

Barbecue is serious business in North Carolina. In the southern part of the state, cooks make a vinegar and mustard sauce; in the northeastern part, vinegar and pepper flakes are used. Only in the western part of the state, however, will you find a barbecue sauce made with tomatoes, such as this one.

PREP: 15 minutes ★ **GRILL:** 25 minutes
MAKES 4 main-dish servings

I can (15 ounces) tomato sauce

$\frac{1}{3}$ cup cider vinegar

3 tablespoons honey

2 tablespoons olive oil

I teaspoon dry mustard

$\frac{3}{4}$ teaspoon salt

$\frac{3}{4}$ teaspoon ground black pepper

$\frac{1}{4}$ teaspoon liquid smoke

I chicken ($3\frac{1}{2}$ pounds), cut into 8 pieces and skin removed from all but wings

I. Prepare grill. In nonreactive 2-quart saucepan, combine tomato sauce, vinegar, honey, oil, dry mustard, $\frac{1}{2}$ teaspoon salt, $\frac{1}{2}$ teaspoon pepper, and liquid smoke; heat to boiling over medium heat. Boil 2 minutes; remove from heat. (Makes about 2 cups sauce.) Reserve 1 cup sauce to serve with chicken.

2. Sprinkle chicken with remaining $\frac{1}{4}$ teaspoon each salt and pepper. Arrange chicken on grill over medium heat and grill, turning occasionally, 15 minutes. Continue to grill, turning and brushing chicken every 2 minutes with barbecue sauce, until juices run clear when thickest part of chicken is pierced with tip of knife, 10 to 15 minutes longer. Serve with reserved barbecue sauce.

EACH SERVING WITHOUT EXTRA SAUCE: About 491 calories, 49g protein, 11g carbohydrate, 27g total fat (7g saturated), 154mg cholesterol, 685mg sodium.

EACH $\frac{1}{4}$ CUP SAUCE: About 73 calories, 1g protein, 11g carbohydrate, 4g total fat (0g saturated), 0mg cholesterol, 540mg sodium.

Chicken Fricassée

Chicken Fricassée, chicken that is fried and then stewed with chopped vegetables in a creamy white sauce, is a traditional Southern dish that is served in many homes. Enjoy it over hot buttery noodles.

PREP: 20 minutes ★ **COOK:** 1 hour
MAKES 6 main-dish servings

1 chicken (3½ pounds), cut into 8 pieces and
  excess fat removed

½ teaspoon salt

2 tablespoons butter or margarine

1 medium onion, coarsely chopped

2 stalks celery, sliced

2 carrots, peeled and sliced

2 tablespoons all-purpose flour

1 can (14½ ounces) chicken broth or 1¾ cups
  Old-Fashioned Chicken Broth (page 45)

½ cup heavy cream

⅛ teaspoon ground black pepper

1 tablespoon fresh lemon juice

2 tablespoons chopped fresh parsley

4 cups wide egg noodles, cooked as label directs

1. Sprinkle chicken with salt. In 12-inch skillet, melt butter over medium-high heat. Add chicken to skillet, in batches if necessary, and cook until browned, about 4 minutes per side. With slotted spoon, transfer chicken pieces to plate as they are browned. Pour off all but 3 tablespoons drippings from skillet.

2. Reduce heat to medium; add onion, celery, and carrots to skillet. Cook, stirring, until vegetables begin to soften, about 5 minutes.

3. Add flour and cook, stirring, 1 minute. Add chicken broth and cook, stirring until browned bits are loosened from bottom of pan. Return chicken and vegetables to skillet along with any juices on plate; heat to boiling. Reduce heat; cover and simmer, turning pieces occasionally, until chicken is tender, 40 to 45 minutes.

4. Transfer chicken to large, deep platter and cover with foil to keep warm. Add cream and pepper to sauce in skillet and whisk until blended; heat to boiling. Reduce heat and simmer until sauce thickens slightly, about 5 minutes. Stir in lemon juice. Pour sauce over chicken; sprinkle with parsley. Serve over hot noodles.

EACH SERVING: About 542 calories, 37g protein, 26g carbohydrate, 31g total fat (12g saturated), 163mg cholesterol, 628mg sodium.

Chicken Cacciatore

Chicken cacciatore (hunter's style) is found on the menu of nearly every Italian-American restaurant. In Italy the dish was often prepared with freshly shot guinea fowl or pheasant, but in the States it is usually prepared with chicken. Use white mushrooms or other favorite varieties. Soft polenta or white rice makes a fine accompaniment to this dish.

PREP: 15 minutes ★ **COOK:** 45 minutes
MAKES 4 main-dish servings

2 tablespoons olive oil

1 chicken (3½ pounds), cut into 8 pieces and skin
  removed from all but wings

3 tablespoons all-purpose flour

1 medium onion, finely chopped

4 garlic cloves, crushed with garlic press

8 ounces mushrooms, trimmed and thickly sliced

1 can (14 to 16 ounces) tomatoes

½ teaspoon dried oregano, crumbled

½ teaspoon salt

¼ teaspoon dried sage

⅛ teaspoon ground red pepper (cayenne)

1. In nonstick 12-inch skillet, heat oil over medium-high heat until very hot. On waxed paper, coat chicken with flour, shaking off excess. Add chicken to skillet and cook until golden brown, about 3 minutes per side. With slotted spoon, transfer chicken pieces to bowl or plate as they are browned.

2. Add onion and garlic to skillet. Reduce heat to medium-low and cook, stirring occasionally, until onion is tender, about 5 minutes. Add mushrooms; cook, stirring frequently, until just tender, about 3 minutes.

3. Add tomatoes with their juice, breaking them up with side of spoon. Add oregano, salt, sage, ground red pepper, and chicken; heat to boiling over high heat. Reduce heat; cover skillet and simmer until juices run clear when thickest part of chicken is pierced with tip of knife, about 25 minutes.

4. Transfer chicken to warm serving bowl. Spoon sauce over chicken.

EACH SERVING: About 371 calories, 44g protein, 18g carbohydrate, 13g total fat (3g saturated), 133mg cholesterol, 608mg sodium.

Country Captain

Nineteenth-century cookbook author Eliza Leslie attributes Country Captain to a British army captain who brought the recipe back to England after his tour of duty in India. Proud Georgians, however, disagree with this story. They claim the mysterious captain sailed into the famous port city of Savannah during the lucrative spice-trading period and entrusted his recipe to friends. Whatever its true origin, curried chicken in a tomato-based sauce has a blend of spices and flavors typical of East Indian cooking.

PREP: 30 minutes ★ **BAKE:** 1 hour
MAKES 8 main-dish servings

2 tablespoons plus 1 teaspoon vegetable oil

2 chickens (3½ pounds each), each cut into 8 pieces and skin removed from all but wings

2 medium onions, chopped

1 large Granny Smith apple, peeled, cored, and chopped

1 large green pepper, chopped

3 large garlic cloves, finely chopped

1 tablespoon grated, peeled fresh ginger

3 tablespoons curry powder

½ teaspoon coarsely ground black pepper

¼ teaspoon ground cumin

1 can (28 ounces) plum tomatoes in puree

1 can (14½ ounces) chicken broth or 1¾ cups Old-Fashioned Chicken Broth (page 45)

½ cup dark seedless raisins

1 teaspoon salt

¼ cup chopped fresh parsley

1. In nonreactive 8-quart Dutch oven, heat 2 tablespoons oil over medium-high heat until very hot. Add chicken, in batches, and cook until golden brown, about 5 minutes per side. With slotted spoon, transfer chicken pieces to bowl as they are browned.

2. Preheat oven to 350°F. In same Dutch oven, heat remaining 1 teaspoon oil over medium-high heat. Add onions, apple, green pepper, garlic, and ginger; cook, stirring frequently, 2 minutes. Reduce heat to medium; cover and cook 5 minutes longer.

3. Stir in curry powder, black pepper, and cumin; cook 1 minute. Add tomatoes with their puree, broth, raisins, salt, and chicken. Heat to boiling over high heat; boil 1 minute. Cover and place in oven. Bake 1 hour. Sprinkle with parsley.

EACH SERVING: About 347 calories, 43g protein, 19g carbohydrate, 11g total fat (2g saturated), 133mg cholesterol, 825mg sodium.

Fried Chicken

Almost every Southerner has a special recipe for fried chicken. Some shake it to coat before frying, others batter it and a few crumb and bake it. Even cooks who agree that frying chicken is the best way to cook it disagree on the amount of oil that should be used. Some immerse their chicken completely in oil, while others fry it in just enough oil to reach halfway up the sides of the chicken. But all southern cooks agree on one thing: the best frying pan is a very well-seasoned cast-iron skillet, preferably one that has been handed down for generations.

PREP: 15 minutes ★ **COOK:** 20 minutes per batch plus 8 minutes
MAKES 8 main-dish servings

4 cups vegetable oil

1½ cups milk

2 cups all-purpose flour

1¾ teaspoons salt

1 teaspoon baking powder

¾ teaspoon ground black pepper

2 chickens (3 pounds each), each cut into 8 pieces

1 can (14½ ounces) chicken broth or 1¾ cups
    Old-Fashioned Chicken Broth (page 45)

1. In deep 12-inch skillet, heat oil over medium heat to 360°F on deep-fat thermometer. Meanwhile, pour ½ cup milk into pie plate. On waxed paper, combine 1¾ cups flour, 1 teaspoon salt, baking powder, and ½ teaspoon pepper. Dip chicken in milk, then coat well with flour mixture. Repeat, dipping and coating chicken twice.

2. Carefully place one-third of chicken pieces, skin side down, in hot oil. Cover and cook until underside of chicken is golden brown, about 5 minutes. Turn chicken, skin side up. Reduce heat to medium-low to maintain 300°F temperature. Cook 8 to 10 minutes longer for white meat; 13 to 15 minutes longer for dark meat, turning pieces every 4 to 5 minutes, until well browned on all sides and juices run clear when thickest part of chicken is pierced with tip of knife. With spatula or tongs, loosen chicken from skillet bottom. Transfer chicken pieces, skin side up, to paper towels to drain; keep warm. Repeat with remaining chicken.

3. Prepare gravy: Spoon 2 tablespoons oil from skillet into 2-quart saucepan. Over medium heat, with wooden spoon, stir remaining ¼ cup flour into oil until blended. Cook, stirring constantly, until flour is light brown. With wire whisk, gradually stir in remaining 1 cup milk, broth, remaining ¾ teaspoon salt, and remaining ¼ teaspoon pepper. Cook, stirring constantly, until gravy has thickened and boils. (Makes 2⅔ cups gravy). Serve gravy with chicken.

EACH SERVING: About 657calories, 46g protein, 26g carbohydrate, 40g total fat (9g saturated), 138mg cholesterol, 942mg sodium.

Fried Chicken

Our thanks go to the Spaniards for bringing the first chickens to Florida by way of the West Indies. The English colonists also brought chickens to the New World, as they were easy to bring onboard ship and could be killed for food, if necessary. The English preferred baking and boiling chickens. It was the Scottish who enjoyed frying chickens and who likely shared this custom when they settled in the South. And just as likely, the African-American plantation cooks who were allowed to raise chickens observed this efficient cooking method and tried it out for themselves with great success.

In 1872, Annabella P. Hill offered a recipe for frying chicken in batter, instructing to first half-fry the chicken in boiling oil "then dip it in a thin fritter batter and finish the frying." She then recommended a water-based pan gravy to be served alongside. The Maryland custom of serving fried chicken with a creamy white gravy was recorded by B. C. Howard in *Fifty Years in a Maryland Kitchen*. In true Maryland fashion, the sauce is served in its own gravy dish alongside the chicken—not spooned on top.

More than one hundred years later, all agree that fried chicken is one of the South's most famous and beloved dishes.

Chicken Pudding

One-half pound of flour, one quart of milk, four eggs, six ounces of butter, one large or two small chickens. Season very highly with pepper and salt. Serve immediately upon baking. Line the dish with the chicken, pour batter over it. Have the dish hot before the chicken is put in.

—**Good Housekeeping Everyday Cook Book**, 1903

Plantation Chicken 'n' Dumplings

Fricassée a chicken, add homemade dumplings, and you have many a Southerner's favorite dish. Before baking powder was invented in the 1850s, Southerners rolled out dumpling dough, cut it into strips, and cooked it up flat, slippery, and chewy. Today dumplings are usually lowered into simmering broth by the spoonful and cooked until light and puffy.

PREP: 15 minutes ★ **COOK:** 1 hour
MAKES 6 main-dish servings

2 tablespoons vegetable oil

6 large bone-in chicken breast halves (3¼ pounds), skin removed

4 large carrots, peeled and cut into 1-inch pieces

2 large stalks celery, cut into ¼-inch-thick slices

1 medium onion, finely chopped

1 cup plus 2 tablespoons all-purpose flour

2 teaspoons baking powder

1 teaspoon salt

½ teaspoon dried thyme

1 large egg

1½ cups milk

2 cups water

1 can (14½ ounces) low-sodium chicken broth or 1¾ cups **Old-Fashioned Chicken Broth** (page 45)

¼ teaspoon ground black pepper

1 package (10 ounces) frozen peas

1. In 8-quart Dutch oven, heat 1 tablespoon oil over medium-high heat. Add 3 chicken breast halves and cook until golden brown, about 5 minutes per side. With slotted spoon, transfer chicken pieces to bowl as they are browned. Repeat with remaining chicken.

2. Add remaining 1 tablespoon oil to drippings in Dutch oven. Add carrots, celery, and onion; cook, stirring frequently, until vegetables are golden brown and tender, about 10 minutes.

3. Meanwhile, prepare dumplings: In small bowl, combine 1 cup flour, baking powder, ½ teaspoon salt, and thyme. In cup, with fork, beat egg with ½ cup milk. Stir egg mixture into flour mixture until just blended.

4. Return chicken to Dutch oven; add water, broth, pepper, and remaining ½ teaspoon salt. Heat to boiling over high heat. Drop dumpling mixture by rounded tablespoons on top of chicken and vegetables to make 12 dumplings. Reduce heat; cover and simmer 15 minutes.

5. With slotted spoon, transfer dumplings, chicken, and vegetables to serving bowl; keep warm. Reserve broth in Dutch oven.

6. In cup, blend remaining 2 tablespoons flour with remaining 1 cup milk until smooth; stir into broth in Dutch oven. Heat to boiling over high heat; boil 1 minute to thicken slightly. Add peas and heat through. Pour sauce over chicken and dumplings.

EACH SERVING: About 437 calories, 46g protein, 38g carbohydrate, 10g total fat (3g saturated), 137mg cholesterol, 951mg sodium.

Creole Chicken and Sausage Gumbo

Since the first pots of gumbo in the late eighteenth century, this Cajun stew was known for being a melting pot of flavors. *Gumbo* is derived from the African word *gombo* ("okra" in Bantu), which is fitting since okra is often used to thicken the pot. The Choctaw Indians thickened it another way: with ground sassafras leaves (filé powder). The French added andouille, a highly seasoned smoked pork sausage, and the Spanish contributed their special blend of spices. An authentic gumbo gets its rich flavor from a roux that is made in a skillet—usually black iron—by slowly browning flour in fat until it's deep brown. From there on, it's up to the individual cook. Most toss in chicken pieces, spicy sausages, and often shrimp and ham. Our recipe is unique, as the flour is browned (without any fat) in the oven instead of in a roux.

PREP: 1 hour 10 minutes plus cooling
COOK: 1 hour 30 minutes
MAKES 18 cups or 12 main-dish servings

²⁄₃ cup all-purpose flour

1 chicken (3¹⁄₂ pounds), cut into 8 pieces

12 ounces fully cooked andouille or kielbasa sausage, cut into ¹⁄₂-inch-thick slices

6 cups canned chicken broth or Old-Fashioned Chicken Broth (page 45)

1 can (6 ounces) tomato paste

2 cups water

2 medium onions, thinly sliced

12 ounces okra, sliced, or 1 package (10 ounces) frozen cut okra, thawed

1 large yellow pepper, chopped

4 stalks celery with leaves, cut into ¹⁄₄-inch-thick slices

³⁄₄ cup chopped fresh parsley

4 garlic cloves, thinly sliced

2 bay leaves

1¹⁄₂ teaspoons salt

1 teaspoon dried thyme

1 teaspoon ground red pepper (cayenne)

1 teaspoon ground black pepper

¹⁄₂ teaspoon ground allspice

1 can (14 to 16 ounces) tomatoes, drained and chopped

¹⁄₂ cup finely chopped green-onion tops

2 tablespoons distilled white vinegar

3 cups regular long-grain rice, cooked as label directs

1. Preheat oven to 375°F. Place flour in oven-safe 12-inch skillet (if skillet is not oven-safe, wrap handle with double layer of foil). Bake until flour begins to brown, about 25 minutes. Stir with wooden spoon, breaking up any lumps. Bake, stirring flour every 10 minutes, until it turns nut brown, about 35 minutes longer. Remove flour from oven and cool. Press flour through sieve to remove any lumps.

2. Heat nonreactive 8-quart Dutch oven over medium-high heat until very hot. Cook chicken, skin side down first, in batches, until golden brown, about 5 minutes per side. Transfer chicken pieces to large bowl as they are browned. Add sausage to Dutch oven and cook over medium heat, stirring constantly, until lightly browned, about 5 minutes. With slotted spoon, transfer sausage to chicken in bowl.

3. Reduce heat to medium-low. Gradually stir in browned flour, about 3 tablespoons at a time; cook, stirring constantly, 2 minutes.

4. Immediately add broth, stirring until browned bits are loosened from bottom of pan. Blend tomato paste with water; add to Dutch oven. Stir in onions, okra, yellow pepper, celery, ¹⁄₄ cup parsley, garlic, bay leaves, salt, thyme, ground red pepper, black pepper, and allspice. Add sausage, chicken, and tomatoes; heat to boiling over high heat. Reduce heat; simmer until liquid has thickened, about 1 hour.

5. Add remaining ¹⁄₂ cup parsley, green onions, and vinegar; heat through. Remove from heat; cover and let stand 10 minutes. Discard bay leaves. Serve gumbo in bowls over rice.

EACH SERVING: About 447 calories, 27g protein, 28g carbohydrate, 25g total fat (8g saturated), 107mg cholesterol, 1,357mg sodium.

◄ *Creole Chicken and Sausage Gumbo*

"All Aboard...Dinner is now being served!"

The day was November 3, 1842. The Baltimore & Ohio Railroad pulled out of Baltimore with company executives on board (at a rapid rate of 25 miles an hour) for a 178-mile ride. No stop was planned, so guests were served an elegant cold repast. It was on that day that the first meal was served on a train, as it chugged its way into the history books. From that first year, dining in dining cars rapidly caught on. By the year 1930, it hit its peak: 1,700 dining cars on 63 different railroads served over 80 million meals!

It is no wonder this new way of dining in an elegant restaurant on wheels became a memorable experience. The décor matched the best dining establishments: gilded Victorian drawing rooms with plush velvet seats in the early days and art deco at its best in the 1930s. Passengers were pampered by experienced, courteous, impeccably dressed crews, and they dined on seven-course dinners prepared with the finest fresh food, which was often loaded on the train at stops along the way.

Each line had its own signature specials: fresh crab cakes on the Baltimore & Ohio, fresh trout on the Santa Fe, prime beefsteak on the Union Pacific, and big baked, stuffed potatoes on the Northern Pacific. There was traditional chicken pie on the Great Northern, lobster Newburg on the New York Central, juicy sugar-cured ham on the Southern Pacific, and luscious fresh strawberry shortcake on the Pullman Company Line. Among the lucky travelers there was no doubt: "Nothing could be finer than dining in the diner!"

San Francisco Stir-Fry Chicken

During the Gold Rush, many Chinese immigrants cooked for the well-to-do, incorporating recipes and techniques from their homeland into the dishes they prepared. Stir-fries soon became a part of America's food melting pot.

PREP: 20 minutes ★ **COOK:** 10 minutes
MAKES 4 main-dish servings

I pound skinless, boneless chicken breast halves

2 tablespoons soy sauce

2 tablespoons dry sherry

2 teaspoons cornstarch

2 teaspoons grated, peeled fresh ginger

1/4 teaspoon sugar

1/4 teaspoon crushed red pepper

2 tablespoons vegetable oil

6 green onions, cut into 2-inch pieces

I green pepper, cut into 1/2-inch pieces

I red pepper, cut into 1/2-inch pieces

1/4 cup dry-roasted unsalted peanuts

I. With knife held in position almost parallel to work surface, cut each chicken breast half crosswise into 1/8-inch-thick slices. In medium bowl, combine soy sauce, sherry, cornstarch, ginger, sugar, and crushed red pepper; add chicken, tossing to coat.

2. In 12-inch skillet, heat 1 tablespoon oil over medium-high heat until very hot. Add green onions and red and green peppers. Cook, stirring frequently (stir-frying), until vegetables are tender-crisp, 2 to 3 minutes. With slotted spoon, transfer vegetables to bowl.

3. Increase heat to high and add remaining 1 tablespoon oil to skillet; heat until very hot. Add chicken mixture and stir-fry until chicken loses its pink color throughout, 2 to 3 minutes. Return vegetables to skillet; heat through. To serve, transfer chicken and vegetables to warm platter and sprinkle with peanuts.

EACH SERVING: About 277 calories, 30g protein, 9g carbohydrate, 13g total fat (2g saturated), 66mg cholesterol, 594mg sodium.

Arroz con Pollo

In early-twentieth-century America, the increasing influence of Spanish culture nationwide gave rise to dishes such as arroz con pollo (chicken with rice). In true Spanish tradition, our skillet dish contains chicken, rice, peas, and tomatoes, which turn the rice a pinkish red.

PREP: 15 minutes ★ COOK: 40 minutes
MAKES 4 main-dish servings

1 tablespoon vegetable oil
1 chicken (3½ pounds), cut into 8 pieces and skin removed from all but wings
1 medium onion, finely chopped
1 red pepper, chopped
1 garlic clove, finely chopped
⅛ teaspoon ground red pepper (cayenne)
1 cup regular long-grain rice
1 can (14½ ounces) chicken broth or 1¾ cups Old-Fashioned Chicken Broth (page 45)
¼ cup water
1 strip (3" by ½") lemon peel
¼ teaspoon dried oregano
¼ teaspoon salt
1 cup frozen peas
¼ cup chopped pimiento-stuffed olives (salad olives)
¼ cup chopped fresh cilantro
lemon wedges

1. In 5-quart Dutch oven, heat oil over medium-high heat until very hot. Add chicken and cook until golden brown, about 5 minutes per side. With slotted spoon, transfer chicken pieces to bowl as they are browned.

2. Reduce heat to medium. Add onion and red pepper to Dutch oven and cook until tender, about 5 minutes. Stir in garlic and ground red pepper; cook 30 seconds. Add rice; cook, stirring, 1 minute. Stir in broth, water, lemon peel, oregano, salt, and chicken; heat to boiling. Reduce heat; cover and simmer until juices run clear when thickest part of chicken is pierced with tip of knife, about 20 minutes longer.

3. Stir in peas; cover and heat through. Remove from heat and let stand 5 minutes.

4. Transfer chicken to serving bowl. Sprinkle with olives and cilantro; serve with lemon wedges.

EACH SERVING: About 387 calories, 26g protein, 48g carbohydrate, 9g total fat (2g saturated), 81mg cholesterol, 927mg sodium.

Chicken à la King

It's fitting that a dish as elegant as chicken à la king would have many wanting to claim it as their own. Some credit Foxhall Keene, son of Wall Street broker James R. Keene, for coming up with the idea, then asking Delmonico's to prepare it for him. He called it chicken à la Keene. Another tale credits Chef George Greenwald of New York's Brighton Beach Hotel with making it for the proprietors, Mr. and Mrs. E. Clark King III. And still another story suggests that Claridge's restaurant in London made the first chicken à la king for James R. Keene, when his horse won the 1881 Grand Prix. This famous dish was—and often still is—ladled from a silver chafing dish onto toast points, over rice, or into flaky patty shells.

PREP: 15 minutes ★ COOK: 20 minutes
MAKES 8 servings

6 tablespoons butter or margarine
8 ounces mushrooms, trimmed and sliced
¼ cup chopped green pepper
6 tablespoons all-purpose flour
3 cups half-and-half
4 cups cubed, cooked chicken or turkey
1 jar (4 ounces) chopped pimientos, drained
2 egg yolks
2 tablespoons medium-dry sherry
1 teaspoon salt
8 frozen patty shells, warmed as package directs

1. In 10-inch skillet, melt butter over medium heat. Add mushrooms and green pepper; cook, stirring, until tender, about 5 minutes.

2. Add flour and cook, stirring, 1 minute. Gradually stir in half-and-half. Cook, stirring constantly with wooden spoon, until sauce has thickened. Add chicken and pimientos. Heat to boiling, stirring often. Reduce heat to low; cover and simmer 5 minutes.

3. In cup, with fork, stir yolks until mixed; stir in ¼ cup sauce. Gradually pour yolk mixture into sauce, stirring vigorously until well blended and smooth. Cook, stirring, until sauce has thickened.

4. Stir in sherry and salt. Spoon chicken mixture into patty shells.

EACH SERVING: About 589 calories, 28g protein, 27g carbohydrate, 41g total fat (14g saturated), 172mg cholesterol, 662mg sodium.

Chicken Curry

In *The Virginia House-Wife*, Mary Randolph tells her readers how to make a dish of curry in the East Indian manner. In *Direction for Cookery,* Eliza Leslie includes a recipe for chicken curry that contains many of the spices used to make curry powder: "two table-spoonfuls of powdered ginger, one table-spoonful of fresh turmeric, a teaspoonful of ground black pepper; some mace, a few cloves, some cardamom seeds, and a little cayenne pepper with a small portion of salt."

PREP: 15 minutes plus cooling ★ **COOK:** 1 hour 15 minutes
MAKES 6 main-dish servings

---

1 chicken (3½ pounds), cut into 8 pieces

4 medium onions, finely chopped

2 carrots, peeled and finely chopped

2 stalks celery with leaves, finely chopped

8 parsley sprigs

1 lime

4 tablespoons butter or margarine

2 Granny Smith apples, peeled, cored, and chopped

3 garlic cloves, finely chopped

1 tablespoon curry powder

3 tablespoons all-purpose flour

½ cup half-and-half or light cream

⅓ cup golden raisins

2 tablespoons mango chutney, chopped

2 teaspoons minced, peeled fresh ginger

½ teaspoon salt

pinch ground red pepper (cayenne)

1. In 5-quart Dutch oven, combine chicken, one-fourth of onions, carrots, celery, and parsley sprigs with just enough *water* to cover. Heat to boiling over high heat. Reduce heat; partially cover and simmer, turning once, until chicken loses its pink color throughout, 25 to 30 minutes. With slotted spoon, transfer chicken to bowl. When cool enough to handle, remove and discard skin and bones; with hands, shred chicken.

2. Meanwhile, strain broth through sieve into bowl; discard vegetables. Return broth to Dutch oven. Heat to boiling; boil until reduced to 2 cups. Skim and discard fat from broth; reserve broth.

3. From lime, grate ½ teaspoon peel and squeeze 5 teaspoons juice; reserve.

4. In 12-inch skillet, melt butter over medium heat. Add remaining three-fourths of onions, apples, garlic, and curry powder; cook, stirring, until apples are tender,

about 10 minutes. Sprinkle with flour, stirring to blend. Gradually add 2 cups reserved broth, stirring constantly until broth has thickened and boils. Stir in reserved lime peel and juice, half-and-half, raisins, chutney, ginger, salt, and ground red pepper. Reduce heat; simmer, stirring occasionally, 5 minutes. Add chicken and heat through.

EACH SERVING: About 379 calories, 30g protein, 33g carbohydrate, 14g total fat (7g saturated), 117mg cholesterol, 449mg sodium.

Chicken Enchiladas

The word *enchilada,* Spanish for "filled with chile," first appeared here in print in 1885. By the mid-twentieth century, enchiladas were a popular dish in Mexican-American restaurants. And hostesses discovered that it was the perfect buffet dish for casual at-home supper parties.

PREP: 15 minutes ★ **BAKE:** 20 minutes
MAKES 4 main-dish servings

---

1 can (4 to 4½ ounces) chopped mild green chiles, undrained

¾ cup loosely packed fresh cilantro leaves and stems

3 green onions, sliced

2 tablespoons sliced pickled jalapeño chiles

2 tablespoons fresh lime juice

¼ teaspoon salt

⅓ cup water

4 (8-inch) flour tortillas

8 ounces cooked chicken or turkey, shredded (2 cups)

¼ cup heavy or whipping cream

3 ounces Monterey Jack cheese, shredded (¾ cup)

1. Preheat oven to 350°F. Grease 11" by 7" baking dish.

2. In blender, combine chiles, cilantro, green onions, pickled jalapeños, lime juice, salt, and water; puree until smooth. Transfer to 8-inch skillet and heat to boiling over medium heat; boil 2 minutes. Dip one side of each tortilla in sauce; spread 1 tablespoon sauce over other (dry) side of tortillas; top with chicken. Roll up tortillas and place, seam side down, in prepared baking dish.

3. Stir cream into remaining sauce in skillet; spoon over filled tortillas. Cover with foil and bake 15 minutes. Remove foil; sprinkle with cheese and bake until cheese melts, about 5 minutes longer.

EACH SERVING: About 402 calories, 30g protein, 23g carbohydrate, 21g total fat (9g saturated), 106mg cholesterol, 713mg sodium.

Brunswick Stew

Brunswick Counties in both North Carolina and Virginia lay claim to creating this famous southern stew. Most historians document 1828 as the year when Dr. Creed Haskins of the Virginia State Legislature asked Jimmy Matthews to stir up a batch of squirrel stew for a political rally. Over time, the squirrel has disappeared from the pot and been replaced by chicken or rabbit.

PREP: 30 minutes ★ **COOK:** 40 minutes
MAKES 6 servings

3 slices bacon

I chicken (3½ pounds), cut into 8 pieces

½ teaspoon dried thyme

½ teaspoon salt

I medium onion, chopped

½ cup chopped carrot

½ cup chopped celery

I tablespoon minced garlic

2 cans (14½ ounces each) stewed tomatoes

I cup canned chicken broth or **Old-Fashioned Chicken Broth** (page 45)

I cup frozen baby lima beans

I cup frozen cut okra

I cup fresh or frozen corn kernels

dash Worcestershire sauce

dash hot pepper sauce

I. In nonreactive 6-quart Dutch oven, cook bacon over medium-high heat until crisp. With slotted spoon, transfer bacon to paper towels to drain. Crumble and set aside.

2. Sprinkle chicken with thyme and salt. Add chicken to drippings in Dutch oven, in batches if necessary; cook over medium-high heat until golden brown, about 3 minutes per side. With slotted spoon, transfer chicken pieces to bowl as they are browned.

3. Discard all but 1 tablespoon drippings from pan; reduce heat to medium. Add onion, carrot, and celery to Dutch oven; cook, stirring, 3 minutes. Stir in garlic; cook 30 seconds. Return chicken to pan. Stir in tomatoes and broth; heat to boiling. Reduce heat; cover and simmer until juices run clear when thickest part of chicken is pierced with tip of knife, about 30 minutes. Stir in lima beans, okra, and corn; cover and simmer 10 minutes. Stir in bacon, Worcestershire, and hot pepper sauce.

EACH SERVING: About 447calories, 38g protein, 28g carbohydrate, 21g total fat (6g saturated), 107mg cholesterol, 843mg sodium.

Turkey Tetrazzini

In the early 1900s, chicken Tetrazzini was created and named after the Italian opera singer Luisa Tetrazzini, who was extremely popular at that time. By 1923 (and perhaps in an even earlier edition), *The Original Boston Cooking-School Cook Book* contained a recipe for a turkey, mushroom, and spaghetti dish baked in a rich cream sauce. With the rising popularity of ethnic food during the twentieth century, this dish became a frequent offering on Italian-American restaurant menus.

PREP: 30 minutes ★ **BAKE:** 30 minutes
MAKES 6 main-dish servings

4 tablespoons butter or margarine

¼ cup all-purpose flour

2¾ cups canned chicken broth or **Old-Fashioned Chicken Broth** (page 45)

¼ cup dry white wine

¼ teaspoon dried thyme

pinch ground nutmeg

½ cup heavy or whipping cream

I small onion, chopped

10 ounces mushrooms, trimmed and cut into quarters

8 ounces linguine, cooked as label directs

12 ounces cooked turkey, coarsely chopped (3 cups)

3 tablespoons freshly grated Parmesan cheese

I. Preheat oven to 400°F. In 2-quart saucepan, melt 3 tablespoons butter over medium heat. Stir in flour and cook, stirring occasionally, 3 minutes. With wire whisk, whisk in broth, wine, thyme, and nutmeg until smooth. Heat to boiling, whisking constantly. Reduce heat and simmer, whisking frequently, 5 minutes. Stir in cream; set sauce aside.

2. In 10-inch skillet, melt remaining 1 tablespoon butter over medium heat. Add onion and cook until tender, about 5 minutes. Add mushrooms and cook, stirring occasionally, 10 minutes longer.

3. In 2- to 2½-quart baking dish, combine linguine, mushroom mixture, and turkey. Stir in sauce; sprinkle with Parmesan. Bake until bubbly, about 30 minutes.

EACH SERVING: About 458 calories, 30g protein, 37g carbohydrate, 21g total fat (11g saturated), 104mg cholesterol, 648mg sodium.

Giving Thanks since 1621

The year was 1621 and the place was Plymouth, Massachusetts. The colonists had survived their first year in the New World, so Governor William Bradford decided it was "time to feast." He invited Chief Massasoit and ninety-two braves of the Wampanoag tribe to join them "to give thanks to God." Some say the celebration lasted as long as three days. They feasted on roast duck and goose, venison (supplied by their guests), clams, oysters, eel, leeks, watercress, corn bread, popcorn, wild plums, and homemade sweet wine. Historians believe that wild turkey may have been served at this first Thanksgiving, as "the governor sent four men on fowling" to bring back food for the feast. On the next recorded Day of Thanks at the Plymouth Colony on July 30, 1623, turkey was definitely served, along with cranberries and pumpkin pie.

On November 26, 1789, George Washington proclaimed the first national Thanksgiving observance. And Sarah Josepha Hale, who was the forty-year editor of Godey's Lady's Book in the nineteenth century, lobbied president Lincoln to make Thanksgiving a national holiday. Centuries later, the tradition continues.

Old-Time Turkey with Giblet Gravy

(pictured on page 110)

Colonial America had an affinity for turkey. Some Native Americans caught wild turkey; others domesticated it. The name appears to be a corruption of the word *furkee*, which is Native American for "turkey." For a moist bird, we prefer to bake the stuffing separately.

PREP: I hour ★ **ROAST:** 3 hours 45 minutes
MAKES I4 main-dish servings

Country Sausage and Corn Bread Stuffing (page 109)
I turkey (14 pounds)
I¹/₂ teaspoons salt
¹/₂ teaspoon coarsely ground black pepper
Giblet Gravy (page 109)

I. Prepare Country Sausage and Corn Bread Stuffing and set aside.

2. Preheat oven to 325°F. Remove giblets and neck from turkey; reserve for making Giblet Gravy. Rinse turkey inside and out with cold running water and drain well; pat dry with paper towels.

3. Loosely spoon some stuffing into neck cavity. Fold neck skin over stuffing; fasten neck skin to turkey back with one or two skewers.

4. Loosely spoon remaining corn bread stuffing into body cavity (bake any leftover stuffing in small covered casserole during last 30 minutes of roasting time). Fold skin over cavity opening; skewer closed, if necessary. Tie legs and tail together with string; push drumsticks under band of skin, or use stuffing clamp. Secure wings to body with string, if desired.

5. Place turkey, breast side up, on rack in large roasting pan (17" by 11½"). Sprinkle salt and pepper on outside of turkey. Cover with loose tent of foil.

6. Roast about 3 hours 45 minutes. Start checking for doneness during last hour of roasting. Place stuffing (in casserole) in oven after turkey has roasted 3 hours. Bake until heated through, about 30 minutes.

7. To brown turkey, remove foil during last hour of roasting; baste occasionally with pan drippings. Turkey is done when temperature on meat thermometer inserted in thickest part of thigh, next to body, reaches 180°F and juices run clear when thickest part of thigh is pierced with tip of knife. (Breast temperature should be 170°F; stuffing temperature 160° to 165°F.)

8. While turkey is roasting, prepare giblets and neck for Giblet Gravy.

9. Transfer turkey to large platter; keep warm. Let stand at least 15 minutes to set juices for easier carving. Prepare Giblet Gravy.

I0. Serve turkey with stuffing and gravy.

EACH SERVING WITHOUT SKIN, STUFFING, OR GRAVY: About I43 calories, 25g protein, 0g carbohydrate, 4g total fat (Ig saturated), 65mg cholesterol, 145mg sodium.

Country Sausage and Corn Bread Stuffing

Heat 12-inch skillet over medium-high heat until very hot. Add *1 pound pork sausage meat* and cook, breaking up sausage with side of spoon, until browned, about 10 minutes. With slotted spoon, transfer sausage to large bowl. Discard all but 2 tablespoons sausage drippings.

Add *4 tablespoons butter or margarine, 3 stalks celery,* coarsely chopped, *1 large onion (12 ounces),* coarsely chopped, and *1 red pepper,* coarsely chopped, to skillet. Cook, stirring occasionally, until vegetables are golden brown and tender, about 10 minutes. Stir in *1 can (14½ ounces) chicken broth* or *1¾ cups Old-Fashioned Chicken Broth* (page 45), *½ teaspoon coarsely ground black pepper,* and *¾ cup water.* Heat to boiling, stirring until browned bits are loosened from bottom of skillet.

Add vegetable mixture, *1 package (14 to 16 ounces) corn bread stuffing mix,* and *¼ cup chopped fresh parsley* to sausage in bowl; stir to combine well. Use to stuff turkey or serve in baking dish. Spoon stuffing into greased 13" by 9" baking dish. Cover with foil. Makes about 12 cups stuffing.

EACH ½ CUP STUFFING: About 137 calories, 4g protein, 15g carbohydrate, 7g total fat (2g saturated), 13mg cholesterol, 414mg sodium.

Giblet Gravy

In 3-quart saucepan, combine *gizzard, heart, neck,* and *4 cups water;* heat to boiling over high heat. Reduce heat; cover and simmer 45 minutes. Add *liver* and cook 15 minutes longer. Strain giblet broth through sieve into large bowl. Pull meat from neck; discard bones. Cover and refrigerate meat and broth separately.

To make gravy, remove rack from roasting pan. Strain *pan drippings* through sieve into 4-cup glass measuring cup or medium bowl. Add *1 cup giblet broth* to hot roasting pan and heat to boiling, stirring until browned bits are loosened from bottom of pan; add to drippings in measuring cup. Let stand until fat separates from meat juice, about 1 minute. Spoon *2 tablespoons fat* from drippings into 2-quart saucepan; skim and discard any remaining fat. Add *remaining giblet broth* and enough *water* to drippings in cup to equal 3 cups.

Heat fat in saucepan over medium heat; stir in *2 tablespoons all-purpose flour* and *½ teaspoon salt.* Cook, stirring, until flour turns golden brown. With wire whisk, gradually whisk in *meat-juice mixture* and cook, whisking, until gravy has thickened slightly and boils; boil 1 minute. Stir in reserved giblets and neck meat; heat through. Pour gravy into gravy boat. Makes about 3½ cups gravy.

EACH ¼ CUP GRAVY: About 70 calories, 7g protein, 2g carbohydrate, 3g total fat (1g saturated), 0g fiber, 63mg cholesterol, 140mg sodium.

Rock Cornish Hens with Wild Rice Stuffing

By the mid-nineteenth century, poultry was so readily available that the "only on Sundays" chicken became plentiful enough to eat every day. In 1965, Donald John Tyson crossed the White Rock with a Cornish game cock, creating a juicy, tasty little bird that weighed between one and two pounds. His specialty item commanded a higher price than regular chickens and was ready for market in thirty days instead of the forty-two days chicken took.

PREP: I hour ★ **ROAST:** 50 minutes
MAKES 8 main-dish servings

Wild Rice and Mushroom Stuffing (opposite)

4 Cornish hens (1½ pounds each)

¼ cup honey

2 tablespoons fresh lemon juice

2 tablespoons dry vermouth

½ teaspoon salt

¼ teaspoon dried thyme

1. Prepare Wild Rice and Mushroom Stuffing; set aside.

2. Preheat oven to 400°F. Remove giblets and necks from hens; reserve for another use. With poultry shears, cut each hen lengthwise in half. Rinse hen halves with cold running water; pat dry with paper towels.

3. With fingertips, carefully separate skin from meat on each hen half to form pocket; spoon some stuffing into each pocket. Place hens, skin side up, in two large roasting pans (17" by 11½").

4. In small bowl, combine honey, lemon juice, vermouth, salt, and thyme. Brush hens with some honey mixture. Roast hens, basting occasionally with remaining honey mixture and drippings in pan, until juices run clear when thickest part of thigh is pierced with tip of knife, about 50 minutes, rotating pans between upper and lower oven racks halfway through roasting.

EACH SERVING: About 521 calories, 37g protein, 30g carbohydrate, 28g total fat (8g saturated), 191mg cholesterol, 554mg sodium.

Wild Rice and Mushroom Stuffing

In 3-quart saucepan, melt *1 tablespoon butter or margarine* over medium heat. Add *1 small onion*, finely chopped, and cook until tender, about 5 minutes. Add *1 pound mushrooms*, trimmed and chopped, and cook, stirring occasionally, until tender, about 10 minutes.

Meanwhile, rinse *1 cup (6 ounces) wild rice*; drain. To mixture in saucepan, add wild rice, *1 can (14½ ounces) chicken broth* or *1¾ cups Old-Fashioned Chicken Broth* (page 45), and *¼ teaspoon salt*; heat to boiling over high heat. Reduce heat; cover and simmer until rice is tender and all liquid has been absorbed, 45 to 50 minutes. Stir in *¼ cup chopped fresh parsley*. Makes 4 cups stuffing.

◄ *Old-Time Turkey with Giblet Gravy (page 108)*

Turkey Potpie with Cornmeal Crust

A chicken pie recipe appears in the 1796 book *American Cookery* by Amelia Simmons, the first cookbook written by an American and printed here. Her recipe begins with: "Roll one inch thick pastry No. 8 and cover a deep dish." The chicken pieces and butter are layered and covered with another layer of thick pastry. It is then baked for one and a half hours. Our recipe uses turkey instead of chicken because we love the richer taste of turkey. You could substitute an equal amount of chicken, if you prefer.

PREP: 30 minutes ★ **BAKE:** 35 minutes
MAKES 10 main-dish servings

1 tablespoon vegetable oil

1 medium rutabaga (1 pound), peeled and cut into ½-inch pieces

3 carrots, peeled and cut into ½-inch pieces

1 large onion (12 ounces), chopped

1 pound all-purpose potatoes (3 medium), peeled and cut into ½-inch pieces

2 large stalks celery, chopped

¾ teaspoon salt

1 pound cooked turkey or chicken, cut into ½-inch pieces (4 cups)

1 package (10 ounces) frozen peas

1 can (14½ ounces) chicken broth or 1¾ cups Old-Fashioned Chicken Broth (page 45)

1 cup milk

¼ cup all-purpose flour

¼ teaspoon ground black pepper

⅛ teaspoon dried thyme

Cornmeal Crust (opposite)

1 large egg, beaten

1. Prepare potpie filling: In nonstick 12-inch skillet, heat oil over medium-high heat. Add rutabaga, carrots, and onion; cook, stirring, 10 minutes. Stir in potatoes, celery, and ½ teaspoon salt; cook, stirring frequently, until rutabaga is tender-crisp, about 10 minutes longer. Spoon into 13" by 9" baking dish; add turkey and peas.

2. In 2-quart saucepan, heat broth to boiling. In small bowl, blend milk and flour until smooth. Stir milk-flour mixture into broth; add pepper, thyme, and remaining ¼ teaspoon salt. Heat to boiling over high heat, stirring. Stir sauce into chicken-vegetable mixture in baking dish.

3. Prepare Cornmeal Crust. Preheat oven to 425°F.

4. On lightly floured surface, with floured rolling pin, roll dough into rectangle about 4 inches larger than top of baking dish. Place dough rectangle over filling. Trim edge, leaving 1-inch overhang. Fold overhang under and flute edge. Brush crust with some beaten egg. If desired, reroll trimmings; cut into decorative shapes to garnish top of pie. Brush dough cutouts with egg. Cut several slits in crust to allow steam to escape during baking.

5. Place potpie on foil-lined cookie sheet to catch any overflow during baking. Bake potpie until crust is golden brown and filling is hot and bubbling, 35 to 40 minutes. During last 10 minutes of baking, cover edges of crust with foil to prevent overbrowning.

EACH SERVING: About 416 calories, 21g protein, 42g carbohydrate, 18g total fat (5g saturated), 60mg cholesterol, 644mg sodium.

Cornmeal Crust

In large bowl, combine *1½ cups all purpose-flour, ¼ cup cornmeal,* and *¾ teaspoon salt.* With pastry blender or two knives used scissor-fashion, cut in *⅔ cup vegetable shortening* until flour mixture resembles coarse crumbs. Sprinkle *6 to 7 tablespoons cold water,* 1 tablespoon at a time, over flour mixture, mixing with fork after each addition until dough is just moist enough to hold together.

Roast Duck with Cherry-Port Sauce

When the colonists arrived in America, they were surprised to see so many ducks in the skies. No wonder early cookbooks such as *The Good Housekeeper, or, the Way to Live Well, and to be Well While We Live* included two recipes: Duck to Roast and Duck to Stew.

PREP: 10 minutes ★ **COOK:** 2 hours 30 minutes
MAKES 4 main-dish servings

1 fresh or frozen (thawed) duck, (about 4½ pounds)

½ teaspoon dried thyme

¼ teaspoon salt

¼ teaspoon ground black pepper

Giblet Broth (opposite)

2 Bosc pears, each cut into quarters and cored

2 teaspoons sugar

¼ cup finely chopped shallots

⅓ cup port wine

¼ cup dried tart cherries

1. Preheat oven to 350°F. Remove giblets and neck from duck; reserve for making Giblet Broth. Discard fat from body cavity. Rinse duck inside and out with cold running water and drain well; pat dry with paper towels. With duck, breast side up, lift wings up toward neck, then fold wing tips under back of duck so they stay in place. With two-tine fork, prick skin in several places to drain fat during roasting. Sprinkle ¼ teaspoon dried thyme inside body cavity.

2. With string, tie legs and tail together. Place duck, breast side up, on rack in medium roasting pan (14" by 10"). Sprinkle with salt, pepper, and remaining ¼ teaspoon thyme.

3. Roast 2½ hours, occasionally spooning off fat from pan. Duck is done when temperature on meat thermometer inserted in thickest part of thigh, next to body, reaches 180° to 185°F.

4. Meanwhile, prepare Giblet Broth. After duck has roasted 2 hours, place pears in small baking dish and sprinkle with sugar. Bake until tender, about 30 minutes. Transfer duck and pears to platter. Let stand 15 minutes to set juices for easier carving.

5. Prepare cherry-port sauce: Discard fat from roasting pan. Add shallots; cook over medium-high heat, stirring, 2 minutes. Stir in port, dried cherries, and Giblet Broth. Heat to boiling, stirring until browned bits are loosened from bottom of pan; simmer 5 minutes. Pour into sauce boat.

6. Serve duck and pears with sauce.

Giblet Broth

In 2-quart saucepan, combine *duck giblets* (except liver) and *neck, 1 can (14½ ounces) chicken broth or 1¾ cups Old-Fashioned Chicken Broth* (page 45) and *2 cups water;* heat to boiling over high heat. Reduce heat to low; simmer, uncovered, 1½ hours (if liquid evaporates too quickly, add *½ cup water*). Strain broth through sieve into small bowl. Discard giblets. Makes ½ to ¾ cup broth.

EACH SERVING: About 790 calories, 39g protein, 25g carbohydrate, 57g total fat (19g saturated), 171mg cholesterol, 685mg sodium.

Holiday Goose
à l'Orange

In the early days in the South, many a bride received a pair of down geese as a special gift. They provided stuffing for heirloom feather beds and pillows and quills for writing. Popular, too, were recipes for roasted goose for special occasions, such as one from the 1870s that begins: "On the day before Christmas, kill a fat goose and dress it."

PREP: 30 minutes ★ ROAST: 4 hours 30 minutes
MAKES 10 main-dish servings

1 fresh or frozen (thawed) goose (about 12 pounds)

5 medium oranges, each cut in half

1 bunch fresh thyme

4 bay leaves

1/2 teaspoon dried thyme

1 1/4 teaspoons salt

1/2 teaspoon coarsely ground black pepper

3 tablespoons orange-flavored liqueur

2 tablespoons cornstarch

1/2 cup orange marmalade

1. Preheat oven to 400°F. Remove giblets and neck from goose; reserve for another use. Trim and discard fat from body cavity and any excess skin. Rinse goose inside and out with cold running water and drain well; pat dry with paper towels. With goose, breast side up, lift wings up toward neck, then fold wing tips under back of goose so wings stay in place. Place 6 orange halves, thyme sprigs, and bay leaves in body cavity. Tie legs and tail together with kitchen string. Fold neck skin over back. With two-tine fork, prick goose skin in several places to drain fat during roasting.

2. Place goose, breast side up, on rack in large roasting pan (17" by 11½"). In cup, combine dried thyme, 1 teaspoon salt, and pepper; rub mixture over goose. Cover goose and roasting pan with foil. Roast 1 hour 30 minutes. Turn oven control to 325°F; roast 2 hours longer.

3. Meanwhile, in small bowl, from remaining 4 orange halves, squeeze ¾ cup juice. Stir in 1 tablespoon liqueur, cornstarch, and remaining ¼ teaspoon salt; set aside. In cup, mix orange marmalade with remaining 2 tablespoons liqueur. Remove foil and roast goose 45 minutes. Remove goose from oven and turn oven control to 450°F. Brush marmalade mixture over goose. Roast goose until skin is golden brown and crisp, about 10 minutes longer. Transfer goose to warm platter; let stand 15 minutes to set juices for easier carving.

4. Prepare sauce: Remove rack from roasting pan. Strain pan drippings through sieve into 8-cup measuring cup or large bowl. Let stand until fat separates from meat juice; skim and reserve fat for another use (there should be about 5 cups fat). Measure meat juice; if necessary, add enough *water* to meat juice to equal 1 cup. Return meat juice to pan and add reserved orange-juice mixture. Heat sauce to boiling over medium heat, stirring; boil 1 minute. Serve sauce with goose. Remove skin before eating, if desired.

EACH SERVING OF GOOSE WITHOUT SKIN OR SAUCE: About 460 calories, 50g protein, 12g carbohydrate, 25g total fat (8g saturated), 170mg cholesterol, 345mg sodium

EACH TABLESPOON ORANGE SAUCE: About 5 calories, 0g protein, 1g carbohydrate, 0g total fat, 0mg cholesterol, 20mg sodiumm.

Chapter 6

From the Butcher's Block

Meat has always been a major part of the American diet. Early on, wild game was plentiful, and the settlers, who brought their love of meat with them to the New World, took full advantage. When supplies began to dwindle, the colonists began raising pork, mutton, and beef, with pork the most plentiful and popular of the three. The smokehouse, built away from the main house, supplied succulent smoked hams and slabs of bacon that were enjoyed during the long, cold winters. Meat was served at least once a day: rib-sticking stews, New England boiled-beef-and-vegetables, wursts and sauerkraut in German settlements in New York and Pennsylvania, and hog and hominy suppers in the South.

During the nineteenth century, known as the "bountiful harvest" century, Americans moved West, built ranches, and raised cattle on the open range. Beef and other meats were packed into railroad cars and transported to cities and towns nationwide, making it possible for almost everyone to have fresh meat.

Simple, straightforward preparations, such as frying, braising, stewing, and roasting, remained popular. But with the greater availability of meat in the early twentieth century, homemakers became more creative, inspired by women's magazines and food manufacturers who provided hostesses with never-fail and elegant ways to prepare and present dishes, such as crown roast of pork stuffed with a savory sausage dressing.

During the depression, meat was often stretched into meat-and-potato pies, ground-meat casseroles, and vegetable-meat stews. After World War II, however, meat dishes with European, Middle Eastern, and Southeast Asian influences were enjoyed.

In the 1960s, meats went gourmet. This was due in large part to Julia Child and her entertaining, instructive television series *The French Chef*. With her help, housewives across America wowed guests with specialties such as Beef Wellington and Beef Bourguignon. But by the end of the century, health concerns brought leaner beef and pork, with hardly a trace of visible fat, to the market. As the century came to a close, celebrity chefs taught us how to bring back the flavor by blackening, marinating, brining, and dry rubbing almost every type of meat, thereby continuing America's love of meat.

◄ *Roasted Prime Ribs of Beef*

Roasted Prime Ribs of Beef

(pictured on page 116)

In the late nineteenth century, beef was often on the menu—and it still is. In our recipe, roast beef is served the most impressive way, as roasted prime ribs of beef with Yorkshire Pudding. The English colonists loved pudding and often served Yorkshire Pudding with their beef roast. The recipe for this savory pan pudding hasn't changed much. The key is the delectable pan drippings that are stirred into the custard mixture. James Beard advises in *American Cookery:* "The first three ribs are considered the best, although in my opinion, a larger roast is preferable—the first five ribs, well trimmed, so that carving will be easy."

PREP: 15 minutes ★ **ROAST:** 2 hours 30 minutes
MAKES 8 main-dish servings

---

1 (3-rib) beef rib roast from small end (5½ pounds), trimmed and chine bone removed

1 teaspoon salt

½ teaspoon dried rosemary, crumbled

¼ teaspoon ground black pepper

1 lemon

1½ cups fresh bread crumbs (about 3 slices bread)

½ cup chopped fresh parsley

2 garlic cloves, finely chopped

1 tablespoon olive oil

2 tablespoons Dijon mustard

Creamy Horseradish Sauce (opposite)

Yorkshire Pudding (opposite)

1. Preheat oven to 325°F. In medium roasting pan (14" by 10"), place rib roast, fat side up. In small bowl, combine salt, rosemary, and pepper. Use to rub on roast.

2. Roast until meat thermometer inserted in thickest part of meat (not touching bone) reaches 140°F, about 2 hours 30 minutes. Internal temperature of meat will rise to 145°F (medium) upon standing. Or roast until desired degree of doneness.

3. About 1 hour before roast is done, prepare bread coating: From lemon, grate ½ teaspoon peel and squeeze 1 tablespoon juice. In small bowl, combine lemon peel and juice, bread crumbs, parsley, garlic, and oil. Remove roast from oven; evenly spread mustard on top of roast. Press bread-crumb mixture onto mustard-coated roast. Roast 1 hour longer or until desired doneness.

4. Meanwhile, prepare Creamy Horseradish Sauce.

5. When roast is done, transfer to warm large platter and let stand 15 minutes to set juices for easier carving.

6. Meanwhile, prepare Yorkshire Pudding. Serve alongside roast and Creamy Horseradish Sauce.

EACH SERVING: About 352 calories, 39g protein, 5g carbohydrate, 18g total fat (7g saturated), 112mg cholesterol, 508mg sodium.

Creamy Horseradish Sauce

In small bowl, combine *1 bottle (6 ounces) white horseradish*, drained, *½ cup mayonnaise, 1 teaspoon sugar,* and *½ teaspoon salt*. Whip *½ cup heavy or whipping cream*; fold into horseradish mixture. Makes about 1⅔ cups.

EACH TABLESPOON: About 49 calories, 0g protein, 1g carbohydrate, 5g total fat (2g saturated), 9mg cholesterol, 74mg sodium.

Yorkshire Pudding

Turn oven control to 450°F. In medium bowl, with wire whisk, combine *1½ cups all-purpose flour* and *¾ teaspoon salt*. Add *1½ cups milk* and *3 large eggs*, beaten. Beat until smooth. Pour *3 tablespoons drippings* from roast beef pan into 13" by 9" baking pan; bake 2 minutes. Remove pan from oven; pour batter over drippings. Bake until puffed and lightly browned, about 25 minutes. Cut into squares. Makes 8 accompaniment servings.

EACH SERVING: About 183 calories, 6g protein, 20g carbohydrate, 8g total fat (4g saturated), 90mg cholesterol, 246mg sodium.

Roasted Beef Tenderloin

The most tender of all cuts of beef—the tenderloin—has very little fat. Until the 1900s, the traditional way to prepare beef tenderloin was to marinate and then roast it. It was often larded (filled with strips of pork fat) to keep it moist.

PREP: 20 minutes plus marinating ★ **ROAST:** 40 minutes
MAKES 10 main-dish servings

MARINADE & BEEF

2 cups dry red wine

2 tablespoons olive oil

I medium onion, sliced

I tablespoon chopped fresh rosemary leaves

2 garlic cloves, crushed with garlic press

2 bay leaves

I whole beef tenderloin (about 4 pounds),* trimmed

¼ cup cracked black peppercorns

HORSERADISH-TARRAGON SAUCE

⅔ cup mayonnaise

½ cup sour cream

2 to 3 tablespoons chopped fresh tarragon leaves

2 tablespoons bottled white horseradish, drained

I tablespoon Dijon mustard

1. Prepare marinade: In jumbo (2-gallon) ziptight plastic bag, combine red wine, oil, onion, rosemary, garlic, and bay leaves. Add tenderloin, turning to coat. Seal bag, pressing out as much air as possible. Place bag in shallow baking dish; refrigerate at least 4 hours or overnight, turning bag occasionally.

2. Preheat oven to 425°F. Remove meat from marinade; turn thinner end of meat under to make meat an even thickness. With string, tie tenderloin at 2-inch intervals to help hold its shape. Place peppercorns on waxed paper. Press tenderloin into peppercorns, turning to coat.

3. Place tenderloin on rack in large roasting pan (17" by 11½"); roast until meat thermometer inserted in center of meat reaches 140°F, 40 to 45 minutes. Internal temperature of meat will rise to 145°F (medium) upon standing. Or roast until desired doneness. Transfer tenderloin to warm large platter; let stand 10 minutes to set juices for easier slicing.

4. Meanwhile, prepare horseradish-tarragon sauce: In small bowl, combine mayonnaise, sour cream, tarragon, horseradish, and mustard; stir until well blended. Cover and refrigerate if not serving right away.

5. To serve, remove string and cut tenderloin into slices. Serve with horseradish-tarragon sauce.

*If you buy an untrimmed tenderloin, it should weigh 6 to 6½ pounds to yield about 4 pounds trimmed.

EACH SERVING WITH SAUCE: About 495 calories, 44g protein, 3g carbohydrate, 34g total fat (10g saturated), 137mg cholesterol, 250mg sodium.

Filet Mignon with Béarnaise Sauce

An exemplar of haute cuisine, filet (thick slice) mignon (dainty) was frequently on the menus in the premiere dining spots in twentieth-century America. It made its debut at New York's Architectural League on February 9, 1899, as *Filet Mignon Sauté à la Périgueux*. It remains to this day an elegant presentation. Filet mignon is from the narrow, small end of the beef fillet. In this recipe, the filet is accompanied by a traditional béarnaise sauce, which resembles a thick hollandaise that is made with tarragon vinegar and white wine instead of lemon juice.

PREP: 5 minutes ★ **COOK:** 25 minutes
MAKES 4 main-dish servings

Béarnaise Sauce (below)

4 beef tenderloin steaks (filet mignon), 1½ inches thick (6 ounces each), trimmed

½ teaspoon salt

¼ teaspoon coarsely ground black pepper

1 tablespoon olive oil

1. Prepare Béarnaise Sauce; keep warm.

2. Sprinkle steaks with salt and pepper. In nonstick 12-inch skillet, heat oil over high heat until very hot. Add steaks and cook, without turning, until browned, about 7 minutes. Turn steaks and cook 7 minutes longer for medium-rare or until desired doneness. Transfer to plates; keep warm.

3. To serve, spoon Béarnaise Sauce over meat.

EACH SERVING: About 302 calories, 35g protein, 0g carbohydrate, 17g total fat (5g saturated), 105mg cholesterol, 381mg sodium.

Béarnaise Sauce

In nonreactive 1-quart saucepan, combine *½ cup tarragon vinegar*, *⅓ cup dry white wine*, and *2 finely chopped shallots*; heat to boiling over high heat. Boil until liquid has reduced to ¼ cup, about 7 minutes. With back of spoon, press mixture through fine sieve into medium bowl.

With wire whisk, beat in *3 large egg yolks*, *¼ cup water*, and *pinch of ground black pepper*. Set bowl over saucepan of simmering water. Heat, whisking constantly, until egg-yolk mixture bubbles around edge and has thickened, about 10 minutes. Reduce heat to very low. With wire whisk, whisk in *½ cup cold butter (1 stick)*, cut into 8 pieces (do not use margarine), one piece at a time, whisking to incorporate each piece of butter completely before adding more. Stir in *1 tablespoon chopped fresh tarragon*. Makes 1 cup.

EACH TABLESPOON: About 68 calories, 1g protein, 1g carbohydrate, 7g total fat (4g saturated), 55mg cholesterol, 60mg sodium.

Beef Wellington

Several countries claim Beef Wellington as their own, including England, Ireland, Australia, and New Zealand. The often-assumed English origin appears dubious. English cookbook author Jane Garmey admitted in 1981 that she had not been able to find any reference to this dish in any British cookbook. Craig Claiborne was convinced that this elegant extravaganza has authentic Irish roots, as food writer Theodora FitzGibbon presents *Steig* (Steak) Wellington in her cook book *Irish Traditional Food*. As one story goes, this dish was a favorite of the Duke of Wellington, who was born in Ireland in 1769. Just when it was first served in America is not clear, but we do know that in the 1960s, Julia Child featured it on her TV show and that President Nixon declared Beef Wellington his favorite dish. Women's magazines touted it as perfect for holidays. By the 1980s, its popularity waned, but this dish still appears in all its glory on some restaurant menus. The directions for preparing Beef Wellington have remained the same over the centuries: Take the finest filet of beef tenderloin, roast it, spread it with foie gras and a layer of duxelles (sautéed chopped mushrooms), and wrap it all up in a sheet of rich, flaky pastry. Bake until golden and serve with bordelaise sauce.

Mom's Pot Roast

Early cookbooks often featured recipes for braised beef, such as the one from Fannie Merritt Farmer's 1896 *The Boston Cooking-School Cook Book*. She advised, "[Begin] with 3 Lbs. beef from lower part of round or face of rump. Wipe meat, sprinkle with salt and pepper, dredge with flour, and brown entire surface in pork fat. When turning meat, avoid piercing with fork or skewer, which allows the inner juices to escape. Place on trivet in deep granite pan or in earthen pudding-dish, and surround with vegetables, peppercorns, and three cups boiling water; cover closely, and bake four hours in very slow oven, basting every half-hour, and turn after second hour. Throughout the cooking, the liquid should be kept below the boiling point. Serve with Horseradish Sauce or with brown sauce made from the liquor in pan." Today we still braise beef in a similar fashion, but now we call it pot roast.

PREP: 25 minutes ★ **BAKE:** 3 hours
MAKES 8 main-dish servings

I tablespoon vegetable oil

I boneless beef chuck cross-rib pot roast or boneless chuck eye roast (4 pounds), trimmed

I large onion (12 ounces), coarsely chopped

I carrot, peeled and coarsely chopped

I stalk celery, coarsely chopped

2 garlic cloves, finely chopped

I can (15 ounces) crushed tomatoes

½ cup canned chicken broth or Old-Fashioned Chicken Broth (page 45)

I teaspoon salt

½ teaspoon dried thyme, crumbled

¼ teaspoon ground black pepper

I bay leaf

1. Preheat oven to 350°F. In nonreactive 5-quart Dutch oven, heat oil over high heat until very hot. Add roast and cook until browned on all sides, about 8 minutes. Transfer roast to plate.

2. Add onion, carrot, and celery to Dutch oven; cook, stirring, over medium-high heat until lightly browned, about 3 minutes. Add garlic; cook, stirring, until fragrant, about 20 seconds. Return roast to Dutch oven; add tomatoes, broth, salt, thyme, pepper, and bay leaf; heat to boiling. Cover and place in oven. Bake, turning roast once, until roast is tender, about 3 hours.

3. When roast is done, transfer to large platter and keep warm. Discard bay leaf. Skim and discard fat from liquid in Dutch oven. Transfer half of vegetables and liquid to blender; cover, with center part of cover removed to let steam escape, and puree until smooth. Pour pureed mixture back into Dutch oven and stir until combined; heat to boiling. Cut meat into thin slices and serve with vegetables and sauce.

EACH SERVING: About 304 calories, 35g protein, 6g carbohydrate, 15g total fat (5g saturated), 114mg cholesterol, 573mg sodium.

Steak Diane

If you were lucky enough to dine at New York City's '21' Club in the late 1940s, (known as the '21' back then) you would likely have seen this steak (with its flaming brandy sauce) being served from a gleaming copper chafing dish.

PREP: 10 minutes ★ **COOK:** 20 minutes
MAKES 4 main-dish servings

2 beef rib-eye steaks, ¾ inch thick (about 12 ounces each), trimmed

salt

ground black pepper

4 tablespoons butter or margarine

¼ cup brandy

2 small shallots, minced

3 tablespoons chopped fresh chives

½ cup dry sherry

1. With meat mallet or with rolling pin, between two sheets of plastic wrap or waxed paper, pound steaks to ¼-inch thickness. Sprinkle both sides of steaks with salt and pepper.

2. In chafing dish or 12-inch skillet, melt 2 tablespoons butter over high heat. Add 1 steak; cook until browned, 3 to 4 minutes per side.

3. Pour 2 tablespoons brandy over steak and carefully ignite with match. When flaming stops, stir in half of shallots and half of chives. Cook, stirring constantly, until shallots are tender, about 1 minute. Add ¼ cup sherry; heat through.

4. Place steak on warm dinner plate and pour one-fourth of sherry mixture over. Keep warm. Repeat with remaining rib-eye steak.

EACH SERVING: About 377 calories, 27g protein, 2g carbohydrate, 23g total fat (11g saturated), 110mg cholesterol, 205mg sodium.

New York Strip with Maître d'Hôtel Butter

Whether you know this steak as Kansas City strip, New York strip, or shell steak, one thing is for sure, it's guaranteed to be flavorful. It is often served with maître d'hôtel butter: a blend of butter, lemon, parsley, and sometimes pepper and chives. In French, maître d' hôtel butter means "master of the house" (the headwaiter in a fine restaurant who runs the front of the house).

PREP: 10 minutes plus chilling ★ **COOK:** 10 minutes
MAKES 4 servings

¼ **cup butter or margarine, softened**

1 **tablespoon chopped fresh parsley**

¼ **teaspoon freshly grated lemon peel**

1½ **teaspoons fresh lemon juice**

4 **boneless beef strip (shell) steaks, 1 inch thick (about 8 ounces each), trimmed**

½ **teaspoon salt**

¼ **teaspoon ground black pepper**

1. In small bowl, beat butter, parsley, and lemon peel and juice with wooden spoon until well blended. Transfer butter mixture to waxed paper and shape into log about 3 inches long. Wrap, twisting ends of waxed paper to seal. Refrigerate until firm, about 2 hours.

2. For grilling: Prepare grill. Sprinkle steaks with salt and pepper. Place steaks on grill over medium-high heat; grill steaks 5 to 6 minutes per side for medium-rare or until desired doneness.

3. For cast-iron skillet: Heat 12-inch cast-iron skillet over medium-high heat until very hot. Sprinkle steaks with salt and pepper. Add steaks; cook 5 to 6 minutes per side for medium-rare or until desired doneness.

4. Cut chilled butter into ½-inch-thick slices. Top each steak with pat of butter and serve.

EACH SERVING: About 383 calories, 43g protein, 0g carbohydrate, 22g total fat (11g saturated), 147mg cholesterol, 523mg sodium.

Deviled Short Ribs

In eighteenth- and nineteenth-century England, Deviled Bones (as Deviled Short Ribs were known in those days) were popular dinner fare. Craig Claiborne elaborates on this preparation in *The New York Times Food Encyclopedia:* "The bones were generally those of cold poultry, game, or beef. The pieces of meat were covered with one of three kinds of devil sauces: a slightly thickened brown devil sauce made of mustard, chutney, and Worcestershire; a wet devil sauce made of cream, curry powder, and mustard; or a white devil sauce made with cream, mustard, mushroom ketchup, and Worcestershire." Our deviled ribs are marinated in a mustard-based sauce for several hours and cooked until nice and tender.

PREP: 10 minutes plus marinating ★ **ROAST:** 2 hours 45 minutes
MAKES 6 main-dish servings

6 **tablespoons spicy brown mustard**

2 **tablespoons cider vinegar**

2 **tablespoons green jalapeño chile sauce**

2 **teaspoons Worcestershire sauce**

4 **pounds beef chuck short ribs**

¾ **teaspoon ground black pepper**

1½ **cups fresh bread crumbs (about 3 slices bread)**

1. In small bowl, combine 3 tablespoons mustard, vinegar, 1 tablespoon jalapeño sauce, and Worcestershire; with wire whisk, whisk until blended. Transfer to ziptight plastic bag; add short ribs, turning to coat. Seal bag, pressing out as much air as possible. Refrigerate at least 1 hour or up to 24 hours to marinate.

2. Preheat oven to 425°F. Arrange ribs on rack in medium roasting pan (14" by 10"); brush with remaining marinade from bag. Roast 40 minutes. Turn oven control to 325°F; roast 1 hour 20 minutes longer.

3. In small bowl, combine remaining 3 tablespoons mustard, remaining 1 tablespoon jalapeño sauce, and pepper. Brush on tops of ribs. Press bread crumbs onto coated ribs; roast until crumbs are crisp and lightly browned, about 45 minutes longer.

EACH SERVING: About 762 calories, 34g protein, 6g carbohydrate, 64g total fat (27g saturated), 143mg cholesterol, 400mg sodium.

Blackened Steaks

French Canadians who were exiled from Arcadia (Nova Scotia) in the 1750s for refusing to swear allegiance to the British crown settled in the low bayou country near New Orleans. These transplanted Canadians soon became known as Cajuns and their cooking was highly spiced and distinctive.

PREP: 5 minutes ★ **COOK:** 10 minutes
MAKES 4 main-dish servings

1 teaspoon dried thyme, crumbled

1 teaspoon onion powder (not onion salt)

½ teaspoon salt

½ teaspoon ground black pepper

¼ teaspoon ground red pepper (cayenne)

¼ teaspoon sugar

4 boneless beef strip (shell) steaks, 1 inch thick
  (8 ounces each), trimmed

2 teaspoons olive oil

1. In bowl, combine thyme, onion powder, salt, black pepper, ground red pepper, and sugar. Use to rub on both sides of steaks.

2. In 12-inch cast-iron skillet, heat oil over medium-high heat until very hot. Add steaks; cook 5 to 6 minutes per side for medium-rare or until desired doneness.

EACH SERVING: About 293 calories, 37g protein, 1g carbohydrate, 14g total fat (5g saturated), 98mg cholesterol, 362mg sodium.

Shaker Flank Steak

The Shakers formed communities throughout New England in the nineteenth century. They were known for their simple approach to living, their many inventions (including the clothespin), and their strict religious beliefs. Pure, wholesome food was their daily fare. Our recipe for flank steak simmered in a fresh vegetable sauce illustrates the Shakers' love of straightforward cooking using homegrown foods.

PREP: 20 minutes ★ **COOK:** 1 hour 45 minutes
MAKES 4 servings

1 beef flank steak (1¼ pounds)

½ teaspoon salt

½ teaspoon ground black pepper

2 tablespoons all-purpose flour

2 tablespoons vegetable oil

1 medium onion, chopped

1 carrot, peeled and chopped

1 stalk celery, chopped

1 cup water

⅓ cup ketchup

1 to 2 tablespoons fresh lemon juice

1. Sprinkle flank steak with ¼ teaspoon salt and ¼ teaspoon pepper. Coat steak lightly with flour, shaking off excess flour.

2. In 12-inch skillet, heat oil over medium-high heat until very hot. Add steak and cook until browned, about 4 minutes per side. Transfer steak to plate.

3. Reduce heat to medium-low. To drippings in skillet, add onion, carrot, and celery. Cook, stirring, until vegetables have lightly browned, about 2 minutes. Stir in water and ketchup. Return steak to skillet; heat to boiling. Reduce heat; cover and simmer, turning once, until meat is tender, about 1 hour 30 minutes.

4. Transfer steak to cutting board. Turn off heat; stir lemon juice, remaining ¼ teaspoon salt, and remaining ¼ teaspoon pepper into sauce in skillet. Slice steak thinly across grain. Transfer to warm platter. Spoon some sauce over meat; serve remaining sauce alongside.

EACH SERVING: About 378 calories, 29g protein, 15g carbohydrate, 22g total fat (7g saturated), 74mg cholesterol, 642mg sodium.

Chicken-Fried Steak with Milk Gravy

Not chicken at all, but beef steak pounded thin, then battered and fried until crispy and golden, just like fried chicken. It's been a staple on menus in the Deep South for decades and is almost always served with a creamy milk pan gravy.

PREP: 10 minutes ★ **COOK:** 20 minutes
MAKES 6 main-dish servings

¾ cup all-purpose flour

1½ teaspoons salt

1 teaspoon paprika

1 teaspoon coarsely ground black pepper

⅛ teaspoon ground red pepper (cayenne)

6 beef cubed steaks (6 ounces each)

½ cup vegetable oil

½ cup beef broth

2 cups milk

1. Preheat oven to 200°F. Line jelly-roll pan with paper towels. On waxed paper, combine flour, salt, paprika, black pepper, and ground red pepper. Reserve 3 tablespoons seasoned-flour mixture. Coat cubed steaks with remaining flour mixture, shaking off excess.

2. In 12-inch skillet, heat oil to 375°F. Cook steaks, two at a time, 2 minutes; turn and cook 1 minute longer. Transfer steaks to paper towel–lined jelly-roll pan to drain; place in oven. Repeat with remaining steaks, transferring each batch to jelly-roll pan in oven when done.

3. Discard all but 2 tablespoons oil from skillet. Reduce heat to medium-high. Stir in reserved flour mixture; cook, stirring, 1 minute. With wire whisk, whisk in broth until browned bits are loosened from bottom of skillet; boil 1 minute. Whisk in milk and heat to boiling; boil 2 minutes. Makes 2 cups.

4. Place steaks on platter and serve with gravy.

EACH SERVING WITH GRAVY: About 385 calories, 38g protein, 16g carbohydrate, 18g total fat (5g saturated), 103mg cholesterol, 757mg sodium.

Swiss Steak

Contrary to its name, this dish doesn't have any Swiss roots. In England, "swissing" refers to the technique of smoothing out cloth by running it between rollers. In much the same manner, round steak is pounded before being cooked to make Swiss Steak.

PREP: 25 minutes ★ **COOK:** 1 hour 30 minutes
MAKES 6 servings

1 boneless round steak, ½ inch thick (1½ pounds), trimmed and cut into 6 pieces

¾ teaspoon salt

½ teaspoon ground black pepper

¼ cup all-purpose flour

¼ cup olive oil

1 medium onion, halved and sliced

½ pound mushrooms, trimmed and sliced

1 green pepper, sliced

2 garlic cloves, minced

½ teaspoon dried thyme

¾ cup dry red wine or beef broth

1 can (14½ ounces) stewed tomatoes

1. Sprinkle steaks with ½ teaspoon salt and pepper. Coat lightly with flour, shaking off excess.

2. In 12-inch skillet, heat oil over medium-high heat until hot. Cook steaks, in batches, until browned, about 4 minutes per batch. Transfer to plate.

3. Reduce heat to medium. Add onion, mushrooms, green pepper, garlic, thyme, and remaining ¼ teaspoon salt. Cook, stirring, until vegetables are tender, about 6 minutes. Add wine; cook, stirring until browned bits are loosened from bottom of pan, about 1 minute. Stir in stewed tomatoes.

4. Return steaks to skillet, pressing them down into the liquid and vegetables; heat to boiling. Reduce heat; cover and simmer until steaks are fork-tender, 1 hour to 1 hour 15 minutes, stirring occasionally.

EACH SERVING: About 290 calories, 26g protein, 15g carbohydrate, 14g total fat (3g saturated), 61mg cholesterol, 506mg sodium.

Beef Pizzaiolo

When servicemen and women returned home from their European tours of duty after World War II, pizzerias increased in numbers and popularity. Every city and town in America (no matter how large or small) seemed to have at least one pizzeria offering Neapolitan cuisine. Beef pizzaiolo shares its topping's main ingredients of tomatoes, peppers, and onions with that of its "cousin," pizza.

PREP: 15 minutes ★ **COOK:** 25 minutes
MAKES 4 main-dish servings

2 boneless beef top loin steaks, ¾ inch thick
    (10 ounces each), trimmed

½ teaspoon salt

¼ teaspoon coarsely ground black pepper

I tablespoon olive oil

I large onion (12 ounces), cut in half and sliced

I small red pepper, cut into I-inch pieces

I small green pepper, cut into I-inch pieces

2 garlic cloves, crushed with garlic press

½ cup canned chicken broth or Old-Fashioned Chicken
    Broth (page 45)

2 tablespoons red wine vinegar

I teaspoon sugar

8 cherry tomatoes, each cut in half

½ cup loosely packed fresh basil leaves, chopped, plus
    additional sprigs

I. Pat steaks dry with paper towels. Sprinkle steaks with ¼ teaspoon salt and black pepper.

2. Heat nonstick 12-inch skillet over medium-high heat until hot. Add steaks; cook 4 minutes. Turn steaks over; cook 4 to 5 minutes longer for medium-rare or until desired doneness. Transfer steaks to platter; cover with foil to keep warm.

3. In same skillet, heat oil over medium heat until hot. Add onion, red and green peppers, garlic, and remaining ¼ teaspoon salt; cook, stirring often, until vegetables are tender and golden, about 10 minutes.

4. Increase heat to medium-high. Stir in broth, vinegar, sugar, and cherry tomatoes; heat to boiling. Cook 1 minute. Remove skillet from heat and stir in chopped fresh basil.

5. To serve, slice steaks and arrange on 4 dinner plates; top with pepper mixture. Garnish with basil sprigs.

EACH SERVING: About 315 calories, 32g protein, 16g carbohydrate, 13g total fat (4g saturated), 88mg cholesterol, 450mg sodium.

Grillades and Grits

Welcome to Louisiana, where Sunday brunch is a weekly ritual and grillades and grits is almost always on the menu. The only variable is the meat: the Cajuns often use pork, the Creole restaurants in New Orleans serve white veal, and the Afro-Americans use baby beef. All, however, serve it on top of a mound of grits with a ladleful of brown tomato sauce over all. The French word *grillade* means "broiled meat" and dates back to the seventeenth century.

PREP: 15 minutes ★ **COOK:** I hour
MAKES 4 main-dish servings

4 beef minute steaks (6 ounces each)

½ teaspoon salt

¼ teaspoon ground black pepper

3 teaspoons vegetable oil

I medium onion, chopped

I green pepper, chopped

I stalk celery, chopped

2 garlic cloves, finely chopped

I can (14 to 16 ounces) tomatoes in puree

I cup beef broth

I teaspoon Worcestershire sauce

2 bay leaves

I tablespoon red wine vinegar

hot cooked old-fashioned or quick hominy grits

I. Sprinkle beef with salt and black pepper. In nonstick 12-inch skillet, heat 1 teaspoon oil over medium-high heat until very hot. Add steaks and cook until browned, about 2 minutes per side, transferring steaks to plate as they are browned.

2. Add remaining 2 teaspoons oil to skillet; reduce heat to medium. Add onion; cook, stirring, 5 minutes. Add green pepper, celery, and garlic; cook, stirring, 3 minutes. Add tomatoes with their puree, breaking them up with side of spoon. Stir in broth, Worcestershire, and bay leaves. Increase heat to high; heat to boiling.

3. Return steaks to skillet; reduce heat. Cover and simmer 40 minutes. Transfer steaks to platter; keep warm. Increase heat to high; stir in vinegar and heat to boiling. Boil until sauce has thickened, about 5 minutes. Discard bay leaves. To serve, spoon sauce over steaks and pass grits separately.

EACH SERVING: About 437 calories, 37g protein, 13g carbohydrate, 26g total fat (9g saturated), 107mg cholesterol, 772mg sodium.

Meat Loaf Surprise

"Surprise" variations of favorite recipes became very popular in the mid-1900s. Sometimes mashed potatoes were piped on top of ground-meat pies, while other times potatoes were rolled up inside a meat loaf jelly-roll fashion. Our Meat Loaf Surprise contains not only potatoes but a layer of spinach too.

PREP: 30 minutes ★ BAKE: 1 hour 15 minutes
MAKES 8 main-dish servings

1½ pounds all-purpose potatoes (about 3 large), peeled and cut into 2-inch pieces

¼ cup milk

2 tablespoons butter or margarine

1¼ teaspoons salt

¼ teaspoon ground black pepper

1 can (14½ ounces) diced tomatoes

½ cup water

2 pounds ground beef chuck

2 large eggs

¾ cup seasoned dried bread crumbs

¼ cup freshly grated Parmesan cheese

1 garlic clove, minced

1 package (10 ounces) frozen chopped spinach, thawed and squeezed dry

1. In 3-quart saucepan, combine potatoes and enough *water* to cover; heat to boiling over high heat. Reduce heat to low; cover and simmer until potatoes are fork-tender, 10 to 15 minutes. Drain potatoes and return to saucepan. Add milk, butter, ½ teaspoon salt, and ⅛ teaspoon pepper. With potato masher, mash potatoes until mixture is smooth; set aside.

2. Preheat oven to 350°F. In blender or in food processor with knife blade attached, puree tomatoes with their juice and water until smooth.

3. In large bowl, mix ground beef, eggs, bread crumbs, Parmesan, garlic, ½ teaspoon salt, remaining ⅛ teaspoon pepper, and ½ cup tomato mixture until well combined but not overmixed.

4. On 14" by 12" sheet of waxed paper, pat meat mixture into 11" by 9" rectangle. Spread mashed potatoes over meat rectangle leaving 1-inch border all around. Spoon spinach over potatoes; sprinkle with remaining ¼ teaspoon salt.

5. Starting at a narrow end, roll up layered meat mixture jelly-roll fashion, lifting waxed paper and using long metal spatula to help loosen meat from waxed paper. Carefully place rolled meat loaf, seam side down, in 13" by 9" baking dish.

6. Pour remaining tomato mixture over and around meat loaf. Bake 1 hour 15 minutes. Let stand 10 minutes to set juices for easier slicing.

EACH SERVING: About 374 calories, 30g protein, 24g carbohydrate, 17g total fat (8g saturated), 138mg cholesterol, 955mg sodium.

Nana's Meat Loaf

According to James Beard, the meat loaf we know today did not become a mainstay of our diet until the twentieth century. Properly prepared, meat loaf resembles a good pâté: highly seasoned, firm and moist, and equally delicious hot or cold. What's the secret to a tender and tasty loaf? Always, always use ground chuck. Our recipe comes from the "Susan, Our Teenage Cook" series, which ran in *Good Housekeeping* magazine for decades.

PREP: 15 minutes ★ BAKE: 1 hour
MAKES 8 main-dish servings

2 pounds ground beef chuck

2 large eggs

2 cups fresh bread crumbs (about 4 slices bread)

2 green onions, finely chopped

1 medium onion, finely chopped

¾ cup ketchup

¼ cup milk

2 tablespoons bottled white horseradish

1½ teaspoons salt

1 teaspoon dry mustard

1. Preheat oven to 400°F. In large bowl, combine ground beef, eggs, bread crumbs, green onions, onion, ¼ cup ketchup, milk, horseradish, salt, and dry mustard just until well blended but not overmixed.

2. Spoon mixture into 9" by 5" metal loaf pan, pressing firmly. Spread remaining ½ cup ketchup on top of loaf. Bake 1 hour. Let meat loaf stand 10 minutes to set juices for easier slicing.

EACH SERVING: About 283 calories, 27g protein, 15g carbohydrate, 13g total fat (5g saturated), 125mg cholesterol, 845mg sodium.

◀ *Meat Loaf Surprise*

Salisbury Steak

In the late nineteenth century, Dr. James Henry Salisbury served Civil War soldiers who suffered with stomach problems chopped beef patties. The beef came from disease-free animals and didn't contain connective tissue, fat, or cartilage. Later he advised all Americans to eat beef three times a day for better health. This simple seasoned ground-beef patty, which carries Dr. Salisbury's name, appeared in print around 1888.

PREP: 25 minutes ★ COOK: 35 minutes
MAKES 4 main-dish servings

1 large onion (12 ounces), halved

1¼ pounds ground beef chuck

¼ cup finely crushed saltine crackers (about 6 crackers)

¼ cup milk

1 large egg, lightly beaten

½ teaspoon salt

¼ teaspoon ground black pepper

1 tablespoon vegetable oil

10 ounces mushrooms, trimmed and sliced

1 can (14½ ounces) beef broth

3 tablespoons all-purpose flour

1 teaspoon Worcestershire sauce

1. Mince enough onion to equal ¼ cup. Thinly slice remaining onion. In large bowl, combine minced onion, ground beef, crushed crackers, milk, egg, ¼ teaspoon salt, and ⅛ teaspoon pepper just until well blended but not overmixed. Shape mixture into 4 oval patties, about ¾ inch thick, handling meat as little as possible.

2. In nonstick 12-inch skillet, heat oil over medium-high heat. Add beef patties; cook until browned, about 4 minutes per side, reducing heat if necessary. With spatula, transfer patties to plate. Discard all but 2 tablespoons drippings from skillet. Add sliced onion, mushrooms, remaining ¼ teaspoon salt, and remaining ⅛ teaspoon pepper to skillet. Cover; cook over medium-low heat, stirring occasionally, until onion is tender, about 10 minutes.

3. In small bowl, blend broth and flour until smooth; add to skillet. Heat to boiling, stirring constantly. Return patties to skillet, pressing them down into sauce. Reduce heat to low; simmer, turning once, until patties are cooked through, about 10 minutes.

EACH SERVING: About 408 calories, 35g protein, 20g carbohydrate, 21g total fat (7g saturated), 149mg cholesterol, 835mg sodium.

Beef Stroganoff

This dish was named in honor of a member of the Stroganov family, who were affluent Russian merchants. Stroganoff usually begins with the finest beef tenderloin, which is quickly cooked in a hot skillet and covered with sour cream sauce that is flavored with fresh or dried tarragon and paprika. Sometimes a splash of brandy is added, as in our classic rendition.

PREP: 15 minutes ★ COOK: 30 minutes
MAKES 4 main-dish servings

1 pound beef tenderloin, trimmed

2 tablespoons butter or margarine

1 medium onion, thinly sliced

¾ cup canned chicken broth or Old-Fashioned Chicken Broth (page 45)

1 teaspoon Hungarian sweet paprika

4 ounces mushrooms, trimmed and sliced

1 tablespoon fresh lemon juice

1 tablespoon brandy

½ teaspoon dried tarragon, crumbled

½ teaspoon salt

⅛ teaspoon ground black pepper

½ cup sour cream

3 teaspoons chopped fresh dill or flat-leaf parsley

1. Cut tenderloin into ⅜-inch-thick slices, then cut into 1½" by ⅜" strips.

2. In 12-inch skillet, melt butter over medium heat. Add half of beef (do not crowd); cook until browned on both sides, about 4 minutes, using slotted spoon to transfer meat to bowl as it is browned. Repeat with remaining beef strips.

3. Reduce heat to medium-low. Stir in onion and cook until tender, about 5 minutes. Add ¼ cup broth and paprika; cook, stirring, until onion is very tender, about 5 minutes longer.

4. Add mushrooms, lemon juice, brandy, tarragon, salt, and pepper. Cook, stirring, until mushrooms are tender and almost all liquid has evaporated, about 8 minutes.

5. Stir in beef, remaining ½ cup broth, sour cream, and 2 teaspoons dill. Cook until heated through (do not boil), about 2 minutes. To serve, sprinkle with remaining 1 teaspoon dill.

EACH SERVING: About 336 calories, 26g protein, 7g carbohydrate, 21g total fat (11g saturated), 99mg cholesterol, 599mg sodium.

Oven Beef Stew

Our forefathers served a one-pot stew called beef with dumplings. They simmered cubes of beef with a simple bouquet of vegetables in a large pot and added a layer of dumplings for the last fifteen minutes of cooking. It wasn't until the late 1800s that the technique of browning the beef, then finishing the stew in the oven became popular.

PREP: 30 minutes ★ **BAKE:** 2 hours
MAKES 6 main-dish servings

2½ **pounds beef chuck, trimmed and cut into 2-inch pieces**
1 **teaspoon salt**
¼ **teaspoon ground black pepper**
4 **teaspoons vegetable oil**
1 **tablespoon butter or margarine**
1 **large onion (12 ounces), chopped**
1 **stalk celery, chopped**
2 **garlic cloves, finely chopped**
½ **teaspoon dried thyme**
2 **tablespoons all-purpose flour**
2 **cups canned chicken broth or Old-Fashioned Chicken Broth (page 45)**
1 **tablespoon tomato paste**
1 **bay leaf**
4 **large carrots, peeled and cut into 2-inch pieces**
1 **pound all-purpose potatoes, peeled and cut into 2-inch pieces**
1 **tablespoon chopped fresh parsley**

1. Preheat oven to 375°F. Pat beef dry with paper towels. In bowl, toss beef with ½ teaspoon salt and pepper.

2. In nonreactive 5-quart Dutch oven, heat 2 teaspoons oil over medium-high heat. Add half of beef; cook until well browned, about 5 minutes, using slotted spoon to transfer meat to bowl as it is browned. Repeat with remaining beef, adding 2 teaspoons oil if necessary.

3. Reduce heat to medium; add butter and heat until melted. Add onion, celery, garlic, thyme, and remaining ½ teaspoon salt. Cook until onions and celery are tender, about 5 minutes. Stir in flour; cook 1 minute. Stir in broth, tomato paste, and bay leaf; cook, stirring until browned bits are loosened from bottom of pot.

4. Return beef to Dutch oven; heat to boiling. Cover tightly and bake 1 hour. Stir in carrots and potatoes; cover and bake until meat and vegetables are fork-tender, about 1 hour. Sprinkle with parsley.

EACH SERVING: About 375 calories, 32g protein, 26g carbohydrate, 16g total fat (6g saturated), 100mg cholesterol, 910mg sodium.

Spiced Beef (or Beef a la Mode)

One piece of the round of beef (known as the "pot roast"), weighing from three to five pounds. Put two tablespoons of butter in stewing kettle over a hot fire; when butter melts, brown the meat on both sides. Remove the meat temporarily and add flour to the butter; let it brown and thicken, then add three pints of boiling water, one bay leaf, one sprig of celery, some parsley, and one large onion with a clove stuck in it, two carrots, one turnip, one tablespoon of salt and one shake of pepper. Replace the meat in this liquid at once and let it simmer for at least six hours. Turn the meat over and stir it occasionally. The secret of the success with this dish is slow cooking. When finished it should be as tender as bread. Place the meat on a hot platter, strain the gravy over it and serve garnished with sliced boiled carrots and sprigs of parsley. The gravy should be thick and of a dark brown color.

—**Good Housekeeping Everyday Cook Book,** 1903

Cottage Pie

This recipe is similar to one of Ireland's most favorite dishes, shepherd's pie, which is made with a savory lamb filling and topped with puffs of mashed potatoes. Cottage pie is usually made with ground beef. In Fannie Farmer's original cookbook, it is made with chopped roasted beef that is sandwiched between two layers of mashed potatoes: one layer is the crust and the other's the topping.

PREP: 40 minutes ★ **BAKE:** 20 minutes
MAKES 4 main-dish servings

2 pounds all-purpose potatoes (6 medium), peeled and cut into quarters

½ **cup milk**

3 tablespoons butter or margarine

¼ **cup plus 1 tablespoon freshly grated Parmesan cheese**

1 teaspoon salt

¼ **plus** ⅛ **teaspoon ground black pepper**

1 medium onion, chopped

2 carrots, peeled and chopped

1 pound ground beef chuck

2 tablespoons tomato paste

2 tablespoons all-purpose flour

¼ **cup dry red wine**

1 cup canned chicken broth or Old-Fashioned Chicken Broth (page 45)

¼ **teaspoon dried thyme**

1 cup frozen peas

1. Preheat oven to 425°F. In 4-quart saucepan, combine potatoes and enough *water* to cover; heat to boiling. Boil until potatoes are tender, about 20 minutes; drain and return to saucepan. With potato masher, mash potatoes with milk and 2 tablespoons butter. Stir in ¼ cup Parmesan, ½ teaspoon salt, and ¼ teaspoon pepper; set mashed potatoes aside.

2. Meanwhile, in nonstick 10-inch skillet, melt remaining 1 tablespoon butter over medium heat. Add onion and carrots; cook until vegetables are tender, about 5 minutes. Add ground beef and cook over medium-high heat, breaking up meat with side of spoon, until beef is no longer pink, about 5 minutes. Skim and discard fat. Add tomato paste and cook, stirring, 1 minute. Add flour and cook, stirring, 1 minute longer. Stir in wine and cook until wine has evaporated. Add broth, thyme, remaining ½ teaspoon salt, and remaining ⅛ teaspoon pepper, stirring until browned bits are loosened from bottom of skillet. Heat to boiling; stir in peas.

3. Transfer beef mixture to 9-inch deep-dish pie plate. Spoon mashed potatoes on top; spread evenly. Sprinkle with remaining 1 tablespoon Parmesan. Place pie on foil-lined cookie sheet and bake until slightly browned, about 20 minutes.

EACH SERVING: About 554 calories, 34g protein, 50gcarbohydrate, 24g total fat (12g saturated), 107mg cholesterol, 1,282mg sodium.

Tamale Pie

The roots of this pie date back to the Aztecs in Tenochtitlán (Mexico City), who served Cortés *tamalli,* meat that is coated with cornmeal dough and steamed inside a softened cornhusk. As early as 1612, Native Americans in Virginia served tamales, which over time evolved into tamale pie. During World War I, cooks appreciated this spicy main-dish pie because they could skimp on the meat or omit it if money was tight. Recipes for tamale pies differ: some have only a bottom layer of cornmeal batter, while others have cornmeal on top also. By the mid-twentieth century, tamale pie became a popular offering in school cafeterias.

PREP: 25 minutes ★ **BAKE:** 45 minutes
MAKES 6 main-dish servings

2 teaspoons vegetable oil
I medium onion, chopped
I pound ground beef chuck
I tablespoon chili powder
I teaspoon ground cumin
I cup medium-hot salsa
I can (15¼ to 16 ounces) whole-kernel corn, drained
4 cups water
I cup cornmeal
I teaspoon salt
½ cup shredded Cheddar cheese

I. Preheat oven to 350°F. In nonstick 12-inch skillet, heat oil over medium-high heat. Add onion and cook until tender and golden, about 5 minutes. Stir in ground beef and cook, breaking up meat with side of spoon, until meat has browned, about 5 minutes. Skim and discard any fat. Stir in chili powder and cumin; cook 2 minutes longer. Remove from heat; stir in salsa and corn.

2. In 2-quart saucepan, heat water to boiling. With wire whisk, gradually whisk in cornmeal and salt. Cook over medium heat, whisking frequently, 5 minutes.

3. Pour half of cornmeal mixture into shallow 2-quart casserole. Spoon beef mixture over cornmeal, spoon remaining cornmeal over beef, and sprinkle Cheddar on top. Bake 45 minutes. Remove casserole from oven and let stand about 15 minutes for easier serving.

EACH SERVING: About 334 calories, 21g protein, 33g carbohydrate, 13g total fat (5g saturated), 57mg cholesterol, 1,026mg sodium.

Chili con Carne

According to food historians Waverley Root and Richard de Rochemont, chili con carne dates back to around 1850 in San Antonio, Texas. It gained popularity at an exhibit of an authentic San Antonio chilley [*sic*] stand at the 1893 Chicago World's Fair. It is believed that chili really took off when a German immigrant in New Braunfels, Texas, created chili powder. It then became easy to spice up the pot with just a dash of this new ingredient. Texans usually prefer cubed or shredded meat in their chili, but midwesterners often choose ground meat, as in our recipe.

PREP: 20 minutes ★ **COOK:** 35 minutes
MAKES 6 main-dish servings

I tablespoon olive oil
I medium onion, chopped
2 garlic cloves, finely chopped
2 green peppers, chopped
2 pounds ground beef chuck
3 pickled jalapeño chiles, seeded and finely chopped (2 tablespoons)
3 tablespoons chili powder
2 teaspoons unsweetened cocoa
1¼ teaspoons salt
¾ teaspoon ground coriander
½ teaspoon dried oregano
¼ teaspoon ground red pepper (cayenne)
I can (14 to 16 ounces) tomatoes, chopped

I. In nonstick 12-inch skillet, heat oil over medium heat. Add onion and garlic; cook, stirring occasionally, until onion is tender, about 5 minutes. Add green peppers and cook, stirring, until tender-crisp, about 5 minutes longer.

2. Add ground beef and cook, breaking up meat with side of spoon, until meat is no longer pink. Stir in pickled jalapeños, chili powder, cocoa, salt, coriander, oregano, and ground red pepper; cook 1 minute. Add tomatoes with their juice; heat to boiling. Reduce heat; simmer, stirring occasionally, until slightly thickened, 15 to 20 minutes.

EACH SERVING: About 326 calories, 33g protein, 10g carbohydrate, 18g total fat (6g saturated), 94mg cholesterol, 758mg sodium.

Barbecued Beef Brisket

Our ancestors barbecued (cooked over an open fire) for centuries. The word *barbecue* comes from the Spanish word *barbacoa*, meaning "framework of sticks." Originally, a *barbacoa* was a latticework bench, but it later became a place on which to grill meat. In America, the word *barbecue* first appeared in print in 1655 but, of course, the Native Americans were barbecuing long before Columbus. Less than a century later, barbecues became social gatherings—often political ones. Texas has always been known for its grand barbecues, many times with beef brisket slow-roasting over a pit for hours until meltingly tender.

PREP: 15 minutes ★ **COOK/GRILL:** 3 hours 35 minutes
MAKES 12 main-dish servings

BRISKET

1 fresh beef brisket (4¹⁄₂ pounds), trimmed

1 medium onion, cut into quarters

1 large carrot, peeled and cut into 1¹⁄₂-inch pieces

1 bay leaf

1 teaspoon whole black peppercorns

¹⁄₄ teaspoon whole allspice

CHUNKY BBQ SAUCE

1 tablespoon vegetable oil

1 large onion (12 ounces), finely chopped

3 garlic cloves, finely chopped

2 tablespoons minced, peeled fresh ginger

1 teaspoon ground cumin

1 can (14¹⁄₂ ounces) tomatoes in puree, chopped

1 bottle (12 ounces) chili sauce

¹⁄₃ cup cider vinegar

2 tablespoons light (mild) molasses

2 tablespoons brown sugar

2 teaspoons dry mustard

1 tablespoon cornstarch

2 tablespoons water

1. Prepare brisket: In 8-quart Dutch oven, place brisket, onion, carrot, bay leaf, peppercorns, allspice, and enough *water* to cover; heat to boiling over high heat. Reduce heat; cover and simmer until meat is tender, about 3 hours.

2. Meanwhile, prepare chunky BBQ sauce: In nonstick 12-inch skillet, heat oil over medium heat. Add onion and cook, stirring occasionally, until tender, about 10 minutes. Add garlic and ginger; cook, stirring, 1 minute. Stir in cumin; cook 1 minute. Stir in tomatoes with their puree, chili sauce, vinegar, molasses, brown sugar, and dry mustard; heat to boiling over high heat. Reduce heat; simmer, stirring occasionally, 5 minutes.

3. Meanwhile, in cup, blend cornstarch and water until smooth. Stir cornstarch mixture into sauce. Heat to boiling, stirring; boil 1 minute. Cover and refrigerate sauce if not using right away. Makes about 4 cups.

4. When brisket is done, transfer to platter. If not serving right away, cover and refrigerate until ready to serve.

5. Prepare grill. Place brisket on grill (preferably one with a cover). Cover and cook over medium heat 10 minutes. Turn brisket and cook 5 minutes longer. Spoon 1 cup barbecue sauce on top of brisket; cook until brisket is heated through, about 5 minutes. (Do not turn brisket after topping with sauce.) Reheat remaining sauce in small saucepan on grill. Slice brisket thinly across the grain and serve with sauce.

EACH SERVING: About 241 calories, 26g protein, 6g carbohydrate, 11g total fat (4g saturated), 81mg cholesterol, 174mg sodium.

EACH 1/4 CUP SAUCE: About 61 calories, 1g protein, 13g carbohydrate, 1g total fat (0g saturated), 0mg cholesterol, 328mg sodium.

New England Boiled Dinner (page 134) ▶

New England Boiled Dinner

(pictured on page 133)

The nineteenth century was known as the "bountiful harvest" century. Farmwives had many creative ways to preserve their bountiful garden vegetables and meats for the upcoming winter. According to Evan Jones in *American Food,* originally New England boiled dinner was prepared with preserved beef. Maine cooks rubbed a piece of beef with coarse salt, covered it with heavily salted water, then weighted it with an iron doorstop to keep it submerged for several weeks. They would then simmer the meat for hours over an open fire, adding salt pork, a head of cabbage, whole peeled potatoes, scraped carrots, and peeled white onions. Scrubbed beets were cooked separately so they didn't stain the other vegetables. Down on the farm, this dish is traditionally served for the midday meal, often with a sprinkling of cider vinegar. Today the most common condiments are homemade horseradish sauce or spicy mustard.

PREP: 15 minutes ★ **COOK:** 3 hours 30 minutes
MAKES 8 main-dish servings

---

1 corned beef brisket (4 to 4½ pounds)

1 medium onion studded with 4 whole cloves

2 quarts water

8 medium all-purpose potatoes (2½ pounds), each peeled and cut in half

8 carrots, each peeled and cut in half

1 small rutabaga (2 pounds), peeled, cut in half, and each half cut into 8 wedges

1 small green cabbage (2 pounds), cut into 8 wedges

2 tablespoons chopped fresh parsley

Dijon mustard

bottled white horseradish

1. In 8-quart Dutch oven, place brisket, clove-studded onion, and water; heat to boiling over high heat. With slotted spoon, skim foam from surface. Reduce heat; cover and simmer until brisket is tender, 2 hours 30 minutes to 3 hours.

2. Add potatoes, carrots, and rutabaga to Dutch oven; heat to boiling over high heat. Reduce heat; cover and simmer until vegetables are tender, about 30 minutes. With slotted spoon, transfer brisket and vegetables to deep large platter; keep warm.

3. Heat liquid remaining in Dutch oven to boiling over high heat. Add cabbage; heat to boiling. Cover and cook until cabbage is tender, about 5 minutes.

4. Slice brisket very thinly across the grain. Transfer sliced meat to platter with vegetables. Place cabbage wedges on platter, sprinkle parsley on vegetables, and serve mustard and horseradish alongside.

EACH SERVING: About 587 calories, 35g protein, 43g carbohydrate, 31g total fat (10g saturated), 157mg cholesterol, 1,887mg sodium.

Red Flannel Hash

Stories abound about how red flannel hash got its name. Some say it comes from its color similarity to red flannel underwear. Red flannel hash has always been a popular way to use up New England boiled dinner leftovers. It is the beets, of course, that contribute the authentic red hue to the dish.

PREP: 15 minutes ★ **COOK:** 30 minutes
MAKES 4 main-dish servings

---

3 tablespoons butter or margarine

1 large onion (12 ounces), chopped

2 cups chopped cooked lean corned beef

2 cups chopped cooked all-purpose potatoes

1 cup finely chopped cooked beets

¼ teaspoon coarsely ground black pepper

1 tablespoon chopped fresh parsley

1. In 10-inch skillet, melt butter over medium heat. Add onion and cook, stirring often, until tender, about 5 minutes. Stir in corned beef, potatoes, beets, and pepper until well combined. Cook, pressing hash down firmly with spatula, until bottom of hash has browned, about 15 minutes.

2. With spatula, turn hash over, one small section at a time. Press down with spatula; cook until second side has browned, 5 to 10 minutes longer. Sprinkle with parsley.

EACH SERVING: About 337 calories, 23g protein, 21g carbohydrate, 18g total fat (9g saturated), 89mg cholesterol, 947mg sodium.

Crown Roast of Pork

From the time the settlers arrived in the New World, pork has been a mainstay in the American diet. History has recorded many menus centered around the pork barrel (sides of pork in salt brine), which helped the colonists survive the long, blustery winters. Eating "high on the hog" is a well-worn expression that denotes comfort and plenty. This spectacular roast pays homage to our love of pork.

PREP: 20 minutes ★ **ROAST:** 3 hours 30 minutes
MAKES 14 main-dish servings

---

1 pork rib crown roast (7 pounds)

2½ teaspoons salt

½ plus ⅛ teaspoon ground black pepper

6 tablespoons butter or margarine

4 stalks celery, chopped

1 large onion (12 ounces), chopped

1 pound Golden Delicious apples (3 medium), peeled, cored, and chopped

8 cups fresh bread cubes (about 12 slices firm white bread)

½ cup apple juice

1 large egg, lightly beaten

1 teaspoon poultry seasoning

¼ cup Calvados, applejack brandy, or water

3 tablespoons all-purpose flour

1 can (14½ ounces) chicken broth or 1¾ cups Old-Fashioned Chicken Broth (page 45)

1. Preheat oven to 325°F. Rub roast with 1 teaspoon salt and ¼ teaspoon pepper. Place roast, rib ends down, in large roasting pan (17" by 11½"). Roast 1 hour.

2. Meanwhile, in 5-quart Dutch oven, melt butter over medium heat. Add celery and onion; cook, stirring, until tender, about 5 minutes. Add apples and cook until tender, 6 to 8 minutes longer. Remove Dutch oven from heat. Stir in bread cubes, apple juice, egg, poultry seasoning, 1 teaspoon salt, and ¼ teaspoon pepper. Toss until well combined.

3. Remove roast from oven and turn, rib ends up. Fill cavity of roast with stuffing. (Place any leftover stuffing into greased 1½-quart casserole. Bake leftover stuffing, uncovered, during last 30 minutes of roasting time.)

4. Return pork to oven; roast until meat thermometer inserted in thickest part of roast (not touching bone) reaches 155°F, about 2 hours 30 minutes. Internal temperature of pork will rise to 160°F upon standing. If stuffing browns too quickly, cover with foil.

5. When roast is done, transfer to warm platter. Let stand 15 minutes to set juices for easier carving.

6. Meanwhile, prepare gravy: Pour pan drippings into 2-cup measuring cup or medium bowl (set roasting pan aside); let stand until fat separates from meat juice. Skim off 3 tablespoons fat from drippings. If necessary, add enough melted butter to fat to equal 3 tablespoons. Pour into 2-quart saucepan. Skim and discard any remaining fat from meat juice. Add Calvados to roasting pan. Heat over medium heat, stirring until browned bits are loosened from bottom of pan. Add to meat juice in cup.

7. Into fat in saucepan, with wire whisk, whisk flour, remaining ½ teaspoon salt, and remaining ⅛ teaspoon pepper until blended; cook, stirring, over medium heat 1 minute. Gradually whisk in meat-juice mixture and broth. Heat to boiling, stirring constantly; boil 1 minute. Serve roast with gravy and stuffing.

EACH SERVING: About 406 calories, 32g protein, 19g carbohydrate, 21g total fat (9g saturated), 104mg cholesterol, 716mg sodium.

Pork Crown Roast Tips

Order your roast a few days ahead so the butcher has enough time to prepare it.

A 7-pound pork rib crown roast has 14 to 16 ribs. When preparing the pork roast, your butcher will "french" the ribs (scrape the meat from the ends of the ribs or chops to expose part of the bones). Ask your butcher to grind this meat for you; it can be added to meat loaf or to meatballs.

Request that the decorative paper or aluminum frills be placed in a separate bag, rather than on the tops of the raw rib bones. This way, you can place the clean frills on your finished roast for serving, if you like.

To carve the crown roast, make centered cuts between the ribs so there is an equal portion of meat on both sides of each chop. Spoon some stuffing over the chops after each rib is cut away.

Stuffed Pork Chops

The word *stuffing* first appeared in print in 1538. It replaced the word *forcemeat*, which comes from the French word *farcir* (to stuff). In the Midwest, where pork has always been plentiful and suppers are hearty and generous, stuffing is frequently used to "overstuff" thick pork chops (at least 1 inch thick, please!).

PREP: 20 minutes ★ COOK: 30 minutes
MAKES 4 main-dish servings

4 teaspoons vegetable oil

1 small onion, chopped

1 Golden Delicious apple, peeled, cored, and chopped

pinch dried thyme

2 slices white bread, toasted and cut into 1/4-inch pieces

2 tablespoons plus 1/2 cup canned chicken broth or Old-Fashioned Chicken Broth (page 45)

1 tablespoon spicy brown mustard

4 pork loin chops, 1 inch thick (8 ounces each)

1/4 teaspoon salt

1. In 12-inch skillet, heat 2 teaspoons oil over medium heat. Add onion and cook until tender, about 5 minutes. Add apple and thyme; cook 3 minutes longer. Transfer apple mixture to medium bowl. Wipe skillet clean.

2. Stir bread pieces, 2 tablespoons broth, and mustard into apple mixture. Pat pork dry with paper towels. Holding knife parallel to surface, cut a horizontal pocket in each chop. Stuff apple mixture into pocket of each chop and secure with toothpicks. Sprinkle with salt.

3. In same skillet, heat remaining 2 teaspoons oil over medium heat until hot. Cook chops until they just lose their pink color throughout, about 7 minutes per side.

4. Transfer chops to platter. Keep warm. Increase heat to high. Add remaining 1/2 cup broth to skillet; heat to boiling. Boil broth until reduced to 1/4 cup, 3 to 5 minutes. Pour sauce over chops.

EACH SERVING: About 367 calories, 39g protein, 15g carbohydrate, 15g total fat (4g saturated), 102mg cholesterol, 540mg sodium.

Smothered Pork Chops

"Smothering" foods is common in soul-food cookery. It refers to the technique of simmering meat or poultry in a thickened gravy until the meat is falling off the bone. True Southerners insist that a seasoned black-iron skillet is essential. According to Craig Claiborne, the term *smothered* may have come from the method of weighting down food with a heavy plate topped with at least five pounds to make sure it stays smothered as it cooks.

PREP: 10 minutes ★ COOK: 20 minutes
MAKES 4 main-dish servings

3/4 cup all-purpose flour

1 teaspoon salt

1/4 teaspoon ground black pepper

1/4 teaspoon ground nutmeg

4 pork rib or loin chops, 3/4 inch thick (6 to 8 ounces each)

2 tablespoons butter or margarine

1/2 cup chopped onion

1 cup canned chicken broth or Old-Fashioned Chicken Broth (page 45)

1/4 cup buttermilk

2 tablespoons chopped fresh parsley

1. In large bowl, combine flour, salt, pepper, and nutmeg. Coat each pork chop with flour mixture, shaking off excess. Reserve 2 tablespoons seasoned flour.

2. Meanwhile, in 12-inch skillet, melt butter over medium-high heat. Add pork chops and cook until golden brown, 3 to 5 minutes per side. Transfer chops to plate; keep warm.

3. Reduce heat to medium. Add onion to skillet; cook, stirring, until tender, about 5 minutes. Sprinkle onion with reserved seasoned flour; cook, stirring, 1 minute. Add broth, stirring to loosen any browned bits from bottom of skillet; simmer 1 minute. Stir in buttermilk. Return pork chops to pan. Simmer 6 minutes, turning once, until cooked through. Sprinkle with parsley.

EACH SERVING: About 319 calories, 28g protein, 16g carbohydrate, 15g total fat (7g saturated), 78mg cholesterol, 813mg sodium.

Ham and Grits with Red-Eye Gravy

As the story goes, Andrew Jackson had a cook who sipped whiskey. He once asked his "tipsy" cook to make some ham and gravy "as red as your eyes." Others contend that the gravy got its name from the "red eye" that seems to appear in the midle of the reduced gravy. In the Deep South, sliced ham or ham steak is quickly fried in a cast-iron skillet (usually a black one), then the gravy is made right in the skillet from the ham drippings and a little strong coffee for extra flavor. It is served with a hefty portion of grits alongside for a true plantation breakfast.

PREP: 5 minutes ★ **COOK:** 30 minutes
MAKES 6 main-dish servings

4½ **cups water**

1 **cup old-fashioned hominy grits**

½ **teaspoon salt**

3 **tablespoons butter or margarine**

1 **tablespoon vegetable oil**

6 **slices country ham,** ¼ **inch thick (about 2 ounces each)**

½ **cup strong brewed coffee**

¼ **teaspoon sugar**

1. In 2-quart saucepan, heat 4 cups water to boiling over medium-high heat; slowly stir in grits and salt. Reduce heat to low; cover and cook, stirring occasionally, until thickened, 15 to 20 minutes. Remove from heat. Stir in butter and keep warm.

2. Meanwhile, in 12-inch skillet, heat oil over medium heat until very hot. Cook ham, 3 slices at a time, turning once, until browned; transfer to platter and keep warm.

3. Add coffee, remaining ½ cup water, and sugar to drippings in skillet. Heat to boiling over medium heat, stirring until browned bits are loosened from bottom of skillet. Cook, stirring occasionally, 5 minutes. Serve gravy over ham and grits.

EACH SERVING: About 279 calories, 18g protein, 21g carbohydrate, 13g total fat (5g saturated), 55mg cholesterol, 1,780mg sodium.

Ham Roasting Tips

When shopping for ham, look for "fully cooked" on the label: this means it's ready to serve. To improve the flavor and texture, heat the ham to an internal temperature of 130° to 140°F. If the label says "cook before eating," the meat must be cooked to 160°F.

To carve a whole bone-in ham: Place the ham on a cutting board. Using a carving fork to steady the ham, cut a few slices from the thin side to form a level base. Turn the ham onto its cut surface. Starting at the shank (narrow) end, slice down to the bone and cut out a small wedge of meat. Continue slicing, perpendicular to the bone, cutting thin slices until you reach the bone at the other end. Then, cut the meat along the leg bone to release the slices. For more servings, return the ham to its original position and cut slices to the bone.

Try to use leftovers within 3 or 4 days to avoid the need to freeze them; freezing changes the flavor and the texture of smoked-pork products. Use any frozen ham within 1 month.

Best Barbecue Ribs

Americans love their barbecue, but *barbecue* means different things to different people; it all depends on what part of the country you're from. In the Lone Star State, where you'll hear the familiar "Y'all come for barbecue" almost everywhere you go; beef brisket and pork spareribs dripping with thick, spicy sauce are often on the menu. The tomato-based Texas sauce is spiked with vinegar, sweetened with molasses, tinged with smoke, and laced with plenty of chiles and spice. In the Carolina back country, neighbors slather whole hogs with spicy, vinegary concoctions that don't contain any tomato at all. They then slowly roast the hogs until the meat is falling off the bone, pull the meat off with a large fork, and pile it onto freshly baked buns. Around the Great Lakes, barbecue aficionados add fruitwood to the fire and use a sweeter, less spicy sauce. Due to Asian influences, cooks along the Pacific Coast use barbecue sauces that are often sweet-and-sour. In Kansas City, they season racks of ribs with a spicy dry rub similar to the one in our recipe. Then they slowly smoke the ribs over charcoal, slather them with a thick and spicy tomato sauce, and grill the pork until glazed and tender. No matter which region it comes from, American barbecue can be counted on to be delicious and satisfying.

PREP: 40 minutes plus standing ★ GRILL: 1 hour 10 minutes
MAKES 8 main-dish servings

BARBECUE SAUCE

2 cups ketchup

1 cup apple cider or juice

2 tablespoons Worcestershire sauce

2 tablespoons light (mild) molasses

2 tablespoons cider vinegar

2 tablespoons brown sugar

2 tablespoons yellow mustard

$\frac{1}{2}$ teaspoon ground black pepper

$\frac{1}{4}$ teaspoon ground red pepper (cayenne)

RIBS

2 tablespoons paprika

1 tablespoon brown sugar

2 teaspoons chili powder

2 teaspoons salt

1$\frac{1}{2}$ teaspoons ground black pepper

1 teaspoon ground cumin

$\frac{1}{2}$ teaspoon ground red pepper (cayenne)

4 racks pork baby back ribs (1 pound each)*

1. Prepare barbecue sauce: In 4-quart saucepan, combine ketchup, cider, Worcestershire, molasses, vinegar, brown sugar, mustard, black pepper, and red pepper. Heat to boiling; reduce heat and simmer, stirring occasionally, until sauce thickens slightly, about 30 minutes.

2. Prepare ribs: In small bowl, combine paprika, brown sugar, chili powder, salt, black pepper, cumin, and ground red pepper. Pat ribs dry with paper towels. Sprinkle on both sides with spice mixture. Let stand 30 minutes.

3. Meanwhile, prepare grill.

4. Place 28" by 12" sheet of heavy-duty foil on surface. Place 1 rack of ribs in center of foil. Place 2 ice cubes under ribs. Bring long sides of foil up and fold several times to seal well. Fold in ends to seal tightly. Repeat with three more sheets of foil, 6 ice cubes, and remaining 3 racks of ribs.

5. Place foil packets on grill rack over medium heat. Cover and cook ribs over medium heat 1 hour, carefully turning packets over once with tongs. With kitchen scissors, cut an X in top of each foil packet to release steam; carefully peel back foil. Remove ribs and place directly on grill. Brush ribs with some sauce; cook, brushing and turning frequently, 10 minutes longer. Serve with remaining sauce on the side.

*If available, use St. Louis–cut baby back ribs because they are meatier.

EACH SERVING: About 532 calories, 28g protein, 32g carbohydrate, 33g total fat (12g saturated), 129mg cholesterol, 1,507mg sodium.

Honey-Glazed Ham

In the South, hams are available two ways: country-cured and sugar-cured. Country hams are salt-cured the old-fashioned way. Smithfield hams go through a series of saltings, chillings, and washings, ten days of smoking, and at least six months of aging in a smoke-house. To warrant the coveted Smithfield label, a ham must be prepared in the town of Smithfield, Virginia, although the ham itself may come from the surrounding area. These hams are usually soaked before being cooked to remove some of their salt. Our recipe uses a sugar-cured ham. It comes precooked and ready to heat, glaze, and eat.

PREP: 45 minutes ★ **ROAST:** 3 hours
MAKES 24 main-dish servings

HAM & GLAZE

1 fully cooked smoked whole ham (about 14 pounds)

½ cup packed brown sugar

½ cup honey

1 teaspoon ground ginger

MUSTARD SAUCE

1 cup sour cream

¾ cup mayonnaise

1 jar (8 ounces) Dijon mustard with seeds

1 teaspoon Worcestershire sauce

½ teaspoon coarsely ground black pepper

1. Preheat oven to 325°F. With sharp knife, remove skin and trim fat from ham, leaving ¼-inch-thick layer of fat. Place ham, fat side up, on rack in large roasting pan (17" by 11½"). Bake ham 2 hours 30 minutes.

2. Meanwhile, prepare glaze: In 1-quart saucepan, combine brown sugar, honey, and ginger; heat to boiling over medium-high heat. Boil 1 minute. When bubbling subsides, brush ham with some glaze. Bake ham, brushing occasionally with remaining glaze, until meat thermometer inserted into thickest part of ham (not touching bone) reaches 140°F, 30 minutes to 1 hour longer.

3. Meanwhile, prepare mustard sauce: In medium bowl, stir sour cream, mayonnaise, mustard, Worcestershire, and pepper until combined. Cover and refrigerate until ready to serve. Makes about 2½ cups.

4. Serve ham with mustard sauce.

EACH SERVING WITHOUT SAUCE: About 325 calories, 36g protein, 10g carbohydrate, 15g total fat (5g saturated), 95mg cholesterol, 2400mg sodium.

EACH TABLESPOON MUSTARD SAUCE: About 50 calories, 1g protein, 1g carbohydrate, 5g total fat (1g saturated), 4mg cholesterol, 170mg sodium.

Mustard and Herb Racks of Lamb

Early cookbooks usually included several recipes for mutton, but only occasionally did a recipe for lamb appear. In the 1796 cookbook *American Cookery* by Amelia Simmons, she suggests roasting lamb while frequently basting it with butter and sending it to the table "with a nice salad, green peas, fresh beans, or a colliflower, or asparagus." Here's the classic show-off racks, perfect for a special dinner party. For easier carving, ask your butcher to loosen the backbone from the ribs.

PREP: 10 minutes ★ **ROAST:** 1 hour 5 minutes
MAKES 8 main-dish servings

2 lamb rib roasts (racks of lamb), 8 ribs each
   (2½ pounds each), trimmed

½ teaspoon salt

3 tablespoons butter or margarine

2 cups fine fresh bread crumbs (about 4 slices
   firm white bread)

2 teaspoons dried rosemary, crumbled

¼ teaspoon ground black pepper

2 tablespoons chopped fresh parsley

2 tablespoons Dijon mustard

1. Preheat oven to 375°F. In large roasting pan (17" by 11½"), place roasts, rib side down; sprinkle with salt. Roast lamb 50 minutes.

2. Meanwhile, in 10-inch skillet, melt butter over medium heat. Add bread crumbs, rosemary, and pepper; cook, stirring frequently, until crumbs are golden brown, about 4 minutes. Stir in parsley.

3. Spread mustard on tops of roasts. Press bread-crumb mixture onto mustard, patting so it adheres. Roast lamb until meat thermometer inserted in center of lamb (not touching bone) reaches 140°F, 15 to 20 minutes longer. Internal temperature of meat will rise to 145°F (medium) upon standing. Or roast to desired doneness.

4. When roasts are done, transfer to cutting board and let stand 10 minutes to set juices for easier carving. Cut off backbone from ribs. Transfer roasts to warm platter. To serve, with sharp knife, cut lamb between bones to separate chops.

EACH SERVING: About 311 calories, 27g protein, 7g carbohydrate, 18g total fat (8g saturated), 99mg cholesterol, 436mg sodium.

The Progressive Dinner Party

During the boom years of the 1950s, having a home in suburbia was a must, and so was entertaining one's neighbors. Progressive dinner parties, a dinner that's held in three or four homes, with a different course served in each home were all the rage. Each hostess prepared one course (instead of the whole dinner), so it saved both time and money.

Going from home to home or backyard to backyard makes a progressive dinner party fun. So why not throw one? As the party organizer, you get to choose the hostesses, the theme of the dinner, and usually the menu. Select foods that not only go together but that can be made ahead. Here's the key to a smooth-flowing party: Suggest that the hostess for the subsequent course leave a little early, so she has plenty of time to have the food hot and waiting when everyone arrives at her home.

Chapter 7

A Mess of Fish

The colonists found the waters of North America teeming with a whole host of fish and shellfish, including cod, flounder, sole, sturgeon, shrimp, lobster, oysters, and clams. As it was plentiful and reliable, fish became their "daily bread." Due to the lack of refrigeration, however,

seafood was always eaten the day it was caught and only in the nearby coastal villages and towns. To preserve fish, the colonists either pickled or salted it. The barrels of prepared pickled oysters and salted mackerel and salmon were then transported to the land-locked colonies so they could eat fish also. According to cookbook author Eliza Leslie, it was customary during much of the nineteenth century to begin dinner with a fish course, which often consisted of a large, whole fish served in a buttery sauce that was laden with shrimp, which was never served by itself. By the time Fannie Farmer's first cookbook was published in 1896, fish was eaten as the main course. Her many—and uncomplicated—fish recipes included broiled, fried, baked,

scalloped, and stuffed preparations. Some recipes suggested a sauce for serving alongside the fish, while others recommended a simple drawn butter.

Americans still love their fish but often prefer it more simply prepared. It took us well into the twentieth century to appreciate the fact that some fish is perfectly delicious sautéed in a bit of butter and oil in a hot skillet. Grilling has also become a favorite way to cook fish, either whole, skewered, or filleted. At many celebrations, fish was—and still is—the star. There are traditional clambakes on the New England coast, shad festivals in the East, cioppino cookouts on the beaches of California, salmon fests along Puget Sound, and fabulous fish fries in the South.

Salt-Crusted Baked Snapper

Our forefathers delighted in eating many varieties of fish. Red snapper, a favorite from the Gulf Coast and southern Atlantic, was stuffed, baked, grilled, and tossed into Louisiana fish stews. Following the Civil War, Floridians began catching and selling red snapper, which contributed to its increased popularity. In this recipe, a whole fish is baked under a salt crust, which keeps the fish juicy and moist. Surprisingly, it doesn't taste salty at all.

PREP: 10 minutes ★ **BAKE:** 30 minutes
MAKES 2 main-dish servings

4 cups kosher salt
1 whole red snapper (1½ pounds), cleaned and scaled
1 lemon
3 thyme sprigs

1. Preheat oven to 450°F. Line 13" by 9" baking pan with foil; spread 2 cups salt in bottom of pan.

2. Rinse snapper inside and out with cold running water; pat dry with paper towels. From lemon, cut 3 slices. Cut remaining lemon into wedges. Place lemon slices and thyme in cavity of fish. Place snapper on bed of salt; cover with remaining 2 cups salt. Bake until fish is just opaque throughout when knife is inserted at backbone, about 30 minutes.

3. To serve, tap salt crust to release from top of fish; discard. Slide cake server under front section of top fillet and lift off fillet; transfer to platter. Slide server under backbone and lift it away from bottom fillet; discard. Slide cake server between bottom fillet and skin and transfer fillet to platter. Serve with reserved lemon wedges.

EACH SERVING: About 188 calories, 37g protein, 6g carbohydrate, 3g total fat (1g saturated), 66mg cholesterol, 800mg sodium.

Trout Amandine

(pictured on page 142)

For the colonists, trout was an everyday food. It was so plentiful that they only had to cast their fishing lines into the water to catch "dinner on the spot." By the twentieth century, the wild trout supply had diminished. But there was plenty of farmed trout, so the mountain streams and lakes across the country were able to be restocked. The secret to keeping this delicate fish moist is to first soak it in milk, then cook it fast in a scalding-hot skillet.

PREP: 10 minutes plus standing ★ **COOK:** 20 minutes
MAKES 4 main-dish servings

4 brook or rainbow trout (10 to 12 ounces each), cleaned and scaled
1 cup milk
¼ cup all-purpose flour
½ teaspoon salt
4 tablespoons vegetable oil
¼ cup plus 1 teaspoon fresh lemon juice
4 tablespoons butter or margarine
¼ cup sliced almonds

1. Rinse trout inside and out with cold running water; pat dry with paper towels. Soak fish in milk 10 minutes. On waxed paper, combine flour and salt. Remove trout from milk and coat well with flour mixture, shaking off excess seasoned flour.

2. In 12-inch skillet, heat 2 tablespoons oil over medium heat until very hot. Add 2 trout; cook until just opaque throughout when knife is inserted at backbone, 4 to 5 minutes per side. Transfer to platter; keep warm. Repeat with remaining oil and fish.

3. Pour off any fat remaining in skillet; wipe skillet clean with paper towels. Return skillet to heat; add ¼ cup lemon juice and cook 15 seconds. Add butter and almonds; cook until almonds are golden, about 2 minutes. Add remaining 1 teaspoon lemon juice; pour sauce over fish.

EACH SERVING: About 523 calories, 42g protein, 8g carbohydrate, 35g total fat (11g saturated), 143mg cholesterol, 467mg sodium.

Poached Salmon with Sour Cream–Dill Sauce

The Native Americans appreciated salmon long before the colonists arrived. They would spread open a whole salmon, rub it with sweet ferns, and plank it on driftwood. The fish was then placed over smoldering embers, where it slowly cooked until charred on the outside and succulent and juicy on the inside. Salmon was also dried and smoked to eat later. For this recipe, you'll need a fish poacher to cook the whole fish as it's too long to fit into a skillet. The handles on the poaching rack make it easy to remove the fish from the poacher all in one piece.

PREP: 30 minutes plus chilling ★ **COOK:** 40 minutes
MAKES 16 main-dish servings

10 cups water

2 cups dry white wine or dry vermouth

2 stalks celery, sliced

1 medium onion, cut into quarters

1 large carrot, peeled and sliced

1 lemon, sliced

4½ teaspoons salt

½ teaspoon whole black peppercorns

1 whole salmon (7 to 8 pounds), cleaned and scaled

1 cup sour cream

⅓ cup chopped fresh dill

¼ cup mayonnaise

1 English (seedless) cucumber

1. In 26-inch fish poacher, combine water, wine, celery, onion, carrot, lemon, salt, and peppercorns; heat to boiling over high heat. Cover and cook 10 minutes.

2. Rinse salmon inside and out with cold running water. Place salmon on rack in fish poacher; heat poaching liquid to boiling. Reduce heat; cover and simmer until fish is just opaque throughout when knife is inserted at backbone, about 30 minutes. Lift out poaching rack; using two wide spatulas, transfer salmon to large platter. Cover fish; refrigerate until well chilled, about 2 hours 30 minutes.

3. Meanwhile, prepare sour cream–dill sauce: In a small bowl, combine sour cream and dill. Cover and refrigerate.

4. Carefully peel off skin from top of salmon; discard. Spread mayonnaise evenly over fish. Thinly slice cucumber; arrange slightly overlapping slices on salmon to resemble scales.

5. To serve, slide cake server under front section of top fillet and lift off fillet; transfer to separate platter. Slide server under backbone and lift it away from bottom fillet; discard. Slide cake server between bottom fillet and skin and transfer fillet to platter. Serve with sour cream–dill sauce.

EACH SERVING WITH 1 TABLESPOON SAUCE:
About 312 calories, 28g protein, 1g carbohydrate,
5g total fat (5g saturated), 90mg cholesterol, 255mg sodium.

Sole Roll-ups with Crab Stuffing

The name for this flat fish comes from the French word *sole,* as the shape of the fish somewhat resembles the shape of the sole of one's foot. Various flounders are marketed as sole: butter sole, English sole, lemon sole, and gray sole. The most highly prized sole—and the most expensive—is Dover sole, which is caught in the Atlantic Ocean off the coast of Europe.

PREP: 20 minutes ★ **COOK/BAKE:** 35 minutes
MAKES 6 main-dish servings

2 tablespoons butter or margarine
4 tablespoons finely chopped shallots
8 ounces lump crabmeat, picked over
½ cup fresh bread crumbs (about 1 slice bread)
1 tablespoon chopped fresh parsley
2 teaspoons fresh lemon juice
½ plus ⅛ teaspoon salt
⅛ teaspoon plus pinch ground black pepper
6 sole or flounder fillets (6 ounces each)
1 can (14 to 16 ounces) tomatoes, drained
¼ cup heavy or whipping cream
1 teaspoon chopped fresh tarragon or parsley

1. Preheat oven to 400°F. Grease 13" by 9" baking dish.

2. In nonstick 10-inch skillet, melt 1 tablespoon butter over medium heat. Add 2 tablespoons shallots; cook until tender, about 2 minutes. Transfer to medium bowl. Add crabmeat, bread crumbs, parsley, lemon juice, ¼ teaspoon salt, and ⅛ teaspoon pepper; toss with fork until evenly combined.

3. Sprinkle skinned side of sole fillets with ¼ teaspoon salt. Spoon crabmeat mixture evenly over fillets. Roll up fillets; place, seam side down, in prepared baking dish. Bake until just opaque throughout, about 25 minutes.

4. Meanwhile, in blender, puree tomatoes until smooth. In same 10-inch skillet, melt remaining 1 tablespoon butter over medium heat. Add remaining 2 tablespoons shallots; cook until tender, about 2 minutes. Add pureed tomatoes, remaining ⅛ teaspoon salt, and remaining pinch pepper. Increase heat to high; cook, stirring frequently, until liquid has almost evaporated, about 5 minutes. Stir in cream and heat to boiling. Remove from heat and stir in tarragon.

5. With wide slotted spatula, transfer fish to platter. Stir any juices in baking dish into tomato sauce; spoon sauce over fish.

EACH SERVING: About 298 calories, 41g protein, 7g carbohydrate, 11g total fat (5g saturated), 144mg cholesterol, 665mg sodium.

Sole Roll-ups with Crab Stuffing ▶

Blackened Tuna Steaks

The French Acadians settled along the banks of Louisiana in the mid-1700s. The settlers adapted their love of simple, hearty French country cooking to the local ingredients. One favorite Cajun technique is to blacken food by first seasoning it with lots of black pepper, then searing it in a heavy skillet over high heat. In most homes, the "family" black cast-iron skillet never leaves the range and is used for cooking everything from the daily fish catch to Sunday chicken and juicy payday steaks.

PREP: 10 minutes plus marinating ★ **COOK:** 6 minutes
MAKES 4 main-dish servings

4 large lemons
6 tablespoons olive oil
6 tablespoons chopped fresh parsley
½ teaspoon salt
¼ teaspoon ground black pepper
4 tuna steaks, ¾ inch thick (5 ounces each)

1. From lemons, grate 1 teaspoon peel and squeeze ⅔ cup juice. In 9-inch square baking dish, with wire whisk, whisk lemon peel and juice, 3 tablespoons oil, 5 tablespoons parsley, salt, and pepper until mixed. Add tuna, turning to coat. Cover and refrigerate 45 minutes to marinate, turning occasionally.

2. In 10-inch cast-iron or other heavy skillet, heat remaining 3 tablespoons oil over medium-high heat until hot. Add tuna; cook until pale pink in center (medium), about 3 minutes per side or until desired doneness. Transfer to 4 dinner plates and sprinkle with remaining 1 tablespoon parsley.

EACH SERVING: About 246 calories, 30g protein, 1g carbohydrate, 13g total fat (2g saturated), 48mg cholesterol, 341mg sodium.

Panfried Catfish

There are over two thousand varieties of catfish, all with barbels, which resemble cat's whiskers. Panfried catfish first became popular in the South. It is almost always dredged in cornmeal (white in the South, yellow in the Midwest) and then fried up fast in bubbling oil in a seasoned iron skillet. It is usually brought to the table in a paper napkin–lined basket, with a large helping of hush puppies alongside. (Fry up a batch of ours, see page 220).

PREP: 15 minutes plus standing ★ **COOK:** 20 minutes
MAKES 6 main-dish servings

¾ cup cornmeal
2 tablespoons all-purpose flour
½ teaspoon salt
¼ teaspoon ground black pepper
¼ cup milk
6 catfish fillets (6 ounces each)
4 tablespoons vegetable oil
lemon wedges

1. In ziptight plastic bag, combine cornmeal, flour, salt, and pepper. Pour milk into pie plate. Dip catfish fillets, one at a time, into milk to coat well. Add fish to cornmeal mixture, shaking bag to coat fish thoroughly. Place coated catfish on wire rack set over waxed paper; set aside to dry 20 minutes.

2. In 10-inch skillet, heat 2 tablespoons oil over medium-high heat until hot. Add 3 fillets to skillet; fry until just opaque throughout and golden, 4 to 5 minutes per side. Transfer to paper towels to drain. Repeat with remaining 2 tablespoons oil and remaining catfish. Serve with lemon wedges.

EACH SERVING: About 377 calories, 28g protein, 16g carbohydrate, 22g total fat (4g saturated), 58mg cholesterol, 255mg sodium.

Friday Night Fish Fry

The observance of meatless Fridays by Catholics gave rise to the Friday-night fish fries of the early and mid-twentieth century. In small villages, bustling cities, and the new sprawling suburbs, diners, local cafés, and even elegant restaurants often featured a tempting all-you-can-eat fish fry for one price. The type of fish and seafood offered varied from season to season, region to region, and depended upon the local catch-of-the-day sold by the nearest fishmonger. The fish-fry menu almost always featured fried fillets of white fish, such as trout, perch, or flounder. The fish was piled high on the platters along with fried oysters, shrimp, or scallops (or a combination of all three); thin, crisply fried potatoes; and often crunchy fried balls of corn bread called hush puppies (especially throughout the South). To complete the feast, there was a spicy red sauce and creamy tartar sauce for dipping and some cooling coleslaw. Without a doubt, no one ever left a Friday-night fish fry hungry!

Codfish Cakes

Originally codfish cakes were made with cod, mashed potato, and egg to bind them. The mixture was shaped into balls and lowered into hot oil. In Middle English, *cod* means "bag." Since this hefty fish slightly resembles the shape of a bag, it is possibly a link to its name. The first New England settlers owed much of their fame and fortune to the abundance of cod. Only ten years after the fishing industry began in Gloucester, Massachusetts, in 1623, ships carried over 300,000 cod to market worldwide. We prefer our codfish cakes shaped into patties and browned in just a little oil in a skillet.

PREP: 30 minutes plus chilling ★ **COOK:** 10 minutes
MAKES 4 main-dish servings

3 tablespoons vegetable oil

2 large stalks celery, chopped

1 small onion, chopped

1½ cups fresh bread crumbs (about 3 slices bread)

1 pound cod fillet

1 large egg, lightly beaten

2 tablespoons light mayonnaise

1 tablespoon chopped fresh parsley

1 teaspoon fresh lemon juice

¼ teaspoon hot pepper sauce

½ teaspoon salt

lemon wedges

1. In 12-inch skillet, heat 1 tablespoon oil over medium heat. Add celery and onion; cook, stirring occasionally, until onion is tender and lightly browned, about 10 minutes. Remove from heat.

2. Place two-thirds of bread crumbs on waxed paper. Place remaining crumbs in medium bowl. With tweezers, remove any bones from cod. With large chef's knife, finely chop fish; add to bread crumbs in bowl. Stir in celery-onion mixture, egg, mayonnaise, parsley, lemon juice, pepper sauce, and salt until well combined.

3. Shape fish mixture into four 3-inch patties (mixture will be very soft and moist). Refrigerate patties until firm, at least 30 minutes. Wipe skillet clean.

4. Use bread crumbs on waxed paper to coat patties, patting crumbs to cover. In same skillet, heat remaining 2 tablespoons oil over medium-low heat until hot. Add patties to skillet; cook until browned and cooked through, 5 to 6 minutes per side. Serve with lemon wedges.

EACH SERVING: About 298 calories, 24g protein, 15g carbohydrate, 16g total fat (2g saturated), 105mg cholesterol, 565mg sodium.

Molded Salmon Mousse

Salmon was an important part of the Native American diet. In many tribes, the word for "salmon" and the word for "fish" was the same. Salmon has always been a popular choice for entertaining. In this recipe, it arrives at the table in elegant style: whipped into a creamy mousse, shaped in a fish mold, and all dressed up for a party.

PREP: 30 minutes plus chilling ★ **MAKES** 6 main-dish servings

I envelope unflavored gelatin

I cup heavy or whipping cream

I can (15½ ounces) salmon, drained and flaked

½ cup mayonnaise

½ teaspoon salt

2 teaspoons chopped fresh dill or ¾ teaspoon dill weed

½ teaspoon paprika

½ teaspoon hot pepper sauce

I bunch radishes

2 whole black peppercorns

2 lemons, thinly sliced

1. In small bowl, evenly sprinkle gelatin over ¼ cup cold water; let stand 5 minutes to soften gelatin slightly. Add ½ cup very hot tap water to gelatin mixture and stir until gelatin has completely dissolved, about 3 minutes. Cover and refrigerate until slightly chilled, about 10 minutes.

2. With pastry brush, lightly brush 5½-cup fish or other decorative mold with vegetable oil.

3. In bowl, with mixer at medium speed, beat cream until stiff peaks form. In large bowl, with mixer at medium-high speed, beat salmon, mayonnaise, salt, dill, paprika, hot pepper sauce, and gelatin mixture until smooth, frequently scraping bowl with rubber spatula. Fold in whipped cream. Spoon salmon mixture into mold; smooth top. Cover and refrigerate until set, about 3 hours.

4. To serve, thinly slice radishes; cut slices in half. Unmold mousse onto large platter. Decorate head of fish using peppercorns for eyes. Carefully press radish slices about ⅛ inch deep into mousse in slightly overlapping rows to resemble scales, with rounded end of each radish extended at slight angle. Garnish with lemon slices.

EACH SERVING: About 368 calories, 16g protein, 6g carbohydrate, 33g total fat (12g saturated), 89mg cholesterol, 625mg sodium.

Salmon Croquettes

Flake two cups of cold boiled or canned salmon with a silver fork. Season it with a little salt, mustard and cayenne. Mix it with one cup of thick cream sauce, made by blending together one tablespoon of butter with two tablespoons of flour, and adding gradually one cup of hot rich milk or thin cream. Cook this in a double boiler or saucepan until smooth and thick, seasoning the sauce with salt, pepper and celery salt. Spread the salmon mixture on a buttered platter to cool. Heat one cup of canned peas with three teaspoons of butter, one teaspoon of sugar, two teaspoons of flour and three tablespoons of thin cream. When the salmon is cold, shape a portion into a flat round cake, put a spoon of creamed peas in the center, cover with the salmon, make into a ball, dip in crumbs, beaten egg, and crumbs again, and fry to a golden brown in hot fat. Garnish with parsley.

—Good Housekeeping Everyday Cook Book, 1903

Tuna-Noodle Casserole

In the 1950s, tuna-noodle casserole was almost always on the menu at school cafeterias, diners, church suppers, and Friday-night dinner tables. Chances are the casserole began with a can of mushroom soup and at least one can of tuna. Then the recipes began to differ. Many contained egg noodles and mushrooms, as does ours, while others contained chow mein noodles. Sometimes the casserole was topped with crushed or broken potato chips, and sometimes it was topped with crisp bread crumbs.

PREP: 20 minutes ★ BAKE: 25 minutes
MAKES 6 main-dish servings

1/2 cup coarse fresh bread crumbs
   (about 1 slice bread)
1 tablespoon chopped fresh parsley
4 tablespoons butter or margarine
4 ounces mushrooms, trimmed and sliced (2 cups)
1/4 cup finely chopped shallots
1/4 cup finely chopped celery
1/4 cup finely chopped red pepper
1/3 cup all-purpose flour
3 cups milk
2 cans (6 ounces each) solid white tuna in water,
   drained and flaked
8 ounces wide egg noodles, cooked as label directs
1 teaspoon salt
1/8 teaspoon ground black pepper

1. Preheat oven to 375°F. Butter shallow 1½- to 2-quart baking dish. Spread bread crumbs in jelly-roll pan. Bake until golden, about 5 minutes; cool. Stir in parsley.

2. Meanwhile, in medium saucepan, melt butter over medium heat. Add mushrooms, shallots, celery, and red pepper. Cook, stirring occasionally, until vegetables are tender, about 4 minutes. Stir in flour; cook, stirring, 1 minute. With wire whisk, gradually whisk in milk; heat to boiling. Reduce heat; simmer, whisking occasionally, 1 minute.

3. In large bowl, combine sauce, tuna, noodles, salt, and pepper. Pour mixture into prepared baking dish. Sprinkle with bread crumbs. Bake until crumb topping has browned and filling is bubbling around edges, about 25 minutes.

EACH SERVING: About 405 calories, 25g protein, 42g carbohydrate, 15g total fat (8g saturated), 96mg cholesterol, 670mg sodium.

Maryland Crab Cakes

As far back as the earliest settlers, folks in Maryland have taken pride in serving up some of the best crab cakes in the country. Blue crabs are found all along the Atlantic coast from Massachusetts to the Bahamas, but most are caught along the Virginia coast and in Chesapeake Bay. These delectable crab cakes are made with lump crabmeat, which is made up of large chunks of meat from the body of the crab and is considered the best.

PREP: 15 minutes ★ COOK: 12 minutes
MAKES 4 main-dish servings

2 large eggs
1 tablespoon dry sherry
1 tablespoon finely chopped onion
1/4 teaspoon salt
1 container (16 ounces) lump crabmeat, picked over
1/2 cup coarsely crumbled saltine crackers
   (about 12 crackers)
3 tablespoons butter or margarine
Tartar Sauce (below)

1. In medium bowl, mix eggs, sherry, onion, and salt until blended; add crabmeat and crumbled crackers, stirring just until mixed.

2. In 12-inch skillet, melt butter over medium heat. Drop 4 equal mounds of crab mixture into skillet. With wide spatula, press mounds to form 3½-inch round cakes. Cook until browned and heated through, about 5 minutes per side. Serve with Tartar Sauce.

EACH SERVING WITHOUT SAUCE: About 272 calories, 27g protein, 7g carbohydrate, 14g total fat (7g saturated), 243mg cholesterol, 693mg sodium.

Tartar Sauce

In small bowl, combine 1/2 cup mayonnaise, 1/4 cup finely chopped dill pickle, 1 tablespoon chopped fresh parsley, 2 teaspoons milk, 2 teaspoons distilled white vinegar, 1/2 teaspoon finely chopped onion, and 1/2 teaspoon Dijon mustard until well blended. Serve, or cover and refrigerate up to 2 days. Makes about 3/4 cup.

EACH TABLESPOON: About 68 calories, 0g protein, 0g carbohydrate, 7g total fat (1g saturated), 6mg cholesterol, 125mg sodium.

Lobster Thermidor

Lobster was so plentiful that the settlers found them washed up on the beaches in piles often several feet high, so it didn't take long for America's love of lobster to grow. Napoleon reportedly named this elegant dish after tasting it during *Thermidor*, the eleventh month in the French calendar at the time of the French Revolution.

PREP: 35 minutes ★ **COOK/BROIL:** 30 minutes
MAKES 4 main-dish servings

4 frozen lobster tails (about 6 ounces each), thawed

4 tablespoons butter or margarine

1 shallot, finely chopped

3 tablespoons all-purpose flour

1½ cups half-and-half

¼ cup dry white wine

¼ teaspoon salt

pinch dry mustard

1 tablespoon chopped fresh tarragon

½ cup freshly grated Parmesan cheese

1. Using kitchen scissors, cut away the portion of shell on underside of lobster tails.

2. Into large skillet, fitted with vegetable steamer, pour *1 inch water*. Place lobster tails, meat side up, in steamer; heat to boiling over high heat. Cover and reduce heat; simmer until lobster tails are just cooked through, about 8 minutes. Refrigerate lobster until cool enough to handle.

3. Meanwhile, in 3-quart saucepan, melt butter over medium heat. Add shallot and cook, stirring, until tender, about 2 minutes. Stir in flour and cook until bubbly, about 1 minute. Stir in half-and-half, wine, salt, and dry mustard. Cook, stirring, until sauce has thickened and boils. Reduce heat to low; simmer, stirring often, 5 minutes.

4. Preheat broiler. Remove lobster meat from shells (reserve shells) and cut into bite-size pieces. Stir lobster meat and tarragon into sauce. Place lobster shells on rack in broiling pan. Fill lobster shells with lobster mixture. Sprinkle evenly with Parmesan. Place pan in broiler 5 inches from heat source. Broil until browned and bubbly, about 3 minutes.

EACH SERVING: About 400 calories, 28g protein, 11g carbohydrate, 26g total fat (16g saturated), 141mg cholesterol, 881mg sodium.

Cooking a Live Lobster

In a large saucepot, heat *3 inches water* (or enough to cover lobster) to boiling. Plunge the lobster, head first, into the pot. Reheat to boiling. Reduce the heat to medium; cover and simmer, lifting the lid occasionally to let the steam escape, until the shell turns red, 12 to 15 minutes.

Removing the Lobster Meat

1. Slightly cool the cooked lobster. Break off the claws and legs. With a lobster cracker or nut cracker, crack the large claws; remove the meat. Separate the legs from the joints; push out the meat.

2. Twist off the head from the tail. With kitchen shears, cut away the thin underside shell from the tail and discard. Gently remove the meat from the shell.

3. Make a ¼-inch-deep cut along the (rounded) backside of the meat to expose the dark vein; remove the vein and discard. Reserve any red roe (coral) or greenish-gray liver (tomalley) in a bowl. Cut lobster meat into chunks; place in the same bowl.

4. With your hand, lift out the bony portion from the head shell; add any remaining roe or liver to the lobster meat. Discard the sac and spongy grayish gills from the top of the head.

5. Break the bony portion into several pieces. With a lobster pick or fork, pick out the meat.

6. Reassemble the shell of the head and tail to use as a server for the lobster meat, if you like.

Oyster Pan Roast

Oysters were abundant and very popular with the colonists. Early cookbooks are filled with ways to stew, fry, scallop, and pickle this succulent shellfish. At Monticello, Thomas Jefferson favored his oysters served up in a pie in a thick, creamy filling that was seasoned with wine. Our pan roast is served on toast points in shallow bowls. It resembles the one that has been served at the famed Grand Central Oyster Bar & Restaurant in New York City ever since its doors opened in 1913. Large quantities of this stewlike dish are made behind the bar in pans set over simmering water. Serve it the traditional way—with oyster crackers, if you like.

PREP: 10 minutes ★ **COOK:** 12 minutes
MAKES 6 first-course servings

2 tablespoons butter or margarine

⅓ cup finely chopped shallots or onion

½ teaspoon paprika

½ teaspoon salt

¼ teaspoon celery salt (optional)

¼ cup dry white wine or dry vermouth

2 cups half-and-half or light cream

1 tablespoon tomato paste

1 teaspoon Worcestershire sauce

1 pint shucked oysters with their liquid

2 tablespoons chopped fresh parsley

6 dashes hot pepper sauce or to taste

6 slices firm white bread, toasted and each cut on diagonal in half

1. In 3-quart saucepan, melt butter over medium heat. Add shallots, paprika, salt, and celery salt, if using. Cook, stirring, 3 minutes. Increase heat to high; add wine; boil until liquid has evaporated, about 3 minutes.

2. Reduce heat to medium; stir in half-and-half, tomato paste, and Worcestershire. Heat to boiling; add oysters with their liquid, 1 tablespoon parsley, and hot pepper sauce. Cook just until edges of oysters begin to curl, 3 to 4 minutes.

3. To serve, place the toast slices in 6 shallow soup bowls, top with oyster mixture and sprinkle with remaining 1 tablespoon parsley.

EACH SERVING: About 289 calories, 11g protein, 23g carbohydrate, 16g total fat (9g saturated), 87mg cholesterol, 553mg sodium.

Scallop Pan Roast

Prepare as directed but substitute *1 pound bay or sea scallops* for oysters. If scallops are large, cut in half or into quarters.

Chesapeake Bay Crab Boil

All along the Chesapeake Bay shoreline there are home-style eateries called crab houses. They are often frequented by the locals for pots of this spicy hot specialty. Communal tables are covered with newspapers, and lots of wooden hammers and crackers are provided for cracking open the crab shells and digging out the succulent meat. When preparing this dish, be sure to keep an eye on the crabs as they cook so you can pull them out of the pot as soon as they turn bright red.

PREP: 10 minutes ★ **COOK:** 40 minutes
MAKES 4 main-dish servings

2 medium onions, coarsely chopped

1 carrot, peeled and coarsely chopped

1 stalk celery, coarsely chopped

1 lemon, sliced

$1/2$ cup crab boil seasoning

1 tablespoon crushed red pepper

1 tablespoon salt

1 gallon (4 quarts) water

1 can or bottle (12 ounces) beer

2 dozen live hard-shell blue crabs, rinsed

1. In 12-quart stockpot, combine onions, carrot, celery, lemon, crab boil seasoning, crushed red pepper, salt, water, and beer. Heat to boiling over high heat; cook 15 minutes.

2. Using tongs, transfer crabs to stockpot. Cover; heat to boiling. Boil 5 minutes (crabs will turn red). With tongs, transfer crabs to colander to drain; place on platter.

3. To eat crab, twist off claws and legs, then crack shell to remove meat. Break off flat pointed apron from underside of crab; remove top shell. Discard feathery gills. With kitchen shears or hands, break body in half down center. With fingers or lobster pick, remove meat.

EACH SERVING: About 123 calories, 24g protein, 0g carbohydrate, 2g total fat (0g saturated), 119mg cholesterol, 1,410mg sodium.

Beer Batter–Fried Shrimp

Ever since the seventeenth century, Louisianians have loved shrimp. At first, only those fortunate enough to live near rivers and seacoasts enjoyed it. When advances were made in refrigerated transportation in the early twentieth century, shrimp became more widely available. In our recipe they're dipped into a light beer batter. The yeast in the beer acts as a leavening agent. This results in a light-as-air, crispy fried coating on the outside and perfectly cooked, tender shrimp on the inside.

PREP: 15 minutes ★ **COOK:** 12 minutes
MAKES 6 first-course servings

$1/2$ cup all-purpose flour

$1/2$ cup beer

$1/2$ teaspoon salt

vegetable oil for frying

$1 1/2$ pounds medium shrimp, shelled and deveined

1. In small bowl, with wire whisk, mix flour, beer, and salt until smooth batter forms.

2. In 2-quart saucepan, heat 2 inches vegetable oil until temperature reaches 375°F on deep-fat thermometer.

3. Pat shrimp dry with paper towels. Dip 6 shrimp, one at a time, into batter then carefully lower into hot oil. Fry, turning once, until golden, about 1 minute. Using slotted spoon, transfer shrimp to paper towels to drain. Coat and fry remaining shrimp.

EACH SERVING: About 199 calories, 20g protein, 10g carbohydrate, 9g total fat (1g saturated), 140mg cholesterol, 331mg sodium.

Cooking on the Bayou

The hearty country cooking of the bayou began around 1755, when the French Acadians were expelled from settlements in Nova Scotia and headed south to Louisiana. When they first arrived there, they were called *Cadians*, then *Cagians*, and finally *Cajuns*. They were fishermen and wetland farmers who were determined to preserve their Gallic folkways but at the same time were eager to adapt to their new surroundings. These Cajuns combined their style of French country cooking with the local rice and available seasonings. Cajun cuisine was also influenced by Spanish one-pot dishes (jambalaya closely resembles paella) and the plentiful seafood found in the nearby Gulf waters. Out of this new style of cooking came jambalayas, etouffées, and gumbos galore.

The more sophisticated food from the elegant River Road plantations near the cities was called Creole, as were all New Orleans residents of European descent. Their elegant cuisine was a reflection of the Native American, West Indian Black, Italian, French, Spanish, and German populace.

Unlike the Cajuns, the Creoles used tomatoes as a base for many dishes and fewer spices. Butter and cream were employed to create luxurious, rich sauces based on classic French technique. In some ways, Cajun and Creole cooking were similar. They both took advantage of the abundance of fresh fish and seafood, meats, the various local vegetables, and the region's rice. And, of course, the "holy trinity" of chopped onions, celery, and green bell peppers appeared frequently in Cajun and Creole dishes. Over the years, the Creoles have created some memorable dishes: they turned local pecans into sumptuous pies and sugary pralines, stuffed local fish with spicy crab, fried up French beignets to be served with steaming cups of chickory coffee, and brought flaming ice-cream desserts to the table.

Today you'll find traditional and innovative Cajun and Creole food served up to create memorable "good cooking and good eating" in the small local country kitchens, high-society southern mansions, and elegant restaurants in New Orleans and other cities in bayou country.

Sausage and Shrimp Gumbo

Down in the Louisiana bayou, this thick stewlike dish is a perfect melting pot of ethnic influences. There's the classic French method for making the roux: a mixture of flour and pan drippings that's cooked to a rich mahogany color (and the real secret to a fine gumbo). The word *gumbo* comes from the African (*gombo*) for okra, which is often included in gumbos. The Choctaw Indians contributed their secret thickening ingredient, filé powder, which is made from sassafras leaves. The Caribbeans lent their unique way of combining seasonings. And the Spaniards added their love of rice to the pot, making gumbo the sublime dish it is to this day.

PREP: 20 minutes ★ **COOK:** 40 minutes
MAKES 6 main-dish servings

1 pound hot Italian-sausage links, pricked with fork

3 tablespoons vegetable oil

¼ cup all-purpose flour

2 stalks celery, chopped

1 green pepper, chopped

1 medium onion, chopped

1 can (14½ ounces) chicken broth or 1¾ cups Old-Fashioned Chicken Broth (page 45)

½ cup water

1 package (10 ounces) frozen whole okra

2 teaspoons hot pepper sauce

¼ teaspoon dried thyme

¼ teaspoon dried oregano

1 bay leaf

1 pound large shrimp, shelled and deveined

1 cup regular long-grain rice, cooked as label directs

1. Heat 5-quart Dutch oven over medium-high heat until hot. Add sausages; cook, turning frequently, until well browned, about 10 minutes. Transfer sausages to plate to cool slightly. Cut each sausage into 3 pieces.

2. Discard all but 1 tablespoon of the sausage drippings from Dutch oven. Add oil and heat over medium heat. With wooden spoon, gradually stir in flour and cook, stirring constantly, until flour mixture (roux) is brown (do not let burn). Add celery, green pepper, and onion; cook, stirring occasionally, until vegetables are tender, 8 to 10 minutes.

3. Return sausage to Dutch oven. Gradually stir in broth, water, okra, hot pepper sauce, thyme, oregano, and bay leaf; heat to boiling over high heat. Reduce heat; cover and simmer 15 minutes. Add shrimp; cook, uncovered, until shrimp are opaque throughout, about 2 minutes. Discard bay leaf. Place scoop of rice in large shallow soup bowls and top with gumbo.

EACH SERVING: About 491 calories, 28g protein, 37g carbohydrate, 25g total fat (7g saturated), 138mg cholesterol, 956mg sodium.

Sausage and Shrimp Gumbo ▶

Shrimp Wiggle

"Wiggle," which often refers to anything done in a hurry, is the perfect name for this quick dish. According to James Beard in *American Cookery:* "For many years this was in the repertoire of every coed with a chafing dish and every girl who had a beau to cook for." Recipes for shrimp wiggle appeared in charity cookbooks, in the 1935 book *The Pennsylvania Dutch and Their Cookery*, as well as in the first edition of *The Joy of Cooking*.

PREP: 15 minutes ★ **COOK:** 12 minutes
MAKES 4 main-dish servings

2 tablespoons butter or margarine

1 medium red pepper, finely chopped

4 ounces mushrooms, trimmed and sliced

1/2 cup finely chopped onion

1 small garlic clove, minced

1 pound large shrimp, shelled and deveined

2 tablespoons all-purpose flour

1/2 teaspoon paprika

1 bottle (8 ounces) clam broth

1/4 cup heavy or whipping cream

1 cup frozen peas, thawed

1/2 teaspoon salt

1/8 teaspoon ground black pepper

4 slices whole-wheat or white bread, toasted,
    each cut in half on diagonal

1. In nonstick 12-inch skillet, melt 1 tablespoon butter over medium-high heat. Add red pepper, mushrooms, onion, and garlic; cook, stirring, until vegetables are tender, about 5 minutes. With slotted spoon, transfer vegetable mixture to plate.

2. Add shrimp to skillet; cook, stirring, until shrimp are opaque throughout, 2 to 3 minutes. Transfer to vegetables on plate.

3. Melt remaining 1 tablespoon butter. Stir in flour and paprika until blended. Whisk in clam broth and cream; cook 1 minute. Stir in shrimp, vegetables, peas, salt, and pepper; heat through. Serve with toast points.

EACH SERVING: About 334 calories, 25g protein, 27g carbohydrate, 14g total fat (8g saturated), 176mg cholesterol, 811mg sodium.

California Cioppino

Thanks to the Italian immigrants who settled around San Francisco Bay, this delicious tomato-based seafood dish is now a California tradition. *Cioppino*, which means "fish stew," is always tomato-based, but the seafood it contains depends upon what is the freshest catch of that day. If you can find Dungeness crab in your fish market, cut up one or two cooked crabs (still in the shell) into serving-size pieces and throw them into the pot in place of the shrimp.

PREP: 45 minutes ★ **COOK:** 35 minutes
MAKES 8 main-dish servings

1/3 cup olive oil

2 medium onions, chopped

1 yellow pepper, coarsely chopped

3 garlic cloves, finely chopped

3 strips (3" by 1/2" each) lemon peel

1 can (28 ounces) diced tomatoes

1 bottle (8 ounces) clam broth

1 cup dry white wine

1 cup water

3/4 teaspoon salt

pinch crushed red pepper

16 littleneck or cherrystone clams, scrubbed

24 small mussels, scrubbed and debearded

1 pound striped bass or red snapper fillets, cut into
    2-inch pieces

1/2 pound medium shrimp, shelled and deveined

1/2 pound sea scallops, halved or quartered if large

1/2 cup chopped fresh parsley

2 tablespoons chopped fresh basil

1. In nonreactive 6-quart Dutch oven, heat oil over medium heat. Add onions, yellow pepper, garlic, and lemon peel. Cook, stirring, until onions are tender, about 5 minutes.

2. Increase heat to high; stir in tomatoes, clam broth, wine, water, salt, and crushed red pepper; heat to boiling. Reduce heat; cover and simmer 10 minutes. Reheat to boiling. Add clams; cover and cook 2 minutes. Stir in mussels, bass, shrimp, scallops, and parsley; cover and simmer until fish is just opaque throughout and shellfish opens, 4 to 5 minutes. Discard any clams or mussels that do not open. Remove from heat and stir in basil.

EACH SERVING: About 282 calories, 29g protein, 12g carbohydrate, 13g total fat (2g saturated), 101mg cholesterol, 669mg sodium.

Seafood Newburg

Lobster Newburg was first served at Delmonico's restaurant in New York City in 1876. As the tale goes, Charles Delmonico named it Lobster à la Wenberg in honor of one of his best customers, Ben Wenberg, a West Indies sea captain. Later when the two men quarreled, Charles changed the name by reversing the first three letters to make it Newberg (later the spelling was changed to Newburg). In this recipe, we've added shrimp and scallops, making it Seafood Newburg.

PREP: 20 minutes ★ **COOK:** 15 minutes
MAKES 8 main-dish servings

1 tablespoon butter or margarine

¼ cup finely chopped shallots

1 pound medium shrimp, shelled and deveined

½ pound sea scallops, halved if large

½ teaspoon salt

⅛ teaspoon ground black pepper

¼ cup dry sherry

2 teaspoons tomato paste

1½ cups heavy or whipping cream

½ cup clam broth

½ teaspoon paprika

2 large egg yolks

¾ pound cooked lobster meat, cut into chunks *

1 tablespoon chopped fresh parsley

hot cooked rice

1. In large skillet, melt butter over medium-high heat. Add shallots; cook until tender, about 2 minutes. Stir in shrimp, scallops, ¼ teaspoon salt, and pepper. Cook, stirring, until seafood just begins to color but is not cooked through, 2 to 3 minutes. With slotted spoon, transfer seafood to plate; cover and keep warm.

2. Stir sherry and tomato paste into skillet; heat to boiling. Cook until reduced by half. Stir in 1 cup cream, clam broth, paprika, and remaining ¼ teaspoon salt. Reduce heat to medium; cook 3 minutes.

3. In small bowl, beat egg yolks and remaining ½ cup cream until blended. Add to skillet along with reserved seafood and lobster. Bring to a simmer; simmer 1 minute (do not boil). Stir in parsley. Serve with rice.

*If cooking whole lobsters for meat, about two 1½-pound whole lobsters will yield ¾ pound cooked meat.

EACH SERVING: About 304 calories, 25g protein, 4g carbohydrate, 20g total fat (12g saturated), 228mg cholesterol, 498mg sodium.

Chapter 8

Pasta, Grains & Beans

Pastes, the word for "pasta" in the earliest American cookbooks, was slow to catch on. The English brought over recipes for macaroni, but it wasn't until Thomas Jefferson began serving macaroni pie at White House linners that pasta became familiar and "a food for all classes." One of our earliest pasta factories was built in 1848 in Brooklyn, New York. Italian immigrants influenced pasta's popularity. At first they made fresh pasta from family recipes, then later used imported dried pasta from southern Italy that was made from hard durum wheat. During World War I, pasta imports were halted, which gave rise to numerous pasta factories. Egg noodles were also embraced by the nation thanks to the delicious egg-noodle dishes made by French, Hungarian, and German immigrants.

When the colonists landed in the New World, the Native Americans introduced them to corn and beans, which became staples in their diet. The Pilgrims used corn flour for their bread and porridge, since their wheat and barley crops failed. In fact, corn remained the most popular grain until well into the nineteenth century when wheat became a major crop.

Rice also influenced America's food history. Although it was not popular in England, the colonists grew it as early as 1622. Toward the end of that century, the rice industry began in Charleston, South Carolina. As one story goes, in 1685, Captain John Thurber was blown off course and landed in Charleston. He gave some Madagascar rice to a Charlestonian, who planted it in his garden. According to another story, a Dutch sea captain brought rice to Charleston in 1694. However it happened, rice production flourished until the American Revolution. When the British captured the highly prized city, they sent its entire rice crop back to England. Later, in 1787, Thomas Jefferson smuggled some rice out of Italy in his pockets (risking the death penalty if caught) and also brought rice from Africa. Eventually favorable trade was established, and rice became readily available throughout the states.

◄ *Chicken-Seafood Paella*

Tomato-Sausage Lasagna

Cities, such as New York, Philadelphia, and San Francisco, each have a Little Italy: a close-knit Italian community that was formed at the turn of the century. Back then the streets were crammed with the sights, smells, and sounds of Italian culture and cuisine. The grocers sold pasta and imported cheeses. The butchers sold meats that were seasoned with Italian herbs and rolled and stuffed the way it was done back home. Nearby there were small restaurants similar to the ones in the old country, where one could enjoy an authentic supper, complete with homemade pasta, meat, and cheese dishes. In these communities, there was always a grocer or a butcher willing to explain how to prepare red sauce or lasagna. By the end of World War II, American cooks were layering, saucing, and serving this delectable creation on a regular basis. Our recipe is much like the traditional lasagnas that are still served in southern Italy.

PREP: 1 hour ★ **BAKE:** 45 minutes
MAKES 10 main-dish servings

---

8 ounces hot Italian-sausage links, casings removed

8 ounces ground beef chuck

1 medium onion, chopped

1 can (28 ounces) plum tomatoes

2 tablespoons tomato paste

1¼ teaspoons salt

12 lasagna noodles (10 ounces)

1 container (15 ounces) part-skim ricotta cheese

1 large egg

¼ cup chopped fresh parsley

⅛ teaspoon coarsely ground black pepper

8 ounces part-skim mozzarella cheese, shredded (2 cups)

1. Prepare meat sauce: In 4-quart saucepan, cook sausage, ground beef, and onion over high heat, breaking up sausage and meat with side of spoon, until meat is well browned, about 6 minutes. Discard fat. Add tomatoes with their juice, tomato paste, and 1 teaspoon salt. Heat to boiling, breaking up tomatoes with side of spoon. Reduce heat; cover and simmer, stirring occasionally, 30 minutes.

2. Meanwhile, in large saucepot, cook lasagna noodles as label directs but do not add salt to water. Drain and rinse with cold running water. Return noodles to saucepot with enough *cold water* to cover.

3. Preheat oven to 375°F. In medium bowl, stir ricotta, egg, parsley, remaining ¼ teaspoon salt, and pepper until well combined.

4. Drain noodles on clean kitchen towels. In 13" by 9" baking dish, arrange 6 lasagna noodles, overlapping to fit. Spread with all of ricotta mixture and sprinkle with half of mozzarella; top with half of meat sauce. Cover with remaining 6 noodles and spread with remaining meat sauce. Sprinkle with remaining mozzarella.

5. Cover lasagna with foil and bake 30 minutes. Remove foil; bake until sauce is bubbling and top has lightly browned, about 15 minutes longer. Let stand 15 minutes for easier serving.

EACH SERVING: About 363 calories, 23g protein, 31g carbohydrate, 16g total fat (7g saturated), 74mg cholesterol, 780mg sodium.

Meatballs and Spaghetti

In the nineteenth century, Italian immigrants often sat down to dinners that included spaghetti. To their American neighbors, spaghetti was more exotic than the already familiar egg noodles and macaroni, so it piqued their interest. Fannie Farmer advised her readers in 1896: "Spaghetti may be cooked in any way that macaroni is cooked, but is usually served with tomato sauce. It is cooked in long strips rather than broken in pieces; to accomplish this, hold quantity to be cooked in the hand, and dip ends in boiling salted water; as spaghetti softens it will bend, and may be coiled under water." By the end of World War II, the growing number of Italian communities helped to Americanize spaghetti dinners, which were inexpensive and robust. Frequently the spaghetti arrived heaped on a plate, crowned with meatballs and a fragrant tomato sauce.

PREP: 20 minutes ★ **COOK:** 1 hour
MAKES 6 main-dish servings

Marinara Sauce (opposite)

1½ **pounds ground meat for meat loaf (beef, pork, and/or veal) or ground beef chuck**

1 **cup fresh bread crumbs (about 2 slices bread)**

1 **large egg**

¼ **cup freshly grated Pecorino Romano or Parmesan cheese**

¼ **cup chopped fresh parsley**

1 **garlic clove, finely chopped**

1 **teaspoon salt**

¼ **teaspoon ground black pepper**

2 **teaspoons olive oil**

1 **package (16 ounces) spaghetti**

1. Prepare Marinara Sauce.

2. Meanwhile, prepare meatballs: In large bowl, combine ground meat, bread crumbs, egg, Pecorino, parsley, garlic, salt, and pepper until blended but not overmixed. Shape into twelve 2-inch meatballs, handling meat as little as possible.

3. In nonstick 12-inch skillet, heat oil over medium heat until hot. Add meatballs and cook, turning gently, until browned and just cooked through, about 20 minutes. Stir sauce into meatballs and heat to boiling, stirring to loosen browned bits from bottom of skillet. Reduce heat and simmer 20 minutes.

4. Meanwhile, in large saucepot, cook pasta as label directs. Drain. In serving bowl, gently toss pasta with meatballs and sauce.

EACH SERVING: About 692 calories, 34g protein, 69g carbohydrate, 30g total fat (10g saturated), 129mg cholesterol, 1,077mg sodium.

Marinara Sauce

In nonreactive 3-quart saucepan, heat *2 tablespoons olive oil* over medium heat. Add *1 onion, chopped*, and *1 garlic clove*, finely chopped; cook, stirring, until onion is tender, about 5 minutes.

Stir in *1 can (28 ounces) plum tomatoes with their juice, 2 tablespoons tomato paste, 2 tablespoons chopped fresh basil or parsley*, and *½ teaspoon salt*. Heat to boiling, breaking up tomatoes with side of spoon. Reduce heat; partially cover and simmer, stirring occasionally, until sauce has thickened slightly, about 20 minutes. Makes 3½ cups.

They Called It Macaroni

The word *macaroni* comes from the Italian word *maccheroni*, which means "mixture of elements." It's often used to refer to any type of pasta and appeared in print as early as the sixteenth century.

Thomas Jefferson returned from Europe with a recipe for homemade noodles which, according to his notes, was to be "served like macaroni." His pasta dough was very similar to what we use today: "...two eggs beaten with a wine glass of milk, a teaspoon of salt, and enough hard flour to make a smooth, firm dough..." His writings even included drawings and a detailed description of a pasta machine that shaped the dough into tubes. Following a visit to a cheese dairy, Jefferson brought back notes on cheese making, and he had Parmesan shipped to Virginia from Italy. Years before the influx of Italian immigrants, Jefferson introduced his countrymen to macaroni and cheese, which is now an American tradition.

Mom's Mac 'n' Cheese

Since the early nineteenth century, cookbooks have offered *receipts* (recipes) for baked macaroni layered with butter and cheese (usually Parmesan). It is believed that one of the first sauced macaroni dishes was introduced by Sarah Rutledge in her recipe To Dress Macaroni à la Sauce Blanche in *The Carolina Housewife* in 1847: "...put in first, a layer of macaroni, then one of grated [Parmesan] cheese, then some sauce, and so on until the dish is filled; the last layer must be of cheese and sauce...Ten minutes will bake it in a quick oven." The dish didn't grow in popularity until around 1914, when the importation of Italian pasta was halted due to World War I. It was then that pasta production began here on a large scale. During the depression, everyone ate macaroni and cheese because it was so affordable and delicious. By the 1950s, the macaroni and cheese we have come to love had become an American tradition in school cafeterias and on supper tables nationwide.

PREP: 45 minutes ★ **BAKE:** 20 minutes
MAKES 4 main-dish servings

1 package (8 ounces) elbow macaroni
¾ cup fresh bread crumbs (about 1½ slices bread)
4 tablespoons butter or margarine, melted
1 small onion, finely chopped
1 tablespoon all-purpose flour
¼ teaspoon dry mustard
1 teaspoon salt
⅛ teaspoon ground black pepper
1½ cups milk
8 ounces Cheddar cheese, shredded (2 cups)

1. In 3-quart saucepan, cook macaroni as label directs. Drain well.

2. Preheat oven to 350°F. Grease 9-inch square baking dish or casserole. In small bowl, toss bread crumbs and melted butter until moistened. Set aside.

3. In saucepan, melt remaining 2 tablespoons butter over medium heat. Add onion and cook until tender, about 5 minutes. Add flour, mustard, salt, and pepper; stir until blended. Stir in milk; cook, stirring, until thickened. Remove from heat; stir in cheese.

4. Spoon macaroni into prepared baking dish. Pour cheese sauce over macaroni. Sprinkle crumb mixture over top. Bake until bubbly and top is golden, about 20 minutes. Let stand 15 minutes for easier serving.

EACH SERVING: About 647 calories, 26protein, 55g carbohydrate, 36g total fat (21g saturated), 103mg cholesterol, 1,146mg sodium.

Buttered Noodles

The word *noodle,* which comes from the German *nudel,* first appeared in print in America in 1779. German immigrants, especially those who settled in Lancaster County, Pennsylvania, introduced egg noodles to the New World. These homemade noodles were always rich, tender, and delicious. The recipe was simple: three large eggs were worked into a couple cups of flour with a little salt to make a stiff dough. The dough was rolled out, cut into thin strips, and boiled. Sometimes cooks dropped the noodles into chicken stock (after the chicken was removed) and served the noodles along with the bird, covered with a rich, creamy white sauce. Noodle pudding was another favorite in the mid-nineteenth century. Cooks in the South (and elsewhere) soaked cooked noodles in warm sweetened cream, which was often flavored with a little lemon zest. They mixed the plump noodles with freshly beaten eggs, baked the dish just until it set up, and served the warm pudding with fruit sauce. Today noodles are simple to buy—dried or fresh—and make a great accompaniment to meat when tossed with butter and fresh herbs.

PREP: 10 minutes ★ **COOK:** 25 minutes
MAKES 6 accompaniment servings

12 ounces wide egg noodles

¼ cup chopped fresh parsley

2 tablespoons butter or margarine, cut into pieces

1 teaspoon poppy seeds

½ teaspoon salt

¼ teaspoon coarsely ground black pepper

1. In large saucepot, cook noodles as label directs. Drain.

2. In same saucepot, combine parsley, butter, poppy seeds, salt, and pepper, stirring until butter has melted. Return cooked noodles to saucepot; toss to coat well with parsley mixture.

EACH SERVING: About 251 calories, 8g protein, 41g carbohydrate, 6g total fat (3g saturated), 64mg cholesterol, 293mg sodium.

Fettuccine Alfredo

Alfredo Di Lelio, of Alfredo's restaurant in Rome, Italy, supposedly created this dish in 1914 to restore his wife's appetite after she gave birth to their son. His original creation was made with very rich butter (made by Alfredo himself) and the best *Parmigiano* (but no cream). In 1927, Hollywood actors Douglas Fairbanks and Mary Pickford dined at Alfredo's while on their honeymoon. Before leaving Rome, they presented the restaurateur with a gold-plated spoon inscribed: *"To Alfredo the King of the Noodles July 1927."* It was a headline event, and the international press quickly spread the fame of Alfredo's noodle dish. Within a year, a recipe for the dish appeared in the *Rector Cookbook* here in the U.S. Today most recipes for this sumptuous dish contain a combination of heavy cream and butter.

PREP: 10 minutes ★ **COOK:** 25 minutes
MAKES 6 accompaniment servings

1 package (16 ounces) fresh fettuccine

1½ cups heavy or whipping cream

1 tablespoon butter or margarine

½ teaspoon salt

¼ teaspoon coarsely ground black pepper

¾ cup freshly grated Parmesan cheese

chopped fresh parsley

1. In large saucepot, cook pasta as label directs. Drain.

2. Meanwhile, in 2-quart saucepan, combine cream, butter, salt, and pepper; heat to boiling over medium-high heat. Boil until sauce has thickened slightly, 2 to 3 minutes. In serving bowl, toss pasta with cream sauce and Parmesan. Sprinkle with parsley.

EACH SERVING: About 558 calories, 16g protein, 59g carbohydrate, 29g total fat (17g saturated), 96mg cholesterol, 532mg sodium.

Chicken-Seafood Paella

(pictured on page 160)

Before Columbus's discovery of the New World, Spaniards didn't have tomatoes, and so neither did their paellas. The Spaniards were the first to discover the rich bounty of America and were among the earliest settlers in the Southwest and along Louisiana's Gulf Coast. Their paellas, filled with tomatoes, rice, and spices, influenced the ingredients the Cajuns used in their jambalayas and gumbos during the eighteenth century. Our paella has many of the ingredients of those early gumbo pots: rice, chicken, seafood, tomatoes, and sausage.

PREP: 30 minutes ★ **COOK:** 1 hour
MAKES 8 main-dish servings

- 1 tablespoon olive oil
- 1½ pounds skinless, boneless chicken thighs, cut into 2-inch pieces
- 2 chorizo sausages (3 ounces each)
- 1 medium onion, finely chopped
- 1 red pepper, finely chopped
- 2 garlic cloves, finely chopped
- ¼ teaspoon ground red pepper (cayenne)
- ½ cup canned tomatoes in puree
- ½ cup dry white wine
- 2 cups medium-grain rice
- 4 ounces green beans, cut into 1-inch pieces
- 2½ cups water
- 1 can (14½ ounces) chicken broth or 1¾ cups Old-Fashioned Chicken Broth (page 45)
- 1½ teaspoons salt
- ¼ teaspoon loosely packed saffron threads, crumbled
- ⅛ teaspoon dried thyme
- ½ bay leaf
- 1 pound mussels, scrubbed and debearded
- 12 ounces medium shrimp, shelled and deveined
- ¼ cup chopped fresh parsley
- lemon wedges

1. In deep nonreactive 12-inch skillet, heat oil over medium-high heat until very hot. Add chicken and chorizo; cook until browned, about 10 minutes. With slotted spoon, transfer chicken and chorizo to bowl.

2. Reduce heat to medium. Add onion and red pepper to skillet; cook, stirring frequently, until onion is tender, about 5 minutes. Stir in garlic and ground red pepper; cook 30 seconds. Add tomatoes with their puree and wine; cook, breaking up tomatoes with side of spoon, until liquid has evaporated.

3. Stir rice, green beans, water, broth, salt, saffron, thyme, and bay leaf into skillet. Thinly slice chorizo; return chorizo and chicken to skillet. Heat to boiling over high heat. Reduce heat; cover and simmer 20 minutes.

4. Tuck mussels into paella; cover and cook 3 minutes. Tuck shrimp into paella; cover and cook just until mussels have opened and shrimp are opaque throughout, about 3 minutes longer. Remove from heat and let stand 5 minutes. Discard bay leaf and any mussels that have not opened. Sprinkle paella with parsley and serve with lemon wedges.

EACH SERVING: About 467 calories, 35g protein, 45g carbohydrate, 15g total fat (4g saturated), 146mg cholesterol, 1,110mg sodium.

Jambalaya

According to the Acadian dictionary, the word *jamba-laya* comes from the French word *jambon* (ham), the African word *ya* (rice), and the influence of the Acadian language, where things are often described as *à la*. Our jambalaya has it all, including Andouille sausage and plenty of rice to soak up all the flavors. All jambalayas are first cooked on top of the stove. Some cooks finish the cooking on the stove; while others transfer the jambalaya to the oven, where it bakes until the rice is tender, yet still a bit firm.

PREP: 20 minutes plus cooling ★ **COOK:** 55 minutes
MAKES 6 main-dish servings

8 ounces Andouille or Polish sausage

1 medium onion, finely chopped

1 green pepper, chopped

1 stalk celery, chopped

1 garlic clove, finely chopped

1/8 teaspoon ground red pepper (cayenne)

1 1/2 cups regular long-grain rice

1 can (14 1/2 ounces) chicken broth or 1 3/4 cups
   Old-Fashioned Chicken Broth (page 45)

1 1/4 cups water

1/4 teaspoon salt

1/8 teaspoon dried thyme

1 can (14 to 16 ounces) tomatoes, drained and chopped

1 pound medium shrimp, shelled and deveined

2 green onions, thinly sliced

hot pepper sauce (optional)

1. In nonreactive 5-quart Dutch oven, cook sausage over medium heat until browned, about 10 minutes. With slotted spoon, transfer sausage to paper towels to drain. When cool enough to handle, cut sausage into 1/2-inch-thick pieces.

2. To drippings in Dutch oven, add onion, green pepper, and celery; cook until tender, about 10 minutes. Stir in garlic and ground red pepper; cook 30 seconds. Add rice and cook, stirring, 1 minute. Stir in sausage, broth, water, salt, and thyme; heat to boiling over high heat. Reduce heat; cover and simmer 15 minutes.

3. Stir in tomatoes; cover and cook 5 minutes. Stir in shrimp; cover and cook until shrimp are opaque throughout, about 5 minutes longer. Transfer jambalaya to serving bowl and sprinkle with green onions. Serve with hot pepper sauce, if you like.

EACH SERVING: About 405 calories, 23g protein, 45g carbohydrate, 14g total fat (5g saturated), 122mg cholesterol, 873mg sodium.

Spanish Rice

The Spaniards governed New Orleans during the last half of the eighteenth century. During that time, their style of cooking influenced how food was prepared along the bayou. Tomatoes, rice, chopped celery, green peppers, and onions were often used. The Cajuns adapted Spanish food to suit their taste, spicing things up with a mix of cayenne and black and white peppers. By the 1930s, Spanish rice was a fairly common dish. During the meatless years of World War II, it appeared on dinner tables as the main dish.

PREP: 15 minutes ★ **BAKE:** 35 minutes
MAKES 6 accompaniment servings

4 slices bacon

1 cup chopped onion

1/2 cup chopped green pepper

1/2 cup chopped celery

1 can (14 to 16 ounces) tomatoes

1 can (8 ounces) tomato sauce

2 teaspoons sugar

1/2 teaspoon salt

1 1/3 cups regular long-grain rice

1. Preheat oven to 350°F. Grease 1 1/2-quart casserole. In 12-inch skillet, cook bacon over medium heat until browned. With slotted spoon, transfer bacon to paper towels to drain; crumble.

2. Pour off all but 2 tablespoons drippings from pan. Add onion, green pepper, and celery; cook, stirring often, until tender, about 5 minutes.

3. Drain tomatoes into measuring cup. Add enough *water* to tomato liquid to equal 1 3/4 cups. Coarsely chop tomatoes. Add tomatoes and thin tomato liquid, tomato sauce, sugar, and salt to skillet; heat to boiling. Remove from heat and stir in rice.

4. Pour rice mixture into casserole. Cover and bake until rice is tender and liquid has been absorbed, about 35 minutes. Sprinkle with crumbled bacon.

EACH SERVING: About 256 calories, 6g protein, 43g carbohydrate, 7g total fat (2g saturated), 7mg cholesterol, 638mg sodium.

Chicken Pilau

Rice became popular in the late seventeenth century in South Carolina and Louisiana. Pilau (also plaw, pilaw, pilaf, and pilaff) comes from the Turkish and Persian *pilāw*. Pilaus are steamed rice stews that are made with what's on hand: vegetables and chicken one day (as in our recipe) and pork, seafood, or ham another. Recipe #134 in *Mrs. Hill's Southern Practical Cookery and Receipt Book* is for Rice Pillau that begins with "carve the fowl into joints, as for frying" and she advises "This dish should only be moist. No gravy is required; make it rich with butter."

PREP: 20 minutes ★ **COOK:** 1 hour 5 minutes
MAKES 6 main-dish servings

1 tablespoon vegetable oil

4 small bone-in chicken breast halves (about 2 pounds), skin removed

3 slices bacon, finely chopped

1 large onion (12 ounces), thinly sliced

1 cup regular long-grain rice

1 can (14½ ounces) chicken broth or 1¾ cups Old-Fashioned Chicken Broth (page 45)

½ cup water

½ teaspoon salt

¼ teaspoon coarsely ground black pepper

½ cup loosely packed fresh parsley leaves, chopped

1. In nonstick 12-inch skillet, heat oil over medium-high heat until hot. Add chicken breasts and cook, turning once, until golden, about 6 minutes. Transfer chicken to plate. Reduce heat to medium. Add bacon and cook, stirring frequently, until browned, about 6 minutes. With slotted spoon, transfer bacon to paper towel to drain.

2. Discard all but 1 tablespoon bacon drippings from skillet; return bacon to skillet. Add onion and cook, stirring occasionally, until tender and lightly browned, about 20 minutes. Add rice and stir until evenly coated. Stir in broth, water, salt, and pepper. Return chicken breasts to skillet; heat to boiling over medium-high heat. Reduce heat to medium-low; cover and cook until juices run clear when chicken is pierced with tip of knife and rice is tender, 25 to 30 minutes. Remove from heat.

3. With tongs, transfer chicken to plate. When cool enough to handle, with fingers, tear chicken into shreds.

4. Return chicken to skillet and stir until well combined; heat through. Sprinkle with parsley.

EACH SERVING: About 315 calories, 31g protein, 27g carbohydrate, 8g total fat (12g saturated), 70mg cholesterol, 525mg sodium.

Chinatown Fried Rice

Before the Gold Rush of 1849, there were only a few Chinese in California. But they were quickly followed by thousands more who came to make their fortunes and to help build the transcontinental railroad. In San Francisco many were hired as housemen in middle-class homes. Although they did not prepare Asian-style meals, their Chinese cooking techniques were often incorporated into everyday foods. Their art of using bits and pieces of food in dishes, such as this fried rice, inspired the creation of many others that are still appreciated.

PREP: 20 minutes ★ **COOK:** 20 minutes
MAKES 4 main-dish servings

3 teaspoons vegetable oil

2 large eggs, lightly beaten

8 ounces mushrooms, trimmed and thinly sliced

1 red pepper, finely chopped

1 tablespoon grated, peeled fresh ginger

2 garlic cloves, finely chopped

1½ cups medium-grain white rice, cooked as label directs and cooled

1 cup frozen peas, thawed

2 green onions, thinly sliced

4 ounces sliced cooked ham, cut into 1" by ¼" strips

½ cup canned chicken broth or Old-Fashioned Chicken Broth (page 45)

2 tablespoons soy sauce

1 teaspoon Asian sesame oil

½ cup loosely packed fresh cilantro leaves, chopped (optional)

1. In nonstick 12-inch skillet, heat 1 teaspoon vegetable oil over medium heat until hot. Add eggs and cook, stirring with wooden spoon, until eggs are scrambled, about 2 minutes. Transfer eggs to plate; set aside.

2. In same skillet, heat remaining 2 teaspoons vegetable oil over medium-high heat. Add mushrooms and red pepper; cook, stirring occasionally, until tender and lightly golden, about 10 minutes. Add ginger and garlic; cook, stirring, 1 minute. Add rice, peas, green onions, ham, broth, soy sauce, sesame oil, and scrambled egg. Cook, stirring and fluffing rice with fork, until heated through, about 3 minutes. Toss with cilantro, if desired.

EACH SERVING: About 470 calories, 18g protein, 73g carbohydrate, 11g total fat (3g saturated), 123mg cholesterol, 1,055mg sodium.

Buffet Rice Ring

During the 1960s and early '70s, Julia Child (*The French Chef*) and Graham Kerr (*The Galloping Gourmet*) were welcomed into homes across America, where they taught and enthralled viewers through their television shows. As a result, entertaining at home became more planned, a chance to show off one's culinary skills. Making food look good enough to wow guests was important. This rice ring is a typical made-for-company presentation—simple yet spectacular.

PREP: 15 minutes ★ **COOK:** 25 minutes
MAKES 12 accompaniment servings

2 cups regular long-grain rice

8 ounces carrots (about 3 medium), peeled and finely chopped

½ teaspoon salt

1 teaspoon plus 3 tablespoons butter or margarine

1 red pepper, finely chopped

1 cup frozen peas, thawed

2 tablespoons chopped fresh parsley

1. Cook rice according to package directions.

2. Meanwhile, butter 10- or 12-cup ring mold. In 2-quart saucepan, heat *6 cups water* to boiling over high heat. Add carrots and salt; cook until tender, about 4 minutes. Drain well.

3. In small skillet, melt 1 teaspoon butter over medium heat. Add red pepper and cook until tender, about 5 minutes. Stir in carrots and peas; cook just until vegetables are heated through.

4. In large bowl, toss hot cooked rice, vegetable mixture, parsley, and remaining 3 tablespoons butter until butter has melted and mixture is well combined. Lightly pack mixture into mold; let stand 1 minute.

5. Run thin knife around edge to loosen; invert flat plate on top of mold. Holding the mold and plate together, quickly invert rice ring onto plate. Lift off mold.

EACH SERVING: About 162 calories, 3g protein, 28g carbohydrate, 4g total fat (2g saturated), 9mg cholesterol, 153mg sodium.

Wild Rice with Mushrooms

Wild rice is not a rice at all but the grain of a self-propagating tall grass that grows in the lakes and rivers of the northern Great Lakes region. The Native Americans called it *manomin* or *Meneninee,* which means seed. The French called it crazy oats, and the Americans named it wild rice. Today most wild rice is cultivated in man-made paddies in Minnesota and California. But true wild rice still flourishes in Minnesota and Canada.

PREP: 5 minutes ★ **COOK:** I hour
MAKES 6 accompaniment servings

I cup wild rice

I cup water

I cup canned chicken broth or Old-Fashioned Chicken Broth (page 45)

¼ teaspoon salt

2 tablespoons butter or margarine

I tablespoon finely chopped shallots

8 ounces mushrooms, trimmed and sliced

2 tablespoons chopped fresh parsley

I. Rinse wild rice; drain. In 2-quart saucepan, combine wild rice, water, broth, and salt; heat to boiling over high heat. Reduce heat; cover and simmer until wild rice is tender and some grains have popped, 45 to 60 minutes. Drain if necessary; keep warm.

2. Meanwhile, in 10-inch skillet, melt butter over medium-high heat. Add shallots and cook until tender, about 2 minutes. Add mushrooms; cook, stirring occasionally, until mushrooms are tender and liquid has evaporated, about 5 minutes. Stir mushroom mixture and parsley into wild rice.

EACH SERVING: About 145 calories, 5g protein, 22g carbohydrate, 5g total fat (3g saturated), 10mg cholesterol, 305mg sodium.

Puffy Cheesy Grits

The pioneers were introduced to hominy—hulled corn—by the Native Americans. To make hominy the hull was removed by soaking the corn in a solution of lye that was made from wood ashes. Then they either served it as hominy or ground it into grits. This beloved dish became a breakfast tradition throughout the South, where it was served with a pat of melting butter or a spoonful of red-eye gravy (made by adding coffee to the skillet a ham steak was fried in). Grits were so popular that Sarah Rutledge gave a recipe for grits bread in her 1847 cookbook *The Carolina Housewife.* Southerners have perfected grits by baking them with plenty of cheese until they're hot and puffy, making this a dish to be enjoyed by all—whether you grew up eating grits or not.

PREP: 20 minutes ★ **BAKE:** 45 minutes
MAKES 8 main-dish servings

3½ cups milk

2 cups water

2 tablespoons butter or margarine

I teaspoon salt

I¼ cups quick hominy grits

8 ounces Cheddar cheese, shredded (2 cups)

5 large eggs

I teaspoon hot pepper sauce

¼ teaspoon ground black pepper

I. Preheat oven to 325°F. Lightly grease shallow 2½-quart casserole.

2. In 3-quart saucepan, combine 1½ cups milk, water, butter, and salt; heat to boiling over medium-high heat. With wire whisk, gradually stir in grits, constantly beating to prevent lumps. Reduce heat; cover and cook, stirring occasionally with a wooden spoon, 5 minutes (grits will be very stiff). Remove from heat and stir in Cheddar cheese.

3. In large bowl, with wire whisk, mix eggs, remaining 2 cups milk, hot pepper sauce, and black pepper until blended. Gradually stir grits mixture into egg mixture until well combined.

4. Pour grits mixture into prepared casserole. Bake until knife inserted in center comes out clean, about 45 minutes.

EACH SERVING: About 338 calories, 16g protein, 24g carbohydrate, 20g total fat (11g saturated), 185mg cholesterol, 604mg sodium.

Creole Red Beans and Rice

Red beans were indigenous to the New World. It is believed that the Spaniards took them to Spain, then eventually brought them back to America and encouraged the locals to try the kidney-shaped red beans (*frijoles colorados* or *habichuelas*). This beans-and-rice dish was created by African-American cooks who called it "red and white." It was known as a Monday dish, as the ham bone left over from Sunday's dinner was used to flavor it. The beans, rice, and ham bone were put into a heavy iron pot and left to slowly simmer until the flavors blended and the beans were tasty and tender. The locals still debate which are the proper ingredients and how they should be put together for this dish. Many Southerners prefer the smaller south Louisiana red bean (with its milder flavor) combined with pickled pork (a seasoning made from pork that has marinated in a flavorful brine). Our recipe uses separate pots for the rice and beans, as is favored by many people along the bayou.

PREP: 15 minutes plus overnight to soak beans
COOK: 2 hours 30 minutes ★ **MAKES** 6 main-dish servings

1 package (16 ounces) dry red kidney beans
2 large smoked ham hocks (about 1½ pounds)
1 large onion (12 ounces), chopped
2 large stalks celery with leaves, finely chopped
½ green pepper, finely chopped
4 large garlic cloves, finely chopped
1 bay leaf
½ teaspoon dried thyme
½ teaspoon dried oregano
¼ teaspoon crushed red pepper
6 cups water
¼ teaspoon salt
1 cup regular long-grain rice, cooked as label directs
sliced scallions
hot pepper sauce

1. In large bowl, place beans with enough *water* to cover by 2 inches. Soak overnight.

2. Drain and rinse beans. Place beans in 5-quart Dutch oven. Add ham hocks, onion, celery, green pepper, garlic, bay leaf, thyme, oregano, crushed red pepper, and water; heat to boiling. Reduce heat; partially cover and simmer, stirring occasionally, until beans are tender and creamy, 2 to 2½ hours.

3. With slotted spoon, transfer ham hocks to plate; refrigerate until cool enough to handle. Remove any meat from hocks and chop. Stir meat and salt into beans and heat through.

4. To serve, spoon hot rice into soup bowls and top with bean mixture. Sprinkle with scallions. Serve hot pepper sauce on the side.

EACH SERVING: About 418 calories, 23g protein, 78g carbohydrate, 2g total fat (0g saturated), 4mg cholesterol, 897mg sodium.

Frijoles (Spanish Beans) with Cheese

Boil one pint of pink beans in plenty of cold water. As water boils away, add more (hot) water until beans are very tender. Season to taste with salt and red pepper. Put in frying pan a heaping tablespoon of lard and butter (half of each). When the beans are very hot in the pot, put in one small onion and mash them a little with a spoon, then put them into the boiling grease. Stir well, and allow to brown slightly. Ten minutes before taking from the frying pan, add seven tablespoons of grated American cheese. Serve with slices of hot buttered toast (thin) and sliced cucumbers with French dressing.

—Good Housekeeping Everyday Cook Book, 1903

Boston Baked Beans

For the Puritans, the Sabbath lasted from sundown on Saturday until sundown on Sunday: twenty-four hours when no cooking was permitted. Baked beans was the perfect solution. They were cooked on Saturday morning and scooped up for dinner, then kept warm overnight in the fireplace. Sunday breakfast was simple: more baked beans, codfish cakes, and Boston brown bread. When housewives were too busy to bake beans, they entrusted the task to the local baker. He would pick up the family bean pot on Saturday morning and take it to a community oven, which was frequently located in the basement of a nearby tavern. He would then return the bubbling pot of baked beans that evening, often accompanied by a loaf of freshly steamed Boston brown bread.

PREP: 15 minutes plus overnight to soak beans
BAKE: 3 hours 30 minutes
MAKES 14 accompaniment servings

2 packages (16 ounces each) dry navy (pea) beans

7½ cups water

4 slices bacon, cut into 1-inch pieces or 4 ounces salt pork, finely chopped

2 medium onions, chopped

½ cup dark molasses

⅓ cup packed brown sugar, preferably dark

5 teaspoons salt

4 teaspoons dry mustard

1. In large bowl, place beans with enough *water* to cover by 2 inches. Soak overnight.

2. Preheat oven to 350°F. Drain and rinse navy beans. In 8-quart Dutch oven, combine beans and water; heat to boiling over high heat. Cover and place in oven. Bake 1 hour. Stir in bacon, onions, molasses, brown sugar, salt, and dry mustard.

3. Cover and bake, stirring occasionally, 1 hour. Remove cover and bake until thickened and soupy, 1 hour 30 minutes to 2 hours longer.

EACH SERVING: About 312 calories, 15g protein, 54g carbohydrate, 5g total fat (2g saturated), 4mg cholesterol, 895mg sodium.

Hoppin' John

This popular black-eyed-peas-and-rice dish is traditionally served on New Year's Day in the Deep South. Often a shiny dime is buried inside the pot and whoever discovers it in their portion of Hoppin' John is assured good luck for the year. There are several thoughts about how this dish got its name. Some connect it to the custom of asking guests over on New Year's Day with the casual words "Hop in, John." Others attribute it to the children's ritual of hopping once around the table before sitting down to eat. Today at New Year's Day parties, you will find Hoppin' John as the main attraction, often served up in grand style in the family's silver chafing dish.

PREP: 15 minutes ★ **COOK:** 1 hour
MAKES 18 accompaniment servings

1 tablespoon vegetable oil

2 stalks celery, chopped

1 large onion (12 ounces), chopped

1 red pepper, chopped

2 garlic cloves, finely chopped

1 package (16 ounces) dry black-eyed peas, rinsed and picked through

1 large smoked ham hock (12 ounces)

4 cups water

2 cans (14½ ounces each) chicken broth or 3½ cups Old-Fashioned Chicken Broth (page 45)

2 teaspoons salt

¼ teaspoon crushed red pepper (optional)

1 bay leaf

2 cups regular long-grain rice

1. In 4-quart saucepan, heat oil over medium heat. Add celery, onion, and red pepper. Cook, stirring frequently, until onion is golden, about 10 minutes. Add garlic; cook 2 minutes longer.

2. Add black-eyed peas, ham hock, water, broth, 1 teaspoon salt, crushed red pepper, if using, and bay leaf to celery mixture; heat to boiling over high heat. Reduce heat; cover and simmer, stirring occasionally, until black-eyed peas are tender, about 40 minutes. Discard bay leaf.

3. Meanwhile, prepare rice as label directs with remaining 1 teaspoon salt. (Do not add butter or margarine.)

4. In large bowl, gently combine black-eyed–pea mixture and rice.

EACH SERVING: About 188 calories, 9g protein, 33g carbohydrate, 2g total fat (0g saturated), 3mg cholesterol, 549mg sodium.

Chapter 9

Eat Your Vegetables!

Not knowing what they would find in their new homeland, the Pilgrims brought vegetable seeds for cabbage, string beans (called French beans), peas, onion, and parsnip to the New World. In time, the Virginia colonists planted asparagus, beets, broccoli, cauliflower, cucumbers, and various greens. To minimize their dependency on English imports, the Jamestown settlers learned how to cultivate corn, white and sweet potatoes, winter squash (including pumpkin), tomatoes, and wild greens, such as ramps and fiddlehead ferns.

The colonists learned how to store vegetables in root cellars, pickle and salt-preserve them, and turn cabbage into sauerkraut. Fruit was often turned into preserves, and by the early nineteenth century, fresh vegetables were canned. The popularity of domestic (home) gardening soared by the nineteenth century. In her 1824 regional cookbook, *The Virginia Housewife*, Mary Randolph devoted an entire section to produce. By the end of the century, commercial canneries made it easy to enjoy vegetables effortlessly year-round.

In the 1920s, Clarence Birdseye, a young scientist on assignment in Labrador with the U.S. Fish and Wildlife Service, discovered that his daily catch froze quickly in the Arctic temperatures yet tasted very fresh when thawed. He seized upon this concept and launched the frozen-food industry in 1924. By 1934, consumers were discovering that they could have the flavor, texture, and color of just-picked vegetables any time of the year.

By the 1960s, the way Americans viewed food began to change. We came to appreciate the Chinese technique of stir-frying, which produced tender-crisp vegetables that were nutritious as well as delicious. Julia Child also influenced our appreciation for vegetables cooked in the French manner: until tender instead of soft and tasteless. In 1971, Alice Waters opened Chez Panisse, where the menu was based on fresh, local ingredients very simply prepared. Farmers' markets sprung up across the country by the mid-1970s as more and more consumers demanded fresh, regional produce of uncompromising quality.

Over the last several hundred years we have come full circle: like the colonists, we have gained an appreciation for high-quality fresh vegetables that can be appreciated on a daily basis.

◄ *Asparagus with Hollandaise Sauce*

Asparagus with Hollandaise Sauce

(pictured on page 174)

A member of the lily family, asparagus is one of the most delicate and graceful of vegetables. Its name derives from the Greek word *asparagos* ("shoot" or "stalk") and from the Persian word *asparag* ("sprout"). The Romans, Greeks, and ancient Egyptians all cultivated it. It was known as 'sparagus, then later as sparrow grass. Amelia Simmons has four recipes for asparagus in her 1796 book *American Cookery*. By the mid-nineteenth century, asparagus was being cultivated in America on a large scale. Fannie Farmer offers four simple ways to prepare asparagus in her 1896 cookbook: on toast, in white sauce, with hollandaise sauce, and in fried bread shells with white sauce spooned over. Asparagus with hollandaise sauce remains a favorite way to enjoy this vegetable. For the best flavor, use good-quality butter—never margarine. For an easy variation, steam or boil asparagus and serve it with melted butter and lemon wedges.

PREP: 10 minutes ★ **COOK:** 10 minutes
MAKES 4 accompaniment servings

1 pound asparagus, tough ends trimmed

¼ teaspoon salt

Hollandaise Sauce (opposite)

1. Boil or steam asparagus as directed in box (opposite). Sprinkle with salt; transfer to serving dish. Keep warm.

2. Meanwhile, prepare Hollandaise Sauce. Serve sauce alongside asparagus.

EACH SERVING WITHOUT SAUCE: About 20 calories, 3g protein, 3g carbohydrate, 0g total fat (0g saturated), 0mg cholesterol, 145mg sodium.

Hollandaise Sauce

PREP: 5 minutes ★ **COOK:** 10 minutes ★ **MAKES** scant 1 cup

3 large egg yolks

¼ cup water

2 tablespoons fresh lemon juice

½ cup butter (1 stick), cut into 8 pieces (do not use margarine)

¼ teaspoon salt

1. In heavy nonreactive 1-quart saucepan, with wire whisk, whisk egg yolks, water, and lemon juice until well blended. Cook over medium-low heat, stirring constantly with wooden spoon or heat-safe rubber spatula, until egg-yolk mixture just begins to bubble at edge, 6 to 8 minutes.

2. Reduce heat to low. With wire whisk, whisk in butter one piece at a time, until each addition is incorporated and sauce has thickened. Remove from heat and stir in salt. Strain through sieve, if you like.

EACH TABLESPOON: About 62 calories, 1g protein, 0g carbohydrate, 7g total fat (4g saturated), 55mg cholesterol, 96mg sodium.

To Cook Asparagus

To Steam: In asparagus steamer or 3-quart saucepan fitted with rack, heat *½ inch water* to boiling over medium-high heat; add *1 pound asparagus*, trimmed. Cover and steam until tender-crisp, 8 to 10 minutes (depending on thickness of asparagus).

To Boil: In 12-inch skillet, heat *1 inch water* to boiling over high heat. Add *1 pound asparagus*, trimmed, and *½ teaspoon salt*; heat to boiling. Reduce heat to medium-high; cook, uncovered, until tender-crisp, 5 to 10 minutes (depending on thickness of asparagus). Drain.

Brussels Sprouts with Bacon

Brussels sprouts are a member of the cabbage family. They grow on a stalk, completely covering it with their round heads. Botanical texts date Brussels sprouts back to the sixteenth century. In 1812, Thomas Jefferson planted some and made a notation about it in his garden book. Mrs. Sarah Rorer in *Mrs. Rorer's Philadelphia Cook Book,* advises readers to add ¼ teaspoon of bicarbonate of soda (baking soda) to the cooking water "to render [sprouts] soft."

PREP: 15 minutes ★ **COOK:** 25 minutes
MAKES 10 accompaniment servings

3 containers (10 ounces each) Brussels sprouts, trimmed and cut lengthwise in half

6 slices bacon

1 tablespoon olive oil

2 garlic cloves, finely chopped

½ teaspoon salt

¼ teaspoon coarsely ground black pepper

1. In 4-quart saucepan, heat *2 quarts water* to boiling over high heat. Add Brussels sprouts; heat to boiling. Cook until tender-crisp, about 5 minutes; drain.

2. In 12-inch skillet, cook bacon over medium heat until browned. With slotted spoon, transfer bacon to paper towels to drain; crumble.

3. Discard all but 1 tablespoon bacon drippings from skillet. Add oil and heat over medium-high heat. Add Brussels sprouts, garlic, salt, and pepper. Cook, stirring frequently, until Brussels sprouts are lightly browned, about 5 minutes. Sprinkle with bacon.

EACH SERVING: About 96 calories, 5g protein, 8g carbohydrate, 6g total fat (1g saturated), 4mg cholesterol, 202mg sodium.

Harvard Beets

The origin of the first recipe for Harvard beets is debatable. One tale links it to a seventeenth-century English tavern named Harwood, where this beet dish was on the menu. A Russian émigré who was a customer moved to America and opened a restaurant in Boston in 1846 that he named Harwood. Just as in the English tavern, he served Harwood beets, but due to his Russian accent it sounded like "Harvard." Another tale relates the name to Harvard's crimson team color, which is similar to the bright red of beets. The required size and shape of the beets differs among recipes. Fannie Farmer suggests "thin slices, small cubes, or fancy shapes, using [a] French vegetable cutter."

PREP: 20 minutes ★ **COOK:** 10 minutes
MAKES 6 accompaniment servings

¼ cup sugar

1 tablespoon cornstarch

½ teaspoon salt

⅓ cup cider vinegar

1 tablespoon butter or margarine

1 teaspoon minced onion

3 cups cooked, sliced beets or 2 cans (16 ounces each) sliced beets, drained

In 1-quart saucepan, combine sugar, cornstarch, and salt. Add vinegar in slow, steady stream, stirring until well blended. Add butter and onion. Cook, stirring constantly over medium heat, until sauce has thickened and boils. Reduce heat and simmer 1 minute. Add beets and cook, stirring occasionally, just until heated through.

EACH SERVING: About 82 calories, 1g protein, 16g carbohydrate, 2g total fat (1g saturated), 5mg cholesterol, 255mg sodium.

Yale Beets

Prepare as directed but substitute *½ cup orange juice* for vinegar and substitute *1 teaspoon freshly grated orange peel* for onion.

Pennsylvania-Dutch Hot Slaw

Europeans were eating cabbage as far back as the Middle Ages. The New England colonists stayed close to their British roots and always boiled it. The Amish and Mennonites who settled in the Pennsylvania countryside loved cabbage. They prepared sauerkraut as well as creamy, hot wilted slaw from recipes brought from Germany. It is interesting to note that Pennsylvania-Dutch hot slaw closely resembles the Alsatian dish *émincé de choux verts aux lardons chauds* (hot cabbage and bacon salad). It features a warm bacon dressing, which slightly wilts the shredded cabbage while leaving just a bit of pleasant crunch.

PREP: 10 minutes ★ **COOK:** 10 minutes
MAKES 4 accompaniment servings

3 slices bacon, finely chopped
½ small head green cabbage (16 ounces), cored and
  thinly sliced
1 small onion, chopped
2 tablespoons cider vinegar
¼ cup sugar
½ teaspoon celery seeds
¼ teaspoon salt

1. In 5-quart Dutch oven, cook bacon over medium heat until browned. With slotted spoon, transfer bacon to paper towels to drain.

2. To drippings in pot, add cabbage and onion. Cook, stirring frequently, until cabbage is tender-crisp, about 5 minutes. Stir in vinegar, sugar, celery seeds, salt, and bacon. Cook 1 minute longer.

EACH SERVING: About 178 calories, 3g protein, 20g carbohydrate, 10g total fat (4g saturated), 11mg cholesterol, 277mg sodium.

Cajun Maquechou

The ingredients in this Cajun dish are rather basic: corn, onions, bell pepper, and cream. Translated from the Cajun-French, its name means to "mock cabbage." Its origin is not easily traced. Some believe the dish was brought to Louisiana by the Spaniards and that its name originates from the Spanish word *machica*, a dish of toasted cornmeal that's sweetened with sugar and spices. Others believe the word comes from *maigrichou*, meaning "thin child," for the dish is more like a (thin) soup than a (chunky) stew.

PREP: 20 minutes ★ **COOK:** 45 minutes
MAKES 8 accompaniment servings

4 slices bacon, chopped
1 large onion (12 ounces), chopped
1 large red pepper, chopped
5 cups corn kernels cut from cobs (about 8 ears) or
  3 packages (10 ounces each) frozen whole-kernel corn
1 can (14½ ounces) diced tomatoes, drained
¼ cup heavy cream
¾ teaspoon salt
½ teaspoon sugar
⅛ to ¼ teaspoon ground red pepper (cayenne)
chopped fresh parsley (optional)

1. In nonstick 12-inch skillet, cook bacon over medium heat until crisp. With slotted spoon, transfer bacon to paper towels to drain.

2. To drippings in skillet, add onion and red pepper. Cook, stirring frequently, until vegetables are lightly browned, about 12 minutes.

3. Stir in corn, tomatoes, cream, salt, sugar, and ground red pepper; heat to boiling over high heat. Reduce heat; cover and simmer, stirring occasionally, until corn is tender, about 15 minutes. Stir in bacon and sprinkle with parsley, if using.

EACH SERVING: About 202 calories, 5g protein, 25g carbohydrate, 11g total fat (4g saturated), 18mg cholesterol, 398mg sodium.

Corn Oysters

Scrape sweet corn from the cob, or grate it. Take one coffeecup of corn and two eggs. Make a batter of a little milk and flour, seasoning with salt. Make the batter sufficiently thick to take out with a spoon, and fry in butter. This recipe is enough for five persons.

—**Good Housekeeping Everyday Cook Book,** 1903

Corn Pudding

Corn pudding dates back to the plantations in the Deep South, where corn was freshly picked from the fields and eggs and cream were always on hand. The secret to the creamiest corn pudding is the way the corn is cut off the cob. According to Evan Jones in *American Food*: "In the smoothest, most luscious corn pudding I know, much depends on the amount of liquid in the corn pulp. Some Kentuckians say this delicacy must be made with young field corn, and served as a vegetable. A razor-sharp knife cuts down the center of each row of kernels. No husk or skin is supposed to come close to the finished product. The blunt, non-cutting edge of a knife is used to depress the kernels when the ear is held upright over a bowl. Out spills the tender inside only, to be mixed with eggs, milk or cream, butter, salt, pepper, and a hint of sugar. This mixture is baked in a buttered casserole at about 350°F. for about forty or forty-five minutes. 'When it doesn't shake', say some Southern cooks, 'it is ready.' "

PREP: 25 minutes ★ **BAKE:** 45 minutes
MAKES 8 accompaniment servings

1¼ **teaspoons salt**

2 **cups corn kernels cut from cobs (3 to 4 ears)**

2 **tablespoons all-purpose flour**

2 **tablespoons sugar**

⅛ **teaspoon ground black pepper**

1¾ **cups milk**

¼ **cup heavy or whipping cream**

2 **tablespoons butter or margarine, melted**

3 **large eggs**

1. Preheat oven to 325°F. Lightly grease 8-inch square baking dish.

2. In 2-quart saucepan, heat *1½ cups water* and ½ teaspoon salt to boiling over high heat. Add corn kernels and heat to boiling; boil 2 minutes. Drain; pat corn dry with paper towels.

3. In medium bowl, with wire whisk, combine flour, sugar, remaining ¾ teaspoon salt, and pepper. Gradually whisk in milk, cream, butter, and eggs until smooth. Stir in corn. Pour mixture into prepared baking dish.

4. Place baking dish in medium roasting pan (14" by 10"); place pan on oven rack. Pour enough *boiling water* into roasting pan to come halfway up sides of baking dish. Bake until top is lightly browned and knife inserted in center comes out clean, about 45 minutes.

EACH SERVING: About 170 calories, 6g protein, 15g carbohydrate, 10g total fat (5g saturated), 105mg cholesterol, 451mg sodium.

Corn Custard With Basil

Prepare recipe as above, but substitute basil-flavored milk for the plain milk in Step 3. To prepare basil-flavored milk, in 1-quart saucepan, heat *1¾ cups milk* and *1 cup loosely packed fresh basil sprigs* over medium-high heat until bubbles form around edge. Remove from heat; cover and let steep about 10 minutes. Discard basil.

Liberty and Victory Gardens

With the declaration of World War I in 1917, President Woodrow Wilson named Herbert Hoover the head of the U.S. Food Administration. The task at hand was enormous, as the United States had to feed not only its citizens at home and the armed forces but also its allies. Food preservation was at the top of the list with public relations campaigns announcing that "Food Will Win the War" if Americans practiced the "Gospel of the Clean Plate." Families were urged to plant vegetables in their backyards, and these plots soon became known as liberty gardens.

The success of the liberty garden campaign prompted the government once again to encourage citizens during World War II to plant gardens wherever there was a flower bed, a plowable backyard, or some available land. These newly named victory gardens popped up in some rather unlikely spots, such as the Portland Zoo and Chicago's Arlington Racetrack. About 20 million gardens were planted, which produced about 1 million tons of vegetables that were worth at least $85 million. Not surprisingly, home canning soared during this time: over three-quarters of American families preserved over 165 jars a year. Not only were they able to grow much-needed food, but Americans were also awakened to the glories of enjoying fresh produce, which has been appreciated ever since.

Eggplant Parmigiana

Thomas Jefferson often gets the credit for introducing America to the eggplant. It took a while for folks to become familiar with how to peel it, slice it, fry it, scallop it, stuff it, and bake it. Although Fannie Farmer's 1923 cookbook offers seven recipes for eggplant, eggplant Parmesan is not one of them. Our authentic version undoubtedly gained its fame in the restaurants and groceries in Italian communities known as Little Italies that popped up in cities following World War II.

PREP: 1 hour 30 minutes ★ **BAKE:** 25 minutes
MAKES 6 main-dish servings

---

4 tablespoons olive oil

1 large onion, chopped

1 garlic clove, minced

2 cans (14 to 16 ounces each) tomatoes

2 teaspoons sugar

$\frac{1}{2}$ teaspoon dried oregano

$\frac{1}{2}$ teaspoon dried basil

$\frac{1}{2}$ teaspoon salt

1 cup plain dried bread crumbs

2 large eggs

2 tablespoons water

1 large eggplant (2$\frac{1}{2}$ pounds), cut lengthwise into $\frac{1}{2}$-inch-thick slices

$\frac{1}{2}$ cup freshly grated Parmesan cheese

1 package (8 ounces) mozzarella cheese, cut into $\frac{1}{4}$-inch-thick slices

1. In 10-inch skillet, heat 2 tablespoons oil over medium heat until hot. Add onion and garlic; cook until tender, about 5 minutes. Add tomatoes, sugar, oregano, basil, and salt. Reduce heat; cover and simmer 30 minutes.

2. Place bread crumbs on waxed paper. In small bowl, with fork, beat eggs and water. Dip eggplant slices, one at a time, in egg mixture, then in bread crumbs; repeat to coat each slice twice.

3. Preheat oven to 350°F. Grease 13" by 9" baking dish.

4. In 12-inch skillet, heat remaining 2 tablespoons oil over medium heat. Add eggplant, a few slices at a time, and cook until golden brown, about 5 minutes per side, using slotted spatula to transfer slices to platter as they are browned, adding more oil if necessary.

5. Layer half of eggplant slices in prepared baking dish and cover with half of tomato mixture. Sprinkle with half of Parmesan and top with half of mozzarella. Repeat layers. Cover baking dish with foil; bake 15 minutes. Remove foil; bake until bubbling, about 10 minutes.

EACH SERVING: About 426 calories, 19g protein, 38g carbohydrate, 24g total fat (9g saturated), 107mg cholesterol, 917mg sodium.

Green Bean Casserole with Frizzled Onions

In the mid-twentieth century, the Campbell Soup Company created a simple green-bean bake made with a can of condensed cream of mushroom soup, green beans (either frozen or canned), some milk, canned french fried onions, a little soy sauce, and black pepper. It was then baked and topped with more onions. Our delicious homemade version uses freshly fried onions, fresh green beans, and sautéed mushrooms.

PREP: 50 minutes ★ **BAKE:** 21 minutes
MAKES 6 accompaniment servings

1 medium onion, very thinly sliced

6 tablespoons all-purpose flour

½ cup vegetable oil

⅛ plus ¼ teaspoon salt

1 pound green beans, trimmed and cut in half

2 tablespoons butter or margarine

8 ounces mushrooms, trimmed and sliced

1 large garlic clove, minced

1 cup milk

⅛ teaspoon ground black pepper

1. In large bowl, separate onion slices into rings. Add 4 tablespoons flour to onions; toss to coat, shaking off excess.

2. In 10-inch skillet, heat oil over medium-high heat until hot. Add onions, leaving excess flour in bowl. Cook onions, stirring frequently, until onions are browned, 3 to 5 minutes. With slotted spoon, transfer onions to paper towels to drain. Sprinkle with ⅛ teaspoon salt. Discard oil from skillet.

3. In same skillet, heat *1 inch water* to boiling over high heat. Add beans; heat to boiling. Cook beans, uncovered, until tender-crisp, 4 to 5 minutes. Drain. Rinse with cold running water to stop cooking; drain well and pat dry with paper towels.

4. Preheat oven to 400°F. Lightly grease shallow 2-quart casserole.

5. In same skillet, melt butter over medium heat. Add mushrooms, garlic, and remaining ¼ teaspoon salt. Cook, stirring, until liquid has evaporated and mushrooms begin to brown, about 5 minutes.

6. In small bowl, with wire whisk, blend remaining 2 tablespoons flour and milk until smooth. Stir into mushroom mixture; heat to boiling. Reduce heat to low and simmer, stirring, 5 minutes. Stir in green beans. Turn mixture into prepared casserole. Cover loosely with foil. Bake until bubbling, about 20 minutes. Top with onions; bake until onions are heated through, about 1 minute.

EACH SERVING: About 289 calories, 5g protein, 17g carbohydrate, 24g total fat (6g saturated), 16mg cholesterol, 212mg sodium.

Butter Beans with Bacon

From Lima, Peru, comes the lima bean, which is known as the butter bean down South. The Native Americans combined lima beans with corn, creating the Narrangansett dish *misickquatash* (succotash), a recipe they shared with the colonists. Subsequently, the dish was also known as *sukquttahash* and *msakwitash*. Nowadays in the South, lima beans are skillet-fried in bacon drippings, then simmered until nice and tender.

PREP: 5 minutes ★ **COOK:** 20 minutes
MAKES 4 accompaniment servings

4 slices bacon

1 package (10 ounces) frozen baby lima beans

2 stalks celery, thinly sliced

¼ teaspoon salt

⅛ teaspoon ground black pepper

⅓ cup water

1. In 10-inch skillet, cook bacon over medium heat until browned. With slotted spoon, transfer bacon to paper towels to drain; crumble. Discard all but 1 tablespoon bacon drippings from skillet.

2. To drippings in skillet, add frozen lima beans, celery, salt, and pepper. Cook over medium heat, stirring frequently, until vegetables are tender, about 5 minutes.

3. Add water to skillet; heat to boiling over high heat. Reduce heat and simmer 5 minutes. Spoon bean mixture into serving bowl; sprinkle with crumbled bacon.

EACH SERVING: About 156 calories, 7g protein, 19g carbohydrate, 6g total fat (2g saturated), 8mg cholesterol, 314mg sodium.

Smothered Greens

The tradition of eating "a mess of greens" dates back to the Virginia colonists, who planted mustard, collard, and other greens and cooked them up in a large pot along with a ham hock for flavor. The potlikker (the broth left in the pot), which was rich in vitamins, was enjoyed by the field hands working the plantations. Political tales that connect potlikker with candidates and campaigns abound. A passion for this broth was frequently believed to be a prerequisite for running for office. Governor Huey Long once staged an all-night filibuster, claiming that fried corn pone (corn bread) should be dunked into potlikker for the best results, while others felt it should be crumbled. During the 1932 Democratic National Convention, Franklin D. Roosevelt jokingly suggested that the debate be referred to the Platform Committee for a decision.

PREP: 30 minutes ★ **COOK:** 1 hour 15 minutes
MAKES 10 accompaniment servings

5 pounds assorted greens, such as kale, collard greens, or mustard greens

2 smoked ham hocks (1½ pounds)

1 medium onion

2 quarts water

1 teaspoon salt

hot pepper sauce

1. Remove stems and tough ribs from greens; rinse well with cool running water. Cut into ½-inch pieces.

2. In 8-quart saucepot, combine ham hocks, onion, water, and salt; heat to boiling over high heat. Add greens to pot in batches, stirring to wilt. Heat to boiling. Reduce heat; cover and simmer until very tender, about 1 hour. Discard ham hocks. Serve with hot pepper sauce.

EACH SERVING: About 82 calories, 5g protein, 13g carbohydrate, 3g total fat (1g saturated), 2mg cholesterol, 560mg sodium.

Minted Sugar Snaps

Green peas were one of the first vegetables that the Pilgrims planted in their gardens. American cookbook author Amelia Simmons advised: "All Peas should be picked *carefully* from the vines as soon as dew is off, shelled and cleaned without water, and boiled immediately; they are thus the richest flavored." Our recipe uses tender sugar snap peas, which don't require shelling.

PREP: 15 minutes ★ **COOK:** 5 minutes
MAKES 4 accompaniment servings

1 tablespoon butter or margarine

¼ teaspoon salt

⅛ teaspoon coarsely ground black pepper

1 pound snap peas, strings removed

1 garlic clove, minced

⅓ cup loosely packed fresh mint leaves, finely chopped

½ teaspoon freshly grated lemon peel

¼ teaspoon freshly grated lime peel

In nonstick 12-inch skillet, heat butter, salt, and pepper over medium heat until butter has melted. Add snap peas and cook, stirring, until tender-crisp, about 5 minutes. Remove from heat. Add garlic, mint, and lemon and lime peels; toss well.

EACH SERVING: About 77 calories, 3g protein, 9g carbohydrate, 3g total fat (2g saturated), 8mg cholesterol, 175mg sodium.

French-Fried Onion Rings

Although wild onions were plentiful in the New World, nothing quite compared to the cultivated ones that were eventually brought to the colonies. Even the Native Americans took to them. Early cookbooks usually offered several ways to cook onions: boiled, creamed, fried, stuffed, and baked. It wasn't until the 1906 edition of *The Boston Cooking-School Cook Book* that a recipe for french-fried onions appeared: "Peel onions, cut in one-fourth-inch slices, and separate into rings. Dip in milk, drain, and dip in flour. Fry in deep fat, drain on brown paper, and sprinkle with salt." The recipe is still a favorite today.

PREP: 15 minutes ★ **COOK:** 5 minutes per batch
MAKES 4 accompaniment servings

I jumbo onion (1 pound), cut into ¼-inch-thick slices

vegetable oil for frying

¼ cup milk

I cup all-purpose flour

½ teaspoon salt

I. Separate onion slices into rings. In 4-quart saucepan, heat 2 inches oil over medium heat until temperature reaches 370°F on deep-fat thermometer.

2. Pour milk into large bowl. In ziptight plastic bag, mix flour and salt. Dip one-fourth of onion rings in milk. With tongs, transfer to flour mixture; shake to coat.

3. Carefully drop coated onion rings into hot oil; fry until golden brown, 5 to 7 minutes. With slotted spoon, transfer to paper towels to drain. Repeat dipping, coating, and frying with remaining onion rings. Serve hot.

EACH SERVING: About 487 calories, 4g protein, 26g carbohydrate, 42g total fat (5g saturated), Img cholesterol, 298mg sodium.

Creamed Onions and Peas

In early cookbooks, vegetable recipes were sometimes general suggestions. *The Good Housekeeper* by Sarah Josepha Hale instructed: "Onions are best boiled in milk and water." In 1896, Fannie Farmer offered Onions in Cream: "Prepare and cook as Boiled Onions . . . cover with Cream or Thin White Sauce." Today this preparation is made with small white onions to accompany the Thanksgiving turkey. Our recipe includes a double amount of green peas. If you prefer, use half the amount of peas and double the amount of onions.

PREP: 30 minutes ★ **COOK:** 25 minutes
MAKES 12 accompaniment servings

I container or bag (10 ounces) pearl onions

2 tablespoons butter or margarine

2 tablespoons all-purpose flour

½ teaspoon salt

¼ teaspoon dried thyme

⅛ teaspoon ground nutmeg

⅛ teaspoon ground black pepper

2¼ cups milk

2 bags (16 ounces each) frozen peas, thawed

I. In 12-inch skillet, heat *1 inch water* to boiling over high heat. Add onions; heat to boiling. Reduce heat to low; cover and simmer until tender, 10 to 15 minutes. Drain.

2. When cool enough to handle, peel onions, leaving a bit of root end attached to help onions hold their shape.

3. Meanwhile, in 2-quart saucepan, melt butter over medium heat. Stir in flour, salt, thyme, nutmeg, and pepper until blended; cook, stirring constantly, 1 minute. With wire whisk, gradually stir in milk; cook, stirring, until sauce has thickened slightly and boils.

4. Return onions to skillet. Add sauce and peas; cover and cook, stirring often, over medium-high heat until sauce boils and peas are heated through.

EACH SERVING: About 116 calories, 6g protein, 15g carbohydrate, 4g total fat (2g saturated), 12mg cholesterol, 225mg sodium.

Home Fries

By the 1930s, mobile lunch wagons across America had "lost their wheels" and turned into stationary eateries, which were originally called "dining cars," then later on "diners." Many were dilapidated electric trolley cars that were renovated and patterned after the railroad dining cars. Home fries were then—and still are—a popular menu item. In diners they're also known as "house fries" or "cottage fries." They begin with boiled potatoes that are chopped or sliced, then fried in butter, often with sliced onion added in. Home fries are usually found frying on the back of the grill in generous mounds. If you don't have a grill, a skillet works just fine.

PREP: 30 minutes plus cooling ★ **COOK:** 20 minutes
MAKES 4 accompaniment servings

4 medium all-purpose potatoes (6 ounces each), not peeled

4 tablespoons butter or margarine

I small onion, chopped

¼ teaspoon salt

I. In 4-quart saucepan, combine potatoes and enough *water* to cover; heat to boiling over high heat. Reduce heat; cover and simmer until tender, 15 to 20 minutes. Drain well.

2. Leave potato skins on, if you like. When cool enough to handle, cut potatoes into ¼-inch-thick slices.

3. In 12-inch skillet, melt butter over medium heat. Add potatoes and onion; cook until underside is golden, about 5 minutes. With wide spatula, turn potato mixture. Cook over medium heat, turning several times, until evenly browned. Sprinkle with salt.

EACH SERVING: About 291 calories, 4g protein, 44g carbohydrate, 12g total fat (7g saturated), 31mg cholesterol, 269mg sodium.

Chicago Mash with Onion and Bacon

In Chicago where the El (the elevated commuter train) reigns, down-home diners are a way of life and have been since the early twentieth century. Chicagoans like their mashed potatoes with plenty of browned onion bits and bacon stirred in. Our recipe calls for making the potatoes with warm milk instead of cold. This keeps the potatoes hot and makes them fluffier because more air can be whipped into hot potatoes.

PREP: 15 minutes ★ **COOK:** 25 minutes
MAKES 8 accompaniment servings

4 slices bacon, chopped

1 large onion (12 ounces), chopped

3 pounds all-purpose potatoes (about 9 medium), peeled and cut into 1-inch pieces

1 bay leaf

1 teaspoon salt

1/4 teaspoon coarsely ground black pepper

1 cup milk, warmed

1. In 10-inch skillet, cook bacon over medium heat until browned. With slotted spoon, transfer bacon to paper towels to drain; crumble.

2. To drippings in skillet, add onion; cook, stirring occasionally, over medium heat until onion is tender, about 15 minutes.

3. Meanwhile, in 3-quart saucepan, combine potatoes, bay leaf, and enough *water* to cover; heat to boiling over high heat. Reduce heat to low; cover and simmer until potatoes are tender, about 15 minutes. Drain.

4. Return potatoes to saucepan. Discard bay leaf. Mash potatoes with salt and pepper. Gradually add milk; mash until smooth and well blended. Stir in onion and bacon.

EACH SERVING: About 200 calories, 5g protein, 28g carbohydrate, 8g total fat (3g saturated), 12mg cholesterol, 370mg sodium.

Potato Boats

Early American cookbooks often featured potatoes "baked in the half-shell." To make them, the potatoes were baked, scooped out, mashed with warm milk, then "lighted" with whipped egg whites. Next the potatoes were piled back into their shells, sprinkled with grated cheese, and baked a second time until lightly browned. Other recipes called for stirring cooked meat into the mashed-potato stuffing. Over the years, the egg whites have been omitted, but we're still twice-baking potatoes with shredded cheese and sometimes a sprinkling of paprika on top. They're called by various names: twice-baked potatoes, stuffed baked potatoes, potato boats, and even 'tater boats.

PREP: 15 minutes ★ **BAKE:** 1 hour 15 minutes
MAKES 4 accompaniment servings

4 medium baking potatoes (8 ounces each), scrubbed

3 tablespoons butter or margarine

2 large green onions (12 ounces each), thinly sliced

1/2 cup sour cream

1/4 teaspoon salt

1/4 teaspoon ground black pepper

4 ounces sharp Cheddar cheese, shredded (1 cup)

1/4 teaspoon paprika

1. Preheat oven to 450°F. Prick potatoes with fork. Bake until tender, about 1 hour.

2. Meanwhile, in medium skillet, melt butter over medium heat. Add green onions and cook, stirring, until wilted, about 2 minutes. Set aside.

3. While potatoes are hot, using a pot holder, cut a thin lengthwise slice, about 1/2 inch thick, from each potato. With spoon, scoop out flesh into skillet; reserve shells. Scoop out flesh from tops into skillet. Mash potatoes, sour cream, salt, and pepper until smooth and well blended. Stir in 1/2 cup Cheddar. Spoon mixture into reserved shells, mounding slightly. Place on cookie sheet; sprinkle with remaining 1/2 cup Cheddar and paprika.

4. Bake potatoes until hot and cheese has melted, about 15 minutes.

EACH SERVING: About 459 calories, 14g protein, 49g carbohydrate, 24g total fat (15g saturated), 66mg cholesterol, 440mg sodium.

Steak Fries

In Eliza Leslie's day, fried potatoes started with cold boiled potatoes. In *Directions for Cookery,* she states: "Cold potatoes may be fried in slices or quarters, or broiled on a gridiron. Raw potatoes, when fried, are generally hard, tough and strong." Steak fries became popular in the mid-twentieth century in diners and roadside cafés. The potatoes were thick cut with their skins left on. Their name derives from the fact that they are usually piled high next to one's steak as the ideal accompaniment.

PREP: 15 minutes plus chilling ★ **COOK:** 6 minutes per batch
MAKES 4 accompaniment servings

2 pounds russet or baking potatoes (4 medium),
 scrubbed

3 cups peanut or vegetable oil

1 teaspoon kosher salt

1. Cut each potato lengthwise into quarters, then cut each quarter into 4 long wedges. In large bowl, combine potatoes with enough *cold water* to cover. Refrigerate potatoes at least 2 hours or up to 8 hours.

2. Drain potatoes; transfer to paper towel–lined jelly-roll pan. Pat dry with paper towels.

3. In 5-quart Dutch oven or deep fryer, heat oil over medium heat until temperature reaches 325°F on deep-fat thermometer. Place one-fourth of potatoes in frying basket or fine-mesh sieve. Cook, turning occasionally, until potatoes are tender and edges are slightly crisp and pale golden, about 4 minutes. Transfer to paper towels to drain. Fry remaining potatoes.

4. Preheat oven to 300°F. Heat oil over medium heat until temperature reaches 375°F. Refry one-fourth of potatoes until crisp and golden, 1½ to 2 minutes. Transfer steak fries to paper towel–lined cookie sheet. Keep warm in oven while refrying remaining potatoes. Sprinkle with salt. Serve hot.

EACH SERVING: About 284 calories, 5g protein,
41g carbohydrate, 12g total fat (2g saturated),
0mg cholesterol, 500mg sodium.

Scalloped Potatoes

At the turn of the twentieth century, scalloped potatoes began appearing at church suppers and holiday gatherings throughout America. It closely resembled the French potato dish *gratin dauphinois.* One classic version consists of thinly sliced potatoes that are covered with cream in a garlic-rubbed gratin dish, while another version contains cheese as well as egg. Traditionally, scalloped potatoes were prepared with thinly sliced potatoes that were covered with white sauce and baked until the potatoes were meltingly tender and the top richly browned, as in our recipe. Early cookbooks often suggested lightly sprinkling bread crumbs on top of the dish to give it a nice crisp top.

PREP: 30 minutes ★ **BAKE:** 1 hour 30 minutes
MAKES 6 accompaniment servings

3 tablespoons butter or margarine

1 small onion, chopped

3 tablespoons all-purpose flour

1 teaspoon salt

⅛ teaspoon ground black pepper

1½ cups milk, warmed

2 pounds all-purpose potatoes (6 medium),
 peeled and thinly sliced

1. Preheat oven to 375°F. Grease 9-inch square baking dish or shallow 2-quart casserole.

2. In heavy 2-quart saucepan, melt butter over low heat. Add onion and cook until tender, about 5 minutes. Add flour and cook, stirring, 1 minute. With wire whisk, gradually whisk in milk. Cook over medium heat, stirring constantly, until mixture has thickened and boils. Reduce heat; simmer, stirring frequently, 1 minute. Stir in salt and pepper; remove from heat.

3. Arrange half of potatoes in single layer in prepared dish; pour half of sauce on top. Repeat layers. Cover and bake 1 hour. Remove cover; bake until potatoes are tender and top is golden, about 30 minutes longer.

EACH SERVING: About 199 calories, 5g protein,
28g carbohydrate, 8g total fat (5g saturated),
24mg cholesterol, 484mg sodium.

Bubbe's Potato Latkes

The tradition of serving potato pancakes at Chanukah began with the Ashkenazi Jews of Northern and Eastern European communities. The pancakes commemorate the Maccabees' defeat of the Syrian army and the reclaiming of the Temple of Jerusalem in 165 BC. The Maccabees found only enough oil in the temple to light their menorah for one night, but miraculously it burned for eight. The oil used to fry these traditional pancakes symbolizes this miracle.

PREP: 45 minutes ★ **COOK:** 45 minutes
MAKES about 20 latkes or 10 accompaniment servings

Homemade Applesauce (opposite)
4 large baking potatoes (about 2½ pounds), peeled
1 medium onion
1 large egg
2 tablespoons all-purpose flour or matzoh meal
1 tablespoon minced fresh parsley or dill
1 tablespoon fresh lemon juice
½ teaspoon baking powder
½ teaspoon salt
¼ teaspoon coarsely ground black pepper
¾ cup vegetable oil

1. Prepare Homemade Applesauce; cover and refrigerate until serving time.

2. Finely shred potatoes and onion into colander. With hands, squeeze to remove as much liquid as possible. Place potato mixture in medium bowl; stir in egg, flour, parsley, lemon juice, baking powder, salt, and pepper until well mixed.

3. Preheat oven to 250°F. In 12-inch skillet, heat 3 tablespoons vegetable oil over medium heat until hot but not smoking. Drop potato mixture by scant ¼ cups into hot oil to make 5 latkes. With back of large spoon, flatten each latke into 3-inch round. Cook until underside is golden, 4 to 5 minutes. With slotted spatula, turn latkes and cook until second side is golden brown and crisp, 4 to 5 minutes longer. With spatula, transfer latkes to paper towel–lined cookie sheet to drain; keep warm in oven.

4. Repeat with remaining potato mixture, stirring potato mixture before frying each batch and using 3 tablespoons more oil for each new batch. Serve hot with Homemade Applesauce.

EACH SERVING WITHOUT APPLESAUCE: About 250 calories, 6g protein, 38g carbohydrate, 9g total fat (1g saturated), 43mg cholesterol, 270mg sodium.

Homemade Applesauce

Peel and core *4 large Golden Delicious apples (2 pounds)*; cut each into eighths. In 3-quart saucepan, combine apples, *½ cup apple cider or juice, ¼ cup sugar, and 1 teaspoon fresh lemon juice.* Heat to boiling over high heat. Reduce heat to low; cover and simmer until apples are very tender, 20 to 25 minutes. Remove from heat; with potato masher, coarsely mash apples. Makes 3 cups.

EACH SERVING: About 69 calories, 0g protein, 18g carbohydrate, 0g total fat (0g saturated), 0mg cholesterol, 0mg sodium.

The Shaker Larder

In the nineteenth century, Shaker communities represented simple, unpretentious farm living at its best. The Shakers were a celibate sect who lived in isolated communities in New England and the Midwest. They were successful farmers and superb craftsmen with high standards of excellence. Their cooking was simple but very tasty. Shaker meals were distinguished by vegetables that weren't overcooked and fresh seasonal fruits.

Unlike other farming families, the Shakers enjoyed a wide variety of foods, many exported from faraway places and brought home by their trustees, who traveled widely. The Shakers loved growing, cooking, and preserving foods and were very fond of herbs. Excellent cooks and bakers, they took advantage of their resources to give everyday dishes an epicurean touch, such as apple pie with rosewater and spinach flavored with rosemary. Shaker larders were known to be superior to others of their day. The women canned their own fruits and vegetables and made jams, jellies, relishes, and preserves, always managing to capture a freshness and high quality second to none.

The noonday meal was the most substantial one of the day. It was always a wholesome feast: meat that was often fried and smothered with gravy, vegetables fresh from the garden or home canned, homemade pies (apple was a favorite), brown bread, spoon cakes, and cream cheese. The Shakers worked hard and ate well, but they never prepared food on Sunday, as that was their day to rest.

Creamed Spinach

Often called the "prince" of vegetables, spinach was brought here by the Spanish settlers. The nutritious pluses of spinach have been touted for centuries, but its mildly bitter taste has often prevented it from being a favorite with children. In 1929, the famous cartoonist Elzie Crisler Segar did his part to make this vegetable appeal to the kindergarten crowd. He had his cartoon character Popeye gain his extraordinary strength from eating spinach. Ever since, parents have reminded their kids to "eat their spinach just like Popeye." In our recipe the spinach is creamed by folding it into a luscious white sauce enriched with cream cheese and sour cream.

PREP: 20 minutes ★ COOK: 15 minutes
MAKES 6 accompaniment servings

2 tablespoons butter or margarine

3 large shallots, finely chopped (about ¾ cup)

2 tablespoons all-purpose flour

½ cup milk

¾ teaspoon salt

¼ teaspoon coarsely ground black pepper

⅛ teaspoon ground nutmeg

1 package (3 ounces) cream cheese, softened and cut into pieces

3 packages (10 ounces each) frozen chopped spinach, thawed and squeezed dry

1 cup loosely packed fresh parsley leaves

¼ cup sour cream

1. In 4-quart saucepan, melt butter over medium-low heat. Add shallots and cook, stirring frequently, until tender, about 3 minutes. Add flour and cook, stirring, 1 minute. With wire whisk, gradually whisk in milk; heat to boiling, whisking constantly. Reduce heat and simmer, stirring occasionally, until sauce has thickened and boils, about 2 minutes. Stir in salt, pepper, and nutmeg.

2. Remove from heat; stir in cream cheese until smooth. Stir in spinach, parsley, and sour cream; heat through (do not boil).

EACH SERVING: About 180 calories, 7g protein, 14g carbohydrate, 12g total fat (7g saturated), 33mg cholesterol, 500mg sodium.

Baked Acorn Squash

The Native Americans introduced the colonists to *askutasquash* (squash). Translated literally it means "eaten raw," and that's how it was likely eaten at first. The colonists were pleased to find that the squashes in America were superior to those back home. Even today acorn squash is a favorite, especially when baked and glazed with brown sugar and butter.

PREP: 10 minutes ★ **BAKE:** 35 minutes
MAKES 4 accompaniment servings

2 small acorn squash (1 pound each), each cut lengthwise in half and seeded

2 tablespoons butter or margarine, cut into pieces

¼ cup packed brown sugar

1. Preheat oven to 350°F. Grease 13" by 9" baking dish.

2. Place squash, cut side down, in baking dish; bake 30 minutes. Turn cut side up. Place one-fourth of butter and brown sugar in each cavity. Bake until squash is tender and butter and brown sugar have melted, about 5 minutes longer.

EACH SERVING: About 181 calories, 1g protein, 31g carbohydrate, 7g total fat (4g saturated), 16mg cholesterol, 69mg sodium.

Dixie Squash Pudding

The tender, sweet yellow squash of summer was one of the new vegetables the colonists learned how to cook in America. The squash was picked fresh and thinly sliced. It was then either boiled and mashed with cream and butter, dipped in batter and fried, or mashed and turned into fritters. In the South, squash pudding is a favorite dish that has changed over time. The squash can be thinly sliced, diced, or completely mashed. In some recipes, the pudding is seasoned with salt and pepper and topped with buttered cracker crumbs, while other recipes contain sautéed onion, crisp bacon, jalapeños, cream cheese, Cheddar, or Monterey Jack.

PREP: 25 minutes ★ **BAKE:** 20 minutes
MAKES 8 accompaniment servings

2 tablespoons butter or margarine

1 small onion, finely chopped

2 pounds yellow squash, cut into ½-inch-thick slices

½ teaspoon salt

1 package (3 ounces) cream cheese, cut into ½-inch pieces

¼ cup milk

4 ounces jalapeño Monterey Jack cheese, shredded (1 cup)

½ cup crushed round buttery crackers (about 12 crackers)

1. Preheat oven to 350°F. Lightly grease shallow 2-quart baking dish.

2. In 12-inch nonstick skillet, melt butter over medium heat. Add onion and cook until translucent, about 2 minutes. Add squash and salt; cook, stirring, until tender, about 10 minutes. Remove from heat.

3. Stir cream cheese into squash mixture until melted. Stir in milk, ½ cup Monterey Jack cheese, and ¼ cup crushed crackers. Turn into prepared baking dish. Combine remaining cheese and crushed crackers; sprinkle over top. Bake until hot and top is golden brown, about 20 minutes. Let stand 5 minutes for easier serving.

EACH SERVING: About 192 calories, 7g protein, 10g carbohydrate, 14g total fat (8g saturated), 39mg cholesterol, 371mg sodium.

Fried Green Tomatoes

Green tomatoes were popular in the New England colonies, where they were often picked right before the first frost. The New Englanders liked their green tomatoes baked into a pie with a little sprinkling of sugar and spice and a splash of vinegar. Down South, green tomatoes were usually fried up with a crunchy cornmeal coating. Often served at bountiful plantation breakfasts, fried green tomatoes became a tradition that continues today.

PREP: 20 minutes ★ **COOK:** 3 minutes per batch
MAKES 6 accompaniment servings

6 slices bacon

I large egg white

¼ teaspoon salt

½ cup cornmeal

¼ teaspoon coarsely ground black pepper

3 medium green tomatoes (I pound),
   cut into scant ½-inch-thick slices

I. In 12-inch skillet, cook bacon over medium heat until browned. With slotted spoon, transfer bacon to paper towels to drain; crumble. Set aside skillet with drippings.

2. In pie plate, beat egg white and salt. On waxed paper, combine cornmeal and pepper. Dip tomatoes in egg mixture to coat both sides, then dip into cornmeal mixture, pressing so mixture adheres. Place on waxed paper.

3. Heat bacon drippings in skillet over medium-high heat. Cook tomatoes, in batches, until golden brown, about 1½ minutes per side, transferring them to paper towels to drain.

4. Transfer tomatoes to platter; top with bacon.

EACH SERVING: About 189 calories, 4g protein, 13g carbohydrate, 13g total fat (5g saturated), 15mg cholesterol, 270mg sodium.

Narraganset Succotash

The earliest versions of succotash were made of fresh corn kernels and dried kidney beans that were cooked in bear grease. According to Evan Jones, the oldest succotash recipe (on record) calls for boiling two fowls and includes four pounds of brisket, one turnip, five or six sliced potatoes, two quarts of dried white beans, and four quarts of cooked dried corn. Today recipes use bacon drippings and toss in lima beans instead of kidney beans.

PREP: 15 minutes ★ **COOK:** 30 minutes
MAKES 10 accompaniment servings

5 slices bacon

3 stalks celery, cut into ¼-inch-thick slices

I medium onion, chopped

2 cans (15¼ to 16 ounces each) whole-kernel corn, drained

2 packages (10 ounces each) frozen baby lima beans

½ cup canned chicken broth or Old-Fashioned Chicken Broth (page 45)

¾ teaspoon salt

¼ teaspoon coarsely ground black pepper

2 tablespoons chopped fresh parsley

I. In 12-inch skillet, cook bacon over medium heat until browned. With slotted spoon, transfer to paper towels to drain; crumble.

2. Discard all but 2 tablespoons drippings from skillet. Add celery and onion; cook over medium heat, stirring occasionally, until vegetables are tender and golden, about 15 minutes. Stir in corn, frozen lima beans, broth, salt, and pepper; heat to boiling over high heat. Reduce heat; cover and simmer, until heated through, 5 to 10 minutes longer. Stir in parsley and sprinkle with bacon.

EACH SERVING: About 155 calories, 7g protein, 24g carbohydrate, 5g total fat (2g saturated), 5mg cholesterol, 490mg sodium.

Roasted Winter Vegetables

Settlers would bring in the fall harvest and store many of the vegetables in root cellars in anticipation of the long winter ahead. Most nineteenth-century cookbooks feature recipes for winter squash and other autumn vegetables. They are often boiled in salted water, then served hot with melted butter poured over. Today winter vegetables are often roasted in the oven with a little oil and seasoning until richly caramelized and flavorful.

PREP: 30 minutes ★ **ROAST:** about 45 minutes
MAKES 24 accompaniment servings

3 large red onions, each cut into 12 wedges

2 pounds carrots, peeled and cut into 2" by 1" pieces

2 pounds parsnips, peeled and cut into 2" by 1" pieces

2 red or yellow peppers, cut into 1½-inch pieces

I whole head garlic, separated into cloves and peeled

3 tablespoons olive oil

2 teaspoons salt

¼ teaspoon ground black pepper

1. Preheat oven to 475°F. In large bowl, combine onions, carrots, parsnips, red peppers, and garlic cloves. Add oil, salt, and pepper; toss until evenly coated.

2. Divide vegetable mixture between two jelly-roll pans or large shallow roasting pans. Place pans on two oven racks; roast until vegetable are tender and golden, about 45 minutes, rotating pans between upper and lower racks halfway through cooking time and tossing once.

EACH SERVING: About 65 calories, 1g protein, 12g carbohydrate, 2g total fat (0g saturated), 0mg cholesterol, 210mg sodium.

Vegetable Stir-Fry

The Chinese have always cooked up tasty vegetables. In the mid-nineteenth century, many Chinese immigrants came to America. They prepared meals and performed household chores for well-to-do families. Although they were not allowed to cook their native dishes, they did apply their Asian cooking techniques to many foods. Stir-frying vegetables in a wok in sizzling hot oil allows them to keep their color, texture, and flavor and is a popular technique today.

PREP: 20 minutes ★ **COOK:** 18 minutes
MAKES 4 accompaniment servings

- **1 tablespoon vegetable oil**
- **2 garlic cloves, thinly sliced**
- **1 teaspoon minced, peeled fresh ginger**
- **1 small bunch broccoli (12 ounces), cut into flowerets (about 3 cups)**
- **1 cup water**
- **1 cup peeled and thinly sliced carrots**
- **1 yellow pepper, cut into ½-inch pieces**
- **6 mushrooms, trimmed and thinly sliced**

- **3 green onions, cut on diagonal into 1-inch pieces**
- **2 tablespoons hoisin sauce**
- **¼ teaspoon salt**

In nonstick 12-inch skillet, heat oil over medium-high heat until hot. Add garlic and ginger; cook, stirring frequently (stir-frying), 1 minute. Add broccoli; stir-fry 1 minute. Increase heat to high; add water and cook 3 minutes. Add carrots and yellow pepper; stir-fry until liquid has evaporated, about 6 minutes. Add mushrooms, green onions, hoisin sauce, and salt; stir-fry until vegetables are tender and almost all liquid has evaporated, about 5 minutes longer.

EACH SERVING: About 109 calories, 4g protein, 15g carbohydrate, 4g total fat (1g saturated), 0mg cholesterol, 355mg sodium.

Chapter 10

From the Bread Basket

Corn always grew in America, and as might be expected, it was used for bread making, first by the Native Americans and then by the colonists. The natives baked bread (similar to tortillas) and corn pone (known as Indian bread). By 1750, the colonists had created their own corn bread. Sometime later, yeast, which had been brought back from Europe enabled the colonists to create rye 'n' Injun bread.

Some innovations and inventions also encouraged bread baking. In the 1790s, it was discovered that when pearl ash, a refined form of potash, was added to quick-bread batter, the bread rose up light and high, something never before thought possible. By the 1850s, a leavening called baking powder made bread making almost foolproof and less labor intensive. And a new product called self-rising flour convinced homemakers that they could whip up delicious griddlecakes, cream biscuits, rolls, and all types of tea cakes with ease. Around this same time, Gold Rushers became acquainted with a San Francisco "wonder" bread called sourdough, and word of its goodness quickly spread. By 1886, Sarah T. Rorer declared in her *Philadelphia Cook Book*:

"Bread heads the list of foods for man." Another popular yeast bread was Sally Lunn. Butter and eggs made it rich, and a Turk's head mold made it decorative.

By 1868, yeast was commercially produced, and by the twentieth century, flour had become more refined. The coarser whole-wheat breads were enjoyed by the middle class, while the whiter breads were reserved for society's upper class. To ensure that all bread was nutritious, by the 1940s federal regulations required manufacturers to enrich their breads with the vitamins and minerals lost in the refining process.

Other products were also heading to market, including Wonder Bread sandwich loaf, heat-and-serve rolls, and refrigerated doughs. With time, bakeries began turning out coarser, more nutritious, artisanal breads that were often like those our forefathers had first baked and enjoyed centuries before.

White Bread (Daily Loaf)

In the 1848 edition of *Directions for Cookery in Its Various Branches*, Eliza Leslie advised her readers to bake several loaves of bread at a time, as it was not worthwhile to heat a brick oven for just a loaf or two: "Take one peck or two gallons of fine wheat flour, and sift it into a kneading trough, or into a small clean tub, or a large broad earthen pan . . ." She suggested wrapping each baked loaf in a clean, coarse towel, then standing the breads on their ends to cool. She also advised sprinkling the towels with water to make the crust less dry and hard. Our recipe only makes two loaves, but you can double it, if you wish.

PREP: 25 minutes plus rising ★ **BAKE:** 30 minutes
MAKES 2 loaves, 12 slices each

½ **cup warm water (105° to 115°F)**

2 packages active dry yeast

1 teaspoon plus ¼ cup sugar

2¼ cups milk, heated to warm (105° to 115°F)

4 tablespoons butter or margarine, softened

1 tablespoon salt

about 7½ cups all-purpose or bread flour

1. In large bowl, combine warm water, yeast, and 1 teaspoon sugar; stir well to dissolve. Let stand until foamy, about 5 minutes. Add milk, butter, remaining ¼ cup sugar, salt, and 4 cups flour. Beat well with wooden spoon. Gradually stir in 3 cups flour to make soft dough.

2. Turn dough onto floured surface. Knead until smooth and elastic, about 8 minutes, working in enough of remaining ½ cup flour just to keep dough from sticking.

3. Shape dough into ball; place in greased large bowl, turning dough to grease top. Cover bowl with plastic wrap and let rise in warm place (80° to 85°F) until doubled in volume, about 1 hour.

4. Grease two 9" by 5" metal loaf pans. Punch down dough. Turn dough onto lightly floured surface and cut in half. Shape each half into rectangle about 12" by 7." Roll each up from a short side. Pinch seam and ends to seal. Place dough, seam side down, in prepared pans. Cover pans loosely with greased plastic wrap; let dough rise in warm place until almost doubled, about 1 hour.

5. Meanwhile, preheat oven to 400°F. Bake until browned and loaves sound hollow when lightly tapped on bottom, 30 to 35 minutes. Remove loaves from pans and cool on wire racks.

EACH SLICE: About 187 calories, 5g protein, 34g carbohydrate, 3g total fat (2g saturated), 8mg cholesterol, 323mg sodium.

Cinnamon-Raisin Bread

Prepare as directed but stir *2 cups dark seedless raisins* into yeast mixture with milk. Spread each rectangle with *2 tablespoons butter or margarine*, softened, leaving ½-inch border. In small cup, combine *⅓ cup packed brown sugar* and *1 tablespoon ground cinnamon*; sprinkle over butter. Roll up each loaf from a short side. Pinch seam and ends to seal. Makes 2 loaves, 12 slices each.

EACH SLICE: About 244 calories, 5g protein, 47g carbohydrate, 4g total fat (2g saturated), 11mg cholesterol, 335mg sodium.

Mashed-Potato Loaf

Early American cookbooks often gave instructions for making Irish potato yeast from a boiled potato and yeast, which included a recommendation to let the starter work for half a day before using it to make a loaf of bread for the next day's breakfast. Recipes suggested using some of the potato water for the bread's liquid. Cookbook author Annabella P. Hill gives a recipe in her 1872 book *Southern Practical Cookery and Receipt Book* that includes six Irish potatoes that have been pushed through a sieve. She advises: "This bread keeps well." We agree. Potato breads store well and are nice and moist.

PREP: 1 hour 30 minutes plus rising ★ BAKE: 25 minutes
MAKES 2 loaves, 12 slices each

3 medium all-purpose potatoes (about 1 pound),
    peeled and cut into 1-inch pieces
1 cup warm water (105° to 115°F)
2 packages active dry yeast
2 tablespoons sugar
4¼ teaspoons salt
4 tablespoons butter or margarine, softened
about 9¾ cups all-purpose flour or 8¾ cups bread flour
2 large eggs

1. In 2-quart saucepan, combine potatoes and *4 cups water;* heat to boiling over high heat. Reduce heat; cover and simmer until potatoes are tender, about 15 minutes. Drain, reserving 1 cup potato water. Return potatoes to saucepan; mash until smooth.

2. In large bowl of electric mixer, combine warm water, yeast, and 1 tablespoon sugar; stir to dissolve. Let stand until foamy, about 5 minutes. Stir in 4 teaspoons salt, remaining 1 tablespoon sugar, butter, reserved potato water, and 3 cups flour.

3. With mixer at low speed, beat just until blended. Increase speed to medium; beat 2 minutes, occasionally scraping bowl with rubber spatula. Separate 1 egg. Cover egg white and reserve in refrigerator. Beat in remaining egg, egg yolk, and 1 cup flour to make thick batter; continue beating 2 minutes, frequently scraping bowl. With wooden spoon, stir in mashed potatoes, then 5 cups all-purpose flour or 4 cups bread flour, 1 cup at a time, to make soft dough. (You may want to transfer mixture to larger bowl for easier mixing.)

4. Turn dough onto well-floured surface. Knead until smooth and elastic, about 10 minutes, working in enough of remaining ¾ cup flour just to keep dough from sticking.

5. Shape dough into ball; place in greased large bowl, turning dough to grease top. Cover bowl with plastic wrap and let rise in warm place (80° to 85°F) until doubled in volume, about 1 hour.

6. Grease two 9" by 5" metal loaf pans. Punch down dough. Turn dough onto lightly floured surface and cut in half. Shape each dough half into rectangle about 12" by 7." Roll up from a short side. Pinch seam and ends to seal. Place dough, seam side down, in prepared pans. Cover pans with greased plastic wrap and let dough rise in warm place until doubled, about 40 minutes, or refrigerate up to overnight.

7. Meanwhile, preheat oven to 400°F. (If dough has been refrigerated, remove plastic wrap and let stand about 10 minutes before baking.) Beat reserved egg white with remaining ¼ teaspoon salt; brush over loaves. Bake until golden and loaves sound hollow when lightly tapped on bottom, 25 to 30 minutes. Remove loaves from pans; cool on wire racks.

EACH SLICE: About 231 calories, 6g protein, 43g carbohydrate, 3g total fat (1g saturated), 23mg cholesterol, 439mg sodium.

San Francisco Sourdough

According to one theory, Columbus brought a sourdough starter to the New World in the hold of his ship and is thus credited with introducing sourdough to America. This special bread grew in popularity thanks to the Alaskan sourdoughs: prospectors who carried sourdough starter in their packs so they could bake a batch of bread where and whenever they wanted.

PREP: 30 minutes plus 8 hours for starter plus rising
BAKE: 25 minutes per loaf ★ **MAKES** 2 loaves, 8 slices each

I cup Sourdough Starter (opposite)

1¾ cups warm water (105° to 115°F)

about 6 cups unbleached all-purpose flour or bread flour

I teaspoon active dry yeast

I tablespoon sugar

I tablespoon plus ¼ teaspoon salt

cornmeal for sprinkling

I large egg white

1. Prepare Sourdough Starter. Place 1 cup of starter in large glass or ceramic bowl. Add 1½ cups warm water and 3 cups flour; stir vigorously with wooden spoon. Cover bowl with plastic wrap; let stand in draft-free place 8 to 24 hours. (The longer the starter sits, the tangier the bread.)

2. In small bowl, combine remaining ¼ cup warm water, yeast, and sugar; stir to dissolve. Let stand until foamy, about 5 minutes. Stir 2 cups flour, yeast mixture, and 1 tablespoon salt into starter to make soft dough. Turn dough onto floured surface. Knead until smooth and elastic, about 8 minutes, working in enough of remaining 1 cup flour to make firm dough. Shape dough into ball; place in greased large bowl, turning dough to grease top of dough. Cover bowl with plastic wrap and let rise in warm place (80° to 85°F) until doubled in volume, about 2 hours.

3. Grease 2 large cookie sheets and sprinkle with cornmeal. Punch down dough. Turn dough onto lightly floured surface and cut in half. Shape each half into smooth round ball. Place 1 ball on each prepared cookie sheet. Cover loosely with greased plastic wrap and let dough rise until doubled, about 1 hour 30 minutes.

4. Meanwhile, preheat oven to 425°F. In small bowl, beat egg white with remaining ¼ teaspoon salt; brush over 1 loaf. With serrated knife or single-edge razor blade, cut six ¼-inch-deep slashes in top of 1 loaf to make crisscross pattern. Place 12 ice cubes in 13" by 9" baking pan. Place pan in bottom of oven. Bake slashed loaf until well browned and loaf sounds hollow when lightly tapped on bottom, 25 to 30 minutes. Transfer loaf to wire rack to cool completely. Repeat with remaining loaf.

EACH SLICE: About 205 calories, 6g protein, 41g carbohydrate, 1g total fat (0g saturated), 0mg cholesterol, 475mg sodium.

Sourdough Rolls

Prepare dough as directed through Step 2, but after first rising, cut dough into 24 equal pieces. Shape each piece into smooth round ball and place, 2 inches apart, on greased cookie sheets. Cover loosely with greased plastic wrap and let dough rise until doubled, about 1 hour. Brush with egg-white glaze. Bake until well browned, 20 to 25 minutes. Cool on wire rack. Makes 24 rolls.

EACH ROLL: About 135 calories, 4g protein, 28g carbohydrate, 1g total fat (0g saturated), 0mg cholesterol, 320mg sodium.

Sourdough Starter

PREP: 10 minutes plus 3 days
MAKES about 2 ⅔ cups starter

2 cups warm water (105° to 115°F)

I package active dry yeast

I tablespoon honey

2 cups unbleached all-purpose flour or bread flour

1. In large glass or ceramic bowl, combine warm water, yeast, and honey; stir to dissolve. Let stand until foamy, about 5 minutes. Gradually stir in flour. Cover bowl with clean kitchen towel and let stand in warm place (80° to 85°F) until starter stops bubbling and has a pleasant yeasty, sour aroma, 3 to 4 days. A clear amber liquid will separate from mixture; stir back into starter once a day. Pour starter into clean jar with lid. Place lid loosely on jar and refrigerate until ready to use.

2. To maintain starter, "feed" it once every 2 weeks: Remove jar from refrigerator and pour starter into large glass or ceramic bowl. Whisk in liquid that has separated. Measure out amount of starter needed for recipe. Replace amount used with equal amounts of flour and water. (For example, if recipe uses 1 cup starter, stir in 1 cup unbleached flour and 1 cup water.) Let starter stand at room temperature to become active again, 8 to 12 hours. Use immediately or refrigerate to use within 2 weeks before feeding again.

3. If not baking with starter every 2 weeks, discard or give away 1 cup before feeding. If at any point starter seems sluggish and breads are not rising well, stir 1 teaspoon active dry yeast dissolved in ¼ cup warm water (105° to 115°F) into starter and let stand at room temperature overnight.

Southern Sally Lunn

A recipe for this popular bread was often included in early cookbooks. Several stories exist regarding its origin. One of the more intriguing stories tells of an English girl who sold bread on the streets of Bath by crying *"Sol et Lune! Soleilune."* Another tale suggests that the name comes from *soleil et lune,* French for "sun and moon," referring to the golden top and the whitish bottom of the buns. By the time the tales and bread showed up in America in the nineteenth century, it was called Sally Lunn. Traditionally it is baked in a kugelhopf pan, which is a turban-shaped tube mold with swirled sides.

PREP: 20 minutes plus rising ★ **BAKE:** 40 minutes
MAKES 1 loaf, 16 slices

⅓ cup warm water (105° to 115°F)

1 package active dry yeast

1 teaspoon plus ⅓ cup sugar

½ cup milk, heated to warm (105° to 115°F)

½ cup butter or margarine (1 stick), softened

1¼ teaspoons salt

3¼ cups all-purpose flour

3 large eggs

1. In large bowl, combine warm water, yeast, and 1 teaspoon sugar; stir to dissolve. Let stand until foamy, about 5 minutes.

2. With mixer at low speed or with wooden spoon, beat warm milk, butter, salt, remaining ⅓ cup sugar, and 1¼ cups flour into yeast mixture. Increase mixer speed to medium; beat 2 minutes, occasionally scraping bowl with rubber spatula. Beat in eggs, one at a time, and 1 cup flour; continue beating 2 minutes, occasionally scraping bowl. With spoon, stir in remaining 1 cup flour. Cover bowl with slightly damp clean kitchen towel; let dough rise in warm place (80° to 85°F) until doubled in volume, about 1 hour.

3. Grease and flour 9- to 10-inch tube pan or kugelhopf mold. With spoon, stir down dough; spoon into prepared pan. With well-greased hands, pat dough evenly into pan. Cover pan with slightly damp towel; let rise in warm place until doubled, about 45 minutes.

4. Meanwhile, preheat oven to 350°F. Bake bread until golden and loaf sounds hollow when lightly tapped on bottom, 40 to 45 minutes. With narrow metal spatula, loosen bread from side of pan; remove from pan to cool on wire rack.

EACH SLICE: About 190 calories, 4g protein, 25g carbohydrate, 8g total fat (4g saturated), 56mg cholesterol, 255mg sodium.

Bee-Sting Cake

The German name for this yeast cake is *bienenstich*. As the tale goes, a German baker made the cake and glazed it with a honey, butter, and cream mixture. The sweet glaze attracted a bee, which then stung the baker. And that's how this cake got its name.

PREP: 40 minutes plus rising and cooling ★ **BAKE:** 20 minutes
MAKES 16 servings

CAKE

¼ cup warm water (105° to 115°F)
1 package active dry yeast
1 teaspoon plus ⅓ cup sugar
6 tablespoons butter or margarine, softened
1 large egg
1 large egg yolk
⅓ cup milk
1 teaspoon vanilla extract
¼ teaspoon salt
about 3 cups all-purpose flour

GLAZE

½ cup sugar
6 tablespoons butter or margarine
⅓ cup honey
3 tablespoons heavy or whipping cream
1½ teaspoons fresh lemon juice
1⅓ cups sliced natural almonds

Pastry Cream (page 272), optional

1. Prepare cake: In cup, combine yeast, warm water, and 1 teaspoon sugar; stir to dissolve. Let mixture stand until foamy, about 5 minutes.

2. Meanwhile, in large bowl, with mixer at medium speed, beat butter and remaining ⅓ cup sugar until blended, frequently scraping bowl with rubber spatula. Beat until creamy, about 1 minute. Reduce speed to low; beat in egg and egg yolk (mixture may look curdled). Beat in yeast mixture, milk, vanilla, salt, and 2½ cups flour until blended.

3. Turn dough onto floured surface and knead until smooth and elastic, about 5 minutes, working in enough of remaining ½ cup flour to make slightly sticky dough.

4. Shape dough into ball; place in greased large bowl, turning dough to grease top. Cover bowl with plastic wrap and let rise in warm place (80° to 85°F) until doubled in volume, about 1 hour.

5. Punch down dough; cover and let rest 15 minutes. Meanwhile, grease 13" by 9" baking pan. Line bottom and sides with foil; grease foil.

6. Turn dough into prepared pan. With hands, press dough evenly into pan, making sure to press dough into corners. Cover pan with plastic wrap; let dough rise in warm place until doubled, about 1 hour.

7. Meanwhile, preheat oven to 375°F. Prepare glaze: In 2-quart saucepan, combine sugar, butter, honey, and cream; heat to boiling over medium heat, stirring frequently. When butter has melted, remove from heat; stir in lemon juice. Set aside to cool slightly, about 5 minutes.

8. Evenly pour all but 3 tablespoons glaze over dough; scatter almonds over top. Drizzle remaining glaze over almonds. Place two sheets of foil underneath pan; crimp foil edges to form a rim to catch any overflow during baking. Bake cake until top is brown, 20 to 25 minutes. Cool in pan on wire rack 15 minutes. Run small knife between foil and edges of pan to loosen, then invert cake onto large cookie sheet. Gently peel off foil and discard. Immediately invert cake, almond side up, onto wire rack to cool completely.

9. If filling cake, prepare Pastry Cream. To fill cake, cut horizontally in half with a serrated knife and gently lift off top. Stir pastry cream to loosen. Spread over bottom half of cake. Replace top, cut side down.

EACH SERVING: About 297 calories, 5g protein, 36g carbohydrate, 15g total fat (7g saturated), 54mg cholesterol, 133mg sodium.

Bee-Sting Cake ▶

Monkey Bread

Recipes for Monkey Bread (also known as bubble loaf) began appearing in women's magazines in the mid-1950s. Before long, it was served at brunches and lunches across America. It's made from balls (bubbles) of dough that are dipped in butter, coated with cinnamon-sugar, and layered in a tube pan. There are several tales regarding the origin of the name Monkey Bread. One connects this popular bread with the monkey-puzzle tree (*Araucaria araucana*) which has prickly branches that are not easy to climb. Another legend links it to the fruit of the baobab tree (*Adansonia digitata*) of Africa, which is called monkey bread, while another connects the name to the fact that the bread resembles a pack of monkeys jumbled together. During the Reagan years, the First Lady made it a tradition to serve Monkey Bread at White House Christmas celebrations. She believed that the name of the bread reflected the fact that as you make it you have to monkey around with the dough.

PREP: 40 minutes plus rising ★ **BAKE:** 45 minutes
MAKES 16 servings

¾ **cup warm water (105° to 115°F)**

2 packages active dry yeast

1 teaspoon plus ¾ cup granulated sugar

¾ **cup butter or margarine (1½ sticks), softened**

1 teaspoon salt

about 5½ cups all-purpose flour

3 large eggs

½ **cup packed brown sugar**

1 teaspoon ground cinnamon

1. In large bowl, combine ½ cup warm water, yeast, and 1 teaspoon granulated sugar; stir to dissolve. Let stand until foamy, about 5 minutes. Add remaining ¼ cup warm water and ½ cup butter; mix well. With wooden spoon, stir in remaining ¾ cup granulated sugar, salt, and 2 cups flour just until blended. Gradually beat in eggs and 1 cup flour. Stir in 2¼ cups flour.

2. Turn dough onto lightly floured surface. Knead until smooth and elastic, 8 to 10 minutes, working in enough of remaining ¼ cup flour just to keep dough from sticking. Cut dough in half and cut each half into 16 equal pieces. Cover dough and let rest 15 minutes.

3. Meanwhile, in small bowl, combine brown sugar and cinnamon. Melt remaining ¼ cup butter; set aside. Grease 9- to 10-inch tube pan.

4. Shape each piece of dough into tight ball. Place half of balls in prepared pan; brush with half of melted butter and sprinkle with half of sugar mixture. Repeat with remaining dough, melted butter, and sugar mixture. Cover pan with plastic wrap and let dough rise in warm place (80° to 85°F) until doubled in volume, about 1 hour.

5. Meanwhile, preheat oven to 350°F. Bake until browned and bread sounds hollow when lightly tapped, about 45 minutes. If top browns too quickly, cover with foil during last 15 minutes of baking. Cool in pan on wire rack 10 minutes; remove from pan. Serve warm, or cool on wire rack to serve later. Reheat if desired.

EACH SERVING: About 319 calories, 6g protein, 50g carbohydrate, 11g total fat (6g saturated), 63mg cholesterol, 249mg sodium.

Finger Rolls

Mix one cup of scalded milk with one tablespoon of butter. When cool, add one teaspoon of sugar, one-half teaspoon of salt, four tablespoons of liquid yeast (one-fourth cup), and flour enough to make a soft dough—about three cups. Mix well, knead for fifteen minutes and set in a warm place to rise for three or four hours. When light, knead again. Shape small pieces of dough into balls, then roll on the molding board into a small, long finger roll, pointing the ends. Place the rolls in a shallow pan, let them rise for one hour, or until double in size, brush them over with a little beaten egg to give a glaze, and bake in a hot oven for ten or fifteen minutes.

—Good Housekeeping Everyday Cook Book, 1903

Coffee Cake Wreath

During the 1950s, national cooking contests encouraged home cooks to develop their own recipes and to enter them into competitions for blue ribbons, prizes, and trips to bake-offs. Women's magazines and food corporations often inspired readers with elaborate creations. This recipe, which is reminiscent of that era, turns a rich yeast coffee cake dough into a Christmas wreath that can be filled with either a sweet almond or cinnamon-sugar filling—perfect for Christmas morning. It's typical of the spectacular food presentations of the '50s that turned ordinary cooks into "stars" in their communities and sometimes beyond.

PREP: 40 minutes plus rising ★ **BAKE:** 30 minutes
MAKES I coffee cake, about 16 slices

CAKE

½ cup warm water (105° to 115°F)

2 packages active dry yeast

I teaspoon plus ½ cup sugar

½ cup butter or margarine (1 stick), softened

I large egg

½ teaspoon salt

about 3¼ cups all-purpose flour

choice of filling (opposite)

ICING (OPTIONAL)

I cup confectioners' sugar

2 tablespoons milk

1. In cup, combine warm water, yeast, and 1 teaspoon sugar; stir to dissolve. Let stand until mixture is foamy, about 5 minutes.

2. Meanwhile, in large bowl, with mixer at low speed, beat butter and remaining ½ cup sugar until blended. Increase speed to high; beat until light and fluffy, about 2 minutes, scraping bowl with rubber spatula. Reduce speed to low; beat in egg until blended. Beat in yeast mixture, salt, and ½ cup flour just until blended (batter will look curdled). With wooden spoon, stir in 2½ cups flour until blended.

3. Turn dough onto lightly floured surface. Knead until smooth and elastic, about 8 minutes, working in enough of remaining ¼ cup flour just to keep dough from sticking.

4. Shape dough into ball; place in greased large bowl, turning dough to grease top. Cover bowl with plastic wrap and let dough rise in warm place (80° to 85°F) until doubled in volume, about 1 hour.

5. Meanwhile, prepare filling of choice; cover and refrigerate until ready to use.

6. Punch down dough. Turn dough onto lightly floured surface; cover and let rest 15 minutes. Meanwhile, grease large cookie sheet.

7. With floured rolling pin, roll dough into 18" by 12" rectangle. Spread filling of choice over dough to within ½ inch of edges.

8. Starting at a long side, roll up dough jelly-roll fashion. Carefully lift roll and place, seam side down, on prepared cookie sheet. Shape roll into ring; press ends together to seal. With knife or kitchen shears, cut ring at 1½-inch intervals, up to but not completely through inside dough edge. Gently pull and twist each cut piece to show filling. Dough will be soft; use small metal spatula to help lift pieces. Cover and let dough rise in warm place until risen slightly, about 1 hour.

9. Meanwhile, preheat oven to 350°F. Bake wreath until golden, 30 to 35 minutes. Transfer to wire rack to cool.

10. Prepare icing, if using: In small bowl, mix confectioners' sugar with milk until smooth. When wreath is cool, drizzle with icing.

EACH SLICE WITHOUT FILLING AND ICING: About 176 calories, 3g protein, 26g carbohydrate, 6g total fat (4g saturated), 29mg cholesterol, 136mg sodium.

Sweet Almond Filling

In food processor with knife blade attached, process ½ cup whole blanched almonds and ¼ cup packed brown sugar until almonds are finely ground. Add 4 ounces almond paste, broken into chunks, and 2 large egg whites; process until mixture is smooth. Makes about 1 cup.

EACH TABLESPOON: About 71 calories, 2g protein, 7g carbohydrate, 4g total fat (0g saturated), 0mg cholesterol, 9mg sodium.

Cinnamon-Sugar Filling

In small bowl, combine ½ cup packed brown sugar, ½ cup whole blanched almonds, toasted and chopped, and ½ teaspoon ground cinnamon. After rolling out dough, brush with 2 tablespoons butter or margarine, melted, and sprinkle with sugar mixture. Makes about 1 cup.

EACH TABLESPOON: About 65 calories, 1g protein, 8g carbohydrate, 4g total fat (1g saturated), 4mg cholesterol, 18mg sodium.

Cloverleaf Rolls

(pictured on page 192)

Although these rolls are not mentioned in the first edition of *The Boston Cooking-School Cook Book,* later editions did include clover leaves [*sic*] in the list of possible shapes for dinner rolls. Crescents, braids, twists, bow-nots[*sic*], and other fancy shapes were popular choices too. Muffin-pan cups help the rolls to hold their shape and enable them to puff up high.

PREP: 30 minutes plus rising ★ **BAKE:** 10 minutes
MAKES 24 rolls

½ cup warm water (105° to 115°F)

2 packages active dry yeast

1 teaspoon plus ⅓ cup sugar

¾ cup milk, heated to warm (105° to 115°F)

4 tablespoons butter or margarine, softened

about 3¾ cups all-purpose flour

1½ teaspoons salt

2 large eggs

1 egg yolk mixed with 1 tablespoon water

1. In large bowl, combine warm water, yeast, and 1 teaspoon sugar; stir to dissolve. Let stand until foamy, about 5 minutes.

2. With wooden spoon or mixer at low speed, beat in warm milk, butter, ½ cup flour, remaining ⅓ cup sugar, salt, and eggs to make thick batter; continue beating 2 minutes, frequently scraping bowl with rubber spatula. Gradually stir in 3 cups flour to make soft dough.

3. Turn dough onto lightly floured surface. Knead until smooth and elastic, about 10 minutes, working in enough of remaining ¼ cup flour just to keep dough from sticking.

4. Shape dough into ball; place in greased large bowl, turning dough to grease top. Cover bowl with plastic wrap and let dough rise in warm place (80° to 85°F) until doubled in volume, about 1 hour.

5. Punch down dough; turn onto lightly floured surface; cover and let rest 15 minutes.

6. Grease twenty-four 2½-inch muffin-pan cups. Divide dough in half. Cut 1 dough half into 36 equal pieces; shape each piece into ball. Place 3 balls in each prepared muffin-pan cup. Repeat with remaining dough. Cover and let rise in warm place until doubled, about 30 minutes.

7. Meanwhile, preheat oven to 400°F. Brush rolls with egg-yolk mixture. Bake until golden and rolls sounds hollow when lightly tapped on bottom, 10 to 20 minutes, rotating sheets between upper and lower racks halfway through baking. Serve warm, or cool on wire racks to serve later.

EACH ROLL: About 130 calories, 3g protein, 19g carbohydrate, 4g total fat (2g saturated), 33mg cholesterol, 175mg sodium.

Parker House Rolls

As the story goes, these famous rolls were created by a German baker named Ward, who worked in the newly opened Parker House Hotel in Boston in 1855. He grew annoyed when a guest became unpleasant, and in his rage threw his unfinished rolls into the oven. They puffed up into light, delicious buns that not only put the guest into a good mood but also went on to make his employer, Harvey Parker, famous. In her 1896 cookbook, Fannie Farmer offers this tip: "Parker House Rolls may be shaped by cutting or tearing off small pieces of dough, and shaping round like a biscuit . . . let rise fifteen minutes. With handle of large wooden spoon, or toy rolling-pin, roll through centre of each biscuit, brush edge of lower halves with melted butter, fold, press lightly, place in buttered pan one inch apart, cover, let rise, and bake." The baked rolls often resemble little pocketbooks, which is another name for these delectable morsels. Our recipe features an ever-popular refrigerator dough, which can be refrigerated overnight or baked up right away,

PREP: 35 minutes plus rising ★ **BAKE:** 18 minutes
MAKES 40 rolls

1½ cups warm water (105° to 115°F)

2 packages active dry yeast

1 teaspoon plus ½ cup sugar

1 cup butter or margarine (2 sticks), softened

2 teaspoons salt

about 6 cups all-purpose flour

1 large egg

vegetable oil for brushing

1. In large bowl, combine ½ cup warm water, yeast, and 1 teaspoon sugar; stir to dissolve. Let stand until foamy, about 5 minutes. Stir in remaining 1 cup warm water, ½ cup butter, remaining ½ cup sugar, salt, and 2¼ cups flour. With wooden spoon or mixer at low speed, beat in egg and ¾ cup flour; continue beating 2 minutes, frequently scraping bowl with rubber spatula. Stir in 2½ cups flour to make soft dough.

2. Turn dough onto lightly floured surface. Knead until smooth and elastic, about 10 minutes, working in enough of remaining ½ cup flour just to keep dough from sticking.

3. Shape dough into ball; place in greased large bowl, turning dough to grease top. Cover bowl with plastic wrap and let rise in warm place (80° to 85°F) until doubled in volume, about 1½ hours.

4. Punch down dough and turn over; brush with oil. Cover bowl tightly with greased plastic wrap and refrigerate overnight or up to 24 hours. (Or, if you like, after punching down dough, shape into rolls as in Step 5. Cover and let rise until doubled, about 45 minutes, and bake as in Step 6.)

5. About 2½ hours before serving, melt remaining ½ cup butter in large deep roasting pan (17" by 11½"). On lightly floured surface, with floured rolling pin, roll out dough ½ inch thick. With floured 2¾-inch round biscuit cutter, cut out as many rounds as possible. Knead trimmings together; reroll and cut out more rounds. Dip both sides of each dough round into melted butter; fold rounds in half and arrange in rows in prepared pan, letting rolls touch each other. Cover and let rise in warm place until doubled, about 1½ hours.

6. Meanwhile, preheat oven to 400°F. Bake until golden and rolls sound hollow when lightly tapped on bottom, 18 to 20 minutes. Serve warm, or cool on wire racks to serve later.

EACH ROLL: About 125 calories, 2g protein, 17g carbohydrate, 5g total fat (3g saturated), 18mg cholesterol, 165mg sodium.

Hot Cross Buns

Fannie Farmer's original recipe for hot cross buns contains raisins and currants but no candied fruit. After the rolls are baked and cooled, she suggests decorating them with a simple ornamental-frosting cross. Americans have been baking these buns on Good Friday for generations. Some recipes now suggest slashing the tops of the unbaked rolls in a cross shape, then filling it with white frosting after baking.

PREP: 45 minutes plus rising ★ **BAKE:** 20 minutes
MAKES 25 buns

1 cup warm water (105° to 115°F)

2 packages active dry yeast

1 teaspoon plus ½ cup granulated sugar

1½ teaspoons ground cardamom

1½ plus ⅛ teaspoon salt

½ cup butter or margarine (1 stick), softened

about 4¾ cups all-purpose flour

2 large eggs

½ cup golden raisins

½ cup diced mixed candied fruit

1 cup confectioners' sugar

4 teaspoons water

1. In large bowl, combine warm water, yeast, and 1 teaspoon granulated sugar; stir to dissolve. Let stand until foamy, about 5 minutes. Stir in cardamom, 1½ teaspoons salt, butter, remaining ½ cup granulated sugar, and 1½ cups flour until mixed well. With mixer at low speed, beat just until blended.

2. Separate 1 egg. Cover egg white and reserve in refrigerator. Beat remaining egg, egg yolk, and ½ cup flour into flour mixture. With wooden spoon, stir in 2¼ cups flour to make soft dough.

3. Turn dough onto lightly floured surface. Knead until smooth and elastic, about 10 minutes, working in enough of remaining ½ cup flour just to keep dough from sticking.

4. Shape dough into a ball; place in greased large bowl, turning dough to grease top. Cover bowl with plastic wrap and let rise in warm place (80° to 85°F) until doubled in volume, about 1 hour.

5. Punch down dough. Knead in raisins and candied fruit. Cut dough into 25 equal pieces; cover loosely and let rest 15 minutes.

6. Grease large cookie sheet. Shape dough into balls. Arrange balls, ½ inch apart to allow for rising, in square shape, on prepared cookie sheet. Cover loosely and let rise in warm place until doubled, about 40 minutes.

7. Meanwhile, preheat oven to 375°F. In cup, with fork, beat reserved egg white with remaining ⅛ teaspoon salt; brush over buns. Bake until golden and buns sound hollow when lightly tapped on bottom, about 20 minutes. Transfer to wire racks to cool.

8. When buns are cool, prepare icing: In small bowl, mix confectioners' sugar and water until smooth. Spoon icing into small ziptight plastic bag; snip off one corner (or use a pastry bag fitted with a very small tip) and pipe cross on each bun. Let icing set before serving.

EACH BUN: About 190 calories, 3g protein, 34g carbohydrate, 5g total fat (3g saturated), 27mg cholesterol, 210mg sodium.

Festive Christmas Tree Buns

Prepare dough as directed through Step 5 and shape into balls. To make Christmas tree: Place 1 dough ball at top of lightly greased large cookie sheet. Make second row by centering 2 dough balls directly under first ball, placing them about ¼ inch apart to allow space for rising. Continue making rows, increasing each row by one ball and centering balls directly under previous row, until there are 6 rows in all. Leave space for rising. Use last 4 balls to make trunk of tree. Center 2 rows of 2 balls each under last row. Cover loosely and let rise in warm place until doubled, about 40 minutes. Brush with egg-white mixture and bake as directed. When buns are cool, prepare icing and pipe in zigzag pattern over tree.

EACH BUN: About 190 calories, 3g protein, 34g carbohydrate, 5g total fat (3g saturated), 27mg cholesterol, 210mg sodium.

Pennsylvania-Dutch Sticky Buns

German-speaking immigrants came here by way of the Rhineland and other parts of Germanic Europe, not from Holland, as their name, Pennsylvania Dutch, might suggest. The Mennonites settled in Germantown near Philadelphia, then the Amish, Bohemian Moravians, and others soon followed. The Pennsylvania Dutch became famous for their food specialties. These sticky buns are made with a rich yeast dough that is rolled up with currant filling, sliced, and then baked on top of a brown sugar–pecan mixture. The rolls are served glaze side up. Some believe that the first sticky buns appeared at about the same time that light corn syrup was introduced in 1912. These buns are a tradition in the Pennsylvania-Dutch countryside and in Philadelphia, where they are known as cinnamon buns.

PREP: 1 hour plus rising and overnight to chill
BAKE: 30 minutes ★ **MAKES** 20 buns

DOUGH

¼ cup warm water (105° to 115°F)

1 package active dry yeast

1 teaspoon plus ¼ cup granulated sugar

¾ cup milk

4 tablespoons butter or margarine, softened

1 teaspoon salt

3 large egg yolks

about 4 cups all-purpose flour

FILLING

½ cup packed dark brown sugar

¼ cup dried currants

1 tablespoon ground cinnamon

4 tablespoons butter or margarine, melted

TOPPING

⅔ cup packed dark brown sugar

3 tablespoons butter or margarine

2 tablespoons light corn syrup

2 tablespoons honey

1¼ cups pecans (5 ounces), coarsely chopped

1. Prepare dough: In cup, combine warm water, yeast, and 1 teaspoon granulated sugar; stir to dissolve. Let stand until foamy, about 5 minutes.

2. In large bowl, with mixer at low speed, blend yeast mixture with milk, butter, remaining ¼ cup granulated sugar, salt, egg yolks, and 3 cups flour until blended. With wooden spoon, stir in ¾ cup flour.

3. Turn dough onto lightly floured surface and knead until smooth and elastic, about 5 minutes, working in enough of remaining ¼ cup flour just to keep dough from sticking.

4. Shape dough into ball; place in greased large bowl, turning dough to grease top. Cover bowl with plastic wrap and let dough rise in warm place (80° to 85°F) until doubled in volume, about 1 hour.

5. Meanwhile, prepare filling: In bowl, combine brown sugar, currants, and cinnamon. Reserve melted butter.

6. Prepare topping: In 1-quart saucepan, combine brown sugar, butter, corn syrup, and honey. Heat over low heat, stirring, until brown sugar and butter have melted. Grease 13" by 9" baking pan; pour brown-sugar mixture into pan and sprinkle evenly with pecans; set aside.

7. Punch down dough. Turn dough onto lightly floured surface; cover and let rest 15 minutes. Roll dough into 18" by 12" rectangle. Brush with reserved melted butter and sprinkle with currant mixture. Starting at a long side, roll up jelly-roll fashion; place, seam side down, on surface. Cut dough crosswise into 20 equal slices.

8. Place slices, cut side down, on brown-sugar mixture in prepared baking pan, making four rows of five slices each. Cover pan and refrigerate at least 12 hours or up to 15 hours.

9. Preheat oven to 375°F. Bake buns until golden, about 30 minutes. Immediately place serving tray or jelly-roll pan over top of baking pan and invert; remove pan. Let buns cool slightly to serve warm, or cool on wire rack to serve later.

EACH BUN: About 290 calories, 4g protein, 42g carbohydrate, 12g total fat (5g saturated), 50mg cholesterol, 195mg sodium.

Cinnamon Buns

Prepare and shape dough as directed, omitting topping; bake as directed. Invert baked buns onto cookie sheet; remove baking pan and invert buns onto wire rack. In small bowl, mix *1 cup confectioners' sugar* and *5 teaspoons water* until smooth; drizzle over hot buns.

EACH BUN: About 215 calories, 4g protein, 36g carbohydrate, 6g total fat (3g saturated), 46mg cholesterol, 170mg sodium.

Soft Pretzels

These knot-shaped salted treats can be traced back to Roman times and have long been traditional in Germany and Alsace. The word *pretzel* is German, which some link to the Latin word *pretium,* meaning "reward" or "little gift." Legend has it that a monk from Alsace or northern Italy first twisted the pretzel into its unusual shape so it resembled the folded arms of a person at prayer. The Dutch are usually credited with bringing pretzels to America. The word *pretzel* first appeared here in print around 1824. The first pretzel bakery was founded in Lititz, Pennsylvania, in 1861. And since 1933, most pretzels have been twisted by machine.

PREP: 30 minutes plus rising ★ **BAKE** 16 minutes
MAKES 12 pretzels

2 cups warm water (105° to 115°F)
1 package active dry yeast
1 teaspoon sugar
about 4 cups all-purpose flour
1 teaspoon table salt
2 tablespoons baking soda
1 tablespoon kosher or coarse sea salt

1. In large bowl, combine 1½ cups warm water, yeast, and sugar; stir to dissolve. Let stand until foamy, about 5 minutes. Add 2 cups flour and table salt; beat well with wooden spoon. Gradually stir in 1½ cups flour to make soft dough.

2. Turn dough onto floured surface. Knead until smooth and elastic, about 6 minutes, working in enough of remaining ½ cup flour just to keep dough from sticking.

3. Shape dough into ball; place in greased large bowl, turning dough to grease top. Cover bowl with plastic wrap and let rise in warm place (80° to 85°) until doubled in volume, about 30 minutes.

4. Meanwhile, preheat oven to 400°F. Grease two large cookie sheets. Punch down dough and cut into 12 equal pieces. Roll each piece into 24-inch-long rope. Shape ropes into loop-shaped pretzels.

5. In small bowl, whisk remaining ½ cup warm water and baking soda until soda has dissolved.

6. Dip pretzels in baking soda mixture and place, 1½ inches apart, on prepared cookie sheets; sprinkle lightly with kosher salt. Bake until browned, 16 to 18 minutes, rotating sheets between upper and lower racks halfway through baking. Serve pretzels warm, or cool on wire racks to serve later.

EACH PRETZEL: About 165 calories, 5g protein, 33g carbohydrate, 1g total fat (0g saturated), 0mg cholesterol, 1190mg sodium.

Soft Pretzel Sticks

Prepare dough as directed, but roll each piece into 8-inch-long rope. Dip ropes in baking-soda mixture and place, 2 inches apart, on prepared cookie sheets. Sprinkle with kosher salt. Bake as directed.

Cheese Pizza

Raffaele Esposito supposedly created the first pizza made with pizza dough, tomato, basil, and mozzarella in Naples, Italy, in 1889. Neapolitan immigrants who settled in New York City in the early twentieth century made oversized pizzas—eighteen inches or more in diameter—and sold them by the slice, which made pizza perfect for a quick lunch or snack. Back in Italy, pizzas were nine to ten inches in diameter, served on dinner plates, and eaten with a knife and fork. Brick-oven pizzerias appeared as early as 1905 in Little Italy communities (Lombardi's was the first one in Manhattan). If you have a pizza stone, use it, as it helps to create a crispier crust.

PREP: 50 minutes plus dough rising and resting
BAKE: 15 minutes ★ **MAKES** 2 pizzas, 8 main-dish servings

PIZZA DOUGH

1¼ cups warm water (105° to 115°F)

1 package active dry yeast

1 teaspoon sugar

2 tablespoons olive oil

2 teaspoons salt

about 4 cups all-purpose flour or 3½ cups bread flour

PIZZA SAUCE

1 tablespoon olive oil

1 large garlic clove, finely chopped

1 can (28 ounces) tomatoes in thick puree, chopped

¼ teaspoon salt

cornmeal for sprinkling

¼ cup freshly grated Parmesan cheese

8 ounces mozzarella cheese, shredded (2 cups)

1. Prepare pizza dough: In large bowl, combine ¼ cup warm water, yeast, and sugar; stir to dissolve. Let stand until foamy, about 5 minutes. With wooden spoon, stir in remaining 1 cup warm water, oil, salt, and 1½ cups flour until smooth. Gradually add 2 cups all-purpose flour or 1½ cups bread flour, stirring until dough comes away from side of bowl.

2. Turn dough onto lightly floured surface. Knead until smooth and elastic, about 10 minutes, working in enough of remaining ½ cup flour just to keep dough from sticking. Shape dough into ball; place in greased large bowl, turning dough to grease top. Cover bowl with plastic wrap and let rise in warm place (80° to 85°F) until doubled in volume, about 1 hour.

3. Meanwhile, prepare pizza sauce: In 2-quart saucepan, heat oil over medium-high heat. Add garlic and cook, stirring often, until golden, about 30 seconds. Add tomatoes with puree and salt; heat to boiling over high heat. Reduce heat and simmer, uncovered, 10 minutes. Makes about 3 cups.

4. Punch down dough. Turn onto lightly floured surface and cut in half. Cover and let rest 15 minutes. Or, if not using right away, place dough in large greased bowl, cover loosely with greased plastic wrap, and refrigerate up to 24 hours.

5. Meanwhile, preheat oven to 450°F. Sprinkle two large cookie sheets with cornmeal. Shape each dough half into ball. On one prepared cookie sheet, with floured rolling pin, roll 1 ball of dough into 14" by 10" rectangle. Fold edges in to make 1-inch rim. Repeat with remaining dough ball.

6. Sprinkle dough with Parmesan. Spread pizza sauce over Parmesan and top with mozzarella. Let pizzas rest 20 minutes. Bake pizzas until crust is golden, 15 to 20 minutes, rotating cookie sheets between upper and lower oven racks halfway through baking.

EACH SERVING: About 400 calories, 15g protein, 56g carbohydrate, 13g total fat (5g saturated), 25mg cholesterol, 976mg sodium.

Buttermilk Biscuits

Many nineteenth-century cookbooks give recipes for soda biscuits that use super-carb soda to make them light and airy (one teaspoonful for every quart of flour). In the 1872 edition of Annabella P. Hill's *Southern Practical Cookery and Receipt Book,* she instructs bakers to sift the flour and super-carb soda together, then to "rub into the flour thoroughly a piece of butter the size of a hen's egg; salt to taste; wet the flour with sour milk until a soft dough is formed; make it into thin biscuit, and bake in a quick oven. Work it very little. Always reserve a little flour before putting in the soda to work into the dough, and flour the board." This good advice holds true even today.

PREP: 15 minutes ★ **BAKE:** 12 minutes
MAKES about 18 high biscuits or 36 thin biscuits

2 cups all-purpose flour

2½ teaspoons baking powder

½ teaspoon baking soda

½ teaspoon salt

¼ cup vegetable shortening

¾ cup buttermilk

1. Preheat oven to 450°F. In large bowl, combine flour, baking powder, baking soda, and salt. With pastry blender or two knives used scissor-fashion, cut in shortening until mixture resembles coarse crumbs. Stir in buttermilk, stirring just until mixture forms soft dough that leaves side of bowl.

2. Turn dough onto lightly floured surface; knead 6 to 8 times, just until smooth. With floured rolling pin, roll dough ½ inch thick for high, fluffy biscuits or ¼ inch thick for thin, crusty biscuits.

3. With floured 2-inch biscuit cutter, cut out rounds, without twisting cutter. Arrange biscuits on ungreased cookie sheet, 1 inch apart for crusty biscuits or nearly touching for soft-sided biscuits.

4. Press trimmings together. Reroll; cut out additional biscuits. Bake biscuits until golden, 12 to 15 minutes. Serve biscuits warm.

EACH HIGH BISCUIT: About 83 calories, 2g protein, 12g carbohydrate, 3g total fat (1g saturated), 0mg cholesterol, 178mg sodium.

Baking Powder Biscuits

Prepare as directed but substitute *¾ cup milk* for buttermilk and use *1 tablespoon baking powder;* omit baking soda. Makes about 18 biscuits.

Angel Biscuits

As the name suggests, these can best be described in one word: heavenly! Beginning in the late 1950s, Southern bakers began sharing recipes for the lightest, airiest, most delicious biscuits ever to come out of an oven. They were filed in recipe boxes under different names: Alabama biscuits, riz biscuits, bride's biscuits, and angel biscuits, which is the name usually used today. No one really knows who baked the first angel biscuit, but it is believed to have been a Southern flour miller. They are made from a never-fail recipe of all-purpose flour, three leaveners (baking powder, baking soda, and yeast), vegetable shortening (though some cooks use lard), usually some butter, plus sour milk (or buttermilk). Our recipe recommends patting out the dough to three-quarter-inch thickness, in contrast to regular biscuits that are patted out one-quarter to one-half inch thick.

PREP: 15 minutes plus rising ★ BAKE: 17 minutes
MAKES 2 dozen biscuits

¼ cup warm water (105° to 115°F)

1 package active dry yeast

1 teaspoon sugar

3 cups all-purpose flour

1½ teaspoons baking powder

½ teaspoon baking soda

¼ teaspoon salt

4 tablespoons cold butter or margarine, cut into pieces

2 tablespoons vegetable shortening

1 cup plus 2 tablespoons buttermilk

1. In small bowl, combine warm water, yeast, and sugar; stir to dissolve. Let stand until foamy, about 5 minutes.

2. In large bowl, combine flour, baking powder, baking soda, and salt. Stir until well combined. With pastry blender or two knives used scissor-fashion, cut in butter and shortening until mixture resembles coarse crumbs. Make well in center of mixture; pour in buttermilk and yeast mixture. Stir until well combined.

3. Turn dough onto lightly floured surface; knead several times, just until dough holds together and is smooth and elastic. Place in greased bowl, turning dough to grease top. Cover bowl with plastic wrap and let stand in warm place (80° to 85°F) until doubled in volume, about 1 hour.

4. Punch down dough. Cover and let stand 10 minutes.

5. On lightly floured surface, with floured hands, pat dough out until ¾ inch thick. With 2-inch round biscuit cutter, cut out rounds without twisting cutter. Place biscuits, 2 inches apart, on 2 ungreased large cookie sheets. Reserve trimmings for rerolling. Cover biscuits and let rise until almost doubled, about 30 minutes.

6. Meanwhile, preheat oven to 400°F. Bake biscuits until tops are pale golden, 17 to 20 minutes, rotating sheets between upper and lower racks halfway through baking. Serve warm.

EACH BISCUIT: About 95 calories, 2g protein, 14g carbohydrate, 3g total fat (2g saturated), 6mg cholesterol, 110mg sodium.

Tex-Mex Cheese Biscuits

Cooks in the Deep South know their biscuits and have been baking them since colonial days. In 1872, Annabella P. Hill suggested making cheese biscuits from "One pound of flour, half a pound of butter, half a pound of grated cheese; make up quick, and with very little handling, as puff paste. Roll thin; cut and bake in a quick oven. Salt to taste. " The problem with adding cheese to biscuit dough was that the rich cheese tended to prevent biscuits from becoming light and flaky. It's no wonder then that cheese biscuits were slow to catch on. But in the 1930s, they gained in popularity, and again in the 1980s when Tex-Mex food came into its own and achieved its rightful status as a unique cuisine. As often happens with popular ethnic ingredients, they get combined, so it is not surprising that cheesy biscuits were teamed up with chile peppers in true Tex-Mex style.

PREP: 15 minutes ★ **BAKE:** 13 minutes ★ **MAKES** 20 biscuits

2 cups all-purpose flour

1 tablespoon baking powder

½ teaspoon paprika

½ teaspoon salt

3 tablespoons cold butter or margarine, cut into pieces

2 tablespoons vegetable shortening

4 ounces shredded sharp or extrasharp Cheddar cheese (1 cup)

3 tablespoons drained and chopped pickled jalapeño chiles

¾ cup milk

1. Preheat oven to 450°F. In large bowl, combine flour, baking powder, paprika, and salt. With pastry blender or two knives used scissor-fashion, cut in butter and shortening until mixture resembles coarse crumbs. Stir cheese, chiles, and milk into flour mixture just until ingredients are blended and mixture forms a soft dough that leaves side of bowl.

2. Turn dough onto lightly floured surface. With lightly floured hands, pat dough into 10" by 4" rectangle. With floured knife, cut rectangle lengthwise in half, then cut each half crosswise to make five 2-inch squares. Cut each square diagonally in half to make 20 triangles in all. Place biscuits, 1 inch apart, on ungreased large cookie sheet.

3. Bake until golden, 13 to 15 minutes. Serve biscuits warm, or cool on wire rack to serve later.

EACH BISCUIT: About 104 calories, 3g protein, 11g carbohydrate, 5g total fat (3g saturated), 12mg cholesterol, 207mg sodium.

Homemade Muffins

Early American cookbooks often provided two types of muffin recipes: one that used yeast and another that used baking soda, beaten egg yolks, and stiffly beaten egg whites, which made the muffins as light as yeast ones. Muffins were rather plain, varying only in the type of flour (or meal) used, usually corn, whole-wheat, or rye. In the nineteenth century, Gems became popular. These muffins were always made with graham or whole-wheat flour and resembled today's bran muffins. Occasionally fresh fruit was added to the batter, turning them into Fruit Gems. Gems were always baked in a Gem pan: a heavy cast-iron pan that contains shallow, rounded-bottom, oblong cups. Until the late twentieth century, the American muffin menu was limited to varieties such as oatmeal, date, apple, and corn. Then in the '70s and '80s, muffin mania set in. No longer were muffins simple. Before being baked, extra ingredients, such as shredded vegetables, fruit, jams or jellies, nuts, and even chocolate, were added to the batter. Sometimes the muffins were showered with chocolate chips or coconut, glazed or frosted, or covered with a rich cinnamon streusel. Muffins as we know them today had arrived.

PREP: 10 minutes ★ **BAKE:** 20 minutes
MAKES 12 muffins

2½ cups all-purpose flour

½ cup sugar

1 tablespoon baking powder

½ teaspoon salt

1 cup milk

½ cup butter or margarine (1 stick), melted

1 large egg

1 teaspoon vanilla extract

1. Preheat oven to 400°F. Grease twelve 2½" by 1¼" muffin-pan cups. In large bowl, combine flour, sugar, baking powder, and salt. In medium bowl, with fork, beat milk, melted butter, egg, and vanilla until blended. Add to flour mixture, stirring just until flour is moistened (batter will be lumpy).

2. Spoon batter into prepared muffin-pan cups. Bake until toothpick inserted in center of muffin comes out clean, 20 to 25 minutes. Immediately remove muffins from pan. Serve muffins warm, or cool on wire rack to serve later.

EACH MUFFIN: About 225 calories, 4g protein, 30g carbohydrate, 10g total fat (6g saturated), 41mg cholesterol, 312mg sodium.

Jam-Filled Muffins

Prepare as directed but fill muffin-pan cups one-third full with batter. Drop *1 rounded teaspoon strawberry or raspberry preserves* in center of each; top with remaining batter. Bake as directed.

Blueberry or Raspberry Muffins

Prepare as directed; stir *1 cup blueberries or raspberries* into batter.

Walnut or Pecan Muffins

Prepare as directed; stir *½ cup chopped toasted walnuts or pecans* into batter. Sprinkle with *2 tablespoons sugar* before baking.

Boston Brown Bread

One cup of sour milk, one-half cup of New Orleans molasses, one egg, butter size of walnut, one teaspoon of soda in the milk, and enough graham flour to thicken like cake. Steam three hours; start over cold water.

—**Good Housekeeping Everyday Cook Book**, 1903

Blueberry Hill Scones

Originally a Scottish word, *scone* probably comes from the word *schoonbrot* or *sconbrot,* meaning "fine white bread." To the colonists, scones were small, fairly plain cakes that were leavened either with baking soda and an acid ingredient such as sour milk or with baking powder. They were meant to be eaten piping hot with butter, then later on were enjoyed with clotted cream and jam. Scones were always served at afternoon tea. Traditionally they were baked on a *girdle* (griddle), but today they're usually baked in the oven. Scones did not often appear in early-nineteenth-century American cookbooks, although recipes for biscuits were almost always present.

PREP: 15 minutes ★ **BAKE:** 22 minutes ★ **MAKES** 12 scones

2 cups all-purpose flour

¼ cup sugar

1 tablespoon baking powder

¼ teaspoon salt

4 tablespoons cold butter or margarine, cut into pieces

1 cup blueberries

⅔ cup heavy or whipping cream

1 large egg

½ teaspoon freshly grated lemon peel

1. Preheat oven to 375°F. In large bowl, with fork, mix flour, sugar, baking powder, and salt. With pastry blender or two knives used scissor-fashion, cut butter into dry ingredients until mixture resembles coarse crumbs. Add blueberries and toss to mix.

2. In small bowl, with fork, mix cream, egg, and lemon peel until blended. Slowly pour cream mixture into dry ingredients and stir with rubber spatula just until soft dough forms.

3. With lightly floured hand, knead dough 3 to 4 times in bowl, just until it comes together; do not overmix. Divide dough in half. On lightly floured surface, shape each half into 6-inch round. With floured knife, cut each round into 6 wedges. Place wedges, 1 inch apart, on ungreased large cookie sheet.

4. Bake scones until golden brown, 22 to 25 minutes. Serve warm, or cool on wire rack to serve later.

EACH SCONE: About 190 calories, 3g protein, 23g carbohydrate, 9g total fat (6g saturated), 46mg cholesterol, 220mg sodium.

◀ *Blueberry Hill Scones*

Yankee Popovers

In Fannie Farmer's 1896 cookbook, she suggests using a Dover egg-beater for mixing the Pop-over [*sic*] batter. Her directions for baking popovers are clear: ". . . turn [batter] into hissing hot buttered iron gem pans, and bake thirty to thirty-five minutes in a hot oven. They may be baked in buttered earthen cups, when the bottom will have a glazed appearance. Small round iron gem pans are best for Pop-overs."

PREP: 10 minutes ★ **BAKE:** 1 hour
MAKES 8 medium or 12 small popovers

3 large eggs

1 cup milk

3 tablespoons butter or margarine, melted

1 cup all-purpose flour

1/2 teaspoon salt

1. Preheat oven to 375°F. Generously grease eight 6-ounce custard cups or twelve 2½" by 1¼" muffin-pan cups. Place custard cups in jelly-roll pan for easier handling.

2. In medium bowl, with mixer at low speed, beat eggs until frothy. Beat in milk and melted butter until blended. Gradually beat in flour and salt. (Or, in blender, combine eggs, milk, butter, flour, and salt. Blend until smooth.)

3. Pour about ⅓ cup batter into each prepared custard cup or fill muffin-pan cups half full. Bake 50 minutes, then with tip of knife, quickly cut small slit in top of each popover to release steam; bake 10 minutes longer. Immediately remove popovers from cups, loosening popovers with spatula if necessary. Serve hot.

EACH MEDIUM POPOVER: About 160 calories, 5g protein, 14gcarbohydrate, 9g total fat (5g saturated), 101mg cholesterol, 250mg sodium.

EACH SMALL POPOVER: About 105 calories, 3g protein, 9g carbohydrate, 6g total fat (3g saturated), 67mg cholesterol, 165mg sodium.

Herb Popovers

Prepare as directed, adding *2 tablespoons chopped chives or green onion* to batter in Step 2. Bake as directed.

Herb Popovers ▶

Golden Corn Bread

In an effort to stave off hunger and to become less dependent on supplies (such as wheat flour) that were imported from England, the earliest settlers took lessons in the use of local products from their new Native American friends. Corn was plentiful, so the colonists often used it for bread instead of the more scarce whole-wheat flour. They baked ash cakes right in the fire's ashes, hoecakes on a hoe before the fire, and corn sticks in a mold. Corn pone (later known as corn bread), made from cornmeal, water, and salt, was usually baked directly over hot coals in a spider: a cast-iron skillet with three short legs. Throughout the Deep South, corn bread is still baked in a cast-iron skillet, and corn sticks are baked in a heavy cast-iron mold. Before adding the batter, the skillet is coated with a little shortening or bacon fat and heated up until sizzling hot. When the cold batter is poured in, the batter starts cooking immediately and a tempting golden crust forms. Even today, the best recipes instruct cooks to preheat the pan before adding the batter.

PREP: 10 minutes ★ **BAKE:** 25 minutes
MAKES 8 servings

4 tablespoons butter or margarine

1½ cups cornmeal

1 cup all-purpose flour

2 teaspoons baking powder

1 teaspoon salt

¼ teaspoon baking soda

1¾ cups buttermilk

2 large eggs

1. Preheat oven to 450°F. Place butter in 10-inch cast-iron skillet or 9-inch square baking pan; place in oven just until butter melts, 3 to 5 minutes. Tilt skillet to coat.

2. Meanwhile, in large bowl, combine cornmeal, flour, baking powder, salt, and baking soda. In bowl, with fork, beat buttermilk and eggs until blended. Add melted butter to buttermilk mixture, then add to flour mixture. Stir just until flour is moistened (batter will be lumpy).

3. Pour batter into prepared skillet. Bake until golden at edge and toothpick inserted in center comes out clean, about 25 minutes. Serve warm.

EACH SERVING: About 243 calories, 7g protein, 35g carbohydrate, 8g total fat (4g saturated), 71mg cholesterol, 584mg sodium.

◄ *Golden Corn Bread*

Hush Puppies

Several legends explain how these fried balls of corn bread became known as hush puppies. One tale dates back to the Civil War. Confederate soldiers frequently cooked dinner over an open fire. Whenever Yankee soldiers were nearby, the Southerners would fry up bits of corn bread and throw them to the dogs, giving the command "Hush, puppies!" in order to keep them quiet. Another legend cites the hounds that often went along on hunting and fishing expeditions in the South. Whenever the hounds smelled fish frying, they would loudly yelp. To quiet them, the hunters fried bits of cornmeal batter alongside the fish, then tossed the corn-bread balls to the dogs, while saying "Hush, puppies!" Hush puppies flavored with onion remain a tradition in the South and are often served on the same platter with fried fish or wrapped inside a paper napkin in a wicker breadbasket.

PREP: 15 minutes plus standing ★ **COOK:** 3 minutes per batch
MAKES about 36 hush puppies, 9 servings

vegetable oil for frying
1¾ cups cornmeal, preferably stone ground
¼ cup all-purpose flour
2 teaspoons sugar
1½ teaspoons baking powder
¾ teaspoon salt
½ teaspoon baking soda
¼ teaspoon ground black pepper
pinch ground red pepper (cayenne)
1 cup buttermilk
1 medium onion, grated (½ cup)
2 large eggs

1. In 5- to 6-quart Dutch oven, heat 2 inches oil over medium heat until temperature reaches 350°F on deep-fat thermometer.

2. Meanwhile, in large bowl, combine cornmeal, flour, sugar, baking powder, salt, baking soda, black pepper, and ground red pepper. Whisk until blended.

3. In medium bowl, with wire whisk, whisk buttermilk, onion, and eggs until blended. Add buttermilk mixture to cornmeal mixture; stir until blended. Let batter stand 5 minutes.

4. Meanwhile, preheat oven to 200°F. Line cookie sheet with paper towels. In batches, drop batter by rounded teaspoons into hot oil, using another teaspoon to push batter from spoon. Cook, turning once, until browned and cooked through, 2 to 3 minutes. With slotted spoon, transfer to paper towel–lined cookie sheet; keep warm in oven. Repeat with remaining batter. Serve immediately.

EACH SERVING: About 253 calories, 5g protein, 27g carbohydrate, 14g total fat (2g saturated), 48mg cholesterol, 388mg sodium.

Spoonbread

This popular southern specialty is more like a tender, custardy soufflé than a bread. Some historians believe that its name comes from the Native American word *suppawn*, meaning "porridge." Others think its name is derived from the fact that it's eaten with a spoon. Curiously, this recipe did not appear in cookbooks until the twentieth century.

PREP: 15 minutes plus standing ★ **BAKE:** 40 minutes
MAKES 8 accompaniment servings

3 cups milk
½ teaspoon salt
¼ teaspoon ground black pepper
1 cup cornmeal
4 tablespoons butter or margarine, cut into pieces
3 large eggs, separated

1. Preheat oven to 400°F. Generously grease shallow 1½-quart baking dish.

2. In 4-quart saucepan, combine milk, salt, and pepper; heat to boiling over medium-high heat. Remove from heat; with wire whisk, whisk in cornmeal. Add butter, stirring until melted. Let stand 5 minutes.

3. Whisk egg yolks, one at a time, into cornmeal mixture, until blended. In small bowl, with mixer at high speed, beat egg whites just until soft peaks form when beaters are lifted. Gently fold egg whites, one-half at a time, into cornmeal mixture. Pour into prepared baking dish; spread evenly. Bake until spoonbread is set, about 40 minutes. Serve immediately.

EACH SERVING: About 203 calories, 7g protein, 18g carbohydrate, 11g total fat (6g saturated), 108mg cholesterol, 272mg sodium.

Spoonbread ▶

Cape Cod Cranberry-Nut Loaf

During that first winter in Plymouth, the Pilgrims found several foods growing wild, including cranberries, which grew along the sandy coastline. With the introduction of baking powder in 1856, breads known as lightnin' breads, aerated breads, or quick breads, became popular. Double-acting baking powder, which showed up on the market in 1889, produced a lighter, higher loaf because it made the batter rise once when the liquid and dry ingredients were combined and a second time in the oven, hence its name.

PREP: 20 minutes plus cooling ★ **BAKE:** 55 minutes
MAKES 1 loaf, 12 slices

1 large orange
2½ cups all-purpose flour
1 cup sugar
2 teaspoons baking powder
½ teaspoon baking soda
½ teaspoon salt
2 large eggs
4 tablespoons butter or margarine, melted
2 cups fresh or frozen cranberries, coarsely chopped
¾ cup walnuts, chopped (optional)

1. Preheat oven to 375°F. Grease 9" by 5" metal loaf pan. From orange, grate peel and squeeze ½ cup juice.

2. In large bowl, combine flour, sugar, baking powder, baking soda, and salt. In small bowl, with wire whisk or fork, beat eggs, butter, and orange peel and juice. With wooden spoon, stir egg mixture into flour mixture just until blended (batter will be stiff). Fold in cranberries and walnuts, if using.

3. Spoon batter into prepared pan. Bake until toothpick inserted in center comes out clean, 55 to 60 minutes. Cool bread in pan on wire rack 10 minutes; remove from pan and cool completely on wire rack.

EACH SLICE WITHOUT WALNUTS: About 223 calories, 4g protein, 40g carbohydrate, 5g total fat (3g saturated), 46mg cholesterol, 281mg sodium.

◄ *Cape Cod Cranberry-Nut Loaf*

Lemon Tea Bread

The early settlers brought their memories of afternoon tea, plus recipes for tea sandwiches and sweet treats, to the New World. From 1860 to 1900, many well-to-do families entertained frequently, as they had servants. Since people often had to travel long distances to visit, dinner parties were replaced by afternoon tea parties for the ladies: low tea, which included a plate of thin sandwiches or cakes, and high tea, which featured more substantial foods, such as lobster in pastry. This lemon tea bread is typical of the kind of sweets that were often taken with a cup of tea. It is more like cake than bread, so it can be cut into small squares and set out alongside other pastries.

PREP: 25 minutes ★ **BAKE:** 1 hour 5 minutes
MAKES 1 loaf, 16 slices

2½ cups all-purpose flour
1½ teaspoons baking powder
½ teaspoon baking soda
½ teaspoon salt
½ cup butter or margarine (1 stick), softened
1¼ cups sugar
2 teaspoons freshly grated lemon peel
2 large eggs
1 container (8 ounces) sour cream
1 teaspoon vanilla extract

1. Preheat oven to 350°F. Grease 9" by 5" metal loaf pan; dust with flour.

2. In medium bowl, combine flour, baking powder, baking soda, and salt. In large bowl, with mixer at low speed, beat butter until creamy. Add sugar and lemon peel and beat until fluffy, about 2 minutes.

3. Reduce speed to low and add eggs, one at a time, beating well after each addition, occasionally scraping bowl with rubber spatula. Add flour mixture alternately with sour cream, beginning and ending with flour mixture. Add vanilla. Beat just until smooth, scraping bowl.

4. Spoon batter into prepared pan; spread evenly. Bake until toothpick inserted in center of loaf comes out clean, about 1 hour 5 minutes. Cool loaf in pan on wire rack 10 minutes. Remove from pan and cool completely on wire rack.

EACH SLICE: About 225 calories, 3g protein, 31g carbohydrate, 10g total fat (6g saturated), 48mg cholesterol, 230mg sodium.

Banana Bread

At the Philadelphia Centennial Exposition of 1876, the owners of the Boston Fruit Company introduced the banana, which was wrapped in foil and sold as an exotic fruit for a dime. The company imported large shipments of bananas from Jamaica and other places and wanted to increase the demand for the fruit—and it worked. By the turn of the century, bananas were being shipped nationwide.

PREP: 20 minutes ★ **BAKE:** 1 hour 10 minutes
MAKES 1 loaf, 12 slices

2½ **cups all-purpose flour**

2 **teaspoons baking powder**

¾ **teaspoon salt**

½ **teaspoon baking soda**

1½ **cups mashed very ripe bananas (3 medium)**

¼ **cup milk**

2 **teaspoons vanilla extract**

½ **cup butter or margarine (1 stick), softened**

1 **cup sugar**

2 **large eggs**

1. Preheat oven to 350°F. Grease 9" by 5" metal loaf pan. In medium bowl, combine flour, baking powder, salt, and baking soda. In small bowl, combine bananas, milk, and vanilla.

2. In large bowl, with mixer at medium speed, beat butter and sugar until light and fluffy. Beat in eggs, one at a time. Reduce speed to low; alternately add flour mixture and banana mixture, beginning and ending with flour mixture, occasionally scraping bowl with rubber spatula. Beat just until blended.

3. Pour batter into prepared pan. Bake until toothpick inserted in center comes out clean, about 1 hour 10 minutes. Cool in pan on wire rack 10 minutes; remove from pan and cool completely on wire rack.

EACH SLICE: About 274 calories, 4g protein, 44g carbohydrate, 9g total fat (5g saturated), 57mg cholesterol, 371mg sodium.

Banana-Nut Bread

Prepare bread as directed but fold *1 cup walnuts or pecans (4 ounces),* coarsely chopped, into batter before baking.

Bishop's Bread

Along the American frontier, during the nineteenth century, clergymen frequently visited parishioners by traveling from village to village, often on horseback. As the story goes, early one Sunday morning, a circuit-riding bishop unexpectedly stopped by the home of a Kentucky parishioner just in time for breakfast. His hostess threw together this quick bread from foods she found in her cupboard. Reportedly her bread contained fruit and nuts. Our version also has chocolate bits.

PREP: 20 minutes ★ **BAKE:** 55 minutes
MAKES 1 loaf, 12 slices

1½ **cups all-purpose flour**

1 **teaspoon baking powder**

¼ **teaspoon salt**

1 **cup walnuts or pecans (4 ounces), chopped**

½ **cup red candied cherries, halved**

½ **cup pitted dates, finely chopped**

½ **cup semisweet chocolate chips**

4 **tablespoons butter or margarine, softened**

1 **cup sugar**

3 **large eggs**

1. Preheat oven to 325°F. Grease and flour 9" by 5" metal loaf pan. In medium bowl, combine flour, baking powder, and salt. In small bowl, combine walnuts, cherries, dates, and chocolate chips.

2. In large bowl, with mixer at low speed, beat butter and sugar until well blended and texture of wet sand, about 2 minutes. Add eggs, one at a time, beating well after each addition. Add flour mixture and beat just until blended. Stir in fruit mixture.

3. Turn batter into prepared pan. Bake until toothpick inserted in center comes out clean, 55 to 60 minutes. Cool in pan on wire rack 10 minutes; remove from pan and cool completely on wire rack. Bread is best if wrapped and served the next day.

EACH SLICE: About 319 calories, 5g protein, 46g carbohydrate, 14g total fat (5g saturated), 63mg cholesterol, 146mg sodium.

The Baker's First Ovens

During the seventeenth century, life centered around the hearth, where all of the cooking was done. Bread was an important part of the day's meals, so the ability to bake it at home was critical. The first baker's oven was simply a sheet of tin. It was attached to the hearth and reflected the fire's heat onto the bread. The reflected heat browned the top crust, while the heat from the hearthstone browned the bottom. Next came the Dutch oven: a portable metal box that was set on the hearth with one open side facing the fire. Usually the box was fitted with shelves, which allowed several breads, cakes, or pies to be baked at the same time. Last came the reflecting oven, which was about a foot square and was made of tin. Its rear wall threw the heat from the fire in the front back into the oven. It could be heated to a higher temperature than previous ovens, as its curved canopy radiated even more heat back into the oven. This reflecting oven was also frequently used for roasting.

As the art of brick work continued to develop in the seventeenth century, fixed brick ovens began appearing. One of the first was a brick compartment built into the walls of the fireplace. A fire was lit inside the oven and was allowed to burn until the oven was the right temperature for baking. The ashes were then scraped out and the food put in. The food that needed the longest baking time was slid to the back, while cakes, pies, and cookies were placed in the front. A tight-fitting wooden shield closed off the oven's open side, and the food was then baked by the heat from the hearth.

When the size of homes increased, separate bake ovens were often built. The height of luxury was a bake oven with a hinged iron door and a damper that could be opened and closed at will, regulating the flow of air and the intensity of the fire and the temperature inside the oven.

Later, in the eighteenth century, cookstoves would appear. But the ambience, efficiency, and success of baking in those first masonry ovens would be hard to beat.

Boston Brown Bread

This dark, moist bread was a favorite of the Puritans, who often served it during the Sabbath along with Boston baked beans. Evan Jones cites a recipe for Boston Brown Bread that appeared in a Yankee cookbook that was carried west in a covered wagon: "One cup of sweet milk, One cup of sour, One cup of corn meal, One cup of flour, Teaspoon of soda, Molasses one cup, Steam for three hours, then eat it all up."

PREP: 15 minutes ★ **BAKE:** 55 to 60 minutes
MAKES 1 loaf, 12 slices

1 cup all-purpose flour

1 cup whole-wheat flour

¼ cup sugar

1¼ teaspoons baking soda

½ teaspoon salt

¾ cup dark seedless raisins

1¼ cups buttermilk or plain lowfat yogurt

¾ cup light (mild) molasses

1 large egg

1. Preheat oven to 350°F. Grease 9" by 5" metal loaf pan. In large bowl, combine all-purpose and whole-wheat flours, sugar, baking soda, and salt. Add raisins; stir in buttermilk, molasses, and egg until batter is just mixed (batter will be very wet).

2. Pour batter into prepared pan. Bake until toothpick inserted in center of loaf comes out clean, 55 to 60 minutes. Cool in pan on wire rack 10 minutes. With narrow metal spatula, loosen bread from sides of pan. Remove bread from pan and cool slightly on wire rack to serve warm, or cool completely to serve later.

EACH SLICE: About 190 calories, 4g protein, 42g carbohydrate, 1g total fat (0g saturated), 19mg cholesterol, 270mg sodium.

Sour Cream Coffee Cake

Show-off cakes, such as this buttery sour-cream version with cinnamon-nut swirls, often appeared in women's magazines between 1945 and 1960. They had the wow factor to impress family and friends and a melt-in-your-mouth flavor. Home economists in magazine test kitchens tested recipes and wrote them out so precisely that even novice bakers (of which there were many) could become star hostesses.

PREP: 30 minutes ★ **BAKE:** 1 hour 20 minutes
MAKES 16 servings

---

²⁄₃ plus 1¾ cups sugar

²⁄₃ cup walnuts, finely chopped

1 teaspoon ground cinnamon

3¾ cups all-purpose flour

2 teaspoons baking powder

1 teaspoon baking soda

¾ teaspoon salt

½ cup butter or margarine (1 stick), softened

3 large eggs

2 teaspoons vanilla extract

1 container (16 ounces) sour cream

1. Preheat oven to 350°F. Grease and flour 9- to 10-inch tube pan with removable bottom. In small bowl, combine ²⁄₃ cup sugar, walnuts, and cinnamon. In medium bowl, combine flour, baking powder, baking soda, and salt.

2. In large bowl, with mixer at low speed, beat butter and remaining 1¾ cups sugar until blended, frequently scraping bowl with rubber spatula. Increase speed to high; beat until light and fluffy, about 2 minutes, occasionally scraping bowl. Reduce speed to low; add eggs, one at a time, beating well after each addition. Beat in vanilla.

3. With mixer at low speed, alternately add flour mixture and sour cream, beginning and ending with flour mixture. Beat until smooth, occasionally scraping bowl.

4. Spoon one-third of batter into prepared pan. Sprinkle about ½ cup nut mixture evenly over batter, then top with half of remaining batter. Sprinkle evenly with ½ cup more nut mixture; top with remaining batter, then sprinkle with remaining nut mixture.

5. Bake coffee cake until toothpick inserted in center comes out clean, about 1 hour 20 minutes. Cool in pan on wire rack 10 minutes. Run thin knife around cake to loosen from side and center tube of pan; lift tube to separate cake from pan side. Invert cake onto plate; slide knife under cake to separate from bottom of pan. Turn cake, nut-mixture side up, onto wire rack to cool completely.

EACH SERVING: About 388 calories, 6g protein, 55g carbohydrate, 17g total fat (8g saturated), 68mg cholesterol, 336mg sodium.

Sour Cream Coffee Cake ▶

Sour Cream–Pear Coffee Cake

Early cookbooks did not contain the kinds of coffee cakes we are familiar with today, but there were recipes for muffins, batter cakes, and Sally Lunn. By most accounts, coffee klatches and the cakes served at them were a twentieth-century phenomenon. After World War II, the boom years brought families to suburbia, where making friends with nearby neighbors was a new adventure. On weekdays when husbands were at work, taking time to visit with the ladies over coffee was a frequent affair. Quick coffee cakes, such as this cinnamon-crumb classic, were often the featured specialty.

PREP: 25 minutes ★ **BAKE:** 40 minutes ★ **MAKES** 16 servings

STREUSEL

⅔ cup packed light brown sugar

½ cup all-purpose flour

1 teaspoon ground cinnamon

4 tablespoons butter or margarine, softened

⅔ cup walnuts, toasted and chopped

CAKE

2½ cups all-purpose flour

1½ teaspoons baking powder

½ teaspoon baking soda

½ teaspoon salt

6 tablespoons butter or margarine, softened

1¼ cups granulated sugar

2 large eggs

1½ teaspoons vanilla extract

1⅓ cups sour cream

3 firm but ripe Bosc pears (about 1¼ pounds),*
    peeled, cored, and cut into 1-inch pieces

1. Preheat oven to 350°F. Grease 13" by 9" baking pan; dust with flour.

2. Prepare streusel: In medium bowl, with fork, mix brown sugar, flour, and cinnamon until well blended. With fingertips, work in butter until evenly distributed. Add walnuts and toss to mix; set aside.

3. Prepare cake: In another medium bowl, combine flour, baking powder, baking soda, and salt. In large bowl, with mixer at low speed, beat butter with sugar until blended, frequently scraping bowl with rubber spatula. Increase speed to high; beat until fluffy, about 2 minutes, occasionally scraping bowl. Reduce speed to low; add eggs, one at a time, beating well after each addition. Beat in vanilla.

4. Reduce speed to low. Add flour mixture alternately with sour cream, beginning and ending with flour mixture. Beat until batter is smooth, occasionally scraping bowl. With rubber spatula, gently fold in pears.

5. Spoon batter into prepared pan; spread evenly. Evenly sprinkle with streusel mixture. Bake until toothpick inserted in center comes out clean, 40 to 45 minutes. Cool cake in pan on wire rack 1 hour to serve warm, or cool completely in pan to serve later.

* The pears can be replaced with an equal amount of apples, peaches, or plums, or 2 cups of blueberries.

EACH SERVING: About 352 calories, 5g protein, 50g carbohydrate, 16g total fat (8g saturated), 54mg cholesterol, 253mg sodium.

Cinnamon Doughnuts

Before leaving for the New World, the Pilgrims and the early Dutch colonists spent several years in Holland, where many learned to make doughnuts. They were described in Washington Irving's 1809 *History of New York* as "balls of sweetened dough, fried in hog's fat, and called doughnuts or *oly koeks* [oil cakes]..." It is believed that doughnuts originated in Germany, home of the Pennsylvania-Dutch settlers. Doughnuts called *fossnocks* or *fasnachts* were served on Shrove Tuesday: they were the last sweet allowed before Lent. It is thought that the Pennsylvania Dutch were probably the first to make doughnuts with holes, perfect for dunking into a cup of steaming hot coffee.

PREP: 30 minutes plus chilling ★ **COOK:** 2 minutes per batch
MAKES 24 doughnuts

3 cups all-purpose flour

1 cup sugar

⅓ cup buttermilk

2 large eggs

2 tablespoons vegetable shortening

1 tablespoon baking powder

1 teaspoon baking soda

1 teaspoon salt

½ teaspoon ground nutmeg

vegetable oil for frying

1 cup sugar

1 teaspoon ground cinnamon

1. In large bowl, combine 1½ cups flour, ½ cup sugar, buttermilk, eggs, shortening, baking powder, baking soda, salt, and nutmeg. With mixer at medium speed, beat until smooth, about 1 minute, scraping bowl with rubber spatula. Stir in remaining 1½ cups flour. Cover and refrigerate at least 1 hour for easier handling.

2. In deep-fat fryer or 6-quart Dutch oven, heat 3 to 4 inches oil over medium heat until temperature reaches 370°F on deep-fat thermometer. In large bowl, combine sugar and cinnamon; set aside.

3. Meanwhile, on well-floured surface, with floured rolling pin, roll dough ½ inch thick. With floured 2½-inch doughnut cutter, cut out doughnuts. Reserve trimmings for rerolling.

4. Fry dough rings, four at a time, until golden, 2 to 3 minutes, turning once. With slotted spoon, transfer doughnuts to paper towels to drain. Toss in cinnamon-sugar mixture while still warm.

Doughnut "Holes"

Prepare as directed in Steps 1 through 3; use centers cut from doughnuts. Or use small biscuit cutter instead of doughnut cutter to cut dough into small rounds. Fry and coat with cinnamon-sugar as directed.

EACH DOUGHNUT AND HOLE: About 213 calories, 2g protein, 30g carbohydrate, 10g total fat (1g saturated), 18mg cholesterol, 220mg sodium.

Chapter 11

What's for Dessert Tonight?

Americans have always been in love with dessert. In the original thirteen colonies, desserts were rich and often very English. The colonists enjoyed creamy custard, whipped syllabub, Indian pudding, blueberry buckle, steamed pudding with raisins, mince pie, and soft flummery fruit pudding flavored with sherry. In eighteenth-century America, when a dinner's main course was over, the tabletop was sometimes flipped over to the "clean pie side." Then a dessert, such as a freshly baked pie (made from stewed preserved fruits in the winter and fresh garden fruits in the summer) was offered.

In the nineteenth century in the wealthiest homes, the dessert course was served in the formal European style, often with twenty sweets to choose from, including ice-cream bombes, sponge cakes, fruit pastries, and fancy puddings. In *Directions for Cookery in Its Various Branches*, readers are offered 124 dessert recipes, from custards and pound cakes to puddings and apple pies. Chocolate was also growing in popularity, thanks to Baker's German chocolate, the introduction of cocoa, and America's first mass-produced chocolate bar: the Hershey Bar.

During the early 1900s, Americans still catered to their sweet tooth but with lighter desserts, such as gelatin molds and quick-to-mix pudding desserts. Strawberry shortcake also found favor, as did hand-churned ice cream, which was scooped into dishes and drizzled with fudge sauce.

By the end of World War II, cake mixes were turning novice cooks into proud bakers, many of whom mixed, measured, and baked their way to national fame in bake-offs. Our tastes became more sophisticated as Americans traveled abroad and visited European pastry shops, then came home to tackle their first puff-pastry desserts.

As the century came to a close, we returned to the homey desserts we first loved: pandowdies, buckles, slumps, and betties, sometimes served with vanilla-bean ice cream or a fruit sauce laced with liqueur. Americans will always treasure their desserts—homespun, homemade, or store-bought.

Gingerbread

Many of the earliest recipes for gingerbread contained flour, molasses, and ground ginger. One version, known as common gingerbread, was a stiff dough that was rolled out, cut into strips, then placed flat in a baking pan or coiled to resemble fancy breads that were sold in the eighteenth-century bakeshops. Recipes for soft gingerbread and gingerbread cake are more like our recipe: they contain a mix of warm spices and bake up into a dessert that is not quite a bread, not quite a cake but always simply delicious. Early recipes suggest serving gingerbread warm and plain. But it's even more special with whipped cream or your favorite lemon sauce.

PREP: 10 minutes ★ **BAKE:** 45 minutes ★ **MAKES** 9 servings

2 cups all-purpose flour

½ cup sugar

2 teaspoons ground ginger

1 teaspoon ground cinnamon

½ teaspoon baking soda

½ teaspoon salt

1 cup light (mild) molasses

½ cup butter or margarine (1 stick), cut into 4 pieces

¾ cup boiling water

1 large egg

whipped cream (optional)

1. Preheat oven to 350°F. Grease and flour 9-inch square baking pan.

2. In large bowl, combine flour, sugar, ginger, cinnamon, baking soda, and salt. Stir until blended.

3. In small bowl, combine molasses and butter. Add boiling water and stir until butter melts. Add molasses mixture and egg to flour mixture; whisk until blended.

4. With rubber spatula, scrape batter into prepared pan. Bake until toothpick inserted in center comes out clean, 45 to 50 minutes. Cool in pan on wire rack. Serve warm or at room temperature with whipped cream, if desired.

EACH SERVING WITHOUT WHIPPED CREAM: About 350 calories, 4g protein, 59g carbohydrate, 12g total fat (7g saturated), 51mg cholesterol, 325mg sodium.

◄ *Gingerbread*

Christmas Pudding

Take three-quarters of a pound each of chopped suet, stoned raisins, currants, sugar and dried bread crumbs, one-quarter of a pound of sliced citron, two chopped sour apples and the grated peel of one lemon. Mix together with one-half teaspoon each of cloves and salt. Add six eggs and one gill of rum or brandy. Steam for four hours in two buttered molds. Turn out on a hot dish, sprinkle sugar over the pudding, garnish with a sprig of holly, pour one-half cup of warm brandy over it and set it on fire as it goes to the table. Serve with

German Sauce

Mix the yolks of four eggs with one-eighth of a pound of sugar, add the grated rind of half a lemon. Stir over the fire until the mixture coats the spoon. Serve hot. The pudding may be made some days before the dinner and reheated.

—**Good Housekeeping Everyday Cook Book,** 1903

New Orleans Bread Pudding

(pictured on page 230)

The bread puddings that appear in early American cookbooks are plain and simple: some are made with cracker crumbs; others use bread or biscuit crumbs or sliced bread. Often the bread puddings are baked plain with an egg-and-milk-custard, or they are layered with currants and citron or with grated lemon, then served with a sweet sauce. Annabella Hill, in her 1867 *Southern Practical Cookery and Receipt Book,* advises readers in her bread pudding recipe: "To ascertain whether a pudding is done, pierce it near the centre with a large straw or knife-blade; if no batter adheres to it, the pudding is done." Our bread pudding brings the spirit of New Orleans to the table with brown sugar–praline and toasted pecans.

PREP: 20 minutes plus standing and cooling
BAKE: 45 minutes ★ **MAKES** 8 servings

---

¹/₂ **cup dark seedless raisins**

2 tablespoons bourbon

¹/₃ **cup granulated sugar**

¹/₈ **teaspoon ground nutmeg**

¹/₈ **teaspoon ground cinnamon**

3 large eggs

2 teaspoons vanilla extract

1 pint half-and-half or light cream

3 cups (¹/₂ inch) day-old French bread cubes

¹/₄ **cup packed dark brown sugar**

2 tablespoons butter or margarine

1 tablespoon light corn syrup

¹/₃ **cup pecans, toasted and chopped**

1. In small bowl, combine raisins and bourbon; let stand 15 minutes. Grease 8-inch square baking dish.

2. In large bowl, combine granulated sugar, nutmeg, and cinnamon. Whisk in eggs and vanilla until combined. In cup, set aside 1 tablespoon half-and-half. Add remaining half-and-half to egg mixture and whisk until blended. Stir in bread cubes. Let stand 15 minutes, stirring occasionally. Stir in raisin mixture.

3. Meanwhile, preheat oven to 325°F. Pour bread mixture into prepared dish. Bake until knife inserted near center comes out clean, 45 to 50 minutes. Cool on wire rack 30 minutes.

4. In 1-quart saucepan, combine reserved half-and-half, brown sugar, butter, and corn syrup; heat to boiling over medium heat. Reduce heat and simmer, stirring occasionally, 2 minutes. Remove from heat and stir in pecans. Serve pudding drizzled with praline sauce.

EACH SERVING: About 300 calories, 6g protein, 36g carbohydrate, 16g total fat (7g saturated), 110mg cholesterol, 175mg sodium.

Oven-Steamed Figgy Pudding (Christmas Pudding)

There are five different Christmas puddings in the post–World War I edition of *Mrs. Beeton's Household Management* book. They are brimming with candied fruits, sultanas, raisins, various nuts, sometimes suet, all manner of warm spices, and are often spiked with brandy, rum, or wine. Popular though they were, preparing Christmas pudding was very time consuming, requiring anywhere from four to seven hours of steaming (or boiling). During the Victorian era, other types of puddings were also popular: puddings that featured one fruit or flavor and required only three or four hours of cooking, such as fig pudding, golden pudding flavored with orange marmalade, apple pudding, damson plum pudding, and lemon and honey puddings. Steamed puddings were popular in America from colonial times. Mrs. Rorer's 1886 fig pudding is similar to the English ones, but it also contains baking powder for extra lightness. Her cooking instructions are direct: "turn into a greased mould, and boil continuously for three hours. Serve hot, with Wine or Hard Sauce. Good." A delicious figgy pudding was once an all-day activity of mixing ingredients, then steaming on the stove top. We have shortened the ingredients list, used butter instead of suet, and have simplified the preparation and cooking (oven steaming is easy and foolproof). Of course we have retained the moistness and rich flavor expected of a fine pudding.

PREP: 45 minutes ★ BAKE: 2 hours ★ MAKES 12 servings

2 packages (8 ounces each) dried Calimyrna figs

1¾ cups milk

1½ cups all-purpose flour

1 cup sugar

2½ teaspoons baking powder

1 teaspoon ground cinnamon

1 teaspoon ground nutmeg

1 teaspoon salt

3 large eggs

½ cup butter or margarine (1 stick), melted and cooled slightly

1½ cups fresh bread crumbs (about 3 slices firm white bread)

2 teaspoons freshly grated orange peel

1 teaspoon freshly grated lemon peel

Brandied Hard Sauce, optional (opposite)

1. Preheat oven to 350°F. Grease 2½-quart metal steamed-pudding mold or fluted tube pan.

2. With kitchen shears, cut stems from figs, then cut figs into small pieces. In 2-quart saucepan, combine figs and milk. Cover and cook over medium-low heat, stirring occasionally, 10 to 15 minutes (mixture may look curdled). Do not let mixture boil.

3. Meanwhile, in medium bowl, combine flour, sugar, baking powder, cinnamon, nutmeg, and salt.

4. In large bowl, with mixer at high speed, beat eggs 1 minute. Reduce speed to low; add butter, bread crumbs, orange peel, lemon peel, and fig mixture. Gradually add flour mixture; beat just until blended.

5. Spoon fig mixture into prepared mold; smooth top. Cover mold with sheet of greased foil, greased side down. (If your mold has a lid, grease inside of lid and omit foil.) Place mold in deep medium roasting pan; place pan on oven rack. Pour enough *very hot water* into roasting pan to come 2 inches up side of mold.

6. Bake until pudding is firm and pulls away from side of mold, about 2 hours. Transfer pudding to wire rack. Remove foil; cool 10 minutes. Invert onto cake plate; remove mold.

7. Meanwhile, prepare Brandied Hard Sauce, if desired. Serve pudding warm with sauce on the side.

EACH SERVING WITHOUT HARD SAUCE: About 350 calories, 6g protein, 59g carbohydrate, 11g total fat (3g saturated), 58mg cholesterol, 430mg sodium.

Brandied Hard Sauce

In small bowl, with mixer at medium speed, beat *1½ cups confectioners' sugar, ½ cup butter or margarine (1 stick)* softened, *2 tablespoons brandy*, and *½ teaspoon vanilla extract* until creamy. Refrigerate if not serving right away. Makes about 1 cup.

EACH TABLESPOON: About 105 calories, 0g protein, 11g carbohydrate, 6g total fat (4g saturated), 16 mg cholesterol, 75mg sodium.

Indian Pudding

The settlers were familiar with English porridge, which was made with flour, butter, spices, milk, and sometimes egg. In the New World, they learned how to cook with the locally available ingredients from the Native Americans. They used cornmeal (Indian meal), which was less expensive than flour, to make an English-style pudding called Yankee hasty pudding. The dessert became known as Indian meal pudding, and later Indian pudding. Eliza Leslie offers A Baked Indian Pudding in *Directions for Cookery* that contains molasses, butter, milk, and sifted Indian meal. "Serve it up hot, and eat it with wine sauce, or with butter and molasses."

PREP: 30 minutes ★ **BAKE:** 2 hours ★ **MAKES** 8 servings

⅔ cup cornmeal

4 cups milk

½ cup light (mild) molasses

4 tablespoons butter or margarine, cut into pieces

¼ cup sugar

1 teaspoon ground cinnamon

1 teaspoon ground ginger

½ teaspoon salt

¼ teaspoon ground nutmeg

whipped cream or vanilla ice cream (optional)

1. Preheat oven to 350°F. Lightly grease shallow 1½-quart baking dish.

2. In small bowl, combine cornmeal and 1 cup milk. In 4-quart saucepan, heat remaining 3 cups milk to boiling over high heat. With wire whisk, whisk in cornmeal mixture; heat to boiling. Reduce heat and simmer, stirring frequently with wooden spoon to prevent lumps, until mixture is thick, about 20 minutes. Remove from heat; stir in molasses, butter, sugar, cinnamon, ginger, salt, and nutmeg until well blended.

3. Pour batter into prepared dish, spreading it evenly. Cover with foil. Place dish in small roasting pan; place in oven. Carefully pour enough *boiling water* into roasting pan to come halfway up sides of baking dish. Bake 1 hour. Remove foil and bake pudding until lightly browned and just set, about 1 hour longer.

4. Carefully remove baking dish from water. Cool pudding in pan on wire rack 30 minutes. Serve pudding warm with whipped cream or vanilla ice cream, if desired.

EACH SERVING WITHOUT WHIPPED CREAM OR ICE CREAM: About 255 calories, 5g protein, 35g carbohydrate, 11g total fat (6g saturated), 33mg cholesterol, 270mg sodium.

Rice Pudding

Many early cookbooks include not one but several recipes for rice pudding. There are straightforward recipes for plain rice pudding—similar to ours—that bake in about an hour. There are recipes for rice plum pudding with raisins or currants and for boiled rice pudding that steams in a pudding mold for two hours. There is even farmers' rice pudding, which uses no eggs at all but contains rich cream. In *American Cookery*, Amelia Simmons instructs her readers to bake rice pudding for at least one-and-one half hours, either in a buttered dish or in one that is lined with puff pastry.

PREP: 10 minutes ★ **COOK:** 1 hour 15 minutes
MAKES 4 cups or 6 servings

4 cups milk

½ cup regular long-grain rice

½ cup sugar

¼ teaspoon salt

1 large egg

1 teaspoon vanilla extract

1. In heavy 4-quart saucepan, combine milk, rice, sugar, and salt; heat to boiling over medium-high heat. Reduce heat; cover and simmer, stirring occasionally, until rice is very tender, about 1 hour.

2. In small bowl, lightly beat egg; stir in ½ cup hot rice mixture. Slowly pour egg mixture back into rice mixture, stirring rapidly to prevent curdling. Cook, stirring constantly, until rice mixture has thickened, about 5 minutes (do not boil, or mixture will curdle). Remove from heat; stir in vanilla. Serve warm, or spoon into medium bowl and refrigerate until well chilled, about 3 hours.

EACH SERVING: About 234 calories, 7g protein, 37g carbohydrate, 6g total fat (4g saturated), 58mg cholesterol, 187mg sodium.

Rich Rice Pudding

Prepare and refrigerate as directed. In small bowl, with mixer at medium speed, beat ½ *cup heavy or whipping cream* until soft peaks form. With rubber spatula, gently fold into rice pudding. Refrigerate until ready to serve, up to 4 hours. Makes 8 servings.

Peach-Noodle Kugel

When Jewish immigrants settled in America, they formed communities reminiscent of their native European villages. These enclaves had specialty food markets and restaurants that served traditional specialties, such as *kugel* (pudding), which could be savory or sweet. Savory kugels were usually made with potatoes, carrots, matzoh, or egg noodles. Sweet noodle kugels were sometimes very simple and contained egg noodles, eggs, and a touch of sugar. At other times raisins, grated apple, nuts, or spices were added. Dairy noodle pudding, which was rich and delicious, had a generous amount of sour cream and farmer (or pot) cheese added. Sweet kugels were often sprinkled with cinnamon sugar, which made the topping crunchy and the kitchen fragrant.

PREP: 25 minutes ★ **BAKE:** 45 minutes ★ **MAKES** 10 servings

1 package (8 ounces) wide egg noodles

3 tablespoons butter or margarine

3 large eggs

½ cup sugar

1½ tablespoons grated freshly lemon peel

¼ teaspoon salt

2 cups milk

½ cup dark seedless raisins

STREUSEL TOPPING

2 tablespoons butter or margarine

¼ cup plain dried bread crumbs

½ teaspoon ground cinnamon

1 can (16 ounces) sliced cling peaches, drained

1. Preheat oven to 350°F. Grease 12" by 8" baking dish. Cook noodles as label directs; drain. In large bowl, toss hot noodles with butter.

2. In medium bowl, with wire whisk or fork, beat eggs, sugar, lemon peel, and salt until well mixed; stir in milk and raisins. Stir egg mixture into noodles; pour into prepared dish. Bake 30 minutes.

3. Meanwhile, prepare streusel topping: In small saucepan, melt butter over low heat. Stir in dried bread crumbs and cinnamon.

4. Remove dish from oven; arrange peach slices on top and sprinkle evenly with topping. Bake 15 minutes longer. Let stand about 30 minutes for easier serving.

EACH SERVING: About 289 calories, 7g protein, 43g carbohydrate, 10g total fat (5g saturated), 108mg cholesterol, 190mg sodium.

Floating Island

A creamy custard sauce with one large or several small fluffs of meringue floating on top, *ile flottante* (floating island) is a classic French dessert that was being served in America by the late eighteenth century. Benjamin Franklin refers to a "custard with floating masses of whipped cream or white of eggs" in his personal journal. And Thomas Jefferson was known to enjoy a French dessert he called "snow eggs" (*oeufs à la neige*). Served at elegant dinners in the nineteenth century, it is still popular today. Floating island is often drizzled with a light caramel sauce, as in our recipe.

PREP: 15 minutes plus chilling ★ **COOK/BAKE:** 25 minutes **MAKES** 4 servings

2 cups milk

¾ cup plus 5 tablespoons sugar

5 large egg yolks

¼ teaspoon salt

½ teaspoon vanilla extract

1 large egg white, at room temperature

1. In double boiler over hot (not boiling) water, combine milk, ¾ cup sugar, egg yolks, and salt. Cook, stirring constantly, until mixture thickens and coats a spoon, about 15 minutes. Stir in vanilla.

2. Pour custard into 4 wine goblets or dessert dishes. Cover and refrigerate until well chilled, about 1 hour.

3. Meanwhile, preheat oven to 350°F. In small bowl, with mixer at high speed, beat egg white until soft peaks form when beaters are lifted. Gradually sprinkle in 2 tablespoons sugar, beating until sugar has dissolved.

4. Pour *½ inch cold water* into 8-inch square baking dish. Drop beaten egg white into water in dish in 4 equal mounds. Bake until lightly browned, 7 to 10 minutes.

5. With slotted spoon, carefully remove each meringue from water. Hold spoon over paper towels to drain, then slip meringue into custard in each goblet.

6. In heavy 1-quart saucepan, heat remaining 3 tablespoons sugar over high heat, stirring constantly, until smooth and amber-colored, about 3 minutes. Remove from heat; let stand 2 minutes. With spoon, quickly drizzle sugar syrup in thin strands over each dessert.

EACH SERVING: About 360 calories, 8g protein, 59g carbohydrate, 10g total fat (5g saturated), 283mg cholesterol, 226mg sodium.

Lemon Pudding Cake

This dessert is a true American creation. Around the end of the nineteenth century, Lemon Sponge Pie became popular in Pennsylvania-Dutch communities. Beaten egg whites were folded into a lemony batter and poured into a pie shell. As it baked, the filling separated into two layers: a spongy, cakelike layer formed on top and a creamy, lemony curd layer formed on the bottom. Beginning in the 1930s, recipes for similar desserts, such as Lemon Mystery Pudding, Lemon Pudding Cake, and Lemon Cake Top Pudding began appearing in *Sunset* and other women's magazines and later on in recipe leaflets that food companies, such as Sunkist, handed out. Like those recipes, our version resembles a cake when it goes into the oven, but as it bake, the cake part rises to the top, leaving a creamy lemon pudding layer on the bottom. Pudding cakes are heavenly, delicate, and simply too good to pass by, especially when served warm.

PREP: 20 minutes ★ **BAKE:** 40 minutes ★ **MAKES** 6 servings

3 lemons

¾ cup sugar

¼ cup all-purpose flour

I cup milk

3 large eggs, separated

4 tablespoons butter or margarine, melted

⅛ teaspoon salt

1. Preheat oven to 350°F. Grease 8-inch square baking dish. From lemons, grate 1 tablespoon peel and squeeze ⅓ cup juice. In large bowl, combine sugar and flour. With wire whisk or fork, beat in milk, egg yolks, melted butter, and lemon peel and juice.

2. In small bowl, with mixer at high speed, beat egg whites and salt until soft peaks form when beaters are lifted. With rubber spatula, fold one-fourth of egg whites into lemon mixture; gently fold in remaining egg whites just until blended. Pour batter into prepared baking dish.

3. Place baking dish in small roasting pan; place on rack in oven. Carefully pour enough *boiling water* into roasting pan to come halfway up sides of dish. Bake until top is golden and set, about 40 minutes (batter will separate into cake and pudding layers). Cool in pan on wire rack 10 minutes. Serve hot.

EACH SERVING: About 255 calories, 5g protein, 32g carbohydrate, 12g total fat (7g saturated), 133mg cholesterol, 180mg sodium.

Orange Pudding Cake

Prepare as directed but in Step 1 use ¼ *cup fresh lemon juice, ¼ cup fresh orange juice* and *2 teaspoons freshly grated orange peel.*

Brownie Pudding Cake

America's love of brownies and chocolate likely prompted the development of this variation on pudding cake. Cocoa powder, which was first produced in America in 1828, makes the bottom pudding layer rich and chocolaty and the top layer fudgy.

PREP: 20 minutes ★ **BAKE:** 30 minutes ★ **MAKES** 8 servings

2 teaspoons instant-coffee powder (optional)

2 tablespoons (optional) plus 1¾ cups boiling water

I cup all-purpose flour

¾ cup unsweetened cocoa

½ cup granulated sugar

2 teaspoons baking powder

¼ teaspoon salt

½ cup milk

4 tablespoons butter or margarine, melted

I teaspoon vanilla extract

½ cup packed brown sugar

whipped cream or vanilla ice cream (optional)

1. Preheat oven to 350°F. In cup, dissolve coffee powder in 2 tablespoons boiling water, if using.

2. In bowl, combine flour, ½ cup cocoa, granulated sugar, baking powder, and salt. In 2-cup measuring cup, combine milk, melted butter, vanilla, and coffee, if using. With wooden spoon, stir milk mixture into flour mixture until just blended. Pour into ungreased 8-inch square baking dish.

3. In small bowl, thoroughly combine brown sugar and remaining ¼ cup cocoa; sprinkle evenly over batter. Carefully pour remaining 1¾ cups boiling water evenly over mixture in baking dish; do not stir.

4. Bake 30 minutes (batter will separate into cake and pudding layers). Cool in pan on wire rack 10 minutes. Serve hot with whipped cream, if you like.

EACH SERVING: About 238 calories, 4g protein, 43g carbohydrate, 7g total fat (5g saturated), 18mg cholesterol, 267mg sodium.

Georgia Peach Cobbler

Cobblers are really deep-dish pies that are topped with individual biscuits or with one thick sheet of biscuit dough. Some believe the dessert got its name because of the biscuit topping's resemblance to cobblestones. Americans were baking cobblers by the early nineteenth century. As our recipe suggests, to ensure that the biscuits are cooked through, the filling must be piping hot when the biscuit dough is placed on top.

PREP: 25 minutes ★ **BAKE:** 20 minutes ★ **MAKES** 8 servings

FILLING

½ cup sugar

3 tablespoons cornstarch

1 tablespoon fresh lemon juice

3 pounds (8 large) ripe peaches, peeled, pitted, and thickly sliced

BISCUITS

1½ cups all-purpose flour

¼ cup plus 1 teaspoon sugar

1½ teaspoons baking powder

½ teaspoon baking soda

¼ teaspoon salt

¼ teaspoon ground cinnamon

⅛ teaspoon ground nutmeg

4 tablespoons cold butter or margarine, cut into pieces

¾ cup plus 1 tablespoon heavy or whipping cream

1. Prepare filling: In 3-quart saucepan, combine sugar and cornstarch. Stir in lemon juice and peaches. Heat to boiling over medium-high heat, stirring. Remove from heat and keep warm.

2. Meanwhile, preheat oven to 400°F. Prepare biscuits: In large bowl, combine flour, ¼ cup sugar, baking powder, baking soda, salt, cinnamon, and nutmeg. With pastry blender or two knives used scissor-fashion, cut in butter until mixture resembles coarse crumbs. Add ¾ cup cream, stirring just until mixture forms soft dough that leaves side of bowl.

3. On lightly floured surface, knead dough 6 to 8 times. With floured rolling pin, roll dough into ½-inch-thick rectangle. Cut dough lengthwise in half, then cut crosswise into fourths to make 8 biscuits. With pastry brush, brush with remaining 1 tablespoon cream and sprinkle with remaining 1 teaspoon sugar.

4. Reheat filling until hot. Spoon into 11" by 7" baking dish or shallow 2-quart casserole. Arrange biscuits on top of filling. Place baking dish on foil-lined cookie sheet to catch any overflow during baking. Bake until biscuits are lightly browned and filling is bubbling, 20 to 25 minutes. Cool on wire rack 30 minutes. Serve warm.

EACH SERVING: About 365 calories, 4g protein, 56g carbohydrate, 15g total fat (9g saturated), 49mg cholesterol, 310mg sodium.

Blueberry Cobbler

Prepare biscuits as directed but substitute blueberry filling for peach filling: In 3-quart saucepan, combine *½ cup sugar* and *2 tablespoons cornstarch*. Stir in *1 tablespoon fresh lemon juice*, *¼ cup water*, and *6 cups fresh blueberries (about 3 pints)*, picked over. Heat to boiling over medium-high heat. Remove from heat; keep warm.

Rhubarb-Strawberry Cobbler

Prepare biscuits as directed but substitute rhubarb-strawberry filling for peach filling: In nonreactive 3-quart saucepan, combine *1¼ pounds rhubarb*, cut into 1-inch pieces (4 cups) and *½ cup sugar*; heat to boiling over high heat, stirring. Reduce heat to medium-low; simmer until rhubarb is tender, about 8 minutes.

In cup, blend *1 tablespoon cornstarch* and *¼ cup water* until smooth. Stir cornstarch mixture and *1 pint strawberries*, hulled and quartered, into rhubarb mixture; cook until mixture has thickened and boils, about 2 minutes. Remove from heat; keep warm.

Apple Crisp

A crisp is a fruit pie with a crumbly topping instead of a crust. Crisps began appearing in America in the nineteenth century. The ingredients for the topping mixture varies: some recipes contain oats; others include nuts or spices. The fruit or combination of fruits used are the baker's prerogative; there are no rules when it comes to this very casual dessert. Over the years the recipes haven't changed very much. It is still up to the baker to choose the fruit and to decide whether to use flour, bread crumbs, cookie crumbs, graham-cracker crumbs, or stale cake crumbs for the crumb mixture. Some of the earliest bakers used toasted bread crumbs and many layers to create their crisps.

PREP: 20 minutes ★ **BAKE:** 30 minutes ★ **MAKES** 6 servings

2¾ pounds baking apples (7 medium), peeled, cored, and cut into ¼-inch-thick slices
2 tablespoons fresh lemon juice
¾ cup packed dark brown sugar
2 tablespoons plus ⅓ cup all-purpose flour
½ cup old-fashioned or quick-cooking oats, uncooked
¼ teaspoon ground cinnamon
6 tablespoons butter or margarine, cut into pieces

1. Preheat oven to 425°F. In 1½-quart baking dish, combine apples, lemon juice, ½ cup brown sugar, and 2 tablespoons flour, tossing to coat.

2. In small bowl, stir oats, remaining ⅓ cup flour, and remaining ¼ cup brown sugar until blended. With pastry blender or two knives used scissor-fashion, cut in butter until mixture resembles coarse crumbs. Sprinkle over apple mixture.

3. Bake, uncovered, until apples are tender and topping has lightly browned, 30 to 35 minutes. Cool slightly on wire rack to serve warm.

EACH SERVING: About 370 calories, 2g protein, 65g carbohydrate, 13g total fat (7g saturated), 31mg cholesterol, 130mg sodium.

Pear Crisp

Prepare as directed but substitute *6 large firm-ripe pears (2¾ pounds)*, peeled, cored, and cut into ½-inch-thick slices, for apples. Toss in large bowl instead of baking dish.

Pear-Cranberry Crisp

Prepare as directed for Pear Crisp but add *1 cup fresh or frozen cranberries* to pear slices.

Baked Apple Dumplings

One cup of butter and lard mixed, one quart of flour, salt to taste, three teaspoons of baking powder. Mix with milk. Pare and core apples. Roll out dough to cover each separately and fill the whole with sugar. Grate nutmeg over the top. Put in the pan with water to half cover. Put in that a half cup of sugar, and butter size of an egg. Baste while baking, allowing three-quarters of an hour, and your dumplings will come out with a delicious glaced brown crust. Serve with a hard or a liquid sauce.

—**Good Housekeeping Everyday Cook Book,** 1903

Raspberry Slump

Fruit slumps date back to the mid-eighteenth century and closely resemble cobblers in that they are both a combination of fruit and biscuit dough. Slumps, however, are topped with soft drop biscuits (dumplings) instead of cut-out biscuits and are usually cooked in a covered skillet on top of the stove. Some say the name slump comes from the fact that the fruit filling doesn't contain a thickener, so it slumps on the plate when served. Author Louisa May Alcott named her home in Concord, Massachusetts, Apple Slump and recorded her favorite slump recipe. Hers, of course, used apples, but the dessert is even more delectable when made with fresh raspberries, as is ours. Traditionally slumps are served with heavy cream, which is poured on top.

PREP: 10 minutes ★ **COOK:** 15 minutes ★ **MAKES** 6 servings

BERRIES

Four ½ pints fresh raspberries

½ cup sugar

¼ cup water

1 tablespoon fresh lemon juice

⅛ teaspoon ground cinnamon

DUMPLING DOUGH

1½ cups all-purpose flour

½ cup sugar

2 teaspoons baking powder

¼ teaspoon salt

¾ cup light cream

1. Prepare berries: In 9-inch cast-iron skillet, combine raspberries, sugar, water, lemon juice, and cinnamon.

2. Prepare dumpling dough: In medium bowl, combine flour, sugar, baking powder, and salt. Add cream, stirring just until mixture forms soft dough.

3. Cover skillet and heat berry mixture to boiling over medium heat. Reduce heat to medium-low. Drop tablespoons of dough on top of fruit. Cover and simmer until dumplings are set and tops are dry when tested with fingertip, about 15 minutes. Serve hot or warm.

EACH SERVING: About 343 calories, 5g protein, 68g carbohydrate, 7g total fat (4g saturated), 20mg cholesterol, 271mg sodium.

Blueberry Slump

Prepare as directed but substitute *2 pints fresh blueberries* for raspberries.

Blueberry Buckle

Unlike slumps, pandowdies, and crisps, buckles by most accounts did not show up until around the mid-twentieth century. It's a rich one-layer butter cake that is made with fresh fruit (often blueberries) and sprinkled with a streusel topping. As the cake bakes, it rises, puffs up, and then buckles. The result is a golden cake with blueberries peeking through the crispy topping. The most well-known mention of a buckle appears in Elsie Masterton's 1959 *Blueberry Hill Cookbook.*

PREP: 30 minutes ★ **BAKE:** 35 minutes ★ **MAKES** 12 servings

STREUSEL TOPPING

⅓ **cup all-purpose flour**

⅓ **cup packed brown sugar**

1 **teaspoon ground cinnamon**

3 **tablespoons butter or margarine, cut into pieces**

CAKE

2 **cups all-purpose flour**

2 **teaspoons baking powder**

½ **teaspoon salt**

½ **cup butter or margarine (1 stick), softened**

¾ **cup granulated sugar**

2 **large eggs**

½ **cup milk**

1 **teaspoon vanilla extract**

3 **cups blueberries (about 2 pints), picked over**

1. Prepare streusel topping: In medium bowl, combine flour, brown sugar, and cinnamon. With pastry blender or two knives used scissor-fashion, cut in butter until mixture resembles coarse crumbs.

2. Prepare cake: Preheat oven to 375°F. Grease and flour 13" by 9" baking pan. In medium bowl, combine flour, baking powder, and salt.

3. In large bowl, with mixer at medium speed, beat butter and sugar until blended, frequently scraping bowl with rubber spatula. Increase speed to medium-high; beat until light and fluffy, about 2 minutes. Reduce speed to low; add eggs, one at a time, beating well after each addition, occasionally scraping bowl.

4. In cup, combine milk and vanilla. To egg mixture, add flour mixture alternately with milk mixture, beginning and ending with flour mixture. Beat just until blended, occasionally scraping bowl. Gently fold in blueberries.

5. Spoon batter into prepared baking dish and spread evenly. Sprinkle with topping.

6. Bake until toothpick inserted in center comes out clean, 35 to 40 minutes. Cool in dish on wire rack 30 minutes to serve warm, or cool completely in pan to serve later.

EACH SERVING: About 299 calories, 4g protein, 43g carbohydrate, 13g total fat (7g saturated), 65mg cholesterol, 306mg sodium.

Peach-Raspberry Buckle:

Prepare as directed but substitute *6 medium peaches (6 ounces each)*, peeled, pitted, and cut into ½-inch-thick slices (3 cups) for blueberries. Arrange peaches on top of batter; press into batter. Sprinkle with *1 cup raspberries*; gently press into batter. Sprinkle with topping; bake as directed.

Banana Brown Betty

Betties date back to colonial times. The ingredients used and the way the betties were layered varies from recipe to recipe. Some of the earliest betties were made with toasted bread crumbs and contained multiple layers. In Fanny Farmer's 1896 cookbook, she offers a recipe for Scalloped Apples: buttered bread crumbs are layered in a baking dish with sliced apples, sugar, nutmeg, and lemon juice and peel. It is served with sugar and cream on the side. In subsequent editions, the recipe is called Apple Brown Betty and is almost identical to the Scalloped Apples recipe. Here's one of our favorite betties. It is made with bananas and laced with cinnamon and ginger.

PREP: 35 minutes ★ **BAKE:** 50 minutes ★ **MAKES** 8 servings

8 slices firm white bread, torn into ½-inch pieces

6 tablespoons butter or margarine, melted

I teaspoon ground cinnamon

6 ripe medium bananas, cut into ¼-inch-thick slices (about 4 cups)

⅔ cup packed light brown sugar

2 tablespoons fresh lemon juice

I teaspoon vanilla extract

½ teaspoon ground ginger

1. Preheat oven to 400°F. Lightly grease shallow 2-quart baking dish.

2. In jelly-roll pan, bake bread pieces, tossing several times, until very lightly toasted, 12 to 15 minutes.

3. In medium bowl, combine melted butter and ½ teaspoon cinnamon. Add toasted bread pieces; gently toss until evenly moistened. In large bowl, combine bananas, brown sugar, lemon juice, vanilla, ginger, and remaining ½ teaspoon cinnamon; toss to coat.

4. Spoon ½ cup bread pieces into prepared dish. Top with half of banana mixture, then 1 cup bread pieces. Spoon remaining banana mixture on top; sprinkle with remaining bread pieces, leaving 1-inch border.

5. Cover with foil; bake 40 minutes. Remove foil; bake until bananas are tender and top is brown, about 10 minutes. Cool on wire rack 10 minutes to serve warm.

EACH SERVING: About 410 calories, 3g protein, 53g carbohydrate, 22g total fat (13g saturated), 55mg cholesterol, 365mg sodium.

Apple Brown Betty

Prepare as directed but gently toss bread pieces with ½ *cup butter or margarine (1 stick)*, melted. Substitute *2½ pounds Granny Smith apples (6 medium)*, peeled, cored, and thinly sliced, for bananas and substitute ¼ *teaspoon ground nutmeg* for ginger.

Strawberry Shortcake

From the beginning, the colonists baked shortcake. In the earliest cookbooks they were cut into small round cakes with a tumbler (glass), then baked and served with butter, not berries. Other shortcakes, like ours, were baked in a round cake pan. For her Rich Strawberry Short Cake, Fanny Farmer instructs readers to split the cake, spread it with rich custard sauce and cover with berries that have been sprinkled with powdered sugar. More custard is spread on top, and the shortcake top covers it all. Our shortcake is served the more traditional way: with whipped cream instead of custard.

PREP: 25 minutes ★ **BAKE:** 20 minutes ★ **MAKES** 10 servings

2 cups all-purpose flour

6 tablespoons plus $^1/_3$ cup sugar

2 teaspoons baking powder

$^1/_4$ teaspoon salt

$^1/_3$ cup cold butter or margarine, cut into pieces

$^2/_3$ cup milk

8 cups strawberries (about 2$^1/_2$ pounds)

I cup heavy or whipping cream

1. Preheat oven to 425°F. Grease 8-inch round cake pan.

2. In medium bowl, combine flour, 3 tablespoons sugar, baking powder, and salt. With pastry blender or two knives used scissor-fashion, cut in butter until mixture resembles coarse crumbs. Stir in milk just until mixture forms soft dough that leaves side of bowl.

3. On lightly floured surface, knead dough 10 times. Pat dough evenly in prepared pan; sprinkle with 1 tablespoon sugar. Bake until golden, 20 to 22 minutes.

4. Meanwhile, reserve 4 whole strawberries for garnish; hull remaining strawberries and cut in half or into quarters if large. In medium bowl, toss strawberries with $^1/_3$ cup sugar until sugar has dissolved.

5. Invert shortcake onto surface. With long serrated knife, carefully cut hot shortcake horizontally in half. In bowl, with mixer at medium speed, beat cream just until soft peaks form. Beat in remaining 2 tablespoons sugar.

6. Place bottom half of shortcake, cut side up, on cake plate. Top with half of strawberry mixture and half of whipped cream. Place remaining shortcake layer, cut side down, over strawberry mixture. Spoon remaining strawberry mixture over cake, then top with remaining whipped cream. Garnish with reserved whole strawberries.

EACH SERVING: About 325 calories, 4g protein, 42g carbohydrate, 16g total fat (10g saturated), 51mg cholesterol, 235mg sodium.

Summer Fruit Shortcake

Prepare as directed but substitute *6 cups mixed fruit (about 3 pounds sliced nectarines, sliced peeled peaches, blueberries, blackberries, and/or raspberries)* for strawberries; toss with *$^1/_3$ cup sugar* and *1 to 2 tablespoons fresh lemon juice.*

Individual Shortcakes

Prepare as directed in Steps 1 and 2. On lightly floured surface, with floured hands, pat dough $^3/_4$ inch thick. With floured 2$^1/_2$-inch biscuit cutter, cut out 8 rounds, without twisting cutter. Transfer to cookie sheet; bake until bottoms of shortcakes are golden brown, 15 to 20 minutes. Cut biscuits horizontally in half. Place bottom halves on dessert plates; top with fruit mixture and whipped cream. Replace tops. Makes 8 servings.

EACH SERVING: About 410 calories, 5g protein, 53g carbohydrate, 21g total fat (12g saturated), 64mg cholesterol, 295mg sodium.

Blueberry-Peach Shortcakes

Prepare Individual Shortcakes as directed but substitute blueberries and peaches for strawberries: In 3-quart nonreactive saucepan, combine *2 tablespoons fresh lemon juice* and *1 tablespoon cornstarch;* stir to dissolve. Add *1$^1/_2$ pints blueberries,* picked over, and *$^2/_3$ cup sugar;* heat to boiling over high heat. Boil 1 minute. Remove from heat and stir in *6 medium peaches,* peeled, pitted, and each cut into 8 wedges.

Granny's Apple Pandowdy

Truly American in origin, the pandowdy is a no-frills fruit dessert that is usually made with apples, although occasionally blueberries are used. It is known as an apple grunt or an apple Jonathan in the Northeast. A pandowdy is made up of apple slices that are tossed with cinnamon and nutmeg and sweetened with brown sugar, molasses, or maple syrup. A thin sheet of biscuit or pastry dough is then placed on top. Traditionally the top crust is broken up about halfway through the baking and pushed down into the fruit. This technique is known as "dowdying" (an expression that first appeared in print in 1806). During the last part of baking, the crust becomes crisp and flavorful from the bubbling fruit juice.

PREP: 20 minutes ★ **BAKE:** 40 minutes ★ **MAKES** 6 servings

I cup packed brown sugar

1¼ cups all-purpose flour

I teaspoon salt

I cup water

I teaspoon distilled white vinegar

¼ teaspoon ground cinnamon

dash ground nutmeg

I teaspoon fresh lemon juice

I teaspoon vanilla extract

2 tablespoons butter or margarine

2 teaspoons baking powder

3 tablespoons vegetable shortening

¾ cup milk

4 large baking apples, such as Cortland or Rome, peeled, cored, and sliced (about 5 cups)

heavy cream, sour cream, or vanilla ice cream (optional)

1. Prepare sauce for apples: In nonreactive 2-quart saucepan, combine brown sugar, ¼ cup flour, and ¼ teaspoon salt. Add water and vinegar; stir until blended. Cook over medium heat, stirring until thickened, 2 to 3 minutes. Add cinnamon, nutmeg, lemon juice, vanilla, and butter, stirring until butter melts. Set aside.

2. Preheat oven to 375°F. Grease shallow 3- to 3½-quart baking dish. In medium bowl, combine remaining 1 cup flour, baking powder, and remaining ¾ teaspoon salt. With pastry blender or two knives used scissor-fashion, cut in shortening until mixture resembles coarse crumbs. Stir in milk until mixture is moistened but still lumpy.

3. Place apples in prepared dish; pour sauce over. Drop tablespoons of dough on top of apples. Bake until topping has browned, about 40 minutes. Serve warm with heavy cream, sour cream, or vanilla ice cream, if desired.

EACH SERVING: About 407 calories, 4g protein, 71g carbohydrate, 13g total fat (5g saturated), 15mg cholesterol, 620mg sodium.

Fast-Baked Apples with Oatmeal Streusel

Baked apples have always been a favorite dessert in America. In Eliza Leslie's 1848 edition of *Directions for Cookery,* she offers a recipe for baked apples that is still good today: "Take a dozen fine large juicy apples, and pare and core them, but do not cut them in pieces. Put them side by side into a large baking-pan, and fill up with brown sugar the holes from whence you have extracted the cores. Pour into each a little lemon-juice, or a few drops of essence of lemon, and stick in every one a long piece of lemon-peel evenly cut . . . . Bake them about an hour, or till they are tender all through, but not till they break. When done, set them away to get cold. If closely covered they will keep two days. They may be eaten at tea with cream. Or at dinner with a boiled custard poured over them. Or you may cover them with sweetened cream flavoured with a little essence of lemon, and whipped to a froth...so as to conceal them entirely." Our microwave version is quick as well as delicious.

PREP: 8 minutes ★ **MICROWAVE:** 12 minutes
MAKES 4 servings

4 large Rome or Cortland apples (about 10 ounces each)

¼ cup packed brown sugar

¼ cup quick-cooking oats, uncooked

2 tablespoons chopped dates

½ teaspoon ground cinnamon

2 teaspoons butter or margarine

1. Core apples, cutting out a 1¼-inch-diameter cylinder from center of each, cutting almost but not all the way through to bottom. Remove peel from top third of each apple. Place apples in shallow 1½-quart ceramic casserole or 8-inch square baking dish.

2. In small bowl, combine brown sugar, oats, dates, and cinnamon. Fill apple cavities with equal amounts of oat mixture. (Mixture will spill over tops of apples.) Dot each apple with ½ teaspoon butter.

3. Microwave apples, covered, on Medium-High (70% power) until tender, 12 to 14 minutes, turning each apple halfway through cooking time. To serve, spoon cooking liquid from baking dish over apples.

EACH SERVING: About 258 calories, 1g protein, 61g carbohydrate, 3g total fat (1g saturated), 5mg cholesterol, 25mg sodium.

Fast-Baked Apples with Oatmeal Streusel ▶

Rosy Peach Melba Compote

The French chef Escoffier created peach Melba in the 1890s at the Hotel Savoy and named it after the opera singer Nellie Melba. He used vanilla-poached peaches, vanilla ice cream, and raspberry sauce made with a splash of kirsch. According to one account, Escoffier later improved the dish by adding a sprinkling of shredded green almonds. In his book, *A Guide to Modern Cooking,* Escoffier calls the dessert *pêches cardinal,* after the sauce's cordial red color. Serve the compote with scoops of vanilla ice cream, just like the original dessert, if you prefer.

PREP: 15 minutes plus chilling ★ **COOK:** about 5 minutes
MAKES about 6 cups or 8 servings

¾ cup sugar

1 cup water

4 ripe large peaches (about 2 pounds), peeled, pitted, and cut into ½-inch-thick wedges

½ pint raspberries

1½ cups rosé or blush wine

3 tablespoons fresh lemon juice

1. In 1-quart saucepan, combine sugar and water; heat to boiling over high heat. Boil 1 minute. Pour syrup into large bowl; cool to room temperature.

2. Add peaches, raspberries, wine, and lemon juice to syrup; stir gently to combine. Cover and refrigerate at least 2 hours or overnight.

EACH SERVING: About 150 calories, 1g protein, 31g carbohydrate, 0g total fat, 0mg cholesterol, 3mg sodium.

◄ *Rosy Peach Melba Compote*

Baked Alaska with Red-Raspberry Sauce

It is interesting to note that there is a scientific principle behind the dish we know as Baked Alaska that can be traced to scientist Benjamin Thompson. He explored the insulating properties of air trapped in sponge cake and in meringue, which keeps the ice cream solid while in the oven. At a White House dinner in 1802, Thomas Jefferson served a puddinglike dish that included "ice cream very good, [pastry] crust wholly dried, crumbled into thin flakes." As for the creator of the dessert itself, some credit Chef Charles Ranhofer of Delmonico's. In 1867 he baked an ice-cream bombe that was covered with meringue and called it a Baked Alaska to commemorate the purchase of Alaska. This dessert appears in Fannie Farmer's 1896 cookbook with instructions to place the sponge cake on a board with white paper covering it: "The board, paper, cake, and meringue are poor conductors of heat, and prevent the cream from melting. Slip from paper on ice cream platter."

PREP: I hour 30 minutes plus freezing ★ **BAKE:** 2 minutes
MAKES 16 servings

ICE-CREAM CAKE

2 pints vanilla ice cream

3 packages (3 to 4½ ounces each) sponge-type ladyfingers

2 pints raspberry sorbet

RED-RASPBERRY SAUCE

I package (10 ounces) frozen raspberries in quick-thaw pouch, thawed

2 tablespoons seedless raspberry jam

I tablespoon orange-flavored liqueur

MERINGUE

4 large egg whites

¾ cup sugar

¼ teaspoon salt

¼ teaspoon cream of tartar

4 teaspoons water

I. Prepare ice-cream cake: Place ice cream in large bowl. Let stand at room temperature to soften slightly, stirring occasionally, until spreadable, about 10 minutes.

2. Meanwhile, split each ladyfinger lengthwise in half. Line bottom and side of 10-inch round baking dish, shallow 1½-quart round casserole, or 9½-inch deep-dish pie plate with about two-thirds of ladyfingers, placing ladyfingers, rounded side out, around side of dish, allowing ladyfingers to extend above rim of baking dish.

3. Spoon ice cream into ladyfinger-lined dish. With narrow metal spatula, smooth top. Cover and freeze until ice cream is firm, about 30 minutes.

4. Place sorbet in large bowl. Let stand at room temperature to soften slightly, stirring occasionally, until spreadable, about 10 minutes. Spoon sorbet on top of ice cream, smoothing with spatula. Top sorbet with remaining ladyfingers. Cover with waxed paper and then foil; freeze until firm, at least 6 hours.

5. Prepare red-raspberry sauce: In food processor with knife blade attached, combine raspberries, jam, and liqueur; puree until smooth. Pour sauce into pitcher; refrigerate until ready to serve. Makes about 1⅓ cups.

6. About 30 minutes before serving, prepare meringue: Preheat oven to 500°F. In large bowl set over simmering water or in top of double boiler, with mixer at medium speed, beat egg whites, sugar, salt, cream of tartar, and water until soft peaks form when beaters are lifted and temperature on thermometer reaches 160°F, 12 to 14 minutes. Transfer bowl to surface. Beat meringue until stiff peaks form, 8 to 10 minutes longer.

7. Remove cake from freezer. Spoon meringue over top of cake; decoratively swirl with back of spoon. Bake until meringue is lightly browned, 2 to 3 minutes. Place cake on heat-safe platter. Serve immediately with sauce.

EACH SERVING: About 250 calories, 4g protein, 40g carbohydrate, 5g total fat (3g saturated), 73mg cholesterol, 95mg sodium.

Baked Alaska with Red-Raspberry Sauce ▶

Crepes Suzette

Etienne Lemaire, Thomas Jefferson's French maître d'hôtel during his presidency in the White House, brought fine French traditions and food to the presidential dinner table. His recipe for *pannequaiques* (crepes) was one of Jefferson's favorites. Lemaire sprinkled each crepe with confectioners' sugar as it came out of the crepe pan and stacked the crepes to keep them warm. Each guest was served a wedge of "crepe pie." Our recipe features crepes simmered in the famous orange–flavored liqueur sauce and presented in a chafing dish. When the sauce is ignited, the raw-alcohol taste burns off, leaving a rich orange essence.

PREP: 30 minutes plus chilling ★ **COOK:** 30 minutes
MAKES 6 servings

BASIC CREPES

3 large eggs

1½ cups milk

⅔ cup all-purpose flour

4 tablespoons butter or margarine, melted

½ teaspoon salt

ORANGE SAUCE

1 orange

4 tablespoons butter or margarine

2 tablespoons sugar

¼ cup Grand Marnier, Cointreau, or other orange-flavored liqueur

1. Prepare basic crepes: In blender, process eggs, milk, flour, 2 tablespoons butter, and salt until smooth, scraping down sides of blender. Transfer batter to medium bowl; cover and refrigerate at least 1 hour or up to overnight to allow flour to absorb liquid.

2. Heat nonstick 10-inch skillet over medium-high heat. Brush bottom of skillet lightly with some remaining butter. With wire whisk, thoroughly stir batter to mix well. Pour scant ¼ cup batter into skillet; tilt pan to coat bottom completely with batter. Cook crepe until top is set and underside is lightly browned, about 1½ minutes.

3. With heat-safe rubber spatula, loosen edge of crepe; turn. Cook until second side has browned, about 30 seconds. Slip crepe onto waxed paper. Repeat with remaining batter, brushing pan lightly with butter before cooking each crepe and stacking crepes between layers of waxed paper. Makes about 12 crepes.

4. Prepare orange sauce: From orange, grate ½ teaspoon peel and squeeze ⅓ cup juice. In nonreactive 12-inch skillet, heat orange peel and juice, butter, and sugar over low heat, stirring until butter melts.

5. Fold crepes into quarters; place in sauce, overlapping if necessary; heat through, turning crepes once.

6. In very small saucepan, heat liqueur over medium heat until hot; remove from heat. Carefully ignite liqueur with long match; pour flaming liqueur over crepes. When flame dies down, transfer crepes to dessert plates.

EACH SERVING: About 311 calories, 7g protein, 22g carbohydrate, 20g total fat (12g saturated), 156mg cholesterol, 411mg sodium.

Cream Puffs

Delicate balls of choux pastry filled with whipped cream or crème patisserie (pastry cream) can be traced back to European filled cream buns. Some were made from a rich choux pastry, while others were simple sweet breakfast buns. Both were traditionally dusted with confectioners' sugar.

PREP: 30 minutes plus standing and cooling
BAKE: 40 minutes ★ **MAKES** 8 servings

CHOUX PASTRY

1 cup water

½ cup butter or margarine (1 stick)

¼ teaspoon salt

1 cup all-purpose flour

4 large eggs

Sublime Hot Fudge Sauce (opposite)

1 quart vanilla ice-cream, slightly softened

1. Preheat oven to 400°F. Grease and flour large cookie sheet.

2. Prepare choux pastry: In 3-quart saucepan, heat water, butter, and salt to boiling over medium heat until butter has melted. Remove from heat. With wooden spoon, vigorously stir in flour all at once, stirring until mixture leaves side of pan and forms a ball. Add eggs to flour mixture, one at a time, beating well after each addition, until mixture is smooth and satiny.

3. Drop pastry by slightly rounded ¼ cups in 8 large mounds, 3 inches apart, on prepared cookie sheet. With moistened finger, gently smooth tops. Bake until deep golden, 40 to 45 minutes. Remove puffs from oven; with tip of knife, make small slit in side of each puff to release steam. Turn off oven. Return puffs to oven and let stand 10 minutes. Transfer puffs to wire rack to cool completely.

4. Meanwhile, prepare Sublime Hot Fudge Sauce. With serrated knife, cut each cooled puff horizontally in half; remove and discard any moist dough inside puffs.

5. To serve, place ½-cup scoop vanilla ice cream in bottom half of each cream puff; replace tops of cream puffs. Spoon fudge sauce over puffs.

EACH SERVING WITH FUDGE SAUCE: About 629 calories, 9g protein, 56g carbohydrate, 44g total fat (26g saturated), 215mg cholesterol, 322mg sodium.

Sublime Hot Fudge Sauce

1 cup heavy or whipping cream

¾ cup sugar

4 squares (4 ounces) unsweetened chocolate, chopped

2 tablespoons light corn syrup

2 tablespoons butter or margarine

2 teaspoons vanilla extract

1. In heavy 2-quart saucepan, combine cream, sugar, chocolate, and corn syrup. Heat to boiling over high heat, stirring constantly. Reduce heat to medium. Cook at a gentle boil, stirring constantly, until sauce has thickened slightly, about 5 minutes.

2. Remove from heat; stir in butter and vanilla until smooth and glossy. Cool completely. Makes about 1¾ cups.

EACH TABLESPOON: About 83 calories, 1g protein, 8g carbohydrate, 6g total fat (4g saturated), 14mg cholesterol, 14mg sodium.

The Ice-Cream Man

One phenomenon of early-twentieth-century America that impacted children was the ice-cream man, who canvassed urban and suburban neighborhoods in a white truck, ringing a bell to herald his arrival. At the first faint chime, kids would rush to gather up (or plead for) some coins and stand in line with their friends from the block. The truck was festooned with brightly colored pictures of the available treats so that the young devotées could study all of the tasty possibilities before finally making a selection—a momentous decision in their young eyes.

In those early days, the brand of ice cream was Good Humor, a company begun in 1920, when Harry Burt (who had created the Jolly Boy Sucker lollipop) set out to make an ice-cream bar that was coated with chocolate. He made one, but it was too messy to hold and eat. At the suggestion of his young son, he inserted a wooden lollipop stick into the bar, and the very first ice-cream-on-a-stick was born. A fleet of twelve trucks was dispatched to make deliveries, and the Good Humor Man became an American tradition.

In 1930, New York businessman M. J. Meehan purchased a majority of shares in the Good Humor Company and took control of the business. In the 1950s and 1960s, the number of trucks expanded, as did the number of tempting ice-cream treats, among them the original Vanilla Ice-Cream Bar, the Toasted Almond Bar, the Strawberry Shortcake Bar, the Candy Crunch Bar, the Vanilla Ice-Cream Sandwich, and the Creamsicle.

In 1961, the business was sold to the Thomas J. Lipton Company. By the 1970s, the ice-cream trucks had been phased out, and Good Humor ice cream was only sold in grocery stores and supermarkets. So ended a golden era for generations of children: delicious ice-cream treats brought right to their door, heralded by the simple ringing of a bell.

Orange Sherbet

The word *sherbet* was not commonly used in America until the mid-nineteenth century, and it was used interchangeably with *sorbet*. Delmonico's restaurant served lemon and orange sorbets (strengthened by sparkling wine, kirsh, or plum brandy) in cups that were made of ice. As Mrs. Marshall's 1885 *Book of Ices* documents, refreshing sorbets would be served halfway through an English or continental dinner in upper class homes. It was usually lemon-water ice that contained a bit of liqueur and was garnished with fruit. By the twentieth century, some states gave sherbet a legal definition: in New York, sherbet must contain milk or a milk product. Our recipe is milk-based and is especially nice because it doesn't require an ice-cream maker.

PREP: 10 minutes plus chilling and freezing
COOK: 10 minutes ★ **MAKES** about 4 cups or 8 servings

1½ **cups milk**

½ **cup sugar**

5 **large oranges**

⅛ **teaspoon salt**

1. In heavy 2-quart saucepan, combine milk and sugar. Cook over medium-high heat, stirring occasionally, until bubbles form around edge and sugar has completely dissolved, about 2 minutes. Pour into medium bowl; press plastic wrap onto surface. Refrigerate until well chilled, at least 1 hour or up to 4 hours.

2. From oranges, grate 1 teaspoon peel and squeeze 2 cups juice. Stir orange peel, juice, and salt into chilled milk mixture. Pour into 9-inch square metal baking pan; cover and freeze until firm, at least 4 hours.

3. With spoon, scoop sherbet into food processor with knife blade attached. Process sherbet until smooth but still frozen. Return sherbet to pan; cover and freeze until firm, 1 to 2 hours longer.

4. To serve, let sherbet stand at room temperature until just soft enough to scoop, about 10 minutes.

EACH SERVING: About 104 calories, 2g protein, 21g carbohydrate, 2g total fat (1g saturated), 6mg cholesterol, 60mg sodium.

Old-Fashioned Vanilla Ice Cream

One of the earliest accounts of ice cream in America appeared around 1745. A guest of Governor Thomas Bladen of Maryland described the dessert: "Dessert no less Curious...Compos'd was some fine Ice Cream which, with the Strawberries and Milk, eat most deliciously." Our founding fathers indulged in ice cream. George Washington owned two pewter ice-cream pots and served "iced creams" at his weekly dinners. Thomas Jefferson returned from France in 1789 with an ice-cream recipe so elaborate that it required eighteen separate steps. He is credited with bringing French-style (custard) ice cream to America. By the mid-1780s, ice cream was commercially produced in New York City. In 1800, one of the first ice-cream parlors opened in Philadelphia, and by the mid-1800s, recipes for freezing creams and jellies began appearing in cookbooks such as Sarah Josepha Hale's *The Good Housekeeper*: "Break ice, in a tub or bucket, in small pieces, and strew a handful of salt among it. Place your mould on this ice..." Ice cream was on its way to becoming a treasured tradition.

PREP: 5 minutes plus chilling and freezing
COOK: 15 minutes ★ **MAKES** about 6½ cups or 13 servings

1 cup sugar
3 tablespoons all-purpose flour
½ teaspoon salt
3 cups milk
3 large eggs
1½ cups heavy or whipping cream
4 teaspoons vanilla extract

1. In heavy 3-quart saucepan, combine sugar, flour, and salt; stir in milk until well blended. Cook over medium heat, stirring frequently, until mixture has thickened and boils. Remove from heat.

2. In medium bowl, with wire whisk, lightly beat eggs; stir in about ½ cup of hot milk mixture. Over medium heat, slowly pour egg mixture back into milk mixture in saucepan, stirring rapidly to prevent curdling. Remove from heat. Strain custard through sieve into large bowl. Press plastic wrap onto surface of custard. Refrigerate until well chilled, about 3 hours or up to overnight.

3. Add heavy cream and vanilla to custard. Freeze in ice-cream maker as manufacturer directs.

EACH SERVING: About 216 calories, 4g protein, 20g carbohydrate, 13g total fat (8g saturated), 95mg cholesterol, 142mg sodium.

Strawberry Ice Cream

Prepare custard for Old-Fashioned Vanilla Ice Cream as directed in Steps 1 and 2. While custard is chilling, in medium bowl, crush *1 quart strawberries*, hulled, with *½ cup sugar* and *2 tablespoons fresh lemon juice*. Refrigerate until well chilled, at least 1 hour or up to 4 hours. Stir strawberry mixture into chilled custard. Freeze in ice-cream maker as manufacturer directs. Makes about 11 cups or 22 servings.

EACH SERVING: About 154 calories, 3g protein, 19g carbohydrate, 8g total fat (5g saturated), 56mg cholesterol, 84mg sodium.

Peach Ice Cream

Prepare custard for Old-Fashioned Vanilla Ice Cream as directed in Steps 1 and 2. When custard is almost chilled, in blender or in food processor with knife blade attached, puree *10 to 12 ripe medium peaches*, peeled, pitted, and cut into pieces, with *½ cup sugar* until smooth. (There should be 3 cups puree.) Add peach puree and *¼ teaspoon almond extract* (omit vanilla) to chilled custard. Freeze in ice-cream maker as manufacturer directs. Makes about 11 cups or 22 servings.

EACH SERVING: About 171 calories, 3g protein, 24g carbohydrate, 8g total fat (5g saturated), 56mg cholesterol, 84mg sodium.

Banana-Split Cake

As ice-cream parlors grew in popularity, so did their special offerings. After 1892, the United Fruit Company began importing large quantities of bananas. In 1915, the editors of the *Soda Water Guide* announced that the banana split was the first fancy soda-fountain–fruit dessert to become popular. A split is traditionally served in an oblong glass dish that has a small lug handle at each end. To make an authentic banana split, begin with a generous layer of long banana slices. Top with three scoops of ice cream (vanilla, chocolate, and strawberry). Dress with various syrups (chocolate, marshmallow, and strawberry are the most popular), sprinkle with ground nuts, crown with whipped cream, and top with maraschino cherries. Our banana-split cake has all of the flair of a delicious banana split but is easier to serve to a crowd.

PREP: 35 minutes plus chilling and freezing
BAKE: 12 minutes ★ **MAKES** 16 servings

Sublime Hot Fudge Sauce (page 253)
14 creme-filled chocolate sandwich cookies
3 tablespoons butter or margarine, melted
1 pint vanilla ice cream
4 ripe medium bananas
1 pint chocolate ice cream
1 pint strawberry ice cream
½ cup heavy or whipping cream
¼ cup walnuts, broken into small pieces
maraschino cherries

1. Preheat oven to 350°F. Prepare Sublime Hot Fudge Sauce; cool completely.

2. In plastic bag, with rolling pin, finely crush cookies. In 9" by 3" springform pan, with fork, stir cookie crumbs and melted butter until evenly moistened. With hand, press cookie mixture firmly onto bottom of springform pan. Bake until crust is slightly darker at edge, 12 to 14 minutes. Place crust in freezer until well chilled, about 30 minutes.

3. Meanwhile, place vanilla ice cream in refrigerator to soften slightly, about 30 minutes. With narrow metal spatula, evenly spread vanilla ice cream over crust; cover and freeze until firm, about 45 minutes.

4. Cut 3 bananas lengthwise in half. Pour cooled fudge sauce over vanilla ice cream; arrange bananas on top. Cover and freeze cake until fudge sauce is firm, about 1 hour.

5. Meanwhile, place chocolate ice cream in refrigerator to soften slightly, about 30 minutes. Evenly spread chocolate ice cream over fudge sauce and bananas. Cover and freeze until firm, about 20 minutes.

6. Meanwhile, place strawberry ice cream in refrigerator to soften slightly. Spread strawberry ice cream evenly over chocolate ice cream. Cover and freeze until firm, about 3 hours or up to 2 days.

7. To serve, in small bowl, with mixer at medium speed, beat cream until soft peaks form. Cut remaining banana on diagonal into ½-inch-thick slices. Dip small knife in hot water, shaking off excess; run knife around edge of pan to loosen cake. Remove side of pan; place cake on platter. With narrow metal spatula, mound whipped cream over top of cake. Arrange banana slices on whipped cream; sprinkle with walnuts and top with cherries. Let stand about 10 minutes at room temperature for easier slicing.

EACH SERVING: About 324 calories, 4g protein, 38g carbohydrate, 19g total fat (10g saturated), 52mg cholesterol, 158mg sodium.

Chapter 12

A Piece of Cake, A Slice of Pie

 In colonial America, cake was simple: a wedge of dense pound cake, a slice of golden sponge cake, a chunk of fruit-and-nut cake, or perhaps a serving of dark steamed pudding cake. In Eliza Leslie's 1848 book, *Directions for Cookery in Its Various Branches,* she discusses the difficulty of baking cake at home: "Unless you are provided with proper and convenient utensils and materials, the difficulty of preparing cakes will be great, and in most instances a failure...It is safest, when practicable, to send all large cakes to a professional baker's . . ." Despite her concerns, the book has sixty-four cake recipes.

By the early twentieth century, several events had impacted baking cakes at home: the greater availability of baking books, improved home ovens assured more reliable results, newly invented baking powder produced cakes that were lighter and rose higher, and Baker's baking chocolate made cake delicious. Homemakers could now more easily bake an array of spectacular cakes, including angel food cake, cream cake, devil's food cake, and chiffon cake. As the century progressed, European immigrants introduced us to the French genoise and the Viennese linzertorte, state fairs and cake contests brought "mile-high" show-off cakes, and community bake sales overflowed with carrot cakes and upside-down cakes. Moms turned cakes into clowns and trains for birthdays and sliced up ice-cream cakes for afternoon tea. And cake mixes turned homemakers into instant bakers in a matter of minutes.

As for pies, the colonists made both sweet and savory ones, including meat, fish, fowl, game, fruit, vegetable, berry, and custard. Amelia Simmons's 1796 cookbook *American Cookery* offers recipes for fresh fruit pie, minced-meat pie, and citrus custard pie.

The twentieth century was also a good time for pies. Chocolate and butterscotch pies made their debut, along with chiffon pies in the 1920s. Regional pies, such as key lime pie, southern pecan pie, and Mississippi mud pie, developed nationwide popularity that shows no sign of abating.

Americans have always loved homemade pies and cakes, and our appreciation for the classics is perhaps stronger than ever.

Mom's Blue-Ribbon Coconut Cake

Coconut cake has been around since 1830. The first coconut cakes were one-layer butter cakes that contained coconut. In *Directions for Cookery,* Eliza Leslie offers a recipe for Cocoa-Nut [*sic*] Cake, which only has four ingredients: "Cut up and wash a cocoa-nut, and grate as much of it as will weigh a pound. Powder a pound of loaf-sugar. Beat fifteen eggs very light; and then beat into them, gradually, the sugar. Then add by degrees the cocoa-nut; and lastly, a handful of sifted flour." The single most important event that helped popularize coconut desserts was the development of a machine by Franklin Baker of Baker's Coconut Company in Philadelphia in 1895 that uniformly shredded coconut. Over time, coconut cake became two-layer butter cakes. Some were filled with lemon curd, then topped with seven minute icing and a mountain of shredded coconut, while others were filled and covered with fluffy white frosting and coconut.

PREP: 35 minutes plus cooling ★ **BAKE:** 30 minutes
MAKES 12 servings

---

2 cups all-purpose flour

2 teaspoons baking powder

1 teaspoon salt

½ cup vegetable shortening or ½ cup butter or margarine (1 stick), softened

1¼ cups sugar

3 large eggs

1 teaspoon vanilla extract

1 cup milk

Fluffy White Frosting (opposite)

1 package (7 ounces) flaked sweetened coconut

1. Preheat oven to 350°F. Grease and flour two 8-inch round cake pans or one 9-inch square baking pan. (Preheat oven to 325°F if using 9-inch square baking pan.)

2. In bowl, combine flour, baking powder, and salt.

3. In large bowl, with mixer at medium speed, beat shortening and sugar until light and fluffy, about 5 minutes, frequently scraping bowl with rubber spatula. Add eggs, one at a time, beating well after each addition. Beat in vanilla. Reduce speed to low; add flour mixture alternately with milk, beginning and ending with flour mixture. Beat just until blended, scraping bowl.

4. Spoon batter into prepared pans, dividing it evenly. Bake until toothpick inserted in center of cake comes out clean, about 30 minutes for 8-inch layers, or 40 to 45 minutes for 9-inch cake. Cool in pans on wire racks 10 minutes. Run thin knife around layers to loosen from sides of pans. Invert onto racks to cool completely.

5. Meanwhile, prepare Fluffy White Frosting. In small bowl, combine 1 cup coconut and 1 cup frosting. Place one cake layer, rounded side down, on cake plate. With narrow metal spatula, spread frosting mixture over cake layer. Top with remaining cake layer, rounded side up, and spread remaining frosting over side and top of cake. Sprinkle top and side of cake with remaining coconut.

EACH SERVING: About 425 calories, 6g protein, 64g carbohydrate, 17g total fat (8g saturated), 56mg cholesterol, 355mg sodium.

Fluffy White Frosting

Late-nineteenth-century cookbooks, such as the 1886 book *Mrs. Rorer's Philadelphia Cook Book,* give recipes for boiled icings that are made by drizzling boiling hot sugar syrup into beaten egg whites, resulting in billowing fluffs of marshmallow crème. Culinary historian Jean Anderson, in her 1997 *American Century Cookbook,* traces the recipe back to 1930 when the *Good Housekeeping* Institute published a recipe for a Seven-Minute Icing in their book *Meals Tested, Tasted and Approved.* As in our recipe, the ingredients are cooked in a double boiler for exactly seven minutes, then beaten off the heat until shiny, stiff peaks form. The term *icing* not *frosting* was used in early cookbooks. Nowadays the two are used interchangeably.

PREP: 15 minutes ★ **COOK:** 7 minutes ★ **MAKES** about 3 cups

---

2 large egg whites

1 cup sugar

¼ cup water

2 teaspoons fresh lemon juice (optional)

1 teaspoon light corn syrup

¼ teaspoon cream of tartar

1. In medium bowl set over 3- to 4-quart saucepan filled with *1 inch simmering water* (double boiler top or bowl should sit about 2 inches above water), with mixer at high speed, beat egg whites, sugar, water, lemon juice, if using, corn syrup, and cream of tartar until soft peaks form when beaters are lifted and temperature of mixture reaches 160°F on candy thermometer, about 7 minutes.

2. Remove bowl from pan; beat egg-white mixture until stiff, glossy peaks form, 5 to 10 minutes longer.

Cakewalk at the County Fair

In early- and mid-twentieth-century America, county fairs were fun social events not to be missed. The cake pavilion was always one of the busiest areas at the fair, especially when the cake walk was about to begin. Everyone passing by could hear the barker calling out: "Ten cents a chance, fifteen chances for a dollar—now's your chance to win a delicious cake! All proceeds go to the community fund, so come on in!"

The heavenly aromas inside the tent told the whole story: here were cakes made by the best bakers in the county. Many proudly displayed blue or gold ribbons, indicating they had just placed in a competition at the fair.

The cake walk closely resembled a game of musical chairs. As the music played, guests walked past the cakes. When the music stopped, each person hurried to stand by a cake. The lucky person standing next to the cake with the winning number got to take home the cake.

In the pavilion, the cakes were grouped according to their category: sponge cakes, old-fashioned cakes, chocolate cakes, and cut-out cakes were all represented. The angel food, chiffon, and sponge cakes were always the most elegant entries, often displayed on glass pedestal cake stands. There was usually a pink-frosted angel food birthday cake, a golden chiffon cake topped with swirled fluffs of white mountain cream and garnished with long, thin strips of candied lemon peel, plus a daffodil cake with its marbled yellow-and-white sponge interior and sunny yellow buttercream frosting covering it all.

Of course there were always lots of entries in the old-fashioned layer-cake category. A five-layer coconut cake filled with lemon curd and finished with freshly grated coconut often took center stage. Frequently, someone entered a snow-white Lady Baltimore cake with its raisin, fig, and pecan filling or a golden Lord Baltimore cake filled with macaroon crumbs, pecans, almonds, and candied cherries, then covered with peaks of seven-minute frosting. There might also be a three-layer spice cake with lemon fluff icing, a banana-nut creation, a pineapple upside-down cake, or a fresh carrot cake with rich cream cheese frosting. Several pound cakes always made an appearance: a golden cake swirled with mounds of whipped cream and crowned with fresh peach slices and strawberries, a burnt-sugar Bundt cake that was drizzled with a praline glaze, and a brandied pound loaf with a broiled toasted-pecan topping.

Naturally the chocolate category was often the most popular. There was usually a three-layer chocolate marble cake swirled with chocolate buttercream, a red devil's food cake with fudge frosting, a dark Mississippi mud cake, a Black Forest cake with its rich cherry filling, and a chocolate cheesecake with fresh raspberries piled on top.

But perhaps the most fun category of all was the cut-out cakes. Depending on the year, happy clowns, elaborate trains, smiling Santas, jack-o-lanterns, laughing elephants, and even Mickey Mouse was designed, baked, and decorated into delicious show-stopping creations.

With a chance to win a scrumptious cake to take home, it was hard to resist joining in the fun. It's no wonder that the cake walk was always the talk of the fair.

Lady Baltimore Cake

This cake comes with a story. Alicia Rhett Mayberry, a southern belle in Charleston, South Carolina, baked this glorious dried fig, fruit, and nut–filled tiered cake for novelist Owen Wister, who was so enamored of the delicious confection that he described it in a 1906 novel he titled *Lady Baltimore*. Food historian Evan Jones writes that the original recipe may also have become the property of Florence and Nina Ottolengui, who managed Charleston's Lady Baltimore Tea Room for over twenty-five years. As the story goes, each year they shipped Owen Wister a cake as "thanks" for helping make their cake famous. As Jean Anderson writes in the *American Century Cookbook*, the original Lady Baltimore Cake was a yellow cake that was made with whole eggs. More recent versions are silver cakes that are made with egg whites. One of the earliest silver-white recipes appears in the 1922 *Good Housekeeping's Book of Menus, Recipes and Household Discoveries*, which uses rose extract for flavoring. Most recipes for Lady Baltimore Cake use either an old-fashioned boiled frosting or a seven-minute icing.

PREP: 35 minutes plus cooling ★ **BAKE:** 25 minutes
MAKES 8 servings

CAKE

2¼ cups cake flour (not self-rising)

1 tablespoon baking powder

1 teaspoon salt

1 cup milk

1 teaspoon vanilla extract

¼ teaspoon almond extract

4 large egg whites

1½ cups sugar

½ cup vegetable shortening

FILLING AND FROSTING

½ cup candied cherries, chopped

⅓ cup dried figs, chopped

⅓ cup raisins, chopped

¼ cup chopped pecans

2 batches Fluffy White Frosting (page 260)

1. Preheat oven to 375°F. Grease and flour two 8-inch round cake pans; line bottoms with waxed paper.

2. In medium bowl, combine flour, baking powder, and salt. In 1-cup measuring cup, stir milk, vanilla extract, and almond extract.

3. In medium bowl, with mixer at high speed, beat egg whites until soft peaks form when beaters are lifted. Sprinkle in ½ cup sugar, 2 tablespoons at a time, beating until sugar has dissolved and egg whites stand in stiff, glossy peaks when beaters are lifted. Do not overbeat.

4. In large bowl, with mixer at medium speed, beat shortening and remaining 1 cup sugar until light and fluffy, about 5 minutes. Reduce speed to low; add flour mixture alternately with milk mixture, beginning and ending with flour mixture. Beat just until blended, scraping bowl with rubber spatula.

5. With spatula, gently fold one-third of beaten egg whites into batter, then fold in remaining egg whites until blended. Divide batter evenly between prepared pans; spread evenly. Bake until cake springs back when lightly pressed, about 25 minutes. Cool in pans on wire racks 10 minutes. Run thin knife around layers to loosen from sides of pans. Invert onto racks to cool completely.

6. In small bowl, combine cherries, figs, raisins, and pecans; set aside. Prepare Fluffy White Frosting. Stir fruit mixture into 3 cups frosting.

7. With serrated knife, cut each cake layer horizontally in half. Place one layer, rounded side down on cake plate. With narrow metal spatula, spread one-third of fruit mixture over cake layer. Top with second layer, rounded side up, and spread with half of remaining fruit mixture. Top with third layer, rounded side down, and top with remaining fruit mixture. Place remaining cake layer, rounded side up, on top. Spread remaining frosting over side and top of cake.

EACH SERVING: About 745 calories, 9g protein, 142g carbohydrate, 18g total fat (4g saturated), 4mg cholesterol, 550mg sodium.

Classic Devil's Food Cake

(pictured on page 258)

Some believe that this twentieth-century cake was so named because of its color contrast to snowy white angel food cake. Others claim it carries the name "devil" because it is so rich and delicious that it can be regarded as somewhat sinful to eat. Recipes for this cake vary greatly: Some use milk and baking powder, while others use sour milk and baking soda. Some are made with chocolate, while others are made with cocoa. And some are sweetened with white or brown sugar instead of a mix of the two, as in our recipe. A classic 1933 devil's food cake was iced with seven-minute icing, but chocolate buttercream frosting makes it even richer and more chocolaty. We use cocoa and baking soda in our cake, which turns it deep reddish brown. It is sometimes known as red devil's food cake.

PREP: 35 minutes plus cooling ★ **BAKE:** 30 minutes
MAKES 16 servings

2 cups all-purpose flour

1 cup unsweetened cocoa

1½ teaspoons baking soda

½ teaspoon salt

½ cup butter or margarine (1 stick), softened

1 cup packed light brown sugar

1 cup granulated sugar

3 large eggs

1½ teaspoons vanilla extract

1½ cups buttermilk

Chocolate Buttercream Frosting (page 278) or
   Fluffy White Frosting (page 260)

1. Preheat oven to 350°F. Grease three 8-inch round cake pans. Line bottoms with waxed paper; grease paper. Dust pans with flour.

2. In medium bowl, combine flour, cocoa, baking soda, and salt.

3. In large bowl, with mixer at low speed, beat butter and brown and granulated sugars until blended. Increase speed to high and beat until light and fluffy, about 5 minutes. Reduce speed to medium-low; add eggs, one at a time, beating well after each addition. Add vanilla and beat until mixed. Add flour mixture alternately with buttermilk, beginning and ending with flour mixture. Beat just until batter is smooth, occasionally scraping bowl with rubber spatula.

4. Divide batter evenly among prepared pans; spread evenly. Place two pans on upper oven rack and one pan on lower oven rack so pans are not directly above one another. Bake until toothpick inserted in center comes out clean, 30 to 35 minutes. Cool in pans on wire racks 10 minutes. Run thin knife around layers to loosen from sides of pans. Invert onto wire racks. Remove waxed paper; cool completely.

5. Meanwhile, prepare Chocolate Buttercream Frosting. Place one cake layer, rounded side down, on cake plate. With narrow metal spatula; spread ⅓ cup frosting over layer. Top with second layer, rounded side up, and spread with ⅓ cup frosting. Place remaining layer, rounded side up, on top. Spread remaining frosting over side and top of cake.

EACH SERVING WITH CHOCOLATE BUTTERCREAM FROSTING: About 450 calories, 5g protein, 74g carbohydrate, 17g total fat (10g saturated), 72mg cholesterol, 355mg sodium.

Mississippi Mud Cake

Exactly when Mississippi Mud Cake was created is hazy, but it appears to have happened in the Deep South around 1985. The original cake contained cocoa, pecans, and miniature marshmallows, and the frosting was made with a pound of confectioners' sugar, a half pound of butter, cocoa, and pecans. In 1986, Natalie Dupree wrote in *New Southern Cooking* that the top of the cake should be "cracked and dry-looking like Mississippi mud in the hot, dry summer." Our rendition is even richer than the original, due to an extra-generous amount of coconut in the cake layer and frosting. Since the cake is very rich, we recommend serving it in small portions.

PREP: 20 minutes plus cooling ★ **BAKE:** 35 minutes
MAKES 32 servings

MUD CAKE

¾ cup butter or margarine (1½ sticks)

1¾ cups granulated sugar

¾ cup unsweetened cocoa

4 large eggs

2 teaspoons vanilla extract

½ teaspoon salt

1½ cups all-purpose flour

½ cup pecans, chopped

½ cup flaked sweetened coconut

3 cups mini marshmallows

FUDGE TOPPING

5 tablespoons butter or margarine

1 square (1 ounce) unsweetened chocolate

⅓ cup unsweetened cocoa

⅛ teaspoon salt

¼ cup evaporated milk (not sweetened condensed milk) or heavy or whipping cream

1 teaspoon vanilla extract

1 cup confectioners' sugar

½ cup pecans, coarsely broken

¼ cup flaked sweetened coconut

1. Preheat oven to 350°F. Grease and flour 13" by 9" baking pan.

2. Prepare mud cake: In 3-quart saucepan, melt butter over low heat, stirring occasionally. With wire whisk, beat in granulated sugar and cocoa. Remove from heat. Beat in eggs, one at a time; beat in vanilla and salt until well blended. With wooden spoon, stir in flour just until blended. Stir in pecans and coconut (batter will be thick).

3. Spread batter in prepared pan. Bake 25 minutes. Remove pan from oven; sprinkle marshmallows in even layer on top of cake. Return to oven and bake until marshmallows are puffed and golden, about 10 minutes. Cool completely in pan on wire rack.

4. When cake is cool, prepare fudge topping: In 2-quart saucepan, melt butter and chocolate over low heat, stirring frequently until smooth. With wire whisk, stir in cocoa and salt until smooth and blended. Stir in evaporated milk and vanilla (mixture will be thick); beat in confectioners' sugar until blended. Pour hot topping over cooled cake.

5. Cool fudge-topped cake 20 minutes; sprinkle pecans and coconut over top. Serve at room temperature, or refrigerate to serve chilled later. To store, leave cake in pan and wrap. To serve, cut lengthwise into 4 strips, then cut each strip crosswise into 8 pieces.

EACH SERVING: About 205 calories, 3g protein, 25g carbohydrate, 11g fat (5g saturated), 44mg cholesterol, 125mg sodium.

German Chocolate Cake

Contrary to common belief, this cake is not German at all. It's named for the German Sweet Chocolate it contains. According to Jean Anderson, the original recipe for this three-tiered chocolate cake with coconut-pecan filling was submitted to a Dallas newspaper in 1957. The cake was so popular that the sales of German chocolate, then manufactured by General Foods, greatly soared in Texas. A district sales manager passed the recipe on to General Foods headquarters, where it was tested, tasted, and perfected for national release. The recipe has since appeared on every wrapper of the chocolate bar. As to why the chocolate is named "German," in 1789 Dr. James Baker financed the first American chocolate factory and hired Samuel German to develop a sweet chocolate.

PREP: 45 minutes plus cooling ★ **BAKE:** 30 minutes
MAKES 16 servings

2 cups all-purpose flour

1 teaspoon baking soda

¼ teaspoon salt

1¼ cups buttermilk

1 teaspoon vanilla extract

3 large eggs, separated

1½ cups sugar

¾ cup butter or margarine (1½ sticks), softened

4 squares (4 ounces) sweet baking chocolate, melted

Coconut-Pecan Frosting (opposite)

1. Preheat oven to 350°F. Grease three 8-inch round cake pans. Line bottoms with waxed paper; grease and flour waxed paper.

2. In small bowl, combine flour, baking soda, and salt. In 2-cup measuring cup, mix buttermilk and vanilla.

3. In medium bowl, with mixer at medium-high speed, beat egg whites until frothy. Sprinkle in ¾ cup sugar, 1 tablespoon at a time, and beat until soft peaks form when beaters are lifted.

4. In large bowl, with mixer at medium speed, beat butter until creamy. Add remaining ¾ cup sugar and beat until light and fluffy, about 5 minutes. Reduce speed to medium-low; add egg yolks, one at a time, beating well after each addition. Beat in melted chocolate. Reduce speed to low; add flour mixture alternately with buttermilk mixture, beginning and ending with flour mixture. Beat until smooth, occasionally scraping bowl with rubber spatula. With spatula, fold half of beaten egg whites into batter; gently fold in remaining whites.

5. Divide batter evenly among prepared pans. Place two pans on upper oven rack and one pan on lower oven rack so pans are not directly above one another. Bake until toothpick inserted in center comes out almost clean, about 30 minutes. Cool in pans on wire racks 10 minutes. Run thin knife around layers to loosen from sides of pans. Invert onto wire racks. Remove waxed paper; cool completely.

6. Meanwhile, prepare Coconut-Pecan Frosting. Place one cake layer, rounded side down, on cake plate. With narrow metal spatula, spread 1 cup frosting over layer. Top with second cake layer, rounded side up, and spread with 1 cup frosting. Place remaining layer, rounded side up, on top. Spread remaining frosting over side and top of cake.

EACH SERVING: About 505 calories, 5g protein, 53g carbohydrate, 31g total fat (16g saturated), 140mg cholesterol, 320mg sodium.

Coconut-Pecan Frosting

PREP: 5 minutes ★ **COOK:** 15 minutes
MAKES about 3 cups

½ cup butter or margarine (1 stick), cut into pieces

1 cup heavy or whipping cream

1 cup packed light brown sugar

3 large egg yolks

1 teaspoon vanilla extract

1 cup flaked sweetened coconut

1 cup pecans (4 ounces), chopped

1. In 2-quart saucepan, combine butter, cream, and brown sugar. Heat almost to boiling over medium-high heat, stirring occasionally.

2. Meanwhile, place egg yolks in medium bowl. Slowly pour about ½ cup sugar mixture into egg yolks, whisking constantly. Reduce heat to medium-low. Add egg-yolk mixture to saucepan and whisk constantly until thickened (do not boil).

3. Remove saucepan from heat. Stir in vanilla, coconut, and pecans until combined. Cool to room temperature.

EACH TABLESPOON: About 80 calories, 1g protein, 6g carbohydrate, 6g total fat (3g saturated), 25mg cholesterol, 30mg sodium.

Black Forest Cake

The German name for this cake is *Schwarzwälder Kirschtorte.* Many believe this famous dessert comes from Swabia in the heart of Germany's Black Forest, while others believe it originated in Berlin in the 1930s. This baroque creation is made up of chocolate cake layers (often sprinkled with kirsch) that are filled with whipped cream and sweet dark cherries. When the recipe "arrived" in Britain, it quickly appeared on many restaurant dessert menus to rave reviews. Sometime in the mid-twentieth century, it showed up in the fanciest restaurants in the United States and is still featured on many menus today, most notably at the Palm Court in New York's Plaza hotel.

PREP: 1 hour plus overnight to chill ★ **BAKE:** 25 minutes
MAKES 16 servings

CHOCOLATE CAKE

2 cups all-purpose flour

1 cup unsweetened cocoa

2 teaspoons baking powder

1 teaspoon baking soda

½ teaspoon salt

1⅓ cups milk

2 teaspoons vanilla extract

1 cup butter or margarine (2 sticks), softened

2 cups granulated sugar

4 large eggs

CHERRY FILLING

2 cans (16½ ounces each) pitted dark sweet
   cherries (Bing) in heavy syrup

⅓ cup kirsch (cherry brandy)

CREAM FILLING

1½ cups heavy or whipping cream

½ cup confectioners' sugar

2 tablespoons kirsch (cherry brandy)

1 teaspoon vanilla extract

Chocolate Curls (page 299)

1. Preheat oven to 350°F. Grease three 9-inch round cake pans. Line bottoms with waxed paper; grease paper. Dust pans with flour.

2. Prepare chocolate cake: In medium bowl, combine flour, cocoa, baking powder, baking soda, and salt. In 2-cup measuring cup, mix milk and vanilla.

3. In large bowl, with mixer at low speed, beat butter and granulated sugar until blended. Increase speed to high; beat until creamy, about 2 minutes. Reduce speed to medium-low. Add eggs, one at a time, beating well after each addition. Reduce speed to low; add flour mixture alternately with milk mixture, beginning and ending with flour mixture. Beat until smooth, occasionally scraping bowl with rubber spatula.

4. Divide batter evenly among prepared cake pans. Place two pans on upper oven rack and one pan on lower oven rack so pans are not directly above one another. Bake until toothpick inserted in center comes out almost clean, about 25 minutes. Cool in pans on wire racks 10 minutes. Run thin knife around layers to loosen from sides of pans. Invert onto wire racks. Remove waxed paper; cool completely.

5. Meanwhile, prepare cherry filling: Drain cherries in sieve set over bowl. Reserve ½ cup syrup; stir in kirsch. Set syrup mixture aside.

6. Prepare cream filling: In small bowl, with mixer at medium speed, beat cream, confectioners' sugar, kirsch, and vanilla until stiff peaks form when beaters are lifted.

7. Assemble cake: Place one layer, rounded side down, on cake plate; brush with one-third of syrup mixture. Spread with one-third of whipped cream mixture, then top with half of cherries. Top with second layer, rounded side up. Brush with half of remaining syrup mixture; spread with half of remaining cream mixture and top with remaining cherries. Place remaining layer, rounded side up, on top. Brush with remaining syrup mixture. Spoon remaining cream mixture into center, leaving border around edge. Pile chocolate curls in center of cake. Cover and refrigerate overnight.

EACH SERVING: About 472 calories, 6g protein, 61g carbohydrate, 23g total fat (14g saturated), 118mg cholesterol, 367mg sodium.

Daffodil Cake

This marbled angel-and-yellow-sponge cake is an American creation. According to Jean Anderson, Joanne Lamb Hayes, former food editor of *Country Living* magazine, found a recipe for Angel and Sponge Marble (cake) in a small recipe booklet from 1925 entitled *Cake Secrets,* published by Swan's Down Cake Flour. In later editions, it's called Daffodil Cake, with the original name as a subtitle. By the time General Foods acquired Swan's Down Cake Flour and published the 1953 edition of *Cake Secrets,* the recipe was simply called Daffodil Cake and was described as: "A cake that looks and tastes like Spring."

PREP: 15 minutes plus cooling ★ **BAKE:** 35 minutes ★ **MAKES** 12 servings

---

2 to 3 large oranges

1 large lemon

1¼ cups egg whites (about 9 large egg whites)

1½ teaspoons cream of tartar

1 teaspoon vanilla extract

¼ teaspoon salt

1½ cups granulated sugar

1 cup cake flour (not self-rising)

4 large egg yolks

1¼ cups sifted confectioners' sugar

1. Preheat oven to 375°F. From oranges, grate 1 tablespoon plus ½ teaspoon peel and squeeze 1 tablespoon juice. From lemon, grate 2 teaspoons peel and squeeze 1 tablespoon juice. Reserve.

2. In large bowl, with mixer at high speed, beat egg whites, cream of tartar, vanilla, and salt until soft peaks form when beaters are lifted. Sprinkle in granulated sugar, 2 tablespoons at a time, beating until sugar has dissolved and egg whites stand in stiff, glossy peaks when beaters are lifted.

3. Reduce speed to low; gradually beat in flour just until mixture is blended.

4. In another large bowl, with mixer at high speed, beat egg yolks until thick and lemon-colored. With rubber spatula, fold in half of egg-white mixture, 1 tablespoon orange peel, and lemon peel just until blended.

5. In ungreased 10-inch tube pan, alternately drop ½ cups of white and yellow batters. Run narrow metal spatula through batter for marbled effect. Bake until cake springs back when lightly pressed, 35 to 40 minutes.

Invert cake in pan onto large metal funnel or bottle; cool completely in pan. Run thin knife around cake to loosen from side and center tube of pan. Remove from pan and place on cake plate.

6. Prepare orange-lemon glaze: In small bowl, combine confectioners' sugar, reserved orange and lemon juices, and remaining ½ teaspoon orange peel to make a smooth glaze; spoon over cooled cake.

EACH SERVING: About 215 calories, 5g protein, 45g carbohydrate, 2g total fat (1g saturated), 71mg cholesterol, 92mg sodium.

Angel Cake

Beat the whites of eight eggs till frothy. Then add one teaspoon of cream of tartar and continue beating till the whites are perfectly stiff. Gradually add one cup of sugar, beating hard all the time. Sift together three-fourths of a cup of flour and one-fourth of a teaspoon of salt, and fold it lightly into the beaten whites. Flavor with three-fourths of a teaspoon of vanilla and pour into an unbuttered angel cake pan. Put into a rather hot oven and allow the cake to rise quickly. Cool it off slightly, and as soon as the cake begins to brown cover with buttered paper. It will take from forty-five to fifty minutes to bake.

—Good Housekeeping Everyday Cook Book, 1903

Clown Cupcakes

During the early and mid-twentieth century, women's magazines featured fancy cake creations that made it possible even for beginning bakers to make show-off cakes. Our simple clown cupcakes are like those that filled magazines and delighted children at birthday parties.

PREP: 1 hour plus cooling ★ **BAKE:** 20 minutes
MAKES 24 cupcakes

CUPCAKES

2 cups all-purpose flour

2 teaspoons baking powder

1 teaspoon salt

½ cup vegetable shortening or ½ cup butter or margarine (1 stick), softened

1¼ cups sugar

3 large eggs

1 teaspoon vanilla extract

1 cup milk

BUTTERCREAM FROSTING

1 cup butter or margarine (2 sticks), softened

6 cups confectioners' sugar (about one and one-half 16-ounce packages)

½ cup half-and-half or light cream

1 tablespoon vanilla extract

DECORATION

24 orange or red fruit slices, cut lengthwise in half

48 bite-size fruit candies

24 gum balls or jaw breakers

12 red gummy rounds, cut in half

1. Preheat oven to 350°F. Line twenty-four 2½-inch muffin-pan cups with paper liners.

2. In bowl, combine flour, baking powder, and salt.

3. In large bowl, with mixer at medium speed, beat shortening and sugar until light and fluffy, about 5 minutes. Add eggs, one at a time, beating well after each addition. Beat in vanilla. Reduce speed to low; add flour mixture alternately with milk, beginning and ending with flour mixture. Beat just until smooth, frequently scraping bowl with rubber spatula.

4. Divide batter evenly among prepared cups. Bake until toothpick inserted in center comes out clean, 20 to 25 minutes. Cool cupcakes in pans on wire racks 10 minutes. Remove cupcakes from pans and cool on racks.

5. Meanwhile prepare buttercream frosting: In large bowl, with mixer at low speed, beat butter, confectioners' sugar, half-and-half, and vanilla just until blended. Increase speed to medium; beat until frosting is smooth and fluffy, about 1 minute, constantly scraping bowl with rubber spatula. Makes 3¾ cups.

6. With small metal spatula, frost tops of cupcakes. Place 2 fruit slices on either side of each cupcake for clown's hair. Place 2 bite-size fruit candies for eyes and 1 gum ball for nose. Cut each gummy round into mouth shape and place on cupcake.

EACH CUPCAKE WITHOUT CANDIES: About 325 calories, 2g protein, 48g carbohydrate, 14g total fat (7g saturated), 51mg cholesterol, 230mg sodium.

Orange and Lemon Chiffon Cake

Chiffon cake was created in the late 1920s by Harry Baker, a Los Angeles insurance salesman and amateur baker. It was so fabulous that he was hired to bake it for Hollywood functions as well as for the Brown Derby restaurant. He kept his recipe (and secret ingredient) to himself until General Mills purchased the recipe from him in 1947. After perfecting the cake (the secret ingredient turned out to be vegetable oil), the test kitchen home economists created several flavor variations. The recipe was published in a recipe leaflet in 1948 and again in *Betty Crocker's Picture Cookbook* in 1950, where the cake was described as: "the first new cake in a hundred years ... as light as angel food, rich as butter cake." Our cake is a favorite: laced with fresh orange zest and drizzled with orange glaze. For a similar version, instead of glazing the cake, dust it lightly with confectioners' sugar.

PREP: 20 minutes ★ **BAKE:** 1 hour 15 minutes
MAKES 16 servings

2 to 3 large oranges

2 to 3 large lemons

2¼ cups cake flour (not self-rising)

1½ cups granulated sugar

1 tablespoon baking powder

1 teaspoon salt

½ cup vegetable oil

5 large eggs, separated

2 large egg whites

½ teaspoon cream of tartar

ORANGE GLAZE

1 cup confectioners' sugar

1 teaspoon freshly grated lemon peel

¼ teaspoon vanilla extract

about 5 teaspoons orange juice

1. Preheat oven to 350°F. From oranges, grate 1 tablespoon peel and squeeze ½ cup juice. From lemons, grate 1 teaspoon peel and squeeze ¼ cup juice.

2. In large bowl, combine flour, 1 cup granulated sugar, baking powder, and salt. Make a well in center; add orange peel and juice, lemon peel and juice, oil, and egg yolks to well. With wire whisk, stir until smooth.

3. In separate large bowl, with mixer at high speed, beat egg whites and cream of tarter until soft peaks form when beaters are lifted. Sprinkle in remaining ½ cup granulated sugar, 2 tablespoons at a time, beating until sugar has dissolved and egg whites stand in stiff, glossy peaks. With rubber spatula, fold one-third of beaten egg whites into egg-yolk mixture, then fold in remaining egg whites until blended.

4. Scrape batter into ungreased 9- to 10-inch tube pan; spread evenly. Bake until cake springs back when lightly pressed, about 1 hour 15 minutes. Invert cake in pan onto large metal funnel or bottle; cool completely. Run thin knife around cake to loosen from side and center tube of pan. Remove from pan and place on cake plate.

5. Prepare orange glaze: In small bowl, combine confectioners' sugar, lemon peel, vanilla, and enough of orange juice to make smooth glaze. Spoon over cooled cake.

EACH SERVING: About 217 calories, 4g protein, 31g carbohydrate, 9g total fat (1g saturated), 66mg cholesterol, 264g sodium.

Carrot Cake

According to Alan Davidson in *The Oxford Companion to Food,* in the Middle Ages, bakers used carrots instead of the more expensive sugar to sweeten cakes and desserts. During the eighteenth and nineteenth centuries, in British recipe books, baked puddings were sweetened with carrots, parsnips, and other sweet root vegetables. During World War II, the British Ministry of Food provided recipes that used carrots instead of (rationed) sugar to sweeten traditional English Christmas puddings. The fresh carrot cake we know and love today appears to be a cake that was "born" here and gained in popularity around the mid-twentieth century. Whether baked in three layer pans, a thirteen-by-nine-inch baking pan, or a decorative Bundt pan, the recipe usually contains a good amount of freshly grated carrots, vegetable oil, cinnamon, and walnuts. More often than not, it's slathered with a decadent cream cheese frosting, as in our recipe.

PREP: 40 minutes plus cooling ★ **BAKE:** 55 minutes
MAKES 16 servings

2½ cups all-purpose flour
2 teaspoons baking soda
2 teaspoons ground cinnamon
1 teaspoon baking powder
1 teaspoon salt
½ teaspoon ground nutmeg
4 large eggs
1 cup granulated sugar
¾ cup packed light brown sugar
1 cup vegetable oil
¼ cup milk
1 tablespoon vanilla extract
3 cups loosely packed shredded carrots (about 6 medium)
1 cup walnuts (4 ounces), chopped
¾ cup dark seedless raisins
Cream Cheese Frosting (opposite)

1. Preheat oven to 350°F. Grease 13" by 9" baking pan. Line bottom with waxed paper; grease paper. Dust pan with flour. Or grease and flour 10-inch Bundt pan.

2. In medium bowl, combine flour, baking soda, cinnamon, baking powder, salt, and nutmeg.

3. In large bowl, with mixer at medium-high speed, beat eggs and granulated and brown sugars until blended, about 2 minutes, frequently scraping bowl with rubber spatula. Beat in oil, milk, and vanilla. Reduce speed to low; add flour mixture and beat until smooth, frequently scraping bowl. Fold in carrots, walnuts, and raisins.

4. Pour batter into prepared pan; spread evenly. Bake until toothpick inserted in center of cake comes out almost clean, 55 to 60 minutes for 13" by 9" cake, or about 1 hour for Bundt cake. Cool in pan on wire rack 10 minutes. Run thin knife, around cake to loosen from sides of pan. Invert onto rack. Remove waxed paper; cool cake completely.

5. Meanwhile, prepare Cream Cheese Frosting. Transfer cooled cake to cake plate. With narrow metal spatula, spread frosting over sides and top of cake.

EACH SERVING: About 550 calories, 6g protein, 71g carbohydrate, 28g total fat (8g saturated), 77mg cholesterol, 445mg sodium.

Cream Cheese Frosting

In large bowl, with mixer at low speed, beat *3 cups confectioners' sugar, 2 packages (3 ounces each) cream cheese, slightly softened, 6 tablespoons butter or margarine, softened, and 1½ teaspoons vanilla extract* just until blended. Increase speed to medium; beat until smooth and fluffy, about 1 minute, frequently scraping bowl with rubber spatula. Makes about 2½ cups.

Boston Cream Pie

Some historians believe that this pie, which is not a pie at all, dates back to a type of dessert known as pudding-cake-pie. One example is Washington Pie (also called Mrs. Washington's Pie), a "filled" cake sandwiched with raspberry jam and dusted with confectioners' sugar. As the story goes, in 1855, in Boston, the Parker House Hotel's German pastry chef decided to spruce up the hotel's Boston Pie (a two-layer sponge cake that was filled with vanilla custard and dusted with confectioners' sugar) by adding a rich chocolate glaze. His creation was called Parker House Chocolate Pie and Parker House Cream Pie. Over the years this dessert gained other names, including Boston Cream Cake and Boston Cream Pie, but little else has changed. It's still a cake (now a golden sponge) that's called a pie. It is filled with a dense vanilla custard, is blanketed with a shiny, thick, deep-chocolate glaze, and remains the signature dessert at the famed Parker House. Boston Cream Pie is also the official state dessert of Massachusetts.

PREP: 40 minutes ★ **BAKE:** 20 minutes
MAKES 12 servings

1½ **cups all-purpose flour**
1½ **teaspoons baking powder**
¼ **teaspoon salt**
3 **large eggs**
½ **cup water**
3 **tablespoons butter or margarine**
1½ **teaspoons vanilla extract**
1⅓ **cups sugar**
Pastry Cream (opposite)
Chocolate Glaze (opposite)

1. Preheat oven to 350°F. Grease two 8-inch round cake pans. Line bottoms with waxed paper; grease and flour cake pans.

2. In medium bowl, combine flour, baking powder, and salt. In large bowl, with mixer at high speed, beat eggs until light and tripled in volume, about 5 minutes.

3. Meanwhile, in small saucepan, combine water and butter; heat to boiling. Remove from heat; add vanilla.

4. With mixer at high speed, gradually add sugar to eggs. Beat until thick and lemon-colored and mixture forms ribbon when beaters are lifted, 5 to 8 minutes, occasionally scraping bowl with rubber spatula. In two additions, fold in flour mixture just until blended. Pour in water mixture; stir gently until blended.

5. Divide batter evenly between prepared pans. Bake until toothpick inserted in center comes out clean, about 20 minutes. Run thin knife around layers to loosen from sides of pans. Invert onto wire racks. Remove waxed paper; cool completely.

6. Meanwhile, prepare Pastry Cream.

7. When cake is cool, prepare Chocolate Glaze.

8. Place one cake layer, rounded side down, on cake plate; top with pastry cream. Top with second cake layer, rounded side up. Pour glaze over top. With narrow metal spatula, spread glaze evenly to edge, allowing it to drip down side of cake. Let glaze set.

EACH SERVING: About 325 calories, 5g protein, 50g carbohydrate, 12g total fat (7g saturated), 110mg cholesterol, 210mg sodium.

Pastry Cream

In 1-quart heavy saucepan, heat ¾ *cup milk* to boiling over medium heat.

Meanwhile, in large bowl, with wire whisk, beat *2 large egg yolks, 6 tablespoons milk,* and *⅓ cup sugar* until smooth. Whisk in *2 tablespoons all-purpose flour* and *2 tablespoons cornstarch* until combined. Gradually whisk hot milk into egg-yolk mixture until blended.

Return mixture to saucepan; cook over medium heat, whisking constantly, until mixture thickens and boils, about 4 minutes. Reduce heat to low; cook, whisking constantly, 2 minutes.

Remove saucepan from heat; stir in *1 tablespoon butter or margarine* and *1 teaspoon vanilla extract*. Pour pastry cream into shallow dish. Press plastic wrap onto surface of pastry cream to keep skin from forming as it cools. Cool to room temperature. Refrigerate at least 2 hours, or up to overnight. Makes about 1 ½ cups.

Chocolate Glaze

In heavy 1-quart saucepan, heat *3 squares (3 ounces) semisweet chocolate,* coarsely chopped, *3 tablespoons butter or margarine, 1 tablespoon light corn syrup,* and *1 tablespoon milk* over low heat, until chocolate and butter melt and mixture is smooth. Makes about ½ cup.

Boston Cream Pie ▶

Pineapple Upside-Down Cake

Most culinary historians agree that upside-down cakes are a product of the twentieth century. In her *Twentieth Century Cookbook*, Jeanne Anderson describes an advertisement for Gold Medal Flour that she found in a women's magazine dated November 1925. It features a full-page color photograph of a round cake topped with six slices of pineapple, candied red cherries, and a brown-sugar glaze. According to *New York Newsday* writer Marie Bianco, the following year the Hawaiian Pineapple Company (to become Dole Food Company, Inc.) ran a recipe contest and received 2,500 entries for pineapple upside-down cake. Around that same time, entrepreneur John Dole was busy canning pineapple rings that were the perfect size for upside-down cake. In many recipes, the pineapple topping is prepared in a cast-iron skillet on the stove top, the batter is spooned in, and the cake is then baked. Upside-down cakes are also made with other fruits, including apples, plums, pears, peaches, cranberries, and blueberries.

PREP: 30 minutes ★ **BAKE:** 40 minutes ★ **MAKES** 8 servings

2 cans (8 ounces each) pineapple slices in juice

⅓ cup packed brown sugar

8 tablespoons butter or margarine (1 stick), softened

1 cup cake flour (not self-rising)

1 teaspoon baking powder

¼ teaspoon salt

⅔ cup granulated sugar

1 large egg

1 teaspoon vanilla extract

⅓ cup milk

1. Preheat oven to 325°F. Drain pineapple slices in sieve set over bowl. Reserve 2 tablespoons juice. Cut 8 slices pineapple in half and drain on paper towels. Refrigerate remaining pineapple for another use.

2. In 10-inch oven-safe skillet (if skillet is not oven-safe, wrap handle with double layer of foil), heat brown sugar and 2 tablespoons butter over medium heat until melted. Stir in reserved pineapple juice and heat to boiling; boil 1 minute. Remove from heat. Arrange pineapple in skillet, slightly overlapping slices to fit if necessary.

3. In small bowl, combine flour, baking powder, and salt. In large bowl, with mixer at high speed, beat remaining 6 tablespoons butter and granulated sugar until light and fluffy, about 3 minutes, frequently scraping bowl with rubber spatula. Reduce speed to low; beat in egg and vanilla until well blended. Add flour mixture alternately with milk, beginning and ending with flour mixture. Beat just until blended.

4. Spoon batter over pineapple; spread evenly. Bake until toothpick inserted in center comes out clean, 40 to 45 minutes. Run thin knife around cake to loosen from side of skillet; invert onto cake plate. (If any pineapple slices stick to skillet, place on cake.) Serve cake warm or at room temperature.

EACH SERVING: About 302 calories, 3g protein, 46g carbohydrate, 13g total fat (8g saturated), 59mg cholesterol, 267mg sodium.

Plum Upside-Down Cake

Prepare as directed but substitute *1 pound plums*, cut into ½-inch-thick wedges, for pineapple. Heat brown sugar and butter in oven-safe skillet over medium heat until melted. Add plums and increase heat to high. Cook, stirring, until plums are glazed with brown-sugar mixture, about 1 minute.

Apple Upside-Down Cake

Prepare as directed but substitute *3 large Golden Delicious apples (1½ pounds)*, peeled, cored, and cut into ¼-inch-thick wedges, for pineapple. Heat brown sugar and butter in oven-safe skillet over medium heat until melted. Add apple wedges and cook over high heat until apples are fork-tender and begin to brown, 7 to 8 minutes.

Lazy-Daisy Cake

This cake was known by several different names during the twentieth century. Most include the word *lazy*, which refers to its quick and easy one-bowl preparation. Lazy-Daisy Cake was promoted as a convenient spur-of-the-moment dessert, perfect for unexpected guests. The unusual technique of adding a mixture of scalded milk and melted butter to the batter results in a cake with a pleasantly coarse texture. Traditionally, as in our recipe, the cake is covered with a brown sugar–coconut topping then placed under the broiler until nicely browned and bubbling.

PREP: 25 minutes plus cooling ★ **BAKE/BROIL:** 40 minutes
MAKES 12 servings

1⅓ cups all-purpose flour
1½ teaspoons baking powder
½ teaspoon salt
¾ cup plus 2 tablespoons milk
6 tablespoons butter or margarine
3 large eggs
1 cup granulated sugar
1½ teaspoons vanilla extract
½ cup packed light brown sugar
½ teaspoon ground cinnamon
½ cup pecans, finely chopped
½ cup flaked sweetened coconut

1. Preheat oven to 350°F. Grease and flour 9-inch square baking pan.

2. In small bowl, combine flour, baking powder, and salt. In small saucepan, heat ¾ cup milk and 2 tablespoons butter over low heat until butter melts and milk is hot.

3. Meanwhile, in another small bowl, with mixer at medium-high speed, beat eggs and granulated sugar until slightly thickened and pale yellow, about 5 minutes, frequently scraping bowl with rubber spatula. Beat in vanilla.

4. Transfer egg mixture to large bowl. With mixer at low speed, alternately add flour mixture and hot milk mixture to egg mixture, beginning and ending with flour mixture. Beat just until smooth, occasionally scraping bowl with spatula.

5. Pour batter into prepared pan. Bake until toothpick inserted in center comes out clean, 35 to 40 minutes. Place pan on wire rack.

6. Preheat broiler. In 2-quart saucepan, combine brown sugar, cinnamon, remaining 4 tablespoons butter, and remaining 2 tablespoons milk. Heat to boiling over medium heat, stirring occasionally. Remove from heat; stir in pecans and coconut. Spoon topping over hot cake; spread to cover evenly.

7. Place pan on rack in broiling pan. Broil 5 to 7 inches from heat source until topping is bubbly and browned, 1 to 2 minutes, watching carefully and rotating pan as necessary for even browning. Serve warm, or cool on wire rack to serve later.

EACH SERVING: About 282 calories, 4g protein, 40g carbohydrate, 12g total fat (6g saturated), 71mg cholesterol, 252mg sodium.

New York Cheesecake

Europeans have been enjoying some form of cheese-cake since the time of the Ancient Greeks, about 2000 years ago. The earliest ones in America were made several ways: with "new milke & whey it with runnet [rennet] as for an ordinary cheese," as in *Martha Washington's Booke of Cookery;* with cottage cheese, as in *Mrs. Rorer's Philadelphia Cook Book;* and with fresh sweet milk and sour milk curd, as in Fannie Farmer's 1896 book, *The Boston Cooking-School Cook Book.* Not until the twentieth century did smooth and silky New York Jewish delicatessen–style cheesecakes appear. Several establishments featured cheese cakes, made with cream cheese: Reuben's on Fifty-eighth Street, supposedly the first to offer this heavenly creamy version; Junior's in Brooklyn, known for its thin cakelike crust; and Lindy's on Broadway, which was popular for its crisp cookie crust. Our recipe uses a graham-cracker crust, which is the easiest to make.

PREP: 30 minutes plus resting and chilling ★ **BAKE:** 55 minutes
MAKES 16 servings

Baked Graham Cracker–Crumb Crust (page 299)
3 packages (8 ounces each) cream cheese, softened
¾ cup sugar
1 tablespoon all-purpose flour
1½ teaspoons vanilla extract
3 large eggs
1 large egg yolk
¼ cup milk

1. Prepare crust as directed, using 8½- to 9-inch spring-form pan. Turn oven control to 300°F.

2. In large bowl, with mixer at medium speed, beat cream cheese and sugar until smooth and fluffy, about 3 minutes. Beat in flour and vanilla until well combined, scraping bowl with rubber spatula. Reduce speed to low; beat in eggs and egg yolk, one at a time, beating well after each addition. Beat in milk just until blended, occasionally scraping bowl.

3. Pour batter into pan. Bake until edge is set and center jiggles slightly, 55 to 60 minutes. Run thin knife around edge of cheesecake to prevent cracking during cooling. Cool completely in pan on wire rack. Cover and refrigerate until well chilled, at least 4 hours or up to overnight. Remove side of pan to serve.

EACH SERVING: About 275 calories, 5g protein, 19g carbohydrate, 20g total fat (12g saturated), 108mg cholesterol, 230mg sodium.

◄ *New York Cheesecake*

Buttercream Frosting

Old-fashioned buttercream frostings seem to be a twentieth-century creation. Their main ingredient, confectioners' sugar (also called powdered sugar and 10X) was first produced around 1910. Fannie Farmer's 1896 book offers recipes for boiled frostings, seven-minute frostings, and confectioners' sugar frostings that are bound together with raw egg whites or egg yolks, but she does not offer buttercreams. By the 1923 edition, however, she includes six buttercreams that use three basic ingredients: butter, confectioners' sugar, and milk or another liquid. Three are flavored with cocoa, and three are flavored with strong coffee. Back then, frosting was mixed by hand. The Mocha Frosting II recipe begins: "Wash butter and pat until no water flies. Work until creamy, using the hand, and add sugar gradually, while beating constantly." Generally, the older recipes use double the amount of butter and one-fourth the amount of liquid of today's buttercreams.

PREP: 10 minutes ★ MAKES about 2¹/₃ cups

1 package (16 ounces) confectioners' sugar
¹/₂ cup butter or margarine (1 stick), softened
4 to 6 tablespoons milk or half-and-half
1¹/₂ teaspoons vanilla extract

In large bowl, with mixer at medium-low speed, beat confectioners' sugar, butter, and 3 tablespoons milk until smooth and blended. Beat in additional milk as needed for easy spreading consistency. Increase speed to medium-high; beat until light and fluffy.

EACH TABLESPOON: About 70 calories, 0g protein, 12g carbohydrate, 3g total fat (2g saturated), 7mg cholesterol, 25mg sodium.

Lemon Buttercream Frosting

Prepare as directed for Buttercream Frosting, but use *1 to 2 tablespoons milk, 2 tablespoons fresh lemon juice,* and *1 teaspoon freshly grated lemon peel.*

EACH TABLESPOON: About 70 calories, 0g protein, 12g carbohydrate, 3g total fat (2g saturated), 7mg cholesterol, 25mg sodium.

Orange Buttercream Frosting

Prepare as directed for Buttercream Frosting, but substitute *2 tablespoons orange juice* for lemon juice and *1 teaspoon freshly grated orange peel* for lemon peel.

EACH TABLESPOON: About 70 calories, 0g protein, 12g carbohydrate, 3g total fat (2g saturated), 7mg cholesterol, 25mg sodium.

Burnt-Buttercream Frosting

In small skillet, heat *¹/₂ cup butter (1 stick)* over medium heat until melted and lightly browned; cool. Prepare as directed but substitute cooled browned butter for softened butter. Makes 2³/₄ cups.

EACH TABLESPOON: About 70 calories, 0g protein, 12g carbohydrate, 3g total fat (2g saturated), 7mg cholesterol, 25mg sodium.

Chocolate Buttercream Frosting

Prepare as directed for Buttercream Frosting, but beat in either *4 squares (4 ounces) bittersweet chocolate,* melted and cooled, or *3 squares (3 ounces) semisweet chocolate* plus *1 square (1 ounce) unsweetened chocolate,* melted and cooled. Makes 2³/₄ cups.

EACH TABLESPOON: About 75 calories, 0g protein, 12g carbohydrate, 3g total fat (2g saturated), 6mg cholesterol, 20mg sodium.

Pound Cake as Our Mothers Made It

One pound of flour, one pound of butter, one pound of sugar, ten large eggs and about one-fourth of a nutmeg. Cream the butter and sugar together well (our mothers' rolled and sifted loaf sugar is better, but granulated sugar will answer the purpose), then add the well-beaten yolks of the eggs, and add the flour, a little at a time, beating very thoroughly all the while, lastly add the whites of the eggs which have been beaten to a stiff froth that can be cut with a knife, or that will adhere to the vessel in which it has been beaten, being careful not to beat the cake after the whites have been added, but merely to fold in the puff. Flavor with one-fourth of a grated nutmeg, which should be put in before the whites of eggs. Bake in a very moderate oven for one hour. The only improvement that could be made on this recipe would be to use pastry flour (which was not used in mother's time). The best authorities on cake baking declare that good results cannot be obtained without the use of pastry flour.

—**Good Housekeeping Everyday Cook Book**, 1903

Vermont Apple Pie

No apples existed in America until the Pilgrims arrived with apple seeds in 1620. Apple orchards soon followed, with William Blaxton planting one of the first orchards on Beacon Hill in Boston. Later in Rhode Island in 1635 he grew pale green apples called Sweet Rhode Island Greenings (great for pies). Apple orchards spread with the frontier, thanks in large part to John Chapman, who was affectionately known as Johnny Appleseed. He planted apple trees and nurseries over ten thousand square miles from Massachusetts to Fort Wayne, Indiana. Apple pie appears in early American cookbooks. In 1758, according to *The American Heritage Cookbook,* a Swedish parson named Dr. Acrelius wrote home to his folks: "Apple-pie is used through the whole year, and when fresh apples are no longer to be had, dried ones are used. It is the evening meal of children." Our pie is made New England–style, with a Vermont Cheddar crust.

PREP: 1 hour plus chilling ★ **BAKE:** 1 hour 15 minutes
MAKES 10 servings

2½ cups all-purpose flour

**3 ounces shredded extrasharp Cheddar cheese
  (¾ cup)**

½ teaspoon salt

3 tablespoons vegetable shortening

½ cup plus 2 tablespoons cold butter or margarine

4 to 6 tablespoons ice water

6 large Cortland apples (about 3¼ pounds)

1 tablespoon fresh lemon juice

⅔ cup sugar

¼ teaspoon ground cinnamon

1. In medium bowl, combine 2¼ cups flour, Cheddar, and salt. With pastry blender or two knives used scissor-fashion, cut in shortening and ½ cup butter until mixture resembles coarse crumbs. Sprinkle in ice water, 1 tablespoon at a time, mixing lightly with fork after each addition, until dough is just moist enough to hold together. Shape dough into two disks, one slightly larger than the other. Wrap smaller disk in plastic wrap; refrigerate until ready to use.

2. On lightly floured surface, with floured rolling pin, roll larger disk of dough into 13-inch round. Gently roll dough round onto rolling pin and ease into 9½-inch deep-dish pie plate, pressing dough against side of plate. Trim edge, leaving 1-inch overhang. Reserve trimmings for decorating pie, if you like. Cover and refrigerate until firm, at least 30 minutes.

3. Meanwhile, peel, core, and cut apples into ⅜-inch-thick slices. In large bowl, toss apple slices with lemon juice. In small bowl, mix sugar, cinnamon, and remaining ¼ cup flour. Add sugar mixture to apples; toss well to coat. Spoon filling into chilled crust; dot with remaining 2 tablespoons butter.

4. Preheat oven to 425°F. Roll remaining disk of dough into 11-inch round. Cut ¾-inch circle out of center and cut 1-inch slits to allow steam to escape during baking. Center dough over filling. Fold overhang under; make decorative edge.

5. Place pie on foil-lined cookie sheet to catch any overflow during baking. Bake until apples are tender when pierced with knife and pie is bubbly, about 1 hour 15 minutes. If necessary, cover pie loosely with foil during last 10 minutes of baking to prevent overbrowning. Cool on wire rack 1 hour to serve warm, or cool completely to serve later.

EACH SERVING: About 410 calories, 6g protein, 57g carbohydrate, 19g total fat (10g saturated), 40mg cholesterol, 286mg sodium.

Vermont Apple Pie (top) and Georgia Chocolate Pecan Pie (bottom, page 288) ►

Diner Cherry Pie

When the colonists arrived in America they found cherries growing wild. It didn't take long for the colonists to learn how to cultivate them. Since the cherry season is notoriously short, knowing how to preserve or store them was critical. Layering them in hay proved to be remarkably successful. In *Martha Washington's Booke of Cookery*, it says, "to keepe cherries yt [so that] you may have them for tarts at Christmass without Preserveing: Take ye fayrest cherries you can get, fresh from ye tress, wth out bruising, wipe them one by one with a linnen cloth, yn [then] put ym [them] into a barrell of hay & lay them in ranks, first laying hay on the bottom, & then cherries, & yn hay & then cheryes & then hay agayne. ..." Today a delicious cherry pie is possible at any time of the year, thanks to the availability of canned and frozen cherries.

PREP: 25 minutes plus chilling ★ BAKE: 1 hour 20 minutes
MAKES 10 servings

Pastry Dough for 2-Crust Pie (page 298)

2 cans (16 ounces each) pitted tart cherries packed in water

¾ cup sugar

¼ cup cornstarch

⅛ teaspoon ground cinnamon

pinch salt

½ teaspoon vanilla extract

1 tablespoon butter or margarine, cut into pieces

1. Prepare Pastry Dough as directed through chilling.

2. Preheat oven to 425°F. Drain cherries in sieve set over bowl; reserve ½ cup juice. In medium bowl, combine sugar, cornstarch, cinnamon, and salt; stir in reserved cherry juice, cherries, and vanilla until mixed well.

3. On lightly floured surface, with floured rolling pin, roll larger disk of dough into 12-inch round. Gently roll dough round onto rolling pin and ease into 9-inch pie plate, pressing dough against side of plate. Trim edge, leaving 1-inch overhang. Reserve trimmings for decorating pie, if you like. Spoon cherry filling into crust; dot with butter.

4. For lattice top, roll out remaining disk of dough into 12-inch round. With pastry wheel or small knife, cut dough into ½-inch-wide strips. Moisten edge of bottom crust with water. Place half of pastry strips, about ¾ inch apart, across top of pie; press strips at both ends to seal. To complete lattice, place equal number of strips perpendicular (at right angles to) first strips. Trim lattice edges, leaving 1-inch overhang; moisten and press strips at both ends to seal. Turn overhang up and over ends of strips; pinch to seal. Make high stand-up edge to hold in juices.

5. Place pie on foil-lined cookie sheet to catch any overflow during baking. Bake 20 minutes. Turn oven control to 375°F; bake until filling bubbles up in center, about 1 hour longer. If necessary, cover pie loosely with foil during last 20 minutes of baking to prevent overbrowning. Cool on wire rack 1 hour to serve warm, or cool pie completely to serve later.

EACH SERVING: About 267 calories, 4g protein, 49g carbohydrate, 7g total fat (2g saturated), 3mg cholesterol, 149mg sodium.

Very Blueberry Pie

The colonists found blueberries growing wild. They had other names for the berries including hurtleberries, whortleberries, huckleberries, and (possibly) bilberries. According to legend, the colonists purchased berries from the Native Americans by the bushelful. The natives then taught the colonists how to sun-dry blueberries so they could be used in favorite English recipes instead of the unavailable currants and raisins. Many early cookbooks do not include recipes for blueberry pie, but one does appear in Fannie Farmer's 1896 cookbook, where she suggests using one-third molasses and two-thirds sugar for those who prefer the taste of molasses. She also recommends adding six seeded green grapes, cut into small pieces, to improve the flavor of the pie, especially if using huckleberries.

PREP: 25 minutes plus chilling ★ BAKE: 1 hour 20 minutes
MAKES 10 servings

Pastry Dough for 2-Crust Pie (page 298)

¾ cup sugar

¼ cup cornstarch

pinch salt

6 cups blueberries (about 3 pints)

1 tablespoon fresh lemon juice

2 tablespoons butter or margarine, cut into pieces

1. Prepare Pastry Dough as directed through chilling.

2. Preheat oven to 425°F. In large bowl, combine sugar, cornstarch, and salt. Add blueberries and lemon juice; toss to combine.

3. On lightly floured surface, with floured rolling pin, roll larger disk of dough into 12-inch round. Gently roll dough round onto rolling pin and ease into 9-inch pie

plate, pressing dough against side of plate. Trim edge, leaving 1-inch overhang. Reserve trimmings for decorating pie if you like. Spoon blueberry filling into crust; dot with butter.

4. Roll remaining disk of dough into 12-inch round. Cut ¾-inch circle out of center and cut 1-inch slits to allow steam to escape during baking. Center dough over filling. Fold overhang under and make decorative edge.

5. Place pie on foil-lined cookie sheet to catch any overflow during baking. Bake 20 minutes. Turn oven control to 375°F; bake pie until fruit filling bubbles in center and crust is golden, about 1 hour longer. If necessary, cover pie loosely with foil during last 20 minutes of baking to prevent overbrowning. Cool on wire rack 1 hour to serve warm, or cool completely to serve later.

EACH SERVING: About 374 calories, 4g protein, 53g carbohydrate, 17g total fat (8g saturated), 31mg cholesterol, 253mg sodium.

Bumbleberry Pie

Over the years, countless enthusiasts have gone bumbleberry picking—without success. They have, however, found bumbleberry pie listed on menus in mom-and-pop cafés, fancy restaurants, and mountain inns, especially in the Pacific Northwest and Canada. Order a slice and a wedge of double-crusted fruit pie is likely to appear. What's between the crusts depends upon the baker, the season, and which berries were the freshest at the market that particular day. For bumbleberry pie is not made with just one berry but with a mixture, often strawberries, blackberries, blueberries, and raspberries. In most bumbleberry pie recipes, the berries are tossed with sliced apples and sometimes cut-up rhubarb as well. If rhubarb isn't in season, use additional apple chunks.

PREP: 1 hour plus chilling ★ **BAKE:** 1 hour 15 minutes
MAKES 10 servings

Pastry Dough for 2-Crust Pie (page 298)

1 cup plus 2 teaspoons sugar

3 tablespoons cornstarch

2 tablespoons all-purpose flour

2 large **Golden Delicious apples (1 pound), peeled, cored, and cut into ¾-inch pieces**

4 cups assorted berries, such as blueberries, raspberries, blackberries, and strawberries

1 cup (½-inch) diced rhubarb

1 large egg

3 tablespoons milk or light cream

1. Prepare Pastry Dough as directed through chilling.

2. Preheat oven to 425°F. In large bowl, combine 1 cup sugar, cornstarch, and flour. Add apples, berries, and rhubarb; gently toss to combine.

3. On lightly floured surface, with floured rolling pin, roll larger disk of dough into a 12-inch round. Gently roll dough round onto rolling pin and ease into 9-inch pie plate, pressing dough against side of plate. Trim edge, leaving 1-inch overhang. Reserve trimmings for decorating pie, if you like. Spoon berry filling into crust.

4. Roll remaining disk of dough into a 12-inch round. Cut ¾-inch circle out of center and cut 1-inch slits to allow steam to escape during baking. Center dough over filling. Fold overhang under and make decorative edge.

5. In small bowl, with fork, beat egg and milk until blended. Lightly brush top of pie with egg mixture. Arrange decorations, if using, and brush with egg mixture. Sprinkle remaining 2 teaspoons sugar over top of pie.

6. Place pie on foil-lined cookie sheet to catch any overflow during baking. Bake 20 minutes. Turn oven control to 375°F. Bake until filling bubbles and crust is deep golden brown, 55 to 60 minutes longer. If necessary, cover pie loosely with foil during last 20 minutes of baking to prevent overbrowning. Cool on wire rack 2 hours to serve warm, or cool completely to serve later.

EACH SERVING: About 391 calories, 5g protein, 60g carbohydrate, 16g total fat (7g saturated), 47mg cholesterol, 221mg sodium.

Peach Pie

The Spaniards get the credit for bringing peaches to the New World in the sixteenth century; the Native Americans and the new Americans eagerly planted orchards in order to enjoy this delicious stone fruit. In the early 1800s, Thomas Jefferson planted French peach varieties at Monticello. It wasn't long before peach pie recipes appeared in cookbooks, including *Mrs. Rorer's Philadelphia Cook Book:* "Line pie dishes with good plain paste [pastry]. Pare, cut the peaches in halve, and take out the stones, then lay them in the dishes, sprinkle lightly with sugar, add a quarter-cup of water, cover with an upper crust, and bake in a quick oven for thirty minutes; or the peaches may be thoroughly rubbed without paring, slightly mashed and baked without stoning." Be sure to use ripe, flavorful peaches for the best-tasting pie.

PREP: 35 minutes plus chilling ★ **BAKE** 1 hour 5 minutes
MAKES 10 servings

Pastry Dough for 2-Crust Pie (page 298)

¾ **cup sugar**

¼ **cup cornstarch**

pinch salt

3 **pounds ripe peaches, peeled, pitted, and sliced (about 7 cups)**

1 **tablespoon fresh lemon juice**

1 **tablespoon butter or margarine, cut into pieces**

1. Prepare Pastry Dough as directed through chilling.

2. Preheat oven to 425°F. In large bowl, combine sugar, cornstarch, and salt. Add peaches and lemon juice; gently toss to combine.

3. On lightly floured surface, with floured rolling pin, roll larger disk of dough into 12-inch round. Gently roll dough round onto rolling pin and ease into 9-inch pie plate, pressing dough against side of plate. Trim edge, leaving 1-inch overhang. Reserve trimmings for decorating pie, if you like. Spoon peach filling into crust; dot with butter.

4. Roll remaining disk of dough into 12-inch round. Cut ¾-inch circle out of center and 1-inch slits to allow steam to escape during baking. Center dough over filling. Fold overhang under and make decorative edge.

5. Place pie on foil-lined cookie sheet to catch any overflow during baking. Bake 20 minutes. Turn oven control to 375°F; bake until filling bubbles in center, 45 to 60 minutes longer. If necessary, cover pie loosely with foil during last 20 minutes of baking to prevent overbrowning. Cool on wire rack 1 hour to serve warm, or cool completely to serve later.

EACH SERVING: About 365 calories, 4g protein, 53g carbohydrate, 16g total fat (8g saturated), 28mg cholesterol, 235mg sodium.

Plum Pie

Prepare pie as directed but substitute *3 pounds tart plums,* pitted and sliced, for peaches, and use *1 cup sugar.*

Pear Pie

Prepare pie as directed but substitute *3 pounds ripe pears,* peeled, cored, and sliced, for peaches; add *⅛ teaspoon ground nutmeg* to sugar mixture.

Cardamom-Pear Pie

Prepare pie as directed for Pear Pie but substitute *½ teaspoon ground cardamom* for nutmeg.

Strawberry-Rhubarb Pie

The earliest rhubarb pie recipes did not combine rhubarb with other fruits as is commonly done today. Fannie Farmer advises that rhubarb is often first scalded in order to tame its acidity. This also means that less sugar is needed to sweeten the pie. Her later books offer the combination of rhubarb and strawberries, as in our recipe. Rhubarb is one of the first harbingers of spring and is so popular for pies that it is often called the pie plant.

PREP: 30 minutes plus chilling ★ **BAKE:** 1 hour 35 minutes
MAKES 10 servings

Pastry Dough for 2-Crust Pie (page 298)

1 cup plus 1 tablespoon sugar

¼ cup cornstarch

1 pint strawberries, hulled and cut in half if large

1¼ pounds rhubarb, trimmed and cut into ½-inch pieces (4 cups)

2 tablespoons butter or margarine, cut into pieces

1. Prepare Pastry Dough as directed through chilling.

2. Preheat oven to 425°F. In large bowl, combine 1 cup sugar and cornstarch. Add strawberries and rhubarb; gently toss to combine.

3. On lightly floured surface, with floured rolling pin, roll larger disk of dough into 12-inch round. Gently roll dough round onto rolling pin and ease into 9-inch pie plate, pressing dough against side of plate. Trim edge, leaving 1-inch overhang. Reserve trimmings for decorating pie, if you like. Spoon strawberry-rhubarb filling into crust; dot with butter.

4. Roll out remaining disk of dough into 12-inch round. Cut ¾-inch circle out of center and 1-inch slits to allow steam to escape during baking. Center dough over filling. Fold overhang under and make decorative edge. Sprinkle with remaining 1 tablespoon sugar.

5. Place pie on foil-lined cookie sheet to catch any overflow during baking. Bake 20 minutes. Turn oven control to 375°F; bake until filling bubbles in center and crust is golden, 1 hour 15 to 25 minutes longer. If necessary, cover pie loosely with foil during last 20 minutes of baking to prevent overbrowning. Cool on wire rack 1 hour to serve warm, or cool completely to serve later.

EACH SERVING: About 375 calories, 4g protein, 53g carbohydrate, 17g total fat (8g saturated), 31mg cholesterol, 235mg sodium.

Shaker Lemon Pie

Shaker communities were formed in rural America during the nineteenth century. The sect's members believed in trances, fasts, heavenly voices, and other religious signs. The "shakes" induced by their spiritual gyrations led to their being known as Shakers or Shaking Quakers. Their lifestyle was very orderly and simple, and their cooking was pure and wholesome. This pie's uncomplicated lemon filling, made with only three ingredients, is a good example. The key to this pie's success is cutting the lemon slices paper-thin.

PREP: 15 minutes plus standing overnight and chilling
BAKE: 1 hour 2 minutes ★ **MAKES** 8 servings

3 large lemons

1½ cups sugar

Pastry Dough for 1-Crust Pie (page 299)

4 large eggs

1. Slice 1 lemon paper-thin; discard seeds. Remove peel and white pith from remaining 2 lemons; slice paper-thin; discard seeds. In medium bowl, combine sliced lemons and sugar. Cover and let stand overnight until lemons are soft and sugar has dissolved.

2. The next day, prepare Pastry Dough as directed through chilling.

3. Preheat oven to 425°F. On lightly floured surface, with floured rolling pin, roll dough into 12-inch round. Roll dough onto rolling pin and ease into 9-inch pie plate, gently pressing dough against side of plate. Trim edge, leaving 1-inch overhang. Fold overhang under and make decorative edge. Refrigerate or freeze until firm, 10 to 15 minutes.

4. Line pie shell with foil; fill with pie weights or dry beans. Bake 15 minutes. Remove foil with weights; bake until golden, 7 to 10 minutes longer. If pastry puffs up during baking, press it down with back of spoon. Cool on wire rack. Turn oven control to 375°F.

5. Meanwhile, in medium bowl, with wire whisk, beat eggs. Transfer 1 tablespoon beaten egg to cup; set aside. Add lemon mixture to eggs; stir until combined. Pour into cooled pie shell. With fork, decoratively arrange top layer of lemon slices. Brush edge of pastry with reserved egg. Bake pie until filling is slightly puffed and lightly golden, 40 to 45 minutes. Cool on wire rack.

EACH SERVING: About 350 calories, 6g protein, 59g carbohydrate, 12g total fat (5g saturated), 122mg cholesterol, 165mg sodium.

Lemon Meringue Pie

By most accounts, lemon meringue pie was not known until the late nineteenth century. The 1903 *Good Housekeeping Everyday Cook Book* offers a recipe for lemon pie that resembles the lemon meringue pies of today but with one exception: the lemon filling is thickened only with egg yolks, even though cornstarch had been developed over sixty years earlier. In fact, the filling more closely resembles an English lemon curd. As for the meringue, the fluffier, higher, more swirled and peaked, the better. To guarantee that your lemon meringue pie cuts well and doesn't "weep," cook the filling until it's very thick. Also, when spreading the meringue, be sure to push it all the way to the crust (until it touches).

PREP: 45 minutes plus chilling ★ **BAKE:** 30 minutes
MAKES 10 servings

Pastry Dough for 1-Crust Pie (page 299)

4 to 5 lemons

1½ cups sugar

⅓ cup cornstarch

¼ teaspoon plus pinch salt

1½ cups water

3 large egg yolks

2 tablespoons butter or margarine, cut into pieces

4 large egg whites

¼ teaspoon cream of tartar

1. Prepare Pastry Dough as directed through chilling.

2. Preheat oven to 425°F. On lightly floured surface, with floured rolling pin, roll dough into 12-inch round. Gently roll dough onto rolling pin and ease into 9-inch pie plate, gently pressing dough against side of plate. Trim edge, leaving 1-inch overhang. Fold overhang under; make decorative edge. Refrigerate or freeze until firm, 10 to 15 minutes.

3. Line pie shell with foil; fill with pie weights or dry beans. Bake 10 minutes. Remove foil with weights; bake until golden, about 10 minutes longer. If pastry puffs up during baking, press it down with back of spoon. Cool on wire rack. Turn oven control to 400°F.

4. Meanwhile, from lemons, grate 1 tablespoon peel and squeeze ¾ cup juice; set aside. In 2-quart saucepan, combine 1 cup sugar, cornstarch, and ¼ teaspoon salt; stir in water. Cook over medium heat, stirring constantly, until mixture has thickened and boils. Boil 1 minute, stirring constantly. Remove from heat.

5. In small bowl, with wire whisk, beat egg yolks. Stir in ⅓ cup hot cornstarch mixture until blended; slowly pour egg-yolk mixture back into hot cornstarch mixture in saucepan, stirring rapidly to prevent curdling. Place saucepan over low heat and cook, stirring constantly, until filling is very thick, about 4 minutes, or temperature on thermometer reaches 160°F. Remove from heat; stir in butter until melted, then gradually stir in lemon peel and juice until blended. Pour into cooled pie shell.

6. In small bowl, with mixer at high speed, beat egg whites, cream of tartar, and remaining pinch salt until soft peaks form when beaters are lifted. Sprinkle in remaining ½ cup sugar, 2 tablespoons at a time, beating until sugar has completely dissolved and egg whites stand in stiff, glossy peaks when beaters are lifted.

7. Spread meringue over filling to edge of pie shell. Decoratively swirl meringue with back of spoon. Bake until meringue is golden, about 10 minutes. Cool pie on wire rack away from drafts. Refrigerate at least 3 hours for easier slicing or up to 2 days.

EACH SERVING: About 310 calories, 4g protein, 49g carbohydrate, 11g total fat (5g saturated), 82mg cholesterol, 225mg sodium.

Lime Meringue Pie

Prepare as directed but substitute *2 teaspoons grated lime peel* for lemon peel and *½ cup fresh lime juice* for fresh lemon juice.

Key Lime Pie

This famous pie can be traced back to 1856, the year Gail Borden invented sweetened condensed milk. Until then, food poisoning and other illnesses that related to the lack of refrigeration made the consumption of fresh milk products a problem. This was especially true in the Florida Keys, whose isolation made fresh milk hard to come by. Using sweetened condensed milk eliminated the need to cook the custard mixture. In the *American Century Cookbook,* Jean Anderson writes that folks in the Florida Keys are purists about their Key Lime Pie. The original version uses Key lime juice and sweetened condensed milk, is not tinted green, and is baked in a flaky pastry crust. The hot baked pie is topped with a billowy meringue that is baked until golden. Our delectable version is baked in a graham-cracker crust and is topped with whipped cream.

PREP: 20 minutes plus cooling and chilling
BAKE: 25 minutes ★ **MAKES** 10 servings

Baked Graham Cracker–Crumb Crust (page 299)
6 to 8 limes, preferably Key limes
1 can (14 ounces) sweetened condensed milk
2 large eggs, separated
green food coloring (optional)
½ cup heavy or whipping cream
lime slices (optional)

1. Prepare Graham Cracker–Crumb Crust as directed. Cool completely.

2. Preheat oven to 375°F. From limes, grate 2 teaspoons peel and squeeze ½ cup juice. In medium bowl, with wire whisk or fork, beat sweetened condensed milk, lime peel and juice, and egg yolks until mixture thickens. Add a few drops of green food coloring, if you like.

3. In small bowl, with mixer at high speed, beat egg whites until stiff peaks form when beaters are lifted. With rubber spatula, gently fold egg whites into lime mixture.

4. Pour filling into cooled crust; smooth top. Bake until filling is firm, 15 to 20 minutes. Cool on wire rack; refrigerate until well chilled, about 3 hours.

5. In small bowl, with mixer at medium speed, beat cream until stiff peaks form when beaters are lifted. Pipe or spoon whipped cream around edge of pie. Arrange lime slices on whipped cream, if desired.

EACH SERVING: About 300 calories, 6g protein, 36g carbohydrate, 15g total fat (8g saturated), 85mg cholesterol, 210mg sodium.

Coconut Custard Pie

During the early part of the nineteenth century, Americans were baking coconut cakes, and by the end of the century they were turning coconuts into pies. Fannie Farmer's 1896 cookbook includes a Cocoanut [*sic*] Pie. It's actually a two-layer cake that is filled and topped with meringue and freshly grated coconut. She also includes a recipe for a plain custard pie, which was very popular at that time. Her turn-of-the-century recipe is very similar to ours. The difference is that in our recipe coconut is sprinkled over the bottom crust before the custard is poured in.

PREP: 15 minutes plus chilling ★ **BAKE:** 20 minutes ★ **MAKES** 6 servings

Pastry Dough for 1-Crust Pie (page 299)
2½ cups milk
½ cup sugar
3 large eggs
1 teaspoon vanilla extract
½ teaspoon salt
¼ teaspoon ground nutmeg
½ cup flaked sweetened coconut
chopped nuts, ground nutmeg, or whipped cream

1. Prepare Pastry Dough as directed through chilling.

2. Preheat oven to 425°F. On lightly floured surface, with floured rolling pin, roll dough into 12-inch round. Gently roll dough onto rolling pin and ease into 9-inch pie plate, gently pressing dough against side of plate. Trim edge, leaving 1-inch overhang. Fold overhang under; make decorative edge. Refrigerate or freeze until firm, 10 to 15 minutes.

3. In medium bowl, with wire whisk, beat milk, sugar, eggs, vanilla, salt, and nutmeg until blended.

4. Sprinkle coconut evenly over bottom of pie shell. Pour filling into pie shell. Bake until knife inserted 1 inch from edge comes out clean, 20 to 25 minutes. Cool completely on wire rack.

5. To serve, garnish cooled pie with chopped nuts, ground nutmeg, or whipped cream.

EACH SERVING WITHOUT NUTS OR WHIPPED CREAM:
About 405 calories, 10g protein, 47g carbohydrate, 20g total fat (11g saturated), 141mg cholesterol, 464mg sodium.

Banana Cream Pie

By the mid-nineteenth century, bananas frequently arrived at American ports. In 1876, the Boston Fruit Company (later to become United Fruit Company and eventually United Brands) introduced many folks to this then-exotic fruit at the Philadelphia Centennial Exposition. Today the banana is often regarded as America's most popular fruit. Although the origin of vanilla wafer cookies is hazy, most believe that they originated in home kitchens in the South well before 1945, the year that Nabisco first sold them. They became even more recognizable when Nabisco changed the name to 'Nilla Wafers. The famous banana-pudding-and-layered-wafer dessert eventually became banana cream pie in a vanilla-wafer crust.

PREP: 30 minutes plus cooling and chilling
BAKE: 10 minutes ★ **MAKES** 10 servings

Baked Vanilla Wafer–Crumb Crust (page 299)
¾ cup sugar
⅓ cup cornstarch
¼ teaspoon salt
3¾ cups milk
5 large egg yolks
2 tablespoons butter or margarine, cut into pieces
1¾ teaspoons vanilla extract
3 ripe medium bananas
¾ cup heavy or whipping cream

1. Prepare Vanilla Wafer–Crumb Crust as directed. Cool completely.

2. In 3-quart saucepan, combine sugar, cornstarch, and salt; stir in milk until blended. Cook over medium heat, stirring constantly, until mixture has thickened and boils; boil 1 minute.

3. In small bowl, with wire whisk, lightly beat egg yolks; beat in ½ cup hot milk mixture. Slowly pour egg-yolk mixture back into milk mixture, stirring rapidly to prevent curdling. Cook over low heat, stirring constantly, until mixture has thickened, about 2 minute, or temperature on thermometer reaches 160°F. Remove from heat. Add butter and 1½ teaspoons vanilla; stir until butter melts. Transfer to medium bowl. Press plastic wrap onto filling surface.

4. Refrigerate, stirring occasionally, until cool, about 1 hour. Slice 2 bananas. Spoon half of filling into crust. Arrange banana slices on top; spoon remaining filling evenly over bananas. Press plastic wrap onto surface; refrigerate at least 4 hours or up to overnight.

5. In small chilled bowl, with mixer at medium speed, beat cream and remaining ¼ teaspoon vanilla until stiff peaks form when beaters are lifted; spread over filling. Slice remaining banana; arrange around edge of pie.

EACH SERVING: About 385 calories, 6g protein, 45g carbohydrate, 21g total fat (12g saturated), 162mg cholesterol, 275mg sodium.

Georgia Chocolate Pecan Pie

As far back as the sixteenth century, wild pecan trees were found in America. The Native Americans named the nut "*pecan*" (all nuts requiring a stone to crack), included them in their diet, and likely were the first to cultivate them. In the late 1700s, George Washington and Thomas Jefferson planted pecan trees in their respective gardens. It is hard to believe that our ancestors, especially those in the South where pecan trees flourished, did not toss pecans into their beloved brown sugar, molasses, or syrup pies. It wasn't until around 1925, however, that recipes for pecan pie appeared in print. The home economists in the Karo test kitchens most likely created the first pecan pie in the early 1900s using a good amount of corn syrup—light or dark—in every pie. Traveling through Georgia these days, you're likely to find pecan pie on the menu: the classic version or this deep chocolate rendition.

PREP: 45 minutes plus chilling and cooling ★ **BAKE:** 1 hour 10 minutes
MAKES 12 servings

Pastry Dough for 1-Crust Pie (page 299)
4 tablespoons butter or margarine
2 squares (2 ounces) unsweetened chocolate
1¾ cups pecan halves (7 ounces)
¾ cup packed dark brown sugar
¾ cup dark corn syrup
1 teaspoon vanilla extract
3 large eggs

1. Prepare Pastry Dough as directed through chilling.

2. On lightly floured surface, with floured rolling pin, roll dough into 12-inch round. Gently roll dough onto rolling pin and ease into 9-inch pie plate, pressing dough against side of plate. Trim edge, leaving 1-inch overhang. Fold overhang under; make decorative edge. Refrigerate or freeze until firm, 10 to 15 minutes.

3. Preheat oven to 425°F. In heavy 1-quart saucepan, melt butter with chocolate over low heat, stirring frequently, until smooth. Cool slightly.

4. Line pie shell with foil; fill with pie weights or dry beans. Bake 15 minutes. Remove foil with weights; bake until golden, 5 to 10 minutes longer. If shell puffs up during baking, gently press it down with back of spoon. Cool on wire rack. Turn oven control to 350°F.

5. Coarsely chop 1 cup pecans. In large bowl, with wire whisk, mix cooled chocolate mixture, brown sugar, corn syrup, vanilla, and eggs until blended. Stir in chopped pecans and remaining pecan halves.

6. Pour pecan mixture into pie shell. Bake until filling is set around edge but center jiggles slightly, 45 to 50 minutes. Cool on wire rack at least 1 hour for easier slicing.

EACH SERVING: About 395 calories, 5g protein, 43g carbohydrate, 24g total fat (4g saturated), 53mg cholesterol, 225mg sodium.

Classic Pecan Pie

Prepare as directed but omit unsweetened chocolate.

Black Bottom Pie

According to James Beard, recipes for this double-layer custard pie began appearing around the turn of the twentieth century. It was considered company pie, as it required (costly) ice to chill it. The refrigerator was not popular or common until the 1920s. Before that, most people had iceboxes. The first black bottom pies probably appeared in the South. The pie has a bottom layer of rich chocolate custard, a top layer of rum-flavored custard, and is crowned with whipped cream. Refrigerator pies became more commonplace by the mid-twentieth century, when refrigerators became affordable. For a classic touch, sprinkle the pie with chocolate curls (page 299) before serving.

PREP: 40 minutes plus cooling and chilling ★ **BAKE:** 10 minutes
MAKES 10 servings

Chocolate Wafer–Crumb Crust (page 299)
1 teaspoon unflavored gelatin
2 tablespoons cold water
1 1/2 cups milk
3/4 cup sugar
4 large egg yolks
2 squares (2 ounces) unsweetened chocolate, melted
1/2 teaspoon vanilla extract
2 teaspoons dark rum or 1 teaspoon vanilla extract
2 cups heavy or whipping cream

1. Prepare Chocolate Wafer–Crumb Crust as directed. Cool completely.

2. In cup, evenly sprinkle gelatin over cold water; let stand 2 minutes to soften gelatin slightly.

3. Meanwhile, in 2-quart saucepan, combine milk and 1/2 cup sugar; cook over medium heat, stirring, until bubbles form around edge.

4. In small bowl, with wire whisk, lightly beat egg yolks. Beat 1/3 cup hot milk mixture into egg yolks. Slowly pour egg-yolk mixture back into milk mixture, whisking rapidly to prevent curdling. Cook over low heat, stirring constantly, until mixture has thickened slightly and coats back of spoon, about 10 minutes, or temperature on thermometer reaches about 160°F; do not boil, or mixture will curdle.

5. Transfer 1 cup milk mixture to small bowl. Stir in melted chocolate and vanilla until blended. Pour into cooled crust; refrigerate.

6. Over low heat, add softened gelatin to remaining milk mixture in saucepan; stir until gelatin has completely dissolved. Remove from heat; stir in rum. Cool to room temperature, stirring occasionally.

7. In bowl, with mixer at medium speed, beat cream with remaining 1/4 cup sugar until stiff peaks form when beaters are lifted. Whisk half of whipped cream into cooled gelatin mixture. Refrigerate remaining whipped cream. Spread gelatin-cream mixture over chocolate layer. Cover; refrigerate until firm, about 3 hours. To serve, mound remaining whipped cream over filling.

EACH SERVING: About 409 calories, 5g protein, 31g carbohydrate, 31g total fat (18g saturated), 168mg cholesterol, 171mg sodium.

Chocolate Cream Pie

In nineteenth-century cookbooks, chocolate pies were very different from the chocolate custard pies we know today. They were made from two butter-cake layers that were split, spread with chocolate frosting, and stacked. In the *Good Housekeeping Everyday Cook Book,* circa 1903, a recipe for cream pie (similar to ours) appears with a suggestion: "The custard may be flavored with chocolate to make a change." The pie is then topped with meringue and lightly browned in the oven. Our pie is even richer—it's crowned with whipped cream.

PREP: 35 minutes plus cooling and chilling
BAKE: 10 minutes ★ **MAKES** 10 servings

Chocolate Wafer–Crumb Crust (page 299)

¾ cup sugar

⅓ cup cornstarch

½ teaspoon salt

3¾ cups milk

5 large egg yolks

3 squares (3 ounces) unsweetened chocolate, melted

2 tablespoons butter or margarine, cut into pieces

2 teaspoons vanilla extract

1 cup heavy or whipping cream

Chocolate Curls (page 299), optional

1. Prepare Chocolate Wafer–Crumb Crust as directed. Cool completely.

2. Meanwhile, in heavy 3-quart saucepan, combine sugar, cornstarch, and salt; with wire whisk, stir in milk until blended and smooth. Cook over medium heat, stirring constantly, until milk mixture has thickened and boils; boil 1 minute.

3. In small bowl, with wire whisk, lightly beat egg yolks. Beat ½ cup hot milk-sugar mixture into beaten egg yolks. Slowly pour egg-yolk mixture back into milk mixture, stirring rapidly to prevent curdling. Cook over low heat, stirring constantly, until mixture is very thick or until temperature on thermometer reaches 160°F.

4. Remove saucepan from heat; stir in melted chocolate, butter, and vanilla until butter has melted and mixture is smooth. Pour hot chocolate filling into cooled crust; press plastic wrap onto surface. Refrigerate until filling is set, about 4 hours.

5. Meanwhile, make Chocolate Curls, if using.

6. To serve, in small bowl, with mixer at medium speed, beat cream until stiff peaks form when beaters are lifted; spoon over chocolate filling, spreading evenly. Top with chocolate curls, if desired.

EACH SERVING: About 417 calories, 7g protein, 38g carbohydrate, 28g total fat (16g saturated), 171mg cholesterol, 329mg sodium.

◄ *Chocolate Cream Pie*

Grandma's Sweet Potato Pie

Christopher Columbus found the sweet potato growing in South and Central America. He took some of these new-found potatoes back to Spain, where they were soon cultivated. Before long, Britain and other European countries were also growing and enjoying them. The colonists were cultivating sweet potatoes by the 1650s. Surprisingly, recipes for sweet potato pie are lacking in our early cookbooks, even though the colonists could easily have brought recipes with them to America. By 1848, Eliza Leslie included a recipe for Sweet Potato Pudding in *Directions for Cookery* that is made from grated parboiled sweet potatoes, sugar, eggs, wine, and brandy.

PREP: 1 hour plus chilling and cooling ★ **BAKE:** 1 hour
MAKES 10 servings

Pastry Dough for 1-Crust Pie (page 299)
2 medium sweet potatoes (about 8 ounces each), not peeled or 2 cans (16 to 17 ounces each) sweet potatoes, drained
1½ cups half-and-half or light cream
¾ cup packed dark brown sugar
1 teaspoon ground cinnamon
¾ teaspoon ground ginger
¼ teaspoon ground nutmeg
½ teaspoon salt
3 large eggs

1. Prepare Pastry Dough as directed through chilling.

2. Meanwhile, if using fresh sweet potatoes, in 3-quart saucepan, combine sweet potatoes and enough *water* to cover; heat to boiling over high heat. Reduce heat; cover and simmer until tender, about 30 minutes. Drain.

3. Preheat oven to 425°F. On lightly floured surface, with floured rolling pin, roll dough into 12-inch round. Gently roll dough onto rolling pin and ease into 9-inch pie plate, gently pressing dough against side of plate. Trim edge, leaving 1-inch overhang. Fold overhang under; make decorative edge. Refrigerate or freeze until firm, 10 to 15 minutes.

4. When cool enough to handle; peel sweet potatoes and cut into large pieces. In large bowl, with mixer at low speed, beat sweet potatoes until smooth. Add half-and-half, brown sugar, cinnamon, ginger, nutmeg, salt, and eggs; beat until well blended.

5. Line pie shell with foil; fill with pie weights or dry beans. Bake 10 minutes. Remove foil with weights; bake

until golden, about 10 minutes longer. If shell puffs up during baking, gently press it down with back of spoon. Cool on wire rack at least 10 minutes. Turn oven control to 350°F.

6. Spoon sweet-potato filling into cooled pie shell. Bake until knife inserted 1 inch from edge comes out clean, about 40 minutes. Cool on wire rack 1 hour to serve warm, or cool slightly and refrigerate to serve later.

EACH SERVING: About 295 calories, 5g protein, 39g carbohydrate, 13g total fat (7g saturated), 89mg cholesterol, 265mg sodium.

Pilgrim's Pumpkin Pie

It's a well-documented fact that pumpkin pie was served at the Pilgrims' second Thanksgiving in 1623. Amelia Simmons, in her 1796 *American Cookery* book, lists two recipes in the pudding chapter: both simply titled "Pompkin [*sic*]." One uses ingredients similar to today's pies but in larger amounts: "One quart [pumpkin] stewed and strained, 3 pints cream, 9 beaten eggs, sugar, mace, nutmeg, and ginger, laid into a paste [pastry] no. 7 or 3, and with a dough spur [hook], cross and chequer [crosshatch] it, and baked in dishes three quarter of an hour." Thanks to the availability of excellent canned pumpkin, our recipe is more reliable and easier to prepare. You can use one and one-half teaspoons pumpkin-pie spice instead of the cinnamon, ginger, and nutmeg, if you like.

PREP: 25 minutes plus chilling ★ **BAKE:** 1 hour 10 minutes
MAKES 10 servings

Pastry Dough for 1-Crust Pie (page 299)
1 can (16 ounces) solid pack pumpkin (not pumpkin-pie mix)
1 can (12 ounces) evaporated milk
2 large eggs
¾ cup packed brown sugar
1 teaspoon ground cinnamon
½ teaspoon ground ginger
¼ teaspoon ground nutmeg
½ teaspoon salt

1. Prepare Pastry Dough as directed through chilling.

2. Preheat oven to 425°F. On lightly floured surface, with floured rolling pin, roll dough into 12-inch round. Gently roll dough onto rolling pin and ease into 9-inch

pie plate, gently pressing dough against side of plate. Trim edge, leaving 1-inch overhang. Fold overhang under; make high stand-up edge. Refrigerate or freeze until firm, 10 to 15 minutes.

3. Line pie shell with foil; fill with pie weights or dry beans. Bake 15 minutes. Remove foil with weights; bake until golden, 5 to 10 minutes longer. If shell puffs up during baking, gently press it down with back of spoon. Cool on wire rack. Turn oven control to 375°F.

4. In large bowl, with wire whisk, mix pumpkin, evaporated milk, eggs, brown sugar, cinnamon, ginger, nutmeg, and salt until well combined. Place piecrust-lined pie plate on oven rack; carefully pour in pumpkin filling. Bake until knife inserted 1 inch from edge comes out clean, about 50 minutes. Cool on wire rack at least 1 hour or up to 6 hours.

EACH SERVING: About 270 calories, 6 g protein, carbohydrate, 11g total fat (6g saturated), 66mg cholesterol, 280mg sodium.

Servers, Savers, and Breakers

A homemade cake or pie deserves only the best: the perfect cake plate, pie dish, server, or saver. Over the centuries, this philosophy has encouraged silversmiths, houseware manufacturers, and cutlery companies to create various accoutrements for cutting, serving, and storing sweet creations.

Stroll through a National Trust country house in the English countryside, a restored plantation in the Deep South, or the Smithsonian Institute in Washington, D.C., and you're likely to see the crème de la crème of dessert servers: a nineteenth-century footed sterling silver cake basket with a filigree edging of flowers and delicate swing handle; a three-tiered silver cake stand for serving afternoon cakes, sweetmeats, and sandwiches; or a hand-cut crystal pedestal cake stand. Visit a bakeshop in a historic restored village, such as Sturbridge Village in Massachusetts, any day of the week. No matter the time of day, you'll find footed glass cake plates laden with tempting offerings, such as a three-tiered coconut cake, a red devil's food cake with marshmallow frosting, or a mile-high lemon meringue pie.

Now step inside twentieth-century America. In the 1930s, glass manufacturers, such as the Hocking Glass Company, produced depression glass in various colors, shapes, and designs, including cake plates etched with delicate lace patterns. Stop by a 1940s diner for their special pound cake displayed under a sparkling glass dome on a stainless-steel art deco pedestal cake stand. Check out '50s cake plates and savers in the local vintage shop. There's likely to be a metal cake saver with a bright yellow cover decorated with red cherries, just like those that carried many a

cake to a church supper or local cake sale, one of those round plastic cake plates with its clear plastic dome, or a square self-locking aluminum cake saver in a shiny copper color.

At a glance, you can tell that pie plates, too, have also changed over the years. There are tin pie plates (now very collectible) with the name of the advertiser stamped inside, which were popular in the nineteenth and early twentieth centuries. For over a hundred years, clear heat-resistant plates in cobalt blue, amber, or clear glass have proudly taken freshly baked pies to the table, often in wicker holders. And at those mid-twentieth-century bake sales, there was always a collection of pie plates: hand-painted pottery ones, stainless-steel plates, and even handcrafted stoneware pie pans from local artisans.

Note, too, that cake and pie servers have followed similar designs. Silversmiths in Europe and in America in the eighteenth and nineteenth centuries designed decorative sterling silver and silver-plated servers: oblong ones for cakes, triangular ones for pies, and small fluted filigree servers for tarts. There are treasured sterling-handled cake breakers (a popular wedding gift in the South) with long, thin prongs that "cut" the finest angel food perfectly. Many still rely on twentieth century pie and cake servers in more affordable materials, such as stainless, ceramic, or serviceable plastic.

From the elegant Victorian era to modern day, cake and pie servers, savers, and breakers have displayed, served, and stored our homemade cakes and pies in perfect style.

Chocolate Angel Pie

In *American Cookery,* James Beard remarks that Angel Pie, with its baked meringue shell and whipped cream filling is "The most frequently printed of all the pie recipes in sectional cookbooks of the last sixty years." Jean Anderson, in the *American Century Cookbook,* quotes Sylvia Lovegren from *Fashionable Food* in 1995: "One of the prettiest and certainly most popular desserts of the Thirties were meringue tortes (sometimes called meringue cakes, schaum tortes, angel pies or meringue glacées, if they were filled with ice cream)." Anderson also includes the recipe from the 1942 *Good Housekeeping Cook Book* for Chocolate Nut Angel Pie in which the whipped cream filling contains melted semisweet chocolate chips and chopped nuts (filberts, walnuts, or pecans). Our recipe uses cocoa and a little instant espresso powder to flavor the whipped cream.

PREP: 20 minutes plus cooling ★ **BAKE:** 1 hour
MAKES 10 servings

3 large egg whites

¼ teaspoon salt

¼ teaspoon cream of tartar

2¼ cups confectioners' sugar

2½ teaspoons vanilla extract

½ cup unsweetened cocoa

1 teaspoon instant espresso-coffee powder

1 teaspoon hot water

2 cups heavy or whipping cream

2 tablespoons milk

Chocolate Curls (page 299), optional

1. Preheat oven to 300°F. Grease and flour 9-inch metal pie plate.

2. In small bowl, with mixer at high speed, beat egg whites, salt, and cream of tartar until soft peaks form when beaters are lifted. Sprinkle in 1 cup confectioners' sugar, 2 tablespoons at a time, beating until sugar has dissolved. Add 1 teaspoon vanilla; continue to beat egg whites until stiff, glossy peaks form when beaters are lifted.

3. With narrow metal spatula, spread meringue evenly over bottom and against side of pie plate, making a high stand-up edge. Bake meringue 1 hour. Turn off oven; leave meringue in oven 1 hour to dry. Cool meringue completely in pie plate on wire rack.

4. Meanwhile, prepare filling: Sift cocoa with remaining 1¼ cups confectioners' sugar. In cup, dissolve espresso powder in water. In large bowl, with mixer at medium speed, beat heavy cream, espresso mixture, and remaining 1½ teaspoons vanilla just until soft peaks form. Reduce speed to low; gradually beat in cocoa mixture just until thoroughly blended and stiff peaks form (do not overbeat). Beat in milk.

5. Spoon chocolate cream into cooled meringue shell; with rubber spatula, smooth top. If not serving pie right away, cover and refrigerate until ready to serve. Top with chocolate curls, if desired.

EACH SERVING: About 290 calories, 3g protein, 31g carbohydrate, 18g total fat (11g saturated), 66mg cholesterol, 95mg sodium.

Apple Turnovers

Steamed apple dumplings and fried apple pies appear in many early-nineteenth-century cookbooks. Small half-moon turnovers appear to be a twentieth-century creation, often called "children's pies," as they're just the right size for children to eat out of hand. Turnovers similar to ours are found in *Charleston Receipts,* recipes collected by the Junior League of Charleston in 1950. Fannie Farmer does not include any turnovers in her 1923 cookbook. However, in the 1990 *Fannie Farmer Baking Book* by Marion Cunningham, there are six different turnovers, including apple-raisin turnovers that are flavored with red wine and cinnamon. All are made with pastry rounds that are filled and folded in half, then crimped closed with fork tines.

PREP: 1 hour plus chilling ★ **BAKE:** 35 minutes
MAKES 14 turnovers

Pastry Dough for 2-Crust Pie (page 298)

3 tablespoons plus ⅓ cup granulated sugar

2 tablespoons butter or margarine

2 large Granny Smith apples (1½ pounds), peeled, cored, and chopped

1 tablespoon cornstarch

¼ teaspoon ground cinnamon

pinch salt

1 teaspoon fresh lemon juice

1 large egg, beaten

1 cup confectioners' sugar

2 tablespoons warm water

2 teaspoons light corn syrup

½ teaspoon vanilla extract

1. Prepare Pastry Dough as directed through chilling, but in Step 1, add 2 tablespoons granulated sugar along with flour.

2. In 10-inch skillet, melt butter over medium-high heat. Add apples, ⅓ cup granulated sugar, cornstarch, cinnamon, and salt; cook, stirring, until apples are tender, about 8 minutes. Add lemon juice; set aside to cool completely.

3. On lightly floured surface, with floured rolling pin, roll one disk of dough into round about ⅛ inch thick. Using 5-inch round plate as guide, cut out 5 dough rounds. Repeat with remaining dough; reroll trimmings. You should have 14 dough rounds in all.

4. Preheat oven to 400°F. Grease two large cookie sheets.

5. Onto half of each dough round, place 1 heaping tablespoon apple filling; fold dough over filling. With fork tines, firmly press edges together to seal. Place turnovers, 2 inches apart, on prepared cookie sheets. With pastry brush, brush turnovers with beaten egg and sprinkle with remaining 1 tablespoon granulated sugar. Make two 1-inch slits in top of each turnover to allow steam to escape during baking. Bake 15 minutes.

6. Turn oven control to 350°F. Bake until golden brown, 20 to 25 minutes longer. Cool on wire racks.

7. Meanwhile, in small bowl, combine confectioners' sugar, water, corn syrup, and vanilla; stir until smooth and spreadable. Drizzle icing over cooled turnovers; let set before serving.

EACH TURNOVER: About 290 calories, 3g protein, 41g carbohydrate, 13g total fat (6g saturated), 37mg cholesterol, 185mg sodium.

◄ *Apple Turnovers*

Pastry Dough for 2-Crust Pie

In the first American cookbook, Amelia Simmons offers nine recipes for pastes (pastry): six for tarts, two for sweetmeats, and one for a royal pastry, which is especially rich and good for apple cake. In Mrs. Hill's *Southern Practical Cookery and Receipt Book,* a unique way of measuring ingredients appears in her recipe for An Easy Way of Making Crust for Plain Family Pies, No. 5: "Use the weight of nine eggs in flour, and of four eggs in lard or butter. If butter is used, the weight of eight eggs in flour will be enough." Our recipe uses two types of fat: shortening and butter. The shortening makes the dough especially flaky, while the butter contributes great flavor.

PREP: 10 minutes plus chilling
MAKES enough dough for one 9-inch 2-crust pie

2¼ **cups all-purpose flour**

½ **teaspoon salt**

½ **cup cold butter or margarine (1 stick), cut into pieces**

¼ **cup vegetable shortening**

4 to 6 tablespoons ice water

1. In large bowl, combine flour and salt. With pastry blender or two knives used scissor-fashion, cut in butter and shortening until mixture resembles coarse crumbs.

2. Sprinkle in ice water, 1 tablespoon at a time, mixing lightly with fork after each addition, until dough is just moist enough to hold together.

3. Shape dough into two disks, one slightly larger than the other. Wrap each disk in plastic wrap; refrigerate 30 minutes or up to overnight. (If chilled overnight, let stand 30 minutes at room temperature before rolling.)

4. On lightly floured surface, with floured rolling pin, roll larger disk of dough into 12-inch round. Gently roll dough round onto rolling pin and ease into 9-inch pie plate, pressing dough against side of plate. Trim edge, leaving 1-inch overhang. Reserve trimmings for decorating pie, if you like. Spoon filling into crust.

5. Roll remaining disk of dough into 12-inch round. Cut ¾-inch circle out of center and 1-inch slits to allow steam to escape during baking; center dough over filling. Or make desired pie top. Fold overhang under; make decorative edge. Bake as directed in recipe.

EACH 1/10TH PASTRY: About 240 calories, 3g protein, 24g carbohydrate, 15g total fat (7g saturated), 25mg cholesterol, 210mg sodium.

Food-Processor Pastry Dough

In food processor with knife blade attached, pulse flour and salt to mix. Evenly distribute butter and shortening on top of flour mixture; pulse just until mixture resembles coarse crumbs. With processor running, pour *¼ cup ice water* through feed tube. Immediately stop motor and pinch dough; it should be just moist enough to hold together. If not, with fork, stir in up to *2 tablespoons more ice water.* Shape, refrigerate, and roll as directed.

Shortening Pastry Dough

Prepare Pastry Dough as directed but use *¾ cup vegetable shortening* and omit butter; use *1 teaspoon salt.*

EACH 1/10TH PASTRY: About 250 calories, 3g protein, 24g carbohydrate, 16g total fat (4g saturated), 0mg cholesterol, 235mg sodium.

Vinegar Pastry Dough

Prepare Pastry Dough as directed but substitute *1 tablespoon distilled white vinegar* for 1 tablespoon ice water.

EACH 1/10TH PASTRY: About 240 calories, 3g protein, 24g carbohydrate, 15g total fat (7g saturated), 25mg cholesterol, 210mg sodium.

Whole-Wheat Pastry Dough

Prepare Pastry Dough as directed but use *1½ cups all-purpose flour* and *¾ cup whole-wheat flour.*

EACH 1/10TH PASTRY: About 235 calories, 4g protein, 23g carbohydrate, 15g total fat (7g saturated), 25mg cholesterol, 210mg sodium.

Pastry Dough for 1-Crust Pie

PREP: 10 minutes plus chilling
MAKES enough dough for one 9-inch crust

1¼ cups all-purpose flour

¼ teaspoon salt

4 tablespoons cold butter or margarine, cut into pieces

2 tablespoons vegetable shortening

3 to 5 tablespoons ice water

1. In large bowl, combine flour and salt. With pastry blender or two knives used scissor-fashion, cut in butter and shortening until mixture resembles coarse crumbs.

2. Sprinkle in ice water, 1 tablespoon at a time, mixing lightly with fork after each addition, until dough is just moist enough to hold together.

3. Shape dough into disk; wrap in plastic wrap. Refrigerate 30 minutes or up to overnight. (If chilled overnight, let stand 30 minutes at room temperature before rolling.)

4. On lightly floured surface, with floured rolling pin, roll dough into 12-inch round. Gently roll dough round onto rolling pin and ease into 9-inch pie plate, gently pressing dough against side of plate.

5. Make decorative edge. Refrigerate or freeze until firm, 10 to 15 minutes. Fill and bake as directed in recipe.

EACH 1/10TH PASTRY: About 125 calories, 2g protein, 13g carbohydrate, 7g total fat (4g saturated), 12mg cholesterol, 105mg sodium.

Baked Graham Cracker–Crumb Crust

PREP: 10 minutes ★ **BAKE:** 10 minutes
MAKES one 9-inch crust

1¼ cups graham-cracker crumbs (11 rectangular graham crackers)

4 tablespoons butter or margarine, melted

1 tablespoon sugar

1. Preheat oven to 375°F.

2. In 9-inch pie plate, with fork, mix crumbs, melted butter, and sugar until crumbs are evenly moistened.

Press mixture firmly onto bottom and against side of 9-inch pie plate, making small rim.

3. Bake 10 minutes; cool on wire rack. Fill as recipe directs.

EACH 1/10TH CRUST: About 105 calories, 1g protein, 12g carbohydrate, 6g total fat (3g saturated), 12mg cholesterol, 137mg sodium.

Chocolate Wafer–Crumb Crust

Prepare as directed but substitute *1¼ cups chocolate-wafer cookie crumbs (about 24 wafer cookies)* for graham-cracker crumbs.

EACH 1/10TH CRUST: About 108 calories, 1g protein, 12g carbohydrate, 7g total fat (3g saturated), 13mg cholesterol, 130mg sodium.

Baked Vanilla Wafer–Crumb Crust

Prepare as directed but substitute *1¼ cups vanilla-wafer cookie crumbs (about 35 wafer cookies)* for graham-cracker crumbs.

EACH 1/10TH CRUST: About 110 calories, 1g protein, 12g carbohydrate, 7g total fat (3g saturated), 13mg cholesterol, 130mg sodium.

Chocolate Curls

PREP: 15 minutes plus chilling

1 package (6 ounces) semisweet chocolate chips

2 tablespoons vegetable shortening

1. In heavy 1-quart saucepan, combine chocolate chips and shortening; heat over low heat, stirring frequently, until melted and smooth.

2. Pour chocolate mixture into foil-lined or disposable 5¾" by 3¼" loaf pan. Refrigerate until chocolate is set, about 2 hours.

3. Remove chocolate from pan. Using vegetable peeler and working over waxed paper, draw blade across surface of chocolate to make large curls. If chocolate is too cold and curls break, let chocolate stand about 30 minutes at room temperature until slightly softened. To avoid breaking curls, use toothpick or wooden skewer to transfer.

Chapter 13

Our Best Cookies & Candies

Springerles were one of the first *koekjes* ("cookies" or "little cakes") baked by the New York–Dutch colonists. By rolling out a rich cookie dough on wooden boards that were carved with animals, flowers, and figures, the designs were transferred to the dough. In the seventeenth and eighteenth

centuries, there were many other cut-out cookies that began with a rich dough and contained a variety of flavorings, such as coriander, caraway, benne seeds, or ginger. They were quickly baked on a hot griddle, in a brick oven built into the fireplace, or in a free-standing reflector oven placed near an outdoor fire. Baking cookies back then was a tricky business at best, but American bakers were undaunted.

During the nineteenth century, America's cookie repertoire expanded to include large molasses cookies, hermits, oatmeal cookies, shortbread, sand tarts, macaroons, and delicate sugar cookies.

By the early twentieth century, reliable gas and electric stoves made baking cookies easier. Americans baked icebox cookies, Toll House cookies, peanut butter cookies, snickerdoodles, and bar cookies. And in the 1960s, Girl Scouts made their mark by popularizing s'mores.

Candies, known as sweetmeats in England, were also special treats the colonists enjoyed. They included maple-syrup candy, marzipan, and benne-seed candies. In the eighteenth century, caramels, pralines, and lollipops were all the rage, and by the twentieth century, candy jars were being filled with pulled taffy, almond nougats, gumdrops, fudge, divinity, and homemade chocolates.

In the twentieth century, we discovered fast-cook and no-cook candies, such as No-Fail Fudge, which started with a can of sweetened condensed milk and melted chocolate, and Rocky-Road Squares. But that's not all. Penny-candy stores, taffy shops, and fudge shops made it possible to purchase chocolate bars, saltwater taffy, and any kind of freshly made fudge.

Over the years, Americans have never outgrown their love of cookies and candies—and probably never will.

◄ *Chocolate-Walnut Fudge*

Good Housekeeping's Fudgy Brownies

Brownies are a twentieth-century creation. Although a recipe for them does appear in *The Boston Cooking-School Cook Book* of 1896, it doesn't contain chocolate and they aren't bar cookies. Instead, they are "browned" by the addition of Porto Rico molasses and are baked in fancy cake tins. Fanny Farmer's 1906 cookbook offers a recipe for brownies that uses two squares of (melted) Baker's chocolate. It may very well be one of the earliest recipes for chocolate brownies. Our recipe is *Good Housekeeping's* favorite when it comes to fudgy, superrich brownies that have deep chocolate flavor. To make them even more decadent, spread them with praline-pecan icing.

PREP: 10 minutes ★ **BAKE:** 30 minutes
MAKES 24 brownies

1¼ **cups all-purpose flour**

½ **teaspoon salt**

¾ **cup butter or margarine (1½ sticks)**

4 squares (4 ounces) unsweetened chocolate, chopped

4 squares (4 ounces) semisweet chocolate, chopped

2 cups sugar

1 tablespoon vanilla extract

5 large eggs, beaten

1. Preheat oven to 350°F. Grease 13" by 9" baking pan. In small bowl, combine flour and salt.

2. In heavy 4-quart saucepan, melt butter and unsweetened and semisweet chocolates over low heat, stirring frequently, until smooth. Remove pan from heat. With wooden spoon, stir in sugar and vanilla. Add eggs; stir until well mixed. Stir flour mixture into chocolate mixture just blended. Spread batter evenly in prepared pan.

3. Bake until toothpick inserted 1 inch from edge comes out clean, about 30 minutes. Cool completely in pan on wire rack. When cool, cut lengthwise into 4 strips, then cut each strip crosswise into 6 pieces.

EACH BROWNIE: About 206 calories, 3g protein, 26g carbohydrate, 11g total fat (6g saturated), 60mg cholesterol, 121mg sodium.

Praline-Iced Brownies

Prepare brownies as directed; cool. In 2-quart saucepan, heat *5 tablespoons butter or margarine* and *⅓ cup packed brown sugar* over medium-low heat until mixture has melted and bubbles, about 5 minutes. Remove from heat.

With wire whisk, beat in *3 tablespoons bourbon or 1 tablespoon vanilla extract plus 2 tablespoons water;* stir in *2 cups confectioners' sugar* until smooth. With narrow metal spatula, spread topping over room temperature brownies; sprinkle *½ cup pecans,* toasted and coarsely chopped, over topping. Cut brownies lengthwise into 8 strips, then cut each strip crosswise into 8 pieces. Makes 64 brownies.

EACH BROWNIE: About 297 calories, 3g protein, 39g carbohydrate, 15g total fat (8g saturated), 66mg cholesterol, 147mg sodium.

Cookie Jars & Biscuit Boxes

In England, biscuit boxes, biscuit jars, and cracker jars are often made of sterling silver and hand-cut crystal. Known as cookie jars in America, they can be as humble as plain pottery or as elaborate as brightly painted ceramic, wood, or tin. The decorations range from apples to grandmas to colorful, laughing clowns. But no matter how they're shaped, painted, and decorated, they all serve the same purpose: to keep crisp cookies crisp and moist cookies moist.

Visit an English mansion or a London antique fair, and you'll see some of the most elegant cookie containers ever created: an engraved Victorian biscuit box by London silversmiths Martin and Hall (ca. 1869); a crystal Sheffield biscuit jar with a thistle-and-diamond pattern and sterling swing-handle and lid (ca. 1898); cream-colored bisque Wedgwood biscuit jars with hand-painted floral motifs; a ceramic biscuit jar decorated in bright cobalt and topped with a molded pomegranate knob; or transferware cracker and biscuit jars painted with English country scenes by W. T. Copeland.

In America, cookies were generally stored in cardboard oatmeal boxes, coffee or cracker tins, and bread boxes (anything handy that would keep them fresh). But by the twentieth century, a whole new "cookie world" opened up. More and more, cookies were being baked at home, thanks to delicious recipes, the availability of baking chocolate, and reliable stoves. Ever since the Great Depression, when homemakers discovered that it was more economical to make cookies at home than to buy them at bakeries, the demand for containers to keep them fresh had been increasing. The Brush Pottery Company in Roseville, Ohio, came up with a solution in 1929: an green canister embossed with the word *cookies* on the front. It is thought to be the first pottery cookie jar ever made. In 1932, the Hocking Glass Company added a cookie jar with a screw top to its glass-paneled canister set. These early jars were simple, often made of stoneware, with a cylindrical or bean-pot shape, and decorated with leaves and flowers, if at all. But soon, two giants, the Nelson McCoy Pottery Company and the American Bisque Company, each made cookie-jar history by respectively designing approximately three hundred decorative cookie jars. The McCoy jars were often shaped like apples, strawberries, and kettles, while the American Bisque jars were often shaped like people.

From the 1940s on, made-in-America cookie jars have been extremely popular, both as practical containers and as valuable collectibles. Among the most recognizable (and marketable) are nursery-rhyme characters, such as Humpty Dumpty and Bo Peep; barnyard animals, including roosters and pigs; and lovable animals, such as laughing elephants and smiling frogs. Walt Disney's Mickey Mouse and Donald Duck have popped up, as have Cookie Monster and Big Bird. Grannies, chefs, little Dutch girls, Santas, and snowmen have also been turned into ceramic cookie jars. Food manufacturers, including Quaker Oats, Coca-Cola, Green Giant, Blue Bonnet, Aunt Jemima, Nestlé, and Pillsbury all joined the cookie-jar mania by manufacturing cookie jars to advertise their products. Wooden, tin, and plastic cookie jars have also made an appearance, but they have never achieved the same marketability as the decorative ceramic ones.

The cookie jar story doesn't stop here, however. Cookie jars in America "live" on, and hopefully always will, in kitchens, corner cabinets, museums, and cherished collections.

Blondies

Sometime in the 1940s, recipes for bar cookies that were similar to brownies but didn't contain chocolate began appearing. Bursting with brown-sugar flavor, these blonde-colored cookies were delicious. Today's blondies often contain nuts; sometimes chocolate chips or butterscotch chips are added too.

PREP: 10 minutes ★ **BAKE:** 30 minutes
MAKES 24 blondies

1 cup all-purpose flour
2 teaspoons baking powder
1 teaspoon salt
6 tablespoons butter or margarine
1¾ cups packed light brown sugar
2 teaspoons vanilla extract
2 large eggs
1½ cups pecans (6 ounces), coarsely chopped

1. Preheat oven to 350°F. Grease 13" by 9" baking pan. In small bowl, combine flour, baking powder, and salt.

2. In 3-quart saucepan, melt butter over low heat. Remove from heat. With wooden spoon, stir in brown sugar and vanilla; add eggs, stirring until well blended. Stir flour mixture into sugar mixture just until mixed. Stir in pecans. Spread batter evenly in prepared pan.

3. Bake until toothpick inserted 2 inches from edge of pan comes out clean, about 30 minutes. Do not overbake; blondies will firm as they cool. Cool completely in pan on wire rack.

4. When cool, cut lengthwise into 4 strips, then cut each strip crosswise into 6 pieces.

EACH BLONDIE: About 159 calories, 2g protein, 21g carbohydrate, 8g total fat (2g saturated), 25mg cholesterol, 179mg sodium.

Coconut Blondies

Prepare as directed, stirring in ¾ *cup flaked sweetened coconut* with pecans.

Chocolate Chip Blondies

Prepare as directed but in Step 2, let batter cool 15 minutes; stir in *1 package (6 ounces) semisweet chocolate chips.* Proceed as directed.

Shortenin' Bread

Shortbread originated in Scotland and the British Isles. Traditionally it was served at Christmas but was also enjoyed throughout the year. Shortbread cookies are firm but temptingly rich. Sometimes they contain only three ingredients: butter, flour, and white sugar. Other recipes call for ginger, almonds, or brown sugar, as does ours. Originally shortbread dough was pressed into a decoratively carved mold, so that when the cookies were turned out, they were embossed. In Scotland, as far back as the twelfth century, shortbread was baked in round pans (sometimes with fluted edges) and cut into wedges that resembled the hoop petticoats worn by ladies of the court. In those days, they were known as *petty cotes tallis'*; today they are called petticoat tails. In our recipe the shortbread is cut into the traditional "fingers."

PREP: 20 minutes ★ **BAKE:** 23 minutes ★ **MAKES** 24 wedges

¾ cup butter or margarine (1½ sticks), softened
⅓ cup packed dark brown sugar
3 tablespoons granulated sugar
1 teaspoon vanilla extract
1¾ cups all-purpose flour
1 cup pecans (4 ounces), chopped

1. Preheat oven to 350°F. In large bowl, with mixer at medium-low speed, beat butter, brown and granulated sugars, and vanilla until creamy. Reduce speed to low and beat in flour until blended (dough will be crumbly). With wooden spoon, stir dough until it holds together.

2. Divide dough in half. With hand, pat evenly onto bottom of two ungreased 8-inch round cake pans. Sprinkle with pecans; press lightly.

3. Bake until edges are lightly browned and center is firm, 23 to 25 minutes. Transfer pans to wire racks. With small sharp knife, cut each round into 12 wedges. Cool completely in pans on wire racks.

EACH WEDGE: About 130 calories, 1g protein, 12g carbohydrate, 9g total fat (4g saturated), 16mg cholesterol, 60mg sodium.

Blondies ▶

Lemon Bars

Early American cookbooks often included recipes for shortbread and lemon curd. It wasn't until the mid-twentieth century that these two favorites were combined in a bar cookie. The contrast of a buttery shortbread-cookie base and a smooth and tangy lemon filling makes these bars a popular sweet treat. Be sure to cool the bars completely before cutting them. If they are still soft and tender, chill them in the refrigerator for a short while.

PREP: 15 minutes ★ **BAKE:** 30 minutes ★ **MAKES** 36 bars

1½ **cups plus 3 tablespoons all-purpose flour**

½ **cup plus 1 tablespoon confectioners' sugar**

¾ **cup cold butter or margarine (1½ sticks), cut into pieces**

2 **large lemons**

3 **large eggs**

1 **cup granulated sugar**

½ **teaspoon baking powder**

½ **teaspoon salt**

1. Preheat oven to 350°F. Line 13" by 9" baking pan with foil, extending foil over rim; lightly grease foil.

2. In medium bowl, combine 1½ cups flour and ½ cup confectioners' sugar. With pastry blender or two knives used scissor-fashion, cut in butter until mixture resembles coarse crumbs. Transfer crumb mixture to prepared pan. With floured hand, pat firmly onto bottom of pan.

3. Bake until lightly browned, 15 to 17 minutes.

4. Meanwhile, from lemons, grate 1 teaspoon peel and squeeze ⅓ cup juice. In large bowl, with mixer at high speed, beat eggs until thick and lemon-colored, about 3 minutes. Reduce speed to low. Add granulated sugar, remaining 3 tablespoons flour, baking powder, salt, and lemon peel and juice. Beat, occasionally scraping bowl with rubber spatula, until blended. Pour lemon filling over warm crust.

5. Bake until filling is just set and golden around edges, about 15 minutes. Transfer pan to wire rack. Dust remaining 1 tablespoon confectioners' sugar over warm filling. Cool completely in pan on wire rack.

6. When cool, remove lemon bars from pan by lifting edges of foil and place on cutting board. Cut lengthwise into 3 strips, then cut each strip crosswise into 12 pieces.

EACH BAR: About 95 calories, 1g protein, 12g carbohydrate, 4g total fat (3g saturated), 28mg cholesterol, 85mg sodium.

◄ *Lemon Bars*

Grandma's Oatmeal-Raisin Cookies

Although Fanny Farmer's 1896 cookbook included a recipe for oatmeal cookies, they were quite different from the ones we bake today. Her cookies contained lots of flour, only a little oatmeal, and no raisins. The stiff dough was rolled and cut out. By the 1900s, drop oatmeal cookie recipes began appearing. The 1921 edition of *The Settlement Cookbook,* had two oatmeal cookie recipes. Both called for white sugar (not brown), and one of the recipes had raisins and hickory nuts. Like many oatmeal cookie recipes today, ours are made with butter and are brimming with raisins.

PREP: 15 minutes ★ **BAKE:** 15 minutes per batch
MAKES about 24 cookies

¾ **cup all-purpose flour**

½ **teaspoon baking soda**

¼ **teaspoon salt**

½ **cup butter or margarine (1 stick), softened**

½ **cup granulated sugar**

⅓ **cup packed brown sugar**

1 large egg

2 teaspoons vanilla extract

1½ **cups old-fashioned or quick-cooking oats, uncooked**

¾ **cup dark seedless raisins or chopped pitted prunes**

1. Preheat oven to 350°F. In small bowl, combine flour, baking soda, and salt.

2. In large bowl, with mixer at medium speed, beat butter and granulated and brown sugars until light and fluffy. Beat in egg and vanilla until blended. Reduce speed to low; beat in flour mixture just until blended. With wooden spoon, stir in oats and raisins.

3. Drop dough by heaping tablespoons, 2 inches apart, on two ungreased large cookie sheets. Bake until golden, about 15 minutes, rotating cookie sheets between upper and lower oven racks halfway through baking. With wide spatula, transfer cookies to wire racks to cool completely.

4. Repeat with remaining dough.

EACH COOKIE: About 113 calories, 2g protein, 17g carbohydrate, 4g total fat (2g saturated), 19mg cholesterol, 94mg sodium.

Peanut Butter Cookies

In the late nineteenth century, a physician developed a protein substitute for people who had poor teeth and therefore had trouble chewing; it was called peanut butter. In 1903, Ambrose W. Straub invented the first peanut butter machine, and a year after that, peanut butter was promoted as a health food at the St. Louis World's Fair. In 1923, J. L. Rosefield developed a process that prevented peanut butter from separating, which Swift and Company began using for its Peter Pan brand peanut butter. It was at this time that recipes for peanut butter cookies began showing up. Originally the dough was cut into shapes, but by the 1940s a stiffer peanut butter dough was being rolled into balls then crosshatched with a fork. Our cookies are rich, thanks to a generous amount of peanut butter. The dough is also soft enough to be dropped onto cookie sheets, which eliminates the need to roll the dough into balls.

PREP: 15 minutes ★ **BAKE:** 15 minutes per batch
MAKES about 36 cookies

1¼ **cups all-purpose flour**

1 teaspoon baking soda

¼ **teaspoon salt**

1 cup creamy peanut butter

½ **cup butter or margarine (1 stick), softened**

½ **cup packed brown sugar**

¼ **cup granulated sugar**

1 large egg

½ **teaspoon vanilla extract**

1. Preheat oven to 350°F. In small bowl, combine flour, baking soda, and salt.

2. In large bowl, with mixer at medium speed, beat peanut butter, butter, brown and granulated sugars, egg, and vanilla until combined, occasionally scraping bowl with rubber spatula. Reduce speed to low. Add flour mixture and beat just until blended.

3. Drop dough by heaping tablespoons, 2 inches apart, on two ungreased large cookie sheets. With fork, press crisscross pattern into top of each cookie. Bake until lightly browned, 15 to 20 minutes, rotating cookie sheets between upper and lower oven racks halfway through baking. With wide spatula, transfer cookies to wire racks to cool completely.

4. Repeat with remaining dough.

EACH COOKIE: About 100 calories, 3g protein, 9g carbohydrate, 6g total fat (2g saturated), 13mg cholesterol, 114mg sodium.

Grandma's Oatmeal-Raisin Cookies ▶

Chocolate Chip Cookies

In 1930, Ruth Wakefield and her husband purchased a 1709 Cape Cod–style house near Whitman, Massachusetts. At one time it had been a toll house where travelers could get a bite to eat, change their horses, and pay their road tolls. Mrs. Wakefield had a large collection of recipes and loved cooking. Both she and her husband enjoyed having guests in their home, so they decided to open up the Toll House Inn. One day when mixing up a batch of her favorite Butter Drop Do cookies, she stirred two chopped up chocolate bars into the dough figuring that the chocolate bits would melt, thus saving her the task of melting the chocolate beforehand. To her surprise, the chocolate bits didn't melt. Her guests liked the cookies so much that she perfected the recipe, adding two bars of Nestlé semisweet chocolate that were chopped "into the size of peas" and some nuts. After the recipe was published in a Boston newspaper and in her first cookbook in 1930, the sales for Nestlé chocolate bars skyrocketed. By 1939, the Nestlé company was packaging chocolate chips and Ruth Wakefield's recipe was being printed on the back of every package.

PREP: 15 minutes ★ **BAKE:** 10 minutes per batch
MAKES about 36 cookies

1¼ cups all-purpose flour

½ teaspoon baking soda

½ teaspoon salt

½ cup butter or margarine (1 stick), softened

½ cup packed brown sugar

¼ cup granulated sugar

1 large egg

1 teaspoon vanilla extract

1 package (6 ounces) semisweet chocolate chips
   (1 cup)

½ cup walnuts, chopped (optional)

1. Preheat oven to 375°F. In small bowl, combine flour, baking soda, and salt.

2. In large bowl, with mixer at medium speed, beat butter and brown and granulated sugars until light and fluffy. Beat in egg and vanilla until well combined. Reduce speed to low; beat in flour mixture just until blended. With wooden spoon, stir in chocolate chips and walnuts, if using.

3. Drop dough by rounded tablespoons, 2 inches apart, on two ungreased large cookie sheets. Bake until golden around edges, 10 to 12 minutes, rotating cookie sheets between upper and lower oven racks halfway through baking. With wide spatula, transfer cookies to wire racks to cool completely.

4. Repeat with remaining dough.

EACH COOKIE: About 80 calories, 1g protein, 11g carbohydrate, 4g total fat (2g saturated), 13mg cholesterol, 79mg sodium.

White Chocolate–Macadamia Cookies

Prepare as directed but substitute ¾ cup white baking chips for semisweet chocolate chips and 1 cup chopped macadamia nuts (4 ounces) for walnuts.

◄ Chocolate Chip Cookies

Whoopie Pies

This Pennsylvania-Dutch favorite is not a pie at all but two cakelike chocolate cookies that are sandwiched together with a fluffy white filling. According to Betty Groff, cookbook author and owner of Groff's Farm Restaurant, they may have been created by mothers using leftover cake batter to make a few cookies for their children. How they became known as whoopie pies is unclear. Perhaps it's the "whoop of glee" that children express when given such a treat. Our recipe uses a marshmallow crème filling that's reminiscent of moon pies, cookies "as big as the moon," which the Chattanooga Bakery in Tennessee has been making since 1917.

PREP: 30 minutes plus cooling ★ **BAKE** 12 minutes
MAKES 12 whoopie pies

COOKIE DOUGH

2 cups all-purpose flour
1 cup sugar
½ cup unsweetened cocoa
1 teaspoon baking soda
¼ teaspoon salt
¾ cup milk
6 tablespoons butter or margarine, melted
1 large egg
1 teaspoon vanilla extract

MARSHMALLOW CRÈME FILLING

6 tablespoons butter or margarine, slightly softened
1 cup confectioners' sugar
1 jar (7 to 7½ ounces) marshmallow crème
1 teaspoon vanilla extract

1. Preheat oven to 350°F. Grease two large cookie sheets.

2. Prepare cookie dough: In large bowl, with wooden spoon, beat flour, sugar, cocoa, baking soda, salt, milk, butter, egg, and vanilla until smooth.

3. Drop 12 heaping tablespoons dough, 2 inches apart, on each prepared cookie sheet. Bake until puffy and toothpick inserted in center comes out clean, 12 to 14 minutes, rotating sheets between upper and lower oven racks halfway through baking. With wide spatula, transfer cookies to wire racks to cool completely.

4. When cookies are cool, prepare marshmallow crème filling: In large bowl, with mixer at medium speed, beat butter until smooth. Reduce speed to low; gradually beat in confectioners' sugar. Beat in marshmallow crème and vanilla until smooth.

5. Spread 1 rounded tablespoon filling on flat side of 12 cookies. Top with remaining cookies, flat side down.

EACH WHOOPIE PIE: About 365 calories, 4g protein, 59g carbohydrate, 14g total fat (8g saturated), 51mg cholesterol, 290mg sodium.

Snowballs

By the 1950s, buttery cookie balls covered with powdered sugar had become so popular that recipes for them began appearing in community cookbooks across America. They are known by several names: Mexican wedding cakes, Russian tea cakes, nut butter balls, and crispy nougats. Just where the recipe originated remains a mystery. These delicious cookies traditionally contain only a small amount of sugar because they are rolled twice in confectioners' sugar: once while still warm from the oven and again when cool.

PREP: 25 minutes ★ **BAKE:** 20 minutes per batch
MAKES about 4 dozen cookies

1 cup pecans (4 ounces)
1¾ cups confectioners' sugar
1 cup butter (2 sticks), cut into 16 pieces, softened (do not use margarine)
1 teaspoon vanilla extract
2 cups all-purpose flour

1. Preheat oven to 325°F. In food processor with knife blade attached, process pecans and ¼ cup confectioners' sugar until nuts are finely chopped. Add butter and vanilla and process until smooth, scraping down side of processor bowl with rubber spatula. Add flour and process until dough comes together.

2. With floured hands, roll dough into 1-inch balls. Place balls, 1½ inches apart, on ungreased large cookie sheet.

3. Bake until bottoms are lightly browned and tops are very light golden brown, 20 to 22 minutes. With wide spatula, transfer cookies to wire rack to cool slightly.

4. Place remaining 1½ cups confectioners' sugar in pie plate. While cookies are still warm, roll in sugar until coated; place on wire rack to cool completely. When cool, reroll cookies in sugar until thoroughly coated.

5. Repeat with remaining dough.

EACH COOKIE: About 85 calories, 1g protein, 9g carbohydrate, 5g total fat (3g saturated), 10mg cholesterol, 40mg sodium.

Whoopie Pies ▶

Black-and-Whites

Just which year these popular cookies began appearing in bakeshops in New York City and elsewhere on the East Coast (in Boston they are called Half Moons) is hazy. But by the mid-twentieth century, these large golden cookies (up to five inches in diameter) had become a regular feature in many neighborhood bakeries. They are rather cakelike, and the tops are half-coated with vanilla icing and half-coated with chocolate icing.

PREP: 20 minutes plus cooling ★ **BAKE:** 15 minutes per batch
MAKES about 14 cookies

2 cups all-purpose flour

½ teaspoon baking soda

¼ teaspoon salt

10 tablespoons butter or margarine (1¼ sticks), softened

1 cup granulated sugar

2 large eggs

2 teaspoons vanilla extract

½ cup buttermilk

1¾ cups confectioners' sugar

2 tablespoons light corn syrup

8 to 10 teaspoons warm water

¼ cup unsweetened cocoa

1. Preheat oven to 350°F. In small bowl, combine flour, baking soda, and salt.

2. In large bowl, with mixer at medium speed, beat butter and granulated sugar until creamy. Beat in eggs and vanilla until blended. Reduce speed to low; add flour mixture alternately with buttermilk, beginning and ending with flour mixture. Beat just until combined, occasionally scraping bowl with rubber spatula.

3. Drop dough by ¼ cups, about 3 inches apart, on two ungreased large cookie sheets. Bake until edges begin to brown and tops spring back when lightly touched with finger, 15 to 17 minutes, rotating sheets between upper and lower racks halfway through baking. With wide spatula, transfer cookies to wire racks to cool completely.

4. When cookies are cool, prepare glazes: In medium bowl, mix 1¼ cups confectioners' sugar, 1 tablespoon corn syrup, and 5 to 6 teaspoons water, 1 teaspoon at a time, until smooth and of spreading consistency. Turn cookies flat side up. With small metal spatula, spread glaze over half of each cookie. Allow glaze to set 20 minutes.

5. Meanwhile, prepare chocolate glaze: In small bowl, mix remaining ½ cup confectioners' sugar, cocoa, remaining 1 tablespoon corn syrup, and remaining 3 to 4 teaspoons water, 1 teaspoon at a time, until smooth and of spreading consistency. With clean small spatula, spread chocolate glaze over remaining un-iced half of each cookie. Let glazes set completely, at least 1 hour.

EACH COOKIE: About 280 calories, 3g protein, 46g carbohydrate, 9g total fat (6g saturated), 53mg cholesterol, 190mg sodium.

◀ *Black-and-Whites*

Gingersnaps

Late-eighteenth-century recipes for gingersnaps called for rolling out the dough and cutting it into rounds. Nowadays some recipes suggest rolling the dough into logs, chilling it, then slicing the dough into rounds. Still other recipes (like ours) recommend rolling the dough into small balls, then spacing them well apart on cookie sheets. As they bake, they spread out flat. The derivation of the name for these cookies is hazy, though the word *snap* does come from the German *snappen,* which means "seize quickly" (easily). Indeed, these cookies are quick and easy to make as well as delicious.

PREP: 20 minutes ★ **BAKE:** 15 minutes
MAKES 10 large cookies or about 30 small cookies

2 cups all-purpose flour

2 teaspoons ground ginger

1 teaspoon baking soda

½ teaspoon ground cinnamon

½ teaspoon salt

¼ teaspoon ground black pepper (optional)

¾ cup vegetable shortening

½ cup plus 2 tablespoons sugar

1 large egg

½ cup dark molasses

1. Preheat oven to 350°F. In medium bowl, combine flour, ginger, baking soda, cinnamon, salt, and black pepper, if using.

2. In large bowl, with mixer at medium speed, beat shortening and ½ cup sugar until light and fluffy. Beat in egg until blended; beat in molasses. Reduce speed to low; beat in flour mixture just until blended.

3. Place remaining 2 tablespoons sugar on waxed paper. Roll ¼ cup dough into ball; roll in sugar to coat evenly. Repeat with remaining dough to make 10 balls in all. Place balls, 3 inches apart, on ungreased large cookie sheet. Or, for small cookies, roll slightly rounded tablespoons dough into balls and place 2 inches apart on two ungreased cookie sheets.

4. Bake until set, about 15 minutes for large cookies, or 9 to 11 minutes for small cookies, rotating cookie sheets between upper and lower oven racks halfway through baking. Cookies will be very soft and may appear moist in cracks. Cool cookies 1 minute on cookie sheets on wire racks. With wide spatula, transfer cookies to wire racks to cool completely.

EACH LARGE COOKIE: About 323 calories, 3g protein, 42g carbohydrate, 16g total fat (4g saturated), 21mg cholesterol, 258mg sodium.

EACH SMALL COOKIE: About 108 calories, 1g protein, 14g carbohydrate, 5g total fat (1g saturated), 7mg cholesterol, 86mg sodium.

Gingersnaps ▶

Coconut Macaroons

Macaroons that were most likely made with almonds were recorded as early as the eighth century and were very popular in Venice and other cities in Italy during the Renaissance. Their name comes from the Italian *maccherone* and *macarone* (fine paste), from which the word *macaroni* is also derived. These small, sweet egg-white puffs were often served with fine wine or liqueur as a light refreshment, particularly during Passover. As far back as the 1850s, American cookbooks contained recipes for both almond and coconut macaroons, including Eliza Leslie's 1848 edition of *Directions for Cookery*. Her Cocoa-Nut Maccaroons [*sic*] included instructions to grate loaf sugar over their tops before baking them in a brisk (hot) oven. Regardless of the recipe you're using, Fanny Farmer's advice in her macaroon recipe in *The Boston Cooking-School Cook Book* still holds true: "After removing [cookies] from oven, invert paper, and wet with a cloth wrung out of cold water, when macaroons will easily slip off."

PREP: 20 minutes ★ **BAKE:** 25 minutes
MAKES about 30 cookies

- 1 package (7 ounces) flaked sweetened coconut
- ¾ cup sugar
- 3 large egg whites
- 1 teaspoon vanilla extract
- ⅛ teaspoon almond extract

1. Preheat oven to 325°F. Line two large cookie sheets with parchment paper or foil. Spray with nonstick cooking spray.

2. In large bowl, stir coconut, sugar, egg whites, and vanilla and almond extracts until well combined.

3. Drop batter by rounded teaspoons, 1 inch apart, on prepared cookie sheets. Bake until set and light golden, about 25 minutes, rotating cookie sheets between upper and lower oven racks halfway through baking. Cool 1 minute on cookie sheets. With wide spatula, transfer cookies to wire racks to cool completely.

EACH COOKIE: About 54 calories, 1g protein, 8g carbohydrate, 2g total fat (2g saturated), 0mg cholesterol, 22mg sodium.

Chocolate-Coconut Macaroons

Prepare as directed, stirring *2 tablespoons unsweetened cocoa* and *1 square (1 ounce) semisweet chocolate*, grated, into coconut mixture.

Chocolate-Dipped Coconut Macaroons

Melt *4 squares (4 ounces) semisweet chocolate* according to package directions. Dip bottoms of cooled macaroons in melted chocolate, scraping bottoms on edge of bowl to remove excess chocolate. Place macaroons on wax paper–lined cookie sheets, chocolate side up. Let stand until chocolate sets.

Wooden Spoon–Lace Cookies

These delicate confections are called French lace cookies and *crepinettes* (almond lace cookies). When they first appeared is not clear, but there are recipes in mid-twentieth-century cookbooks. In France, the cookies are often made with sliced almonds and confectioners' sugar, while Swedish bakers use ground almonds and white sugar. Once the cookies are baked, they are sometimes rolled around a broom handle to give them a curved shape. In American recipes, the cookies are often made with uncooked oatmeal and brown sugar. Our cookies, however, are made in the Swedish manner. We suggest baking only a few cookies at a time, as they spread out on the cookie sheet.

PREP: 25 minutes plus cooling ★ **BAKE:** 5 minutes per batch
MAKES about 36 cookies

¾ **cup blanched almonds, ground**

½ **cup butter or margarine (1 stick), softened**

½ **cup sugar**

1 **tablespoon all-purpose flour**

1 **tablespoon heavy or whipping cream**

1. Preheat oven to 350°F. Grease and flour two large cookie sheets.

2. In 2-quart saucepan, combine ground almonds, butter, sugar, flour, and cream. Heat over low heat, stirring occasionally, until butter melts. Keep mixture warm over very low heat.

3. Drop batter by rounded teaspoons, about 3 inches apart, on prepared cookie sheets. (Do not place more than six on each cookie sheet.)

4. Bake until edges are lightly browned and centers are just golden, 5 to 7 minutes. Cool cookies 30 to 60 seconds on cookie sheet, until edges are just set. With long, flexible narrow metal spatula, flip cookies over quickly (lacy texture will be on outside after rolling up).

5. Working as quickly as possible, roll each cookie around handle (½-inch diameter) of wooden spoon or dowel. If cookies become too hard to roll, briefly return to oven to soften. As each cookie is shaped, slip off spoon handle and cool completely on wire rack.

6. Repeat with remaining batter.

EACH COOKIE: About 57 calories, 1g protein, 4g carbohydrate, 5g total fat (2g saturated), 7mg cholesterol, 26mg sodium.

Snickerdoodles

These rich cinnamon-sugar cookies were created in New England and Pennsylvania-Dutch communities in the nineteenth century. As they bake, the little balls of dough puff up, then quickly flatten out and crinkle on top. Recipes for these cookies differ: some contain chopped walnuts, hickory nuts, raisins, or currants; others, like ours, are simple and buttery, with only a little vanilla extract and a fine coating of cinnamon-sugar to flavor them. Craig Claiborne believed that the name is derived from the German word *schnecken* (sticky buns.) Early Hudson River Valley community cookbooks called them schnecken noodles, schneckenoodles, or snecke noodles, while in the Midwest, they are called snickerdoodles. Some historians credit this cookie's name to the fact that New England cooks often enjoyed giving dishes whimsical names.

PREP: 25 minutes ★ **BAKE:** 12 minutes per batch
MAKES about 54 cookies

3 **cups all-purpose flour**

2 **teaspoons cream of tartar**

1 **teaspoon baking soda**

1 **cup butter or margarine (2 sticks), softened**

1⅓ **cups plus ¼ cup sugar**

2 **large eggs**

1 **teaspoon vanilla extract**

1½ **teaspoons ground cinnamon**

1. Preheat oven to 375°F. In large bowl, combine flour, cream of tartar, and baking soda.

2. In large bowl, with mixer at medium speed, beat butter and 1⅓ cups sugar until light and fluffy. Beat in eggs, one at a time, beating well after each addition; beat in vanilla. Reduce speed to low; beat in flour mixture until well blended.

3. In small bowl, combine remaining ¼ cup sugar and cinnamon. Roll dough into 1-inch balls. Roll in cinnamon-sugar to coat evenly. Place balls, 1 inch apart, on two ungreased large cookie sheets.

4. Bake cookies until set and slightly crinkled on top, about 12 minutes, rotating cookie sheets between upper and lower oven racks halfway through baking. Cool cookies 1 minute on cookie sheet. With wide spatula, transfer cookies to wire racks to cool completely.

5. Repeat with remaining dough.

EACH COOKIE: About 81 calories, 1g protein, 11g carbohydrate, 4g total fat (2g saturated), 17mg cholesterol, 61mg sodium.

Benne Seed Wafers

In the South Carolina low country you'll rarely hear folks call the main ingredient in these cookies sesame seeds. Instead they refer to them as benne seeds: the name the African slaves called them when the seeds were brought here in the seventeenth century. South Carolina cooks add the seeds to bread, candy, and to these traditional brown-sugar wafers. Be sure to let the cookies rest one minute (for easier handling) before transferring then to wire racks to cool and crisp.

PREP: 30 minutes ★ **BAKE:** 6 minutes per batch
MAKES about 120 cookies

½ **cup sesame seeds**

¾ **cup all-purpose flour**

¼ **teaspoon salt**

½ **cup butter (1 stick), softened (do not use margarine)**

1 **cup packed light brown sugar**

1 **large egg**

1 **teaspoon vanilla extract**

1. Preheat oven to 350°F. Grease two large cookie sheets.

2. Spread sesame seeds in even layer in jelly-roll pan. Bake until light golden, 10 to 12 minutes. Cool in pan on wire rack.

3. In small bowl, combine flour and salt.

4. In medium bowl, with mixer at medium speed, beat butter and brown sugar until creamy. Reduce speed to low; beat in egg and vanilla until well blended. Beat in flour mixture and sesame seeds until combined, occasionally scraping bowl with rubber spatula.

5. Drop dough by rounded half teaspoons, 3 inches apart, on prepared cookie sheets. Bake until light brown and lacy, 6 to 7 minutes, rotating cookie sheets between upper and lower oven racks halfway through baking. Cool on cookie sheet on wire rack 1 minute. With wide spatula, transfer cookies to wire rack to cool completely.

6. Repeat with remaining dough.

EACH COOKIE: About 20 calories, 0g protein, 3g carbohydrate, 1g total fat (1g saturated), 4mg cholesterol, 15mg sodium.

Cookie-Press Cookies

Scandinavian immigrants introduced America to buttery spritz cookies. Half of the fun in preparing them is choosing a decorative disk (or disks) and pressing the cookies out onto cookie sheets. By the mid-twentieth century, these cookies were often the center of attraction on dessert trays, especially around the holidays. The name *spritz* comes from the German word *spritzen*, which means "squirt" or "spray." If you've never used a cookie press, you may need a little practice at first. Experts advise to shape the dough into a roll a little narrower than the diameter of the cookie-press tube. You can easily make hearts, wreaths, and trees by using the various metal disks. Tint the dough different colors if you wish, and sprinkle the cookies with decorating sugar.

PREP: 15 minutes ★ **BAKE:** 10 minutes per batch
MAKES about 60 cookies

---

1 **cup butter or margarine (2 sticks), softened**

¾ **cup confectioners' sugar**

1 **teaspoon vanilla extract**

⅛ **teaspoon almond extract**

2 **cups all-purpose flour**

⅛ **teaspoon salt**

1. Preheat oven to 350°F. In large bowl, with mixer at medium speed, beat butter and confectioners' sugar until light and fluffy. Beat in vanilla and almond extracts. Reduce speed to low; add flour and salt and beat until well combined.

2. Spoon one-third of batter into cookie press fitted with disk of choice. Press out cookies, 1 inch apart, on two large ungreased cookie sheets.

3. Bake until golden brown around edges, 10 to 12 minutes, rotating cookie sheets between upper and lower oven racks halfway through baking. With wide spatula, transfer cookies to wire racks to cool completely.

4. Repeat with remaining dough.

EACH COOKIE: About 48 calories, 0g protein, 5g carbohydrate, 3g total fat (2g saturated), 8mg cholesterol, 36mg sodium.

Raspberry Linzer Thumbprint Cookies

From Linz, Austria, comes the famous linzertorte, a tart made with a nutty, shortbread-type crust that is filled with jam and topped with a pastry lattice. Thumbprint cookies, which became popular during the mid-twentieth century, were typically made from a buttery cookie dough that was mixed with ground nuts (often almonds), then formed into balls and rolled in more ground nuts. Before popping them into the oven, the baker would make an indentation in each cookie with his or her thumb, and then fill it with any favorite jam or jelly. Our thumbprint cookies resemble the classic linzertorte, as they are made with a rich shortbread dough and raspberry jam.

PREP: 45 minutes ⋆ **BAKE:** 20 minutes per batch
MAKES about 48 cookies

1⅓ cups hazelnuts (filberts, about 6 ounces)

½ cup sugar

¾ cup butter or margarine (1½ sticks), cut into pieces

1 teaspoon vanilla extract

¼ teaspoon salt

1¾ cups all-purpose flour

¼ cup seedless red-raspberry jam

1. Preheat oven to 350°F.

2. Place 1 cup hazelnuts in 9-inch square baking pan. Bake until toasted, about 15 minutes. Wrap hot hazelnuts in clean kitchen towel. With hands on outside of towel, roll hazelnuts back and forth to remove most of skins. Cool; separate hazelnuts from skins.

3. In food processor with knife blade attached, process toasted hazelnuts and sugar until nuts are finely ground. Add butter, vanilla, and salt; process just until blended. Add flour and process until evenly combined. Remove knife blade and press dough together with hands.

4. Finely chop remaining ⅓ cup hazelnuts; spread on sheet of waxed paper. Roll dough into 1-inch balls (dough may be slightly crumbly). Roll balls in hazelnuts, gently pressing to coat.

5. Place balls, about 1½ inches apart, on two ungreased large cookie sheets. With thumb, make small indentation in center of each ball. Fill each indentation with ¼ teaspoon jam.

6. Bake until lightly golden around edges, about 20 minutes, rotating cookie sheets between upper and lower oven racks halfway through baking. With wide spatula, transfer cookies to wire racks to cool completely.

7. Repeat with remaining dough balls and jam.

EACH COOKIE: About 75 calories, 1g protein, 7g carbohydrate, 5g total fat (2g saturated), 8mg cholesterol, 40mg sodium.

Gingerbread Cutouts

Early cookbooks often offered several gingerbread cookie recipes. Among them was usually one for gingerbread that was rolled out thin, baked on an inverted drip pan, then cut into strips. It is possible that this recipe was the forerunner of the ever-popular gingerbread cutout cookies that are piled high on holiday cookie platters and often found hanging on Christmas trees. Nowadays gingerbread cookies are decorated with various colors, but in earlier times they were outlined with a thin zigzag of white icing.

PREP: 45 minutes plus cooling and decorating
BAKE: 12 minutes per batch ★ **MAKES** about 36 cookies

½ **cup sugar**
½ **cup light (mild) molasses**
1½ **teaspoons ground ginger**
1 **teaspoon ground allspice**
1 **teaspoon ground cinnamon**
1 **teaspoon ground cloves**
2 **teaspoons baking soda**
½ **cup butter or margarine (1 stick), cut into pieces**
1 **large egg, beaten**
3½ **cups all-purpose flour**
Ornamental Frosting (opposite)

1. In 3-quart saucepan, combine sugar, molasses, ginger, allspice, cinnamon, and cloves; heat to boiling over medium heat, stirring occasionally with wooden spoon. Remove pan from heat; stir in baking soda (mixture will foam up in pan). Add butter; stir until melted. Stir in egg, then flour.

2. On floured surface, knead dough until thoroughly blended. Divide dough in half; wrap one piece in waxed paper and set aside.

3. Preheat oven to 325°F. With floured rolling pin, roll remaining piece of dough slightly less than ¼ inch thick. With floured 3- to 4-inch assorted cookie cutters, cut dough into as many cookies as possible; reserve trimmings for rerolling. Place cookies, 1 inch apart, on two ungreased large cookie sheets. If desired, with drinking straw or skewer, make ¼-inch hole in top of each cookie for hanging.

4. Bake until edges begin to brown, about 12 minutes, rotating cookie sheets between upper and lower oven racks halfway through baking. With wide spatula, transfer cookies to wire racks to cool completely. Repeat with remaining dough and trimmings.

5. When cookies are cool, prepare Ornamental Frosting. Use frosting to decorate cookies as desired. Allow frosting to dry completely, about 1 hour.

EACH COOKIE WITHOUT FROSTING: About 95 calories, 2g protein, 16g carbohydrate, 3g total fat (2g saturated), 13mg cholesterol, 100mg sodium.

Ornamental Frosting

PREP: 8 minutes ★ **MAKES** about 3 cups

1 **package (16 ounces) confectioners' sugar**
3 **tablespoons meringue powder***
⅓ **cup warm water**
assorted food colorings or food color pastes (optional)

1. In bowl, with mixer at medium speed, beat confectioners' sugar, meringue powder, and warm water until stiff and knife drawn through leaves path, about 5 minutes.

2. If desired, tint frosting with food colorings. Keep tightly covered to prevent drying out. With small metal spatula, artists' paintbrushes, or decorating bags with small plain tips, decorate cookies with frosting. (You may need to thin frosting with a little warm water to obtain desired spreading or piping consistency.)

*Meringue powder is available in specialty stores wherever cake-decorating equipment is sold.

EACH TABLESPOON: About 40 calories, 0g protein, 10g carbohydrate, 0g total fat, 0mg cholesterol, 3mg sodium.

Gingerbread Cutouts ▸

Christmas Sugar-Cookie Cutouts

In Amelia Simmons's book *American Cookery,* there are two similar cookie recipes. One of them, Another Christmas Cookey, suggests: "...roll [dough] three quarters of an inch thick, and cut or stamp into shape and size you please, bake slowly fifteen or twenty minutes; tho' hard and dry at first, if put into an earthenware pot, and dry cellar, or damp room, they will be finer, softer and better when six months old." With today's recipes, sugar cookies can be enjoyed warm out of the oven. Or let them cool, then decorate them with icing and all the colorful holiday sugars and edible decorations you can find.

PREP: 1 hour 30 minutes plus chilling
BAKE: 12 minutes per batch
MAKES about 6 dozen cookies

---

3 cups all-purpose flour

½ teaspoon baking powder

½ teaspoon salt

1 cup butter (2 sticks), softened (do not use margarine)

1½ cups sugar

2 large eggs

1 teaspoon vanilla extract

Ornamental Frosting (page 322), optional

colored sugar crystals (optional)

1. In large bowl, combine flour, baking powder, and salt. In separate large bowl, with mixer at low speed, beat butter and sugar until blended. Increase speed to high; beat until light and fluffy, about 5 minutes. Reduce speed to low; beat in eggs and vanilla until mixed. Beat in flour mixture, just until blended, occasionally scraping bowl with rubber spatula.

2. Divide dough into four equal pieces. Shape each into disk; wrap each disk in waxed paper and freeze until firm enough to roll, at least 2 hours or refrigerate overnight.

3. Preheat oven to 350°F. On lightly floured surface, with floured rolling pin, roll one piece of dough until slightly less than ¼ inch thick; refrigerate remaining dough. With floured 3- to 4-inch assorted cookie cutters, cut out as many cookies as possible, reserving trimmings for rerolling. Place cookies, about 1 inch apart, on two ungreased large cookie sheets.

4. Bake cookies until golden around edges, 12 to 15 minutes, rotating cookie sheets between upper and lower oven racks halfway through baking. With wide spatula, transfer cookies to wire racks to cool completely. Use Ornamental Frosting or colored sugar to decorate cookies, if desired.

5. Repeat with remaining cookie dough and trimmings.

EACH COOKIE WITHOUT FROSTING OR SUGAR CRYSTALS: About 60 calories, 1g protein, 8g carbohydrate, 3g total fat (2g saturated), 13mg cholesterol, 45mg sodium.

Icebox Pinwheels

During the 1930s, a time when electric refrigerators were being installed in more and more American kitchens, recipes for icebox cookies began appearing in magazines and cookbooks claiming "...you can now quickly slice and freshly bake from rolls of chilled dough, at a moment's notice." The refrigerator cookies contained nuts, candied fruit, melted chocolate, or a few drops of almond extract or peppermint oil. Chocolate pinwheels were one of the first variations on icebox cookies, and they became an instant winner.

PREP: 35 minutes plus chilling ★ **BAKE:** 10 minutes per batch
MAKES about 48 cookies

2 cups all-purpose flour

1 teaspoon baking powder

¼ teaspoon salt

½ cup (1 stick) plus 1 tablespoon butter or margarine, softened

1 cup sugar

1 large egg

1 teaspoon vanilla extract

1 square (1 ounce) semisweet chocolate

3 tablespoons unsweetened cocoa

1. In small bowl, combine flour, baking powder, and salt. In medium bowl, with mixer at medium speed, beat ½ cup butter and sugar until creamy. Reduce speed to low; beat in egg and vanilla until blended. Beat in flour mixture just until combined, occasionally scraping bowl with rubber spatula. Transfer half of dough to sheet of waxed paper.

2. In 2-quart saucepan, melt chocolate and remaining 1 tablespoon butter over very low heat. Stir in cocoa until combined. Add chocolate mixture to dough in bowl, stirring until blended.

3. Roll chocolate dough between two sheets of waxed paper into 12" by 10" rectangle. Repeat with vanilla dough. Remove top sheets of waxed paper from chocolate and vanilla doughs. Using waxed paper, turn vanilla dough over onto chocolate dough. Peel off top sheet of waxed paper. Using bottom piece of waxed paper to help, roll up doughs together jelly-roll fashion. Wrap dough in plastic wrap and refrigerate until very firm, at least 4 hours or up to overnight.

4. Preheat oven to 375°F. Grease two large cookie sheets.

5. Cut dough crosswise into ¼-inch-thick slices. Place slices, ½ inch apart, on prepared cookie sheets.

6. Bake just until golden, 10 to 12 minutes, rotating cookie sheets between upper and lower oven racks halfway through baking. Cool on cookie sheets on wire racks 5 minutes. With wide spatula, transfer to wire racks to cool completely.

EACH COOKIE: About 61 calories, 1g protein, 9g carbohydrate, 3g total fat (2g saturated), 10mg cholesterol, 46mg sodium.

Penny Candy Store

In the late nineteenth century, hundreds of factories were busy producing candies destined to fill the glass bins and candy jars in mom-and-pop candy stores, corner ice-cream shops, and general stores. Such was the beginning of an American institution that would stand the test of time and be known as penny candy.

In 1880, the Wunderle Candy Company in Philadelphia was making one of the most beloved penny candies: orange, white, and yellow fondant candy corn. Eighteen years later, Gustav Goelitz began mass-producing candy corn. In 1886, in a candy kitchen in Lancaster, Pennsylvania, Milton S. Hershey was turning out high-quality caramels. Some time later, he purchased chocolate-making equipment and began chocolate coating his caramels. Around the same time, the Quaker City Confectionery Company was producing soft and chewy Good & Plenty licorice candies, the oldest branded candy in the United States. Their advertisements featured Choo-Choo Charlie, the engineer, who fueled his train with the pink-and-white candies and steered the confection into candy stores all across America.

In 1896, in a small candy shop in New York City, Austrian immigrant Leo Hirshfield began hand-rolling the first-ever wrapped penny candy in brown and red–striped paper. He named his chewy, chocolaty treat the Tootsie Roll, after his daughter Clara, whose nickname was Tootsie. Just four years later, Milton S. Hershey would once again make candy history by creating the first milk-chocolate bar. He also created chocolate kisses, named for the sound the chocolate made when dropped onto the conveyor belt during manufacturing. In 1901, in California, the King Leo Company began making striped peppermint sticks from their original recipe of "peppermint oil and old-fashioned care."

In the candy shops of the early twentieth century, hard candies came in an array of colorful shapes and sizes: tiny cinnamon red hots; root beer barrels; wrapped butterscotch buttons; orange, lemon, lime, and cherry sour balls; peppermint Lifesavers, and crystalline rock candy on a stick in vivid colors. Chewy candies also made an appearance, including bite-size peanut butter and molasses candies called Mary Janes, multicolored Jujyfruit, and honey-flavored taffy and almond bites named Bit-O-Honey. Fruit-flavored jelly candies were turned into sugared gumdrops, jelly beans, rippled rectangles called Chuckles ("five flavors for five cents"), red and black raspberries, sugar-coated spearmint leaves, red watermelon slices, and jelly rings. Licorice, too, was a regular feature: black gumdrops called Crows, red and black licorice laces, and red and black licorice Scotties all had their fans.

Peanuts and peanut butter popped up in various guises, such as candy-coated peanuts called Boston Baked Beans, Reese's peanut butter cups, and chocolate-coated peanuts named Goobers. Naturally, penny-candy bins often held chocolate treasures: M&M's, Milk Duds, Rocky Roads, Goo Goo Clusters, and Sugar Babies. Other candies were simply silly and fun: tiny wax bottles filled with colorful sugar sips (now called Nik-L-Nips), Chupa Chups suckers in assorted flavors, candy cigarettes, six-inch-long chewy caramels called Cow Tales, and chewable, edible waxy lips.

Seasonal candies also had their place at the penny-candy store. At Christmas, glass candy jars held tiny candy canes, colorful strips of ribbon candy, and little candies that were shaped into Santas, wreaths, and bells. In the spring, yellow marshmallow chicks, chocolate-covered eggs, pastel Robin Eggs, and thin mints decorated with icing flowers made a colorful appearance.

The penny-candy business began in small candy kitchens and grew into a major industry that would bring happy moments and sweet memories for just a few pennies for generations to come. And although old-fashioned penny-candy stores are a rare sight these days, penny-candy treasures can still be found.

Chocolate-Walnut Fudge

(pictured on page 300)

As the story goes, in the late nineteenth century a batch of toffee was being manufactured and something went very wrong. The toffee crystallized, turning grainy instead of silky smooth. Surprisingly, it was a rich golden color and delicious! What had been created was America's first batch of fudge, a mixture of sugar, milk, and butter. Over the years, lots of flavor variations have been developed: chocolate, the all-time favorite; peppermint; coconut; maple sugar; and vanilla nut. Fudge shops began popping up, too, especially in resort communities, such as Atlantic City. In the mid-twentieth century, making fudge became easier, faster, and practically foolproof thanks to sweetened condensed milk.

PREP: 25 minutes plus chilling ★ **MAKES** 64 pieces

1 pound bittersweet chocolate or 16 squares (16 ounces) semisweet chocolate, chopped

1 can (14 ounces) sweetened condensed milk

1 cup walnuts (4 ounces), coarsely chopped

1 teaspoon vanilla extract

⅛ teaspoon salt

1. Line 8-inch square baking pan with plastic wrap; smooth out wrinkles. In heavy 2-quart saucepan, melt chocolate with condensed milk over medium-low heat, stirring constantly, until smooth. Remove from heat.

2. Stir in walnuts, vanilla, and salt. Scrape chocolate mixture into prepared pan; spread evenly. Refrigerate until firm, about 3 hours.

3. Remove fudge from pan by lifting edges of plastic wrap. Invert fudge onto cutting board; discard plastic wrap. Cut fudge into 8 strips, then cut each strip crosswise into 8 pieces. Layer between waxed paper in airtight container. Store at room temperature up to 1 week, or refrigerate up to 1 month.

EACH PIECE: About 67 calories, 1g protein, 8g carbohydrate, 4g total fat (2g saturated), 2mg cholesterol, 13mg sodium.

Creamy Penuche

From the Mexican word *panocha* (raw sugar) comes the name of this popular confection. It's also called Mexican fudge and brown-sugar fudge. Just when and where penuche was created appears to be a mystery. But we do know that authentic south-of-the-border versions contain raw, coarse Mexican sugar. Southern cooks claim that authentic penuche is made by caramelizing white sugar until nutty brown, but recipes often use brown sugar along with cream, butter, and nuts.

PREP: 15 minutes plus cooling ★ **COOK:** 25 minutes
MAKES about 64 pieces

4 tablespoons butter (do not use margarine)

2 cups heavy or whipping cream

2 tablespoons light corn syrup

1½ cups granulated sugar

1½ cups packed dark brown sugar

2 ounces white chocolate or white baking bar, chopped

1½ cups walnuts (6 ounces), toasted and coarsely chopped

1. Grease 8-inch square baking pan. Line pan with foil, extending foil over rim on two opposite sides; grease foil.

2. In heavy 4-quart saucepan, melt butter over medium heat. Add cream, corn syrup, and granulated and brown sugars; cook over high heat, stirring, until sugars have completely dissolved and mixture is bubbling. With pastry brush dipped in cold water, wash down sugar crystals on side of saucepan.

3. Set candy thermometer in place; continue cooking, without stirring, until temperature reaches 234° to 240°F (soft-ball stage), 15 to 20 minutes.

4. Remove saucepan from heat. Without stirring, cool mixture to 210°F, about 8 minutes. Sprinkle chopped white chocolate over mixture; let stand 1 minute.

5. With wooden spoon, stir in walnuts just until mixed (do not overmix). Immediately pour mixture into prepared pan (do not scrape mixture from saucepan).

6. Cool in pan on wire rack until firm but still warm, about 30 minutes. Remove candy from pan by lifting edges of foil and place on cutting board. Cut into 8 strips, then cut each strip crosswise into 8 pieces. Cool completely on foil on wire rack. With spatula, lift candy away from foil. Layer between waxed paper in airtight container. Store at room temperature up to 3 weeks.

EACH PIECE: About 95 calories, 1g protein, 11g carbohydrate, 6g total fat (2g saturated), 12mg cholesterol, 14mg sodium.

Pralines

According to the 1951 edition of *The Original Picayune Creole Cook Book,* these delightful confections originated in the old Creole kitchens of New Orleans. The word *praline,* however, did not. It's of French origin and means "sugared." Numerous recipes (and variations) for these dainty, delicious candies exist. Pralines can be made with white or brown sugar, almonds or peanuts, or coconut and cochineal, which turns the candies pink. If you ever get to the French Quarter in New Orleans, be sure to look for *pralines aux pacanes* (pralines with pecans); they are one of the most authentic versions you will find.

PREP: 15 minutes ★ **COOK:** 25 minutes
MAKES about 40 pralines

- ½ cup butter (1 stick), cut into pieces (do not use margarine)
- 2 cups granulated sugar
- 1 cup packed light brown sugar
- 1 cup heavy or whipping cream
- 2 tablespoons light corn syrup
- 2 cups pecans (8 ounces), toasted and coarsely chopped
- 1 teaspoon vanilla extract

1. Grease two or three cookie sheets.

2. In heavy 3-quart saucepan, combine butter, granulated and brown sugars, cream, and corn syrup; cook over medium heat, stirring occasionally, until sugars have dissolved and syrup is bubbling.

3. Set candy thermometer in place and continue cooking, without stirring, until temperature reaches 230° to 234°F (thread stage), about 8 minutes.

4. Add pecans and vanilla; stir until bubbling subsides. Heat to boiling. Continue cooking until candy temperature reaches 244° to 248°F (firm-ball stage).

5. Remove saucepan from heat and stir vigorously until syrup has thickened and turns opaque, about 3 minutes.

6. Working quickly, drop mixture by tablespoons, at least 1 inch apart, on prepared cookie sheets (stir briefly over low heat if mixture gets too thick). Cool pralines completely. Layer between waxed paper in airtight container. Store at room temperature up to 1 week, or freeze up to 3 months.

EACH PRALINE: About 144 calories, 1g protein, 17g carbohydrate, 9g total fat (3g saturated), 14mg cholesterol, 29mg sodium.

Popcorn Balls

Some historians believe that it is likely that the Native Americans brought popping corn to the first Thanksgiving feast. The colonists called it by several names, including popped corn and parching corn; by 1820 the name popcorn was commonly used. Before long, cooks were adding molasses to the popped corn and shaping it into sweet, crunchy balls. In 1886, candy maker Milton S. Hershey opened the Lancaster Caramel Company in Lancaster, Pennsylvania. About ten years later, he began adding chocolate and vanilla to his caramels. Just when the idea of melting caramels to make popcorn balls occurred isn't clear, but it quickly became the fastest and most foolproof way to make these ever-popular treats.

PREP: 10 minutes ★ **COOK:** 10 minutes ★ **MAKES** 15 balls

- 16 cups salted popped corn
- 1 cup salted cocktail peanuts
- 1 bag (14 ounces) caramels, unwrapped
- 2 tablespoons water

1. Pick over popcorn and discard any unpopped kernels. Grease large deep roasting pan or bowl. In pan, combine popcorn and peanuts

2. In medium microwave-safe bowl, combine caramels and water. Cook in microwave according to package directions, stirring frequently, until smooth. Pour over popcorn; with large spoon toss until evenly coated. Grease hands and shape by cups into 15 balls.

EACH BALL: About 207 calories, 5g protein, 28g carbohydrate, 10g total fat (4g saturated), 2mg cholesterol, 291mg sodium.

Peanut Brittle

Around the turn of the twentieth century, recipes for peanut brittle began appearing; it didn't take long for Americans to embrace it as a favorite candy treat. In the original recipe, raw peanuts are slowly poached in hot sugar syrup, which infuses the candy with lots of peanut flavor. In our recipe, roasted peanuts are stirred into the candy just before it is removed from the heat. The bubbling-hot candy mixture is poured onto a cookie sheet and stretched into a thin rectangle. Traditionally, confectioners use a slab of marble for this step, as the cool temperature of the marble gives more time to stretch the hot mixture before it turns to brittle. Once it hardens, the brittle is broken into pieces just right for eating out of hand.

PREP: 5 minutes plus cooling ★ **COOK:** 30 minutes
MAKES about 1 pound

1 cup sugar

½ cup light corn syrup

¼ cup water

2 tablespoons butter or margarine

1 cup salted peanuts

½ teaspoon baking soda

1. Lightly grease large cookie sheet.

2. In heavy 2-quart saucepan, combine sugar, corn syrup, water, and butter; cook over medium heat, stirring constantly, until sugar has dissolved and syrup is bubbling.

3. Set candy thermometer in place and continue cooking, stirring frequently, until temperature reaches 300° to 310°F (hard-crack stage), 20 to 25 minutes. (Once temperature reaches 220°F, it will rise quickly, so watch carefully.) Stir in peanuts.

4. Remove saucepan from heat and stir in baking soda (mixture will bubble vigorously); immediately pour onto prepared cookie sheet. With two forks, quickly lift and stretch peanut mixture into 14" by 12" rectangle.

5. Cool brittle completely on cookie sheet on wire rack. With hands, break brittle into small pieces. Layer between waxed paper in airtight container. Store at room temperature up to 1 month.

EACH OUNCE: About 146 calories, 2g protein, 22g carbohydrate, 6g total fat (2g saturated), 4mg cholesterol, 103mg sodium.

Gold Rush Nut Brittle

Prepare as directed but use only ¾ *cup salted peanuts*; stir in ¾ *cup sliced blanched almonds* and ¾ *cup pecans*, coarsely broken, with peanuts. Makes about 1¼ pounds.

Bibliography

Adams, Marcia. *Cooking from Quilt Country*. New York: Clarkson N. Potter, 1998.

American Heritage Cookbook and Illustrated History of American Eating & Drinking. New York: American Heritage Publishing, 1964.

Anderson, Jean. *American Century Cookbook*. New York: Clarkson N. Potter, 1997.

Beard, James. *James Beard's American Cookery*. Boston: Little, Brown, 1972.

Charleston Receipts. Collected by the Junior League of Charleston. Charleston, South Carolina: Walker, Evans & Cogswell, 1950.

Child, Julia. *The French Chef Cookbook*. New York: Alfred A. Knopf, 1978.

Claiborne, Craig. *Craig Claiborne's The New York Times Food Encyclopedia*. Compiled by Joan Whitman. New York: Times Books, 1985.

Claiborne, Craig. *Southern Cooking*. New York: Random House, 1987

Claudet, Gabrielle and Claudet, Rita. *Acadian Dictionary*. Houma, LA. 1981.

Cunningham, Marion. *The Fannie Farmer Baking Book*. New York: Alfred A. Knopf, 1990.

Davidson, Alan. *The Oxford Companion to Food*. Oxford: Oxford University Press, 1999.

Farmer, Fannie Merritt. *The Boston Cooking-School Cook Book*. Boston: Little, Brown, 1896.

Farmer, Fannie Merritt; Perkins, Cora d. Farmer, editor. *The Boston Cooking-School Cook Book*. Boston: Little, Brown, 1923.

Good Housekeeping's Book of Menus, Recipes, and Household Discoveries. New York: Good Housekeeping, 1922.

The Good Housekeeping Cook Book. New York: Farrar & Rinehart, 1942.

Good Housekeeping Everyday Cook Book. Arranged by Isabel Gordon Curtis, Associate Editor of *Good Housekeeping*, New York: Hearst Books, a division of Sterling Publishing. Originally published by The Phelps Publishing Co, 1903.

Groff, Betty as told to Diane Stoneback. *Betty Groff Cookbook Pennsylvania German Recipes*. Harrisburg, PA: 2001.

Gutman, Richard J.S. *American Diner Then and Now*. New York: HarperCollins, 1993.

Hale, Sarah Josepha. *The Good Housekeeper, or, The Way to Live Well and to be Well While We Live*. Boston: Otis, Broaders, 1841.

Hein, Peg. *Tastes and Tales of Texas…with Love*. Austin: Hein & Associates, 1984.

Herbst, Sharon Tyler. *The New Food Lover's Companion*, Third Edition. Hauppauge, New York: Barron's Educational Series, 2001.

Hill, Annabella P. *Mrs. Hill's Southern Practical Cookery and Receipt Book*. New York: James O'Kane, 1872.

Jamison, Cheryl Alters, and Jamison, Bill. *American Home Cooking*. New York: Broadway Books, 1999.

Jones, Evan. *American Food: The Gastronomic Story*. New York: E.P. Dutton, 1975.

Kimball, Marie, with Essay by Helen d. Bullock. *Thomas Jefferson's Cook Book*. (reprint). Charlottesville: The University Press of Virginia, 1976.

Lang, Jenifer Harvey, editor. *Larousse Gastronomique*. New York: Crown, 1988.

Leslie, Eliza. *Directions for Cookery in Its Various Branches*. Introduction and Suggested Recipes by Louis Szathmary. New York: Arno Press, a New York Times Company, 1973.

London, Anne, and Bishov, Bertha Kahn, eds. *The Complete American-Jewish Cookbook*. New York: Harper & Row, 1971.

Mariani, John F. *The Encyclopedia of American Food & Drink*. New York: Lebhar-Friedman Books, 1999.

Martha Washington's Booke of Cookery from the seventeenth century and in her keeping from 1749 to 1779. Transcribed by Karen Hess. New York: Columbia University Press, 1981.

Porterfield, James D. *Dining by Rail*. New York: St. Martin's Press, 1993.

Prudhomme, Paul. *Chef Paul Prudhomme's Louisiana Kitchen*. New York: William Morrow, 1984.

Randolph, Mary. *The Virginia House-wife*, facsimile of first edition (1824), along with additional material from the editions of 1825 and 1828. Historical notes and commentaries by Karen Hess. Columbia, SC: University of South Carolina Press, 1984.

Reader's Digest Down Home Cooking The New, Healthier Way. Pleasantville, NY: The Reader's Digest Association, 1994.

River Road Recipes. Collected by the Junior League of Baton Rouge, Louisiana. Baton Rouge, 1959.

Roerig, Fred, and Roerig, Joyce Herndon. *Cook Jars Book II*. Paducah, KY: Collector Books, a Division of Schroeder Publishing Co., 1994.

Root, Waverly, and de Rochemont, Richard. *Eating in America*. New York: The Ecco Press, 1981.

Rorer, Sarah Tyson. *Mrs. Rorer's Philadelphia Cook Book*. Philadelphia: Arnold and Company, 1886.

Rutledge, Sarah. *The Carolina Housewife*. Facsimile of the 1847 Edition, with an Introduction and a Preliminary Checklist of South Carolina Cookbooks Published before 1935 by Anna Wells Rutledge. Columbia, SC: University of South Carolina Press, 1979.

Sax, Richard. *Classic Home Desserts*. Shelburne, Vermont: Chapters, 1994.

Schneider, Mike. *The Complete Cookie Jar Book*. Atglen, PA: Schiffer Publishing, 2003.

Schremp, Gerry. *Celebration of American Food*. Published in cooperation with the Library of Congress. Golden, CO: Fulcrum, 1996.

Simmons, Amelia. *The First American Cookbook: A Facsimile of "American Cookery," 1796* with an essay by Mary Tolford Wilson. New York: Oxford University Press, 1958. Unabridged and unaltered republication: New York: Dover, 1984.

The Original Picayune Creole Cook Book. New Orleans: Times-Picayune, 1954.

The Settlement Cook Book. Compiled by Mrs. Simon Kander. Milwaukee: The Settlement Cook Book Co., 1921.

The Southern Heritage Plain and Fancy Poultry Cook Book. Birmingham: Oxmoor House, 1983,

Trager, James. *The Food Chronology*. New York: Henry Holt, 1995.

Wakefield, Ruth Graves. *Ruth Wakefield's Toll House Tried and True Recipes*. New York: M. Barrows, 1943.

Weaver, William Woys. *Pennsylvania Dutch Country Cooking*. New York: Abbeville, 1993.

Boldface page numbers are illustrations.

Acorn squash, baked, 188
Alciatore, Jules, 23
Alcott, Louisa May, 241
All-American club, 48
Almonds
　　bee-sting cake, 198, 199
　　cinnamon-sugar filling, 201
　　gold rush nut brittle, 328
　　sweet, filling, 201
　　trout amandine, 144
American cooking, trends in, 9–11
Anaya, Ignacio "Nacho," 19
Anderson, Jean, 260, 262, 266, 268, 272, 287, 294
Andouille sausage
　　Creole chicken and sausage gumbo, **102,** 103
　　jambalaya, 168
Angel biscuits, 210
Angel cake, 268
Appetizers, 12–29
　　bite-size quiche Lorraine, 19
　　buffalo chicken wings, 26
　　chafing-dish meatballs, 12, 27
　　chicken liver pâté, 15
　　clams casino, 24
　　classic onion dip, 17
　　deviled eggs, 28
　　dilly shrimp, 25
　　firecracker party mix, 22
　　half-moon empanadas, 12, 18
　　hot Cheddar puffs, 12, 17
　　Maryland crab dip, 14
　　nachos, 19
　　oysters Rockefeller, 23
　　peppery nuts, 20
　　potted shrimp, 16
　　ribbon sandwiches, 29
　　sausage-stuffed mushrooms, 27
　　seven-layer Tex-Mex dip, 15
　　shrimp cocktail, 24
　　south-of-the-border guacamole, 14
　　Swiss fondue, 28
　　Texas cheese straws, 20, 21
Apples
　　baked, dumplings, 240
　　brown betty, 243
　　bumbleberry pie, 283
　　crisp, 240
　　fast-baked, with oatmeal streusel, 246, 247
　　German puffed pancakes, 88
　　granny's, pandowdy, 245

turnovers, 296, 297
upside-down cake, 272
Vermont, pie, 280, 281
Waldorf salad, 72
Applesauce, homemade, 186
Arliss, George, 77
Arroz con pollo, 105
Asparagus, 32
　　cooking, 176
　　cream, of soup, 32
　　creamy, cup, 32
　　with hollandaise sauce, 174, 176
Avocado(s)
　　seven-layer Tex-Mex dip, 15
　　south-of-the-border guacamole, 14

Bacon
　　Brussels sprouts with, 177
　　butter beans with, 181
　　Chicago mash with onion and, 184
　　-corn chowder, 30, 34
　　hot, dressing, 68
Baked acorn squash, 188
Baked eggs au gratin, 83
Baked graham cracker–crumb crust, 299
Baked vanilla wafer–crumb crust, 299
Baker, Harry, 270
Baker, James, 266
Baker, Walter, 266
Baking powder, 193, 223
　　biscuits, 209
Baltimore & Ohio Railroad, dining on, 104
Banana
　　bread, 224
　　brown betty, 243
　　cream pie, 288
　　-nut bread, 224
　　-split cake, 256, 257
Barbecue(d)
　　beef brisket, 132
　　best, ribs, 138, 139
　　chicken, North Carolina style, 96
　　pulled pork sandwiches, 60
　　sauce, 138
Burt, Harry, 254
Barthe, Louis, 43
Basic crepes, 252
Basil
　　-and-dried-tomato chicken salad, 64
　　corn custard with, 179
Bayou, cooking on the, 154

Beans
　　black, soup, 33
　　green
　　　casserole with frizzled onions, 181
　　　three-bean salad, 70
　　kidney
　　　Creole red beans and rice, 172
　　　three-bean salad, 70
　　lima
　　　butter beans with bacon, 181
　　　Narragansett succotash, 190
　　navy
　　　Boston baked, 173
　　　Senate's famous bean soup, 33
　　pinto, seven-layer Tex-Mex dip, 15
　　wax, three-bean salad, 70
Beard, James, 45, 48, 89, 118, 127, 158, 289, 294
Bear Mountain butternut squash soup, 38
Béarnaise sauce, 120
Beef, 116–134. *See also* Ground beef
　　brisket, barbecued, 132
　　cubed steaks, chicken-fried steak with milk gravy, 124
　　deviled short ribs, 122
　　filet mignon with béarnaise sauce, 120
　　flank steak
　　hot open-faced steak sandwiches, 59
　　Shaker, 123
　　minute steaks, grillades and grits, 125
　　mom's pot roast, 121
　　New England boiled dinner, 133, 134
　　New York strip with maître d'hôtel butter, 122
　　oven, stew, 129
　　pizzaiolo, 125
　　prime ribs of, roasted, 116, 118
　　rib-eye steaks
　　"The Original" Pat's King of Steaks Philadelphia cheese steak, 54
　　steak Diane, 121
　　round steak, Swiss steak, 124
　　Salisbury steak, 128
　　skirt steak, fajitas, 60
　　soup, beefy vegetable, 46, 47
　　spiced, 129
　　strip steaks, blackened steaks, 123
　　stroganoff, 128

tenderloin, roasted, 119
top loin steaks, beef pizzaiolo, 125
Wellington, 120
Beer batter-fried shrimp, 154
Bee-sting cake, 198, **199**
Beet(s)
　　Harvard, 177
　　pickled, with eggs, 84
　　Yale, 177
Bell, Glen, 66
Benedict, Lemuel, 83
Benne seed wafers, 320
Berries. *See also* Blueberries; Raspberries; Strawberries
　　bumbleberry pie, 283
Best barbecue ribs, 138, **139**
Betty Crocker, 11, 16
Beverages
　　pineapple punch, 22
　　tea, 55
Beverley, Robert, 69
Billi bi, 43
Birdseye, Charles, 11, 175
Biscuit boxes, 303
Biscuits, 239
　　angel, 210
　　baking powder, 209
　　buttermilk, 209
　　Tex-Mex cheese, 211
Bishop's bread, 224
Bisque, shrimp, 42
Bite-size quiche Lorraine, 19
Black-and-whites, **314,** 315
Black bean soup, 33
Black bottom pie, 289
Blackened
　　steaks, 123
　　tuna steaks, 149
Black-eyed peas, Hoppin' John, 173
Black Forest cake, 267
Blalden, Thomas, 255
Blaxton, William, 280
Blondies, 304, **305**
Blueberries
　　blueberry hill scones, **214,** 215
　　buckle, 242
　　cobbler, 239
　　muffins, 212
　　-peach shortcakes, 244
　　slump, 241
　　very, pie, 282–283
Blue cheese dressing, 75
Borden, Gail, 287
Boston baked beans, 173
Boston brown bread, 9, 173, 215, 225

Boston cream pie, 272, **273**
Brand, William, 43
Brandied hard sauce, 235
Bread pudding, New Orleans, **230**, 234
Breads, 192–229
  biscuits, 239
    angel, 210
    baking powder, 209
    buttermilk, 209
    Tex-Mex cheese, 211
  corn
    golden, **218**, 219
    hush puppies, 220
    spoonbread, 220, **221**
  muffins
    blueberry or raspberry, 212
    homemade, 212, **213**
    jam-filled, 212
    walnut or pecan, 212
  popovers
    herb, 216, **217**
    Yankee, 216
  quick
    banana, 224
    banana-nut, 224
    Bishop's, 224
    Boston brown, 225
  scones, blueberry hill, **214**, 215
  soda, Boston brown, 215
  yeast
    cinnamon-raisin, 194
    cloverleaf rolls, **192, 202**
    finger rolls, 200
    mashed-potato loaf, 195
    monkey bread, 200
    Parker House rolls, 203
    San Francisco sourdough, 196–197
    Southern Sally Lunn, 197
    white (daily loaf), 194
Broccoli, cream, of soup, 32
Broth
  giblet, 114
  old-fashioned chicken, 45
Brownie pudding cake, 238
Brownies
  Good Housekeeping's fudgy, 302
  praline-iced, 302
Brunswick stew, 9, 107
Brussels sprouts, 177
  with bacon, 177
Buffalo chicken wings, 26
Buffet rice ring, 170
Bumbleberry pie, 283
Butter beans, with bacon, 181
Buttercream frosting, 269, 278
Buttered noodles, 166
Buttermilk
  biscuits, 209
  ranch, dressing, 76
Butternut squash
  Bear Mountain, soup, 38
  peeling, 38
Byrd, William, 32

Cabbage, 63
  creamy coleslaw, 69
  Pennsylvania-Dutch hot slaw, 178
  perfection salad, 72
Caesar salad, 63, 67
Caesar-style egg salad, 67
Cajun maquechou, 178
Cajuns, 103, 123, 148, 155, 168, 178
Cake(s), 258–279
  angel, 268
  apple upside-down, 272
  Black Forest, 267
  brownie pudding, 238
  carrot, 271
  classic devil's food, 258, 263
  clown cup, 269
  daffodil, 268
  German chocolate, 266
  Lady Baltimore, 262
  lazy-daisy, 277
  lemon pudding, 238
  Mississippi mud, 264, 265
  mom's blue-ribbon coconut, 260
  New York cheese, 275, 277
  orange and lemon chiffon, 270
  orange pudding, 238
  pineapple upside-down, 274
  plum upside-down, 272
  pound, 279
Cake frostings. *See also* Glazes; Toppings
  burnt-buttercream, 278
  buttercream, 269, 278
  chocolate buttercream, 278
  coconut-pecan frosting, 266
  cream cheese, 271
  fluffy white, 260
  lemon buttercream, 278
  orange buttercream, 278
  ornamental, 322
Cake servers, 293
Cake walk, 261
Cakewalk at the county fair, 261
Calico cheese soup, 34
California cioppino, 158
California dip, 17
Candies, 301, 326–328
  chocolate-walnut fudge, **302**, 326
  creamy penuche, 326
  gold rush nut brittle, 328
  peanut brittle, 328
  popcorn balls, 327
  pralines, 327
Cape Cod cranberry-nut loaf, 223
Cardamom-pear pie, 284
Cardini, Caesar, 67
Carrot(s)
  cake, 271
  chef's salad, 65
  -raisin salad, 68
Casseroles
  green bean, with frizzled onions, 181

overnight cheese strata, 90
  tuna-noodle, 151
Catfish, panfried, 149
Chafing dish, 13, 26
Chafing-dish meatballs, **12**, 27
Chapman, John, 280
Cheddar cheese, 90
  calico, soup, 34
  classic cheese soufflé, 89
  hot, puffs, **12**, 17
  mom's mac 'n' cheese, 165
  overnight cheese strata, 90
  puffy cheesy grits, 171
  Texas cheese straws, 20, 21
  Tex-Mex, biscuits, 211
  tuna melt, 55
Cheese, 79, 90. *See also specific varieties*
  American style, 90
  Welsh rarebit, 88
Cheesecake, New York, **276**, 277
Cheese pizza, 208
Chef's salad, 65
Cherries
  diner, pie, 282
  filling, 267
  roast duck with, -port sauce, 113
Chesapeake bay crab boil, 154
Chicago mash with onion and bacon, 184
Chicken. *See also* Turkey
  à la king, 105
  arroz con pollo, 105
  Baltimore style, 96
  barbecued, North Carolina style, 96
  basil-and-dried-tomato, salad, 64
  Brunswick stew, 107
  Buffalo wings, 26
  cacciatore, 97
  country captain, 98, **99**
  Creole, and sausage gumbo, **102**, 103
  enchiladas, 106
  fricassée, 97
  fried, 100
  herb-roasted, with moist bread stuffing, 95
  liver pâté, 15
  old-fashioned, broth, 45
  pilau, 169
  plantation, 'n' dumplings, 101
  pudding, 101
  salads
    classic, 64
    cobb, **62**, 66
    curry-grape, 64
    lemon-pepper, 64
  San Francisco stir-fry, 104
  -seafood paella, 160, 167
  soups
    -noodle, 44
    and rice, 45
  Sunday roast, **92**, 94
Chicken-fried steak with milk gravy, 124

Child, Julia, 11, 16, 19, 77, 89, 117, 120, 170
Children's pies, 297
Chile peppers, south-of-the-border guacamole, 14
Chili con carne, 131
Chinatown fried rice, 170
Chinese cuisine
  Chinatown fried rice, 170
  egg foo yong, 81
  San Francisco stir-fry chicken, 104
  vegetable stir-fry, 191
Chocolate. *See also* Brownies; Fudge
  angel pie, 294, **295**
  black-and-whites, **314**, 315
  black bottom pie, 289
  Black Forest cake, 267
  brownie pudding cake, 238
  buttercream frosting, 278
  classic devil's food cake, **258**, 263
  coconut macaroons, 318
  cream pie, **290**, 291
  creamy penuche, 326
  curls, 299
  -dipped coconut macaroons, 318
  Georgia, pecan pie, **281**, 288
  German, cake, 266
  glaze, 274
  ice box pinwheels, 324
  Mississippi mud cake, 264, **265**
  sublime hot fudge sauce, 253
  wafer–crumb crust, 299
  -walnut fudge, **300**, 326
  white, -macadamia cookies, 311
  whoopie pies, 312, **313**
Chocolate chip(s)
  bishop's bread, 224
  blondies, 304
  cookies, **310**, 311
Chorizo sausage
  chicken-seafood paella, **160**, 167
  nachos, 19
Choux pastry, 253
Chowders. *See also* Soup(s)
  bacon-corn, **30**, 34
  Manhattan clam, 41
  New England clam, 40
  Yankee fish, 43
Christmas pudding, 233, 235
Christmas sugar-cookie cutouts, 323
Chuck wagon, 54
Chunky gazpacho, 35
Church-supper macaroni salad, 71
Cinnamon
  buns, 206
  croutons, 38
  doughnuts, 229
  -raisin bread, 194
  -sugar filling, 201
Cioppino, California, 158

Claiborne, Craig, 120, 122, 319
Clams
California cioppino, 158
casino, 24
Manhattan, chowder, 41
New England, chowder
Classic cheese soufflé, **78**, 89
Classic chicken salad, 64
Classic devil's food cake, **258**, 263
Classic egg salad, 67
Classic French vinaigrette, 76
Classic onion dip, 17
Cloverleaf rolls, **192**, **202**
Clown cupcakes, 269
Club sandwich
all-American club, 48
origin of, 48
Cobb, Robert, 66
Cobblers. *See also* Pie(s)
blueberry, 239
Georgia peach, 239
rhubarb-strawberry, 239
Cobb salad, **62**, 63, 66
Cocktail buffet tables, 13
Cocktail parties, 13, 17, 20
Coconut
blondies, 304
chocolate-, macaroons, 318
chocolate-dipped,
macaroons, 318
custard pie, 287
macaroons, 318
mom's blue-ribbon, cake, 260
-pecan frosting, 266
Cod
cakes, 149
Yankee fish chowder, 43
Coffee cakes. *See also*
Doughnuts; Sweet rolls
bee-sting cake, 198, **199**
Cape Cod cranberry-nut
loaf, **222**, 223
lemon tea bread, 223
sour cream, 226, **227**
sour cream-pear, 228
wreath, 201
Coleslaw, creamy, 69
Coney Island dog, 49
Cookbooks, first, 10
Cookie jars, 303
Cookie-press cookies, 320
Cookies, 301–325
benne seed wafers, 320
black-and-whites, **314**, 315
blondies, 304, **305**
chocolate chip, **310**, 311
chocolate chip blondies, 304
chocolate -coconut
macaroons, 318
chocolate-dipped coconut
macaroons, 318
Christmas sugar, cutouts, 323
coconut blondies, 304
coconut macaroons, 318
cookie-press, 320
gingerbread cutouts, 322, 323
gingersnaps, 316, 317
Good Housekeeping's fudgy
brownies, 302
Grandmother's oatmeal-
raisin, 308, **309**
ice box pinwheels, 324
lemon bars, **306**, 307
maple sugar, 318
peanut butter, 308
praline-iced brownies, 302
raspberry linzer thumbprint,
321
shortenin' bread, 304
snickerdoodles, 319
snowballs, 312
whoopie pies, 312, **313**
wooden spoon–lace, 319
Corbitt, Helen, 75
Corn, 70, 161
bacon-, chowder, **30**, 34
Cajun maquechou, 178
custard with basil, 179
Iowa, salad, 70
Narragansett succotash, 190
oysters, 179
and Pepper Jack soufflé, 89
pudding, 179
Corn bread
golden, **218**, 219
hush puppies, 220
spoonbread, 220, **221**
Corned beef
red flannel hash, 134
Reuben sandwiches, 53
Cornish hens, rock, with wild
rice stuffing, 111
Cornmeal crust, 112
Cottage cheese, party cheese
mold, 91
Cottage pie, 130
Country captain, 98, **99**
Country hams, 140
Country sausage and corn bread
stuffing, 109
County fair, cakewalk at, 261
Crab
Chesapeake bay, boil, 154
Louis, 65
Maryland
cakes, 151
dip, 14
sole roll-ups with, stuffing, 146
Cranberries
Cape Cod, -nut loaf, **222**, 223
pear-, crisp, 240
Cream cheese
creamy scrambled eggs for a
crowd, 80
frosting, 271
party cheese mold, 91
scrambled eggs with, and
salmon, 80
Creamed onions and peas, 183
Creamed spinach, 188
Cream filling, 267
Cream of broccoli soup, 32
Cream of cauliflower soup, 32
Cream of mushroom soup, 36
Cream of spinach soup, 32
Cream puffs, 253
Cream waffles, 85
Creamy coleslaw, 69
Creamy horseradish sauce, 118
Creamy penuche, 326
Creamy scrambled eggs for a
crowd, 80
Creole chicken and sausage
gumbo, **102**, 103
Creole red beans and rice, 172
Creoles, 155
Crepes
basic, 252
Suzette, 252
Croutons, cinnamon, 38
Crown roast of pork, 135
Cucumbers, wilted dilly, 69
Cunningham, Marion, 297
Cupcakes, clown, 269
Curried egg salad, 67
Curry, chicken, 106
Curry-grape chicken salad, 64
Cut-out cakes, 261

Daffodil cake, 268
Deli-style egg salad, 67
Delmonico, Charles, 159
Denver omelet, 80
Desserts, 230–257. *See also*
Cake(s); Cobblers; Cookies; Ice
cream; Pie(s); Sherbet
apple brown betty, 243
apple crisp, 240
baked apple dumplings, 240
banana brown betty, 243
banana-split cake, 256, **257**
blueberry buckle, 242
blueberry-peach shortcakes,
244
blueberry slump, 241
Christmas pudding, 233
cream puffs, 253
crepes Suzette, 252
fast-baked apples with
oatmeal streusel, 246, **247**
floating island, 237
gingerbread, **232**, 233
granny's apple pandowdy,
245
holiday baked Alaska with
red-raspberry sauce, 250,
251
Indian pudding, 236
individual shortcakes, 244
New Orleans bread pudding,
230, 234
oven-steamed figgy pudding,
235
peach-noodle kugel, 237
peach-raspberry buckle, 242
pear-cranberry crisp, 240
pear crisp, 240
raspberry slump, 241
rice pudding, 236
rich rice pudding, 236
rosy peach Melba compote,
248, 249
strawberry shortcake, 244
summer fruit shortcake, 244
Deviled eggs, 28
Deviled short ribs, 122
Diat, Louis, 40, 65
Dill(y)
egg tea sandwiches, 55
poached salmon with sour
cream-, sauce, 145
shrimp, 25
wilted, cucumbers, 69
Diner cherry pie, 282
Diners, 59
Dining cars, 104
Dinner parties, 16
Dips
Maryland crab, 14
seven-layer Tex-Mex, 15
Dixie squash pudding, 188
Dole, John, 272
Dorgan, T. A., 49
Dough. *See* Pastry dough
Doughnuts. *See also* Coffee
cakes; Sweet rolls
cinnamon, 229
holes, 229
Downing, Lewis, 36
Duck, roast, with cherry-port
sauce, 113
Dumpling dough, 241
Dumplings, plantation chicken
'n,' 101
Dupree, Natalie, 264
Dutch oven, 225

Earl of Sandwich, 50
Easter eggs, dyeing, 91
Egg(s), 78–91
baked, au gratin, 83
Benedict, 83
Caesar-style, salad, 67
chef's salad, 65
classic, salad, 67
creamy scrambled, for a
crowd, 80
curried, salad, 67
deli-style, salad, 67
deviled, 28
dilly, tea sandwiches, 55
dyeing Easter, 91
foo yong, 81
in a hole, 82
huevos rancheros, 82
Mexican-style, salad, 67
omelet
Denver, 80
Italian ham and potato
frittata, 81
pickled beets with, 84
quiche, bite-size, Lorraine, 19
scrambled, with cream
cheese and salmon, 80
western sandwiches, 54
Eggplant parmigiana, 180
Empanadas, half-moon, **12**, 18
Enchiladas, chicken, 106
Entertaining, 13, 16
Escoffier, 249
Esposito, Raffaele, 208
Evelyn, John, 77

Fajitas, steak, 60
Farmer, Fannie, 10, 11, 55, 64,
67, 121, 143, 177, 183, 203, 205,

216, 243, 244, 275, 278, 285, 287, 297, 302, 308, 318
Fast-baked apples with oatmeal streusel, 246, 247
Feltman, Charles, 49
Festive Christmas tree buns, **204**, 205
Fettuccine Alfredo, 166
Feuchtwanger, Antoine, 49
Figs, oven-steamed figgy pudding, 235
Filet mignon with béarnaise sauce, 120
Fillings. *See also* Sauce(s)
    cherry, 267
    cinnamon-sugar, 201
    cream, 267
    marshmallow crème, 312
    sweet almond, 201
Finger rolls, 200
Firecracker party mix, 22
Fish, 142–159. *See also specific varieties*
    billi bi, 43
    Friday night fry, 149
    Yankee, chowder, 43
Fish cakes
    codfish, 149
    Maryland crab, 151
    salmon croquettes, 150
FitzGibbon, Theodora, 120
Flaky turnover pastry, 18
Flat cakes, 86
Floating island, 237
Flounder, 146
Fluffy white frosting, 260
Fondue, Swiss, 28
Food-processor pastry dough, 298
Franklin, Benjamin, 237
French country onion soup, 36, **37**
French-fried onion rings, 182–183
French toast
    pain perdu, 85
    skillet, 84
Fresh tomato soup, 39
Fricassée, 93
    chicken, 97
Friday night fish fry, 149
Fried chicken, 100
Fried green tomatoes, 190
Frijoles, 172
Frittatas, 78
    Italian ham and potato frittata, 81
Fruits. *See also specific varieties*
    salad, 74
        heavenly, 74
    summer, shortcake, 244
Fudge
    chocolate-walnut, **300**, 326
    topping, 264

Garney, Jane, 120
Gazpacho, chunky, 35
Gems, 212
Georgia chocolate pecan pie, **281**, 288

Georgia peach cobbler, 239
German, Samuel, 266
German chocolate cake, 266
German lentil soup, 35
German puffed pancakes, 88
German sauce, 233
Giblet broth, 114
Giblet gravy, 109
Gingerbread, **232**, 233
    cutouts, **322**, 323
Gingersnaps, 316, **317**
Glazes. *See also* Cake frostings; Toppings
    chocolate, 274
    orange, 270
Goelitz, Gustav, 325
Golden corn bread, **218**, 219
Gold rush nut brittle, 328
Good Housekeeping's fudgy brownies, 302
Goose, holiday, à l'orange, 114, **115**
Graham cracker–crumb crust, baked, 299
Grandma's sweet potato pie, 292
Grandmother's oatmeal-raisin cookies, 308, **309**
Granny's apple pandowdy, 245
Grape, curry-, chicken salad, 64
Gravy
    chicken-fried steak with milk, 124
    giblet, 109
    ham and grits with red-eye, 137
Green beans
    casserole with frizzled onions, 181
    three-bean salad, 70
Green goddess dressing, 76
Greens
    smothered, 182
    types of, in salads, 63
Green tomatoes, fried, 190
Greenwald, George, 105
Griddle cakes, 86, **87**
Grillades and grits, 125
Grits
    grillades and, 125
    ham and, with red-eye gravy, 137
    puffy cheese, 171
Groff, Betty, 312
Ground beef
    chafing-dish meatballs, **12**, 27
    chili con carne, 131
    classic hamburgers, 57
    cottage pie, 130
    grilled hamburgers, 57
    meatballs and spaghetti, 164
    meat loaf surprise, 126, 127
    Nana's meat loaf, 127
    seven backyard secrets, 57
    sloppy Joes, 59
    tamale pie, 131
    Tex-Mex burgers, 56, 57
    tomato-sausage lasagna, 162, 163

Gruyère cheese
    Gruyère-spinach soufflé, 89
    Monte Cristo, 51
    Swiss fondue, 28
Guacamole, south-of-the-border, 14
Gumbo, 156
    Creole chicken and sausage, **102**, 103
    sausage and shrimp, 156, **157**

Hale, Sarah Josepha, 39, 108, 183, 255
Half-moon empanadas, **12**, 18
Ham. *See also* Pork
    chef's salad, 65
    Creole red beans and rice, 172
    and grits with red-eye gravy, 137
    honey-glazed, 140
    Italian, and potato frittata, 81
    Monte Cristo, 51
    muffuletta, 51
    roasting tips, 137
    split pea with, soup, 39
Hamburgers
    backyard secrets, 57
    classic, 57
    grilled, 57
    Tex-Mex burgers, **56**, 57
Ham & glaze, 140
Handwerker, Nathan, 49
Harvard beets, 177
Hayes, Joanne Lamb, 268
Hazelnuts, raspberry linzer thumbprint cookies, 321
Heavenly fruit salad, 74
Henson, Steve, 76
Herb popovers, 216, **217**
Herb-roasted chicken with moist bread stuffing, 95
Hero, **52**, 53
Hershey, Milton S., 325, 327
Hill, Annabella P., 100, 195, 209, 211, 234
Hirshfield, Leo, 325
Holiday baked Alaska with red-raspberry sauce, 250, 251
Holiday goose à l'orange, 114, **115**
Hollandaise sauce, 176
    asparagus with, **174**, 176
    eggs Benedict, 83
Home fries, 183
Homemade applesauce, 186
Hominy, 171
Honey-glazed ham, 140
Hoover, Herbert, 11
Hoppin' John, 173
Horseradish, creamy, sauce, 118
Horseradish-tarragon sauce, 119
Hot Cheddar puffs, **12**, 17
Hot cross buns, **204**, 205
Hot dogs, 49
Hot open-faced steak sandwiches, 59
Howard, B. C., 100
Huevos rancheros, 82
Hush puppies, 220

Ice box pinwheels, 324
Ice cream. *See also* Sherbet
    old-fashioned vanilla, 254
    peach, 254
    strawberry, 254
Ice-cream cake, 250, **251**
Ice-cream man, 254
Ice rings, 13
Iowa corn salad, 70
Irving, Washington, 229
Italian ham and potato frittata, 81
Italian sausage
    and shrimp gumbo, 156, **157**
    -stuffed mushrooms, 27
    tomato-sausage lasagna, 162, **163**

Jackson, Andrew, 137
Jambalaya, 168
Jam-filled muffins, 212
Jefferson, Thomas, 10, 79, 153, 161, 165, 177, 180, 237, 250, 252, 255, 284, 288
Jones, Evan, 26, 35, 134, 179, 190, 225, 262

Kalm, Peter, 32
Keene, Foxhall, 105
Keller, Julius, 24
Kentucky hot brown, 58
Kidney beans
    Creole red beans and rice, 172
    three-bean salad, 70
Kielbasa sausage, Creole chicken and sausage gumbo, **102**, 103
Knox, Charles B., 10, 63, 74
Kugel, peach-noodle, 237
Kulakofsky, Reuben, 53

Lady Baltimore cake, 261, 262
Lamb, mustard and herb racks of, 141
Lasagna, tomato-sausage, 162, **163**
Lazy-daisy cake, 277
Lelio, Alfredo Di, 166
Lemaire, Etienne, 252
Lemon(s)
    bars, **306**, 307
    buttercream frosting, 278
    meringue pie, 286
    orange and, chiffon cake, 270
    -pepper chicken salad, 64
    potato salad, 71
    pudding cake, 238
    Shaker, pie, 285
    tea bread, 223
Lentils, German, soup, 35
Leslie, Eliza, 63, 93, 98, 106, 143, 185, 194, 236, 246, 259, 260, 292, 318
Lettuce, 76
Liberty Gardens, 11, 180
Lima beans
    butter beans with bacon, 181
    Narragansett succotash, 190
Limburger, 90

Lime
    key, pie, 287
    meringue pie, 286
Liver, chicken pâté, 15
Lobster
    cooking live, 152
    seafood Newburg, 159
    Thermidor, 152
Long, Huey, 93, 182
Lovegren, Sylvia, 294
Lupo, Salvatore, 51

Macadamia nuts, white
    chocolate- cookies, 311
Macaroni, 165
    church-supper, salad, 71
    mom's mac 'n' cheese, 165
Macaroons
    chocolate-coconut, 318
    chocolate-dipped coconut,
        318
    coconut, 318
Main dish pies
    cottage pie, 130
    tamale pie, 131
    turkey potpie with cornmeal
        crust, 112
Manhattan clam chowder, 41
Maple sugar cookies, 318
Marinade & beef, 119
Marinara sauce, 164
Marshmallow crème filling, 312
Maryland crab cakes, 151
Maryland crab dip, 14
Mashed-potato loaf, 195
Masterton, Elsie, 242
Mayberry, Alicia Rhett, 262
Mayonnaise, 71
Meatballs
    chafing-dish, 12, 27
    and spaghetti, 164
Meat loaf
    Nana's, 127
    surprise, 126, 127
Meehan, M. J., 254
Meringue, 250
    chocolate angel pie, 294, 295
    lemon, pie, 286
    lime, pie, 286
Mexican-American cuisine
    chicken enchilads, 106
    chili con carne, 131
    half-moon empanadas, 18
    huevos rancheros, 82
    Mexican-style egg salad, 67
    nachos, 19
    seven-layer Tex-Mex dip, 15
    south-of-the-border
        guacamole, 14
    steak fajitas, 60
    taco salad, 66
    tamale pie, 131
    Tex-Mex burgers, 57
Mexican-style egg salad, 67
Minted sugar snaps, 182
Mississippi mud cake, 264, 265
Moist bread stuffing, 95
Molded salads, 63, 73
    party cheese mold, 91

perfection salad, 73
    tomato aspic mold, 74
Molded salmon mousse, 150
Mom's blue-ribbon coconut
    cake, 260
Mom's mac 'n' cheese, 165
Mom's pot roast, 121
Monkey bread, 200
Montagu, John, 50
Monte Carlo, 51
Monte Cristo, 51
Monterey Jack cheese, 90
    Southwestern soufflé, 89
Mousse, molded salmon, 150
Mud cake, 264, 265
Muffins
    blueberry or raspberry, 212
    homemade, 212, 213
    jam-filled, 212
    walnut or pecan, 212
Muffuletta, 51
Mushrooms
    cream of, soup, 36
    sausage-stuffed, 27
    wild rice and, stuffing, 111
    wild rice with, 171
Mussels
    billi bi, 43
    chicken-seafood paella, 160,
        167
Mustard and herb racks of lamb,
    141
Mustard sauce, 140

Nachos, 19
Nagreen, Charles, 57
Nana's meat loaf, 127
Narragansett succotash, 190
Nathan's Famous Frankfurter
    Stand, 49
Navy beans
    Boston baked, 173
    Senate's famous bean soup, 33
New England boiled dinner, 133,
    134
New England clam chowder, 40
New Orleans bread pudding,
    230, 234
New Orleans oyster po' boy, 61
New York cheesecake, 276, 277
New York strip with maître
    d'hôtel butter, 122
Noodle(s), 161
    buttered, 166
    chicken-, soup, 44
    peach-, kugel, 237
    for soup, 44
    tuna- casserole, 151
Nuts. See also Almonds;
    Hazelnuts; Macadamia nuts;
    Peanuts; Pecans; Walnuts
    banana-, bread, 224
    Cape Cod cranberry-, loaf, 223
    gold rush, brittle, 328
    peppery, 20

Oatmeal
    fast-baked apples with,
        streusel, 246, 247

grandmother's, -raisin
    cookies, 308, 309
Old-fashioned potato salad, 71
Old-time turkey with giblet
    gravy, 108, 110
Olivieri, Pat, 54
Omelet(s)
    Denver, 80
    Italian ham and potato
        frittata, 81
Onion(s)
    Chicago mash with, and
        bacon, 184
    classic tip, 17
    creamed, and peas, 183
    French country, soup, 36, 37
    French-fried, rings, 182–183
    green bean casserole with
        frizzled, 181
Open-faced sandwiches, 50
Orange
    buttercream frosting, 278
    daffodil cake, 268
    glaze, 270
    holiday goose à l', 114
    and lemon chiffon cake, 270
    pudding cake, 238
    sauce, 252
    sherbet, 254
"The original" Pat's King of
    Steaks Philadelphia cheese
    steak, 54
Ornamental frosting, 322
Oven beef stew, 129
Ovens, first colonial, 225
Oven-steamed figgy pudding, 235
Overnight cheese strata, 90
Oysters
    New Orleans, po' boy, 61
    pan roast, 153
    Rockefeller, 23

Paddleford, Clementine, 53
Paella, chicken-seafood, 160, 167
Pain perdu, 85
Pancakes. See also French toast;
    Waffles
    German puffed, 88
    griddle cakes, 86, 87
    sour cream, 86
Panfried catfish, 149
Parker House rolls, 203
Party cheese mold, 91
Pasta. See Fettuccine; Lasagna;
    Macaroni; Noodle(s);
    Spaghetti
Pastry
    choux, 253
    flaky turnover, 12, 18
Pastry cream, 274
Pastry dough. See also Piecrusts
    dumpling, 241
    food-processor, 298
    for 1-crust pie, 299
    shortening, 298
    for 2-crust pie, 298
    vinegar, 298
    whole-wheat, 298
Pâté, chicken liver, 15

Pea(s). See also Black-eyed peas;
    Sugar snap peas
    creamed onions and, 183
    split, with ham soup, 39
Peach(es)
    blueberry-, shortcakes, 244
    Georgia, cobbler, 239
    ice cream, 254
    -noodle kugel, 237
    pie, 284
    -raspberry buckle, 242
    rosy, melba compote, 248,
        249
Peanut brittle, 328
Peanut butter cookies, 308
Peanuts
    brittle, 328
    popcorn balls, 327
Pear(s)
    cardamon-pear, 284
    -cranberry crisp, 240
    crisp, 240
    pie, 284
    sour cream-, coffee cake, 228
Pecans. See also Walnuts
    blondies, 304, 305
    classic, pie, 289
    coconut-, frosting, 266
    Georgia chocolate, pie, 281,
        288
    gold rush nut brittle, 328
    pralines, 327
    shortenin' bread, 304
    snowballs, 312
Pennsylvania-Dutch hot slaw,
    178
Pennsylvania-Dutch sticky buns,
    206
Penny candy store, 325
Penuche, creamy, 326
Pepper, lemon-, chicken salad, 64
Pepper jack cheese, corn and,
    soufflé, 89
Peppery nuts, 20, 21
Perfection salad, 63, 73
Philadelphia cheese steak, 54
Pickled beets with eggs, 84
Pickled shrimp, 25
Pie(s), 259, 280–299. See also
    Cobblers
    banana cream, 288
    black bottom, 289
    Boston cream, 272, 273
    bumbleberry, 283
    cardamon-pear, 284
    chocolate angel, 294, 295
    chocolate cream, 290, 291
    classic pecan, 289
    coconut custard, 287
    diner cherry, 282
    Georgia chocolate pecan,
        281, 288
    grandma's sweet potato, 292
    key lime, 287
    lemon meringue, 286
    lime meringue, 286
    peach, 284
    pear, 284
    Pilgrim's pumpkin, 292–293

plum, 284
    Shaker lemon, 285
    strawberry-rhubarb, 285
    Vermont apple, 280, **281**
    very blueberry, 282–283
Piecrusts. *See also* Pastry dough
    baked graham
        cracker–crumb, 299
    baked vanilla wafer–crumb,
        299
    chocolate wafer–crumb, 299
    cornmeal, 112
Pie servers, 293
Pilau, chicken, 169
Pilgrim's pumpkin pie, 292–293
Pineapple
    punch, 22
    upside-down cake, 274
Pinto beans, seven-layer Tex-
    Mex dip, 15
Pizza, cheese, 208
Pizzaiolo, beef, 125
Plantation chicken 'n',
    dumplings, 101
Plums
    pie, 284
    upside-down cake, 272
Poached salmon with sour
    cream-dill sauce, 145
Po'boy, New Orleans oyster, 61
Popcorn
    balls, 327
    firecracker party mix, 22
Popovers
    herb, 216, **217**
    Yankee, 216
Poppy-seed dressing, 75
Pork, 135–140. *See also* Bacon;
    Ham
    barbecued pulled,
        sandwiches, 60
    best barbecue ribs, 138, **139**
    crown roast of, 135
    smothered, chops, 136
    stuffed, chops, 136
Potatoes
    boats, 184
    Bubbe's, latkes, 186, **187**
    Chicago mash with onion
        and bacon, 184
    home fries, 183
    Italian ham and, frittata, 81
    lemony, salad, 71
    mashed- loaf, 195
    meat loaf surprise, 127
    old-fashioned, salad, 71
    scalloped, 185
    steak fries, 185
    vichyssoise, 40
Potlikker, 182
Potpie, turkey, with cornmeal
    crust, 112
Potted shrimp, 16
Potting food, 16
Poultry. *See* Chicken; Cornish
    hens; Duck; Goose; Turkey
Pound cake, 279
Praline-iced brownies, 302
Pralines, 327

Pretzels, soft, 207
    sticks, 207
Progressive dinner party, 141
Pudding(s)
    chicken, 101
    Christmas, 233, 235
    corn, 179
    Dixie squash, 188
    Indian, 236
    oven-steamed figgy, 235
    rice, 236
    rich rice, 236
    Yorkshire, 118
Puffy cheesy grits, 171
Pumpkin, Pilgrim's, pie, 292–*293*
Punch, pineapple, 22
Punch bowls, 13

Quiche, bite-size, Lorraine, 19

Raisin(s)
    carrot-, salad, 68
    cinnamon- bread, 194
Ranch buttermilk dressing, 76
Randolph, Mary, 106, 175
Ranhofer, Charles, 250
Raspberries
    linzer thumbprint cookies,
        321
    muffins, 212
    peach-, buckle, 242
    red-, sauce, 250
    slump, 241
Red flannel hash, 134
Red-raspberry sauce, 250
Red snapper, salt-crusted baked,
    144
Regional cooking, 9–10
Rémoulade sauce, 24
Rémoulade verte, 25
Rest-of-the-turkey soup, 48
Reuben sandwiches, 53
Rhubarb
    strawberry-, pie, 285
    -strawberry cobbler, 239
Ribbon sandwiches, 29, 55
Ribs
    best barbecue, 138, 139
    deviled short, 122
Rice, 161
    arroz con, 105
    buffet, ring, 170
    chicken and, soup, 45
    chicken pilau, 169
    Chinatown fried, 170
    Creole red beans and, 172
    Hoppin' John, 173
    jambalaya, 169
    Spanish, 168
    wild
        with mushrooms, 171
        rock cornish hens with,
            stuffing, 111
Rice pudding, 236
Rich rice pudding, 236
Roast duck with cherry-port
    sauce, 113
Roasted beef tenderloin, 119
Roasted prime ribs of beef, **116,**

118
Roasted winter vegetables,
    190–191
Rochemont, Richard de, 131
Rock cornish hens with wild rice
    stuffing, 111
Roosevelt, Franklin D., 182
Root, Waverley, 131
Rorer, Sarah T., 74, 177, 193, 260,
    275
Rosenfield, J. L., 308
Russian dressing, 75
Rutledge, Sarah, 165

St. Louis World's Fair, 49, 57
Salad(s), 62–74. *See also*
    Coleslaw
    basil-and-dried-tomato
        chicken, 64
    Caesar, 67
    Caesar-style egg, 67
    carrot-raisin, 68
    chef's, 65
    church-supper macaroni, 71
    classic chicken, 64
    classic egg, 67
    cobb, **62,** 66
    crab Louis, 65
    curried egg, 67
    curry-grape chicken, 64
    deli-style egg, 67
    fruit, 74
    heavenly fruit, 74
    Iowa corn, 70
    lemon-pepper chicken, 64
    lemony potato, 71
    Mexican-style egg, 67
    molded, 73
    old-fashioned potato, 71
    perfection, 73
    spinach with hot bacon
        dressing, 68
    taco, 66
    three-bean, 70
    tomato aspic, 72
    Waldorf, 72
    wilted dilly cucumbers, 69
Salad dressings
    blue cheese, 75
    classic French vinaigrette, 77
    green goddess, 77
    hot bacon, 68
    poppy seed, 75
    ranch buttermilk, 76
    Russian, 75
    Thousand Island, 76
Salisbury, James Henry, 128
Salisbury steak, 128
Sally Lunn, 197
Salmon
    croquettes, 150
    molded, mousse, 150
    poached, with sour
        cream–dill sauce, 145
    scrambled eggs with cream
        cheese and, 80
Salt-crusted baked snapper, 144
Sandwiches, 48–61
    all-American club, 48

barbecued pulled pork, 60
    classic hamburgers, 57
    dilly egg tea, 55
    grilled hamburgers, 57
    hero, **52,** 53
    hot open-faced steak, 59
    Kentucky hot brown, 58
    Monte Cristo, 51
    muffuletta, 51
    New Orleans oyster po' boy,
        61
    "The Original" Pat's King of
        Steaks Philadelphia cheese
        steak, 54
    Reuben, 53
    ribbon, 29
    sloppy Joes, 59
    Tex-Mex burgers, **56,** 57
    tuna melt, 55
    turkey divan, 50
San Francisco sourdough,
    196–197
San Francisco stir-fry chicken,
    104
Sauce(s). *See also* Fillings
    appetizer
        red cocktail, 25
        rémoulade verte, 25
    dessert
        béarnaise, 120
        brandied hard, 235
        fudge topping, 264
        German, 233
        orange, 252
        red-raspberry, 250
        sublime hot fudge, 253
    main-dish
        barbecue, 138
        hollandaise, 176
        horseradish
            creamy, 118
            -tarragon, 116
        marinara, 164
        mustard, 140
        tartar, 151
Sausage. *See also* Andouille
    sausage; Chorizo sausage;
    Italian sausage
    country, and corn bread
        stuffing, 109
    and shrimp gumbo, 156, **157**
    -stuffed mushrooms, 27
Scalloped potatoes, 185
Scallops
    pan roast, 153
    seafood Newburg, 159
Schmidt, Fred K., 58
Scones, 215
    blueberry hill, **214,** 215
Scrambled eggs with cream
    cheese and salmon, 80
Seafood Newburg, 159
Segar, Elzie Crisler, 188
Senate's famous bean soup, 33
seven-layer Tex-Mex dip, 15
Shaker flank steak, 123
Shaker lemon pie, 285
Shakers, 188, 285
Shellfish. *See* Lobster; Mussels;

Scallops; Shrimp
Shepherd's pie, 130
Sherbet. *See also* Ice cream
    orange, 254
Shortcakes
    blueberry-peach, 244
    individual, 244
    strawberry, 244
    summer fruit, 244
Shortenin' bread, 304
Shortening pastry dough, 298
Shrimp
    beer batter-fried, 154
    bisque, 42
    chicken-seafood paella, **160**,
        167
    cocktail, 24
    dilly, 25
    egg foo yong, 81
    potted, 16
    sausage and, gumbo, 156, **157**
    seafood Newburg, 159
    wiggle, 158
Simmons, Amelia, 10, 112, 141,
    176, 236, 259, 292, 298, 323
Skillet French toast, 84
Sloppy Joes, 59
Smithfield ham, 140
Smothered greens, 182
Smothered pork chops, 136
Snacks. *See also* Appetizers
    firecracker party mix, 22
    nachos, 19
    peppery nuts, 20
    soft pretzels, 207
    soft pretzel sticks, 207
Snickerdoodles, 319
Snowballs, 312
Soft pretzels, 207
Soft pretzel sticks, 207
Sole roll-ups with crab stuffing,
    146
Soufflés
    classic cheese, 89
    corn and pepper jack, 89
    Gruyère-spinach, 89
    Southwestern, 89
Soup(s), 30–48
    bacon-corn chowder, **30**, 34
    Bear Mountain butternut
        squash, 38
    billi bi, 43
    black bean, 33
    calico cheese, 34
    chicken and rice, 45
    chicken-noodle, 44
    chunky gazpacho, 35
    cream of broccoli, 32
    cream of cauliflower, 32
    cream of mushroom, 36
    cream of spinach, 32
    creamy asparagus cup, 32
    French country onion, 36, **37**
    fresh tomato, 39
    German lentil, 35
    Manhattan clam chowder, 41
    New England clam chowder,
        40
    noodles for, 44

old-fashioned chicken
        broth, 45
    rest-of-the-turkey, 48
    Senate's famous bean, 33
    shrimp bisque, 42
    split pea with ham, 39
    vichyssoise, 40
    Yankee fish chowder, 43
Sour cream
    coffee cake, 226, **227**
    pancakes, 86
    -pear coffee cake, 228
    poached salmon with, - dill
        sauce, 145
Sourdough, 193
Sourdough rolls, 196
Sourdough starter, 196–197
Southern Sally Lunn, 197
Southern sweet potatoes, 191
South-of-the-border
    guacamole, 14
Southwestern soufflé, 89
Spaghetti, meatballs and, 164
Spanish rice, 168
Spiced beef, 129
Spinach
    cream, of soup, 32
    creamed, 188
    Gruyère-, soufflé, 89
    with hot bacon dressing, 68
Spoonbread, 220, **221**
Springerles, 301
Squash
    acorn, baked, 188
    butternut
        Bear Mountain, soup, 38
        peeling, 38
    yellow, Dixie, pudding, 188
Steak Diane, 121
Steak fajitas, 60
Steak fries, 185
Stews
    Brunswick, 106
    California cioppino, 158
    chicken pilau, 169
    jambalaya, 168
    oven beef, 129
Stir-fries
    San Francisco, chicken, 104
    vegetable, 191
Straub, Ambrose W., 308
Strawberries
    ice cream, 254
    rhubarb-cobbler, 239
    -rhubarb pie, 285
    shortcake, 244
Streusel
    fast-baked apples with
        oatmeal, 246, **247**
    topping, 242
Stuffed pork chops, 136
Stuffing
    country sausage and corn
        bread, 109
    moist bread, 95
    rock cornish hens with wild
        rice, 111
    sole roll-ups with crab, 146
Sublime hot fudge sauce, 253

Succotash, 9
    Narragansett, 190
Sugar-cured hams, 140
Sugar snap peas, minted, 182
Summer fruit shortcake, 244
Sunday roast chicken, **92**, 94
Sweet almond filling, 201
Sweet potatoes
    grandma's, pie, 292
    Southern, 191
Sweet rolls. *See also* Coffee cakes;
    Doughnuts
    cinnamon buns, 206
    festive Christmas tree buns,
        204, 205
    hot cross buns, **204**, 205
    Pennsylvania-Dutch sticky
        buns, 206
Swiss cheese, 90
    baked eggs au gratin, 83
    bite-size quiche Lorraine, 19
    chef's salad, 65
    fondue, 28
    Monte Cristo, 51
    Reuben sandwiches, 53
    Swiss fondue, 28
    tuna melt, 55
Swiss fondue, 28
Swiss steak, 124

Taco salad, 66
Tamale pie, 131
Tarragon, horseradish-, sauce,
    119
Tartar sauce, 151
Tea, 55, 223
Teahouses, 55
Tea parties, 29, 223
Tearooms, 50
Tennyson, Jeffrey, 57
Terrazzini, turkey, 107
Tetrazzini, Luisa, 107
Tetrazzini, 107
Texas cheese straws, 20, **21**
Tex-Mex cheese biscuits, 211
Thanksgiving, 108
Thompson, Benjamin, 250
Thousand Island dressing, 76
Three-bean salad, 70
Thurber, John, 161
Tomato(es)
    aspic mold, 72
    basil-and-dried-, chicken
        salad, 64
    chunky gazpacho, 35
    fresh, soup, 39
    fried green, 190
    marinara sauce, 164
    -sausage lasagna, 162, **163**
Toppings
    fudge, 264
    streusel, 242
Trager, James, 57
Trout amandine, 144
Tschirky, Oscar, 72
Tuna
    blackened, steaks, 149
    melt, 55
    -noodle casserole, 151
Turkey. *See also* Chicken

all-American club, 48
    divan, 50
    Kentucky hot brown, 58
    old-time, with giblet gravy,
        108, **110**
    potpie with cornmeal crust,
        112
    rest-of-the, soup, 48
    Tetrazzini, 107
Turnovers
    apple, **296**, 297
    flaky pastry, 18
    half-moon empanadas, 18
Twitcher, Jimmy, 50

Upside-down cakes, 272
    apple, 272
    pineapple, 272
    plum, 272

Vanilla wafer–crumb crust,
    baked, 299
Vegetables, 174–191. *See also
    specific varieties*
    beefy, soup, **46**, 47
    roasted winter, 190–191
    stir-fry, 191
Vermont apple pie, 280, **281**
Very blueberry pie, 282–283
Vichyssoise, 40
Victory Gardens, 11, 180
Vinegar pastry dough, 298

Waffles, cream, 85
Wakefield, Ruth, 311
Waldorf salad, 63, 72
Walnuts. *See also* Pecans
    banana-nut bread, 224
    bishop's bread, 224
    Cape Cod cranberry-nut
        loaf, **222**, 223
    chocolate- fudge, 300, 326
    muffins, 212
    peppery nuts, 20, 21
Warm slaw, 63
Washington, George, 288
Washington Pie, 274
Waters, Alice, 175
Wax beans, three-bean salad, 70
Welsh rarebit, 88
Wenberg, Ben, 159
White bread (daily loaf), 194
White chocolate–macadamia
    cookies, 311
Whole-wheat pastry dough, 298
Whoopie pies, 312, **313**
Wild rice with mushrooms, 171
Wilted dilly cucumbers, 69
Wister, Owen, 262
Wooden spoon–lace cookies, 319

Yale beets, 177
Yankee fish chowder, 43
Yankee popovers, 216
Yeast, 193
Yellow squash, Dixie, pudding,
    188
Yorkshire pudding, 118